VIOLENT VICTORIANS

Manchester University Press

Violent Victorians

Popular entertainment
in nineteenth-century London

Rosalind Crone

Manchester University Press

Manchester and New York

distributed in the United States exclusively by Palgrave Macmillan

Copyright © Rosalind Crone 2012

The right of Rosalind Crone to be identified as the author of this work has been asserted by her in accordance with the Copyright, Designs and Patents Act 1988.

Published by Manchester University Press
Oxford Road, Manchester M13 9NR, UK
and Room 400, 175 Fifth Avenue, New York, NY 10010, USA
www.manchesteruniversitypress.co.uk

Distributed in the United States exclusively by
Palgrave Macmillan, 175 Fifth Avenue, New York,
NY 10010, USA

Distributed in Canada exclusively by
UBC Press, University of British Columbia, 2029 West Mall,
Vancouver, BC, Canada V6T 1Z2

British Library Cataloguing-in-Publication Data
A catalogue record for this book is available from the British Library

Library of Congress Cataloging-in-Publication Data applied for

ISBN   978 0 7190 8684 7   hardback
ISBN   978 0 7190 8685 4   paperback

First published 2012

The publisher has no responsibility for the persistence or accuracy of URLs for any external or third-party internet websites referred to in this book, and does not guarantee that any content on such websites is, or will remain, accurate or appropriate.

Typeset in Minion and Harrington
by Carnegie Book Production, Lancaster
Printed in Great Britain
by Bell & Bain Ltd, Glasgow

For my mother, Sheelagh Crone

Contents

List of figures, tables and diagrams

Figures

Tables

Diagrams

Acknowledgements

IDEAS ARE ONLY EVER TRANSFORMED into monographs when support, guidance and most of all time are offered so unselfishly by others to the author. This is even more the case when the idea begins life as a postgraduate project. Over the past ten years I have been frequently surprised by the generosity of supervisors and teachers, peers, curators and librarians, friends and family who not only showed an interest in the project, but actively ensured the research emerged coherently in print.

Violent Victorians began life as an honours dissertation at the University of Queensland in Australia, and was transformed into a doctoral thesis at Cambridge University as a result of generous funding from the Cambridge Australia Trust and St John's College. My global trotting meant that the project benefited from the input of three exceptional supervisors: first, Simon Devereaux, whose work I found inspirational as an undergraduate and who not only provided great encouragement but kept his promise not to laugh at my idea to write my first dissertation on Punch and Judy; second, Larry Klein, whose guidance during my first year in Cambridge smoothed the transition between countries and gave me the confidence to persevere with the doctorate; and third, Peter Mandler, who expertly combined gentle reassurances with fierce intellectual rigour, whose constant (and sometimes unexpected) challenges forced me to delve deeper to uncover the roles of cultural phenomena, and who has stayed true to his words, that there is no such thing as an ex-supervisor.

When I moved to The Open University in 2006 to begin a new research project, I was both touched and grateful for the tremendous support I continued to receive from the Arts Faculty and close colleagues for my research on violent entertainments. Moreover, I have been lucky enough to spend time in both the English and History departments at the OU, which has increased my sensitivity towards the approaches and methods of both disciplines and I hope that some of that sensitivity is reflected in this book.

Further, I would like to mention and specially thank those who have spent large amounts of their own time discussing this project with me, who have shared their own work, published and unpublished, and who have read partial or even whole drafts of my shifting manuscript: Clive Emsley, Margot Finn, Elizabeth Foyster, David Gange, V. A. C. Gatrell, Ben Griffin, Katie Halsey, Gareth Stedman Jones, Pete King, Paul Lawrence, Michael Ledger-Lomas, Donna Loftus, Rohan McWilliam, Iain McCalman, Bob Owens, William St Clair, Gill Sutherland, Deborah Thom, Shaf Towheed and Chris Williams. I would also like to thank the anonymous reviewers of the manuscript at Manchester University Press, whose pertinent comments and suggestions forced me to rethink some central ideas and made that final process a pleasure. Various portions of this book have been presented at a large number of conferences and seminars around the world and I would like to thank both the organisers of those events and those who attended for all their comments and useful feedback.

I would like to thank the staff at Manchester University Press, especially the history editor, Emma Brennan, who helped to transform a rough draft into a book. Librarians and archivists from the following institutions offered invaluable advice during the research process and help in securing images for inclusion in this book: Cambridge University Library (especially the staff in the Rare Books Room); the British Library and British Newspaper Library at Colindale; the Bodleian Library and in particular the curators of the John Johnson Collection; the National Archives; curators of the Harvard Theatre Collection at the Houghton Library, Harvard; the Royal Pavilion and Museums, Brighton and Hove; and Heritage Services at St Edmundsbury Borough Council, including the kind staff at Moyses Hall Museum in Bury St Edmunds, who gave me directions to the site of the Red Barn Murder in Suffolk. Selected material has previously appeared in two articles: 'Mr and Mrs Punch in nineteenth-century England', *Historical Journal*, 49 (2006, Cambridge University Press); and 'From Sawney Beane to Sweeney Todd: murder machines in the mid-nineteenth-century metropolis', *Cultural and Social History*, 7 (2010, Berg Publishers, an imprint of A&C Black Publishers). I would like to thank the publishers for permission to reproduce some of that work here.

Finally, and most importantly, I would like to thank my friends and family, who have not only shown remarkable patience by not asking awkward questions when 'the book' took so long to emerge in print, but have given substantial emotional support and encouragement. In particular, I would like thank John Phillips and Sylvia Williams, who gave me a second home in London, and made research trips to the metropolis so much fun. My sister, Jennifer Honnery, always expressed a genuine interest in this project and never minded discussing ideas over the telephone. When I sorely needed help with the more creative aspects, including the cover design, Jenn immediately came to the rescue, giving the project that final breath of life. My parents, Sheelagh and Richard, have and continue to offer support, emotional and financial, not to mention love, in immeasurable quantities, their incredible generosity extending beyond plane tickets to reading drafts at dawn. In many ways, my mother is responsible for both my career choice and for the character of this book: through stories, books, travel plans and later deep discussion, my mother passed on her love of history to me, and especially her interest in the everyday experience of ordinary people. It seems only fitting and natural that my first substantial work should be dedicated to her. Lastly, I want to thank James Adams, who has had to live with this project from our very first meeting at a graduate seminar in Cambridge where I gave a paper on domestic violence in the nineteenth century. Since then, James graciously endured dates at Madame Tussaud's Chamber of Horrors and in Fleet Street attempting to find the location of Sweeney Todd's barber shop, as well as a longer excursion in a muddy field trying to find the site of the Red Barn Murder. Far from taking flight, James has become the most fervent supporter of *Violent Victorians*; he made this project a high priority in our life together, which resulted in many sacrifices. His love and encouragement, reflected in his repeated statement, 'you've got to finish your book', ensured that the work ended up in print. And he even says that he is looking forward to the next one.

Prologue

I N 1846 A NEW SERIAL APPEARED in Edward Lloyd's popular weekly magazine, the *People's Periodical and Family Library*, under the slightly obscure title, 'The String of Pearls'. Surrounded by other instalments of romantic fiction and short advisory articles on marriage and family matters, it is clear that Lloyd intended it to be read by working- and lower-middle-class men, women and children. The tale proved to be a hit with this audience. Not only was Lloyd encouraged by the profits to successfully republish 'The String of Pearls' as a penny novelette just three years later with the addition of several hundred pages, but the story was also promptly plagiarised by theatrical hacks for performance as a melodrama in London's theatres to the great applause of packed houses of all ages. However, the story was a far cry from what we would today regard as suitable family entertainment.

'The String of Pearls' introduced Londoners to the dastardly character of Sweeney Todd, a barber whose shop was located in busy Fleet Street, the very heart of the growing city of London. Todd was no ordinary barber; each day he murdered selected customers by slitting their throats and using his mechanical barber's chair to throw their bodies into the stone vaults below. After he relieved the victims of their valuables, Todd sliced the bodies into bite-sized chunks and passed the meat through the vaults to the bakehouse which serviced Mrs Lovett's pie shop, where the remains were served up to hungry customers as tasty fillings in the pastries they purchased.

The tale of Sweeney Todd was brutal. No detail was spared in its telling and retelling in different genres to multiple audiences. But, although well known even today, this rather gross presentation of violence sits uncomfortably with the picture historians have traditionally painted of Victorian society. From the late eighteenth century, we are told, English society was subjected to tremendous cultural, social and political change. The pre-industrial social hierarchy and vibrant, inclusive plebeian culture had been swept away with the advancement of an industrial revolution and unprecedented urbanisation. In its wake, there emerged a metropolitan, class-based society. At the same time, significant cultural and intellectual shifts initiated a process of the taming of popular culture from above, and historians have concluded that by the 1820s many of the excesses that had characterised earlier forms of entertainment had been removed or at least subjected to strict regulation. Although inappropriate displays of violence and passion still existed, they argue, these had been successfully pushed to the margins, regarded as minor deviations from the norm of respectability. Yet the character of Sweeney Todd was far from marginal. Nor was he a deviation, a product of an underground culture, located in the underbelly of Victorian society. It is this incongruity that this book sets out to explore.

The late eighteenth and early nineteenth centuries undeniably represented a period of unprecedented change, as evident in crucial legal reforms, in the substantial restructuring of the social hierarchy, and in the transformation of people's behaviour and values more generally. To explain the important contrast between early modern and modern English society, historians have readily applied the framework of the 'civilising process'. The term, 'civilising process', was first coined by sociologist Norbert Elias to describe changing patterns in human behaviour from the late medieval to the modern period. Elias found that in Western societies, as people increasingly sought to suppress so-called 'animal characteristics', manners and attitudes towards bodily functions shifted while aggressiveness and the potential for violence in everyday life declined.[1]

For historians, the 'civilising process' became a convenient term, a short-hand by which to describe the impact of a number of key movements at work from the mid-eighteenth century, such as politeness, sensibility, humanitarianism, evangelism and respectability. Many historians explained how a more disciplined and restrained society emerged during the early decades of the nineteenth century as change was imposed from the top downwards. New values and standards of behaviour adopted by the higher classes slowly trickled down, influencing the lifestyles of those below. In addition, public order necessary for economic progress was enforced by new structures of authority and the extension of the law. Thus, by the Victorian period, society had been largely 'tamed'.

As a framework of analysis, the 'civilising process' has enjoyed a wide application in studies of eighteenth- and nineteenth-century society, used to account for crucial changes in law and punishment, notable alterations in the behaviour of ordinary people and the increasingly active role of the state in the lives of its citizens. Many historians have suggested that the removal of public displays of punishment in the late eighteenth and early nineteenth centuries, the collapse of the infamous Bloody Code during the 1820s and the eventual abolition of public execution in 1868 were the results of the emergence of an increasingly civilised sensibility. The language of sympathy, which included identification with the suffering of the felon, and fears of the brutalisation of the spectators of punishment, infused debates about the reform of the penal law.[2] But the extent to which more polite, disciplined and restrained mores and values trickled down to influence the behaviour of ordinary people remains a point of contention. Recently, Robert Shoemaker argued that Londoners at the turn of the nineteenth century were a more pacified people, less prone to riot and violent mob action than their ancestors of the early eighteenth century, not because they had been persuaded by the rhetoric of politeness, but because rapid urbanisation and population growth had led to greater anonymity in the metropolis and so radically altered patterns of social interaction.[3]

V. A. C. Gatrell has remained similarly suspicious of arguments which give weight to the rise of humanitarianism or sympathy among the higher orders.[4] In his latest study of the satirical and bawdy prints which coloured London culture during the late eighteenth century, Gatrell allocated responsibility for the changing character of popular culture to the rising middle class whose increased wealth and thirst for power encouraged their conscious pursuit of virtue and their moral or hypocritical war on the previously shared entertainments of the people. As he concluded, 'the aggressive symbolism of farts and bums which had sustained the satirical carnivalesque for centuries, along with the humorous celebration of manliness, sex and drink, were displaced by the harmless geniality of the domestic joke and pun, and sexual or bodily vulgarities were relegated to the *doubles entendres* of music hall or saloon bar'.[5] The extent to which the so-called 'enemies' of popular culture succeeded in their attempts to tame it and to eradicate its 'excesses' so early in the nineteenth century will be questioned within the pages of this book. But it is noteworthy that other historians have also noted the enthusiasm with which the nineteenth-century state sought to control the behaviour of its citizens, most evident in new criminal and penal policies, and especially in the extension of the criminal law to cover types of behaviour which had only just come to be perceived as immoral or socially disruptive, including vagrancy, drunkenness and previously legitimate uses of public spaces or thoroughfares, from street games to street selling.[6]

In addition to these wide-ranging accounts of eighteenth- and nineteenth-century society and culture, more specific studies on the incidence and role of violence, namely forms of interpersonal violence, in England have tended to lend further, crucial support to the grand narrative of the 'civilising process'. Despite some early claims that late medieval or even early modern society might have represented a golden age in history, notable for surprisingly low levels of violence, more recent scholars have produced convincing sets of statistical data which demonstrate a dramatic fall in the rates of homicide and serious assaults over the seventeenth, eighteenth and nineteenth centuries.[7] Various studies have shown that the number of victims of fatal violence dropped from around 20 per 100,000 per year in 1200 to approximately 2 per 100,000 per year in 1800, the steepest decline occurring during the seventeenth and eighteenth centuries.[8] Based on these conclusions, many historians of violence have come to the conclusion that the nineteenth century was much less violent than previous centuries and this was most likely the result of a general growing intolerance for violent behaviour which filtered down through society as time progressed.

While it is true that criminal statistics have limits in what they can tell us about the role of violence in English society, in the case of the nineteenth century, historians have shown that this data can shed light on important social perceptions of violence. Although the number of homicides was falling to unprecedented low levels, the rate of crime generally was experiencing a dramatic increase from the late eighteenth century. However, this was most likely the result of a new concern with various types of criminal behaviour, the criminalisation of some previously legitimate forms of behaviour, and the improvement and professionalisation of prosecution procedures.[9] Violent behaviour was more frequently brought to the attention of magistrates and county judges, but public, male-on-male violence, was almost certainly in decline. The authorities were most obviously concerned about the threat public violence posed to the preservation of law and order, especially in a climate of political unrest and growing urban populations. But their campaign was also in part inspired and greatly assisted by the emergence and vigorous promotion of a more self-disciplined and pacific ideal of manhood.[10] From the late eighteenth century until c. 1870, duelling, prizefighting and common tavern brawls became increasingly stigmatised with the triumph of a 'civilising offensive' waged against the 'customary mentality', a previously shared culture which saw violence as a legitimate form of self-expression but which had first been confined to the lower classes and finally to the rough residuum located at the very bottom of society.[11] The success of the 'civilising offensive', it has been argued, can be found in the sets of official criminal statistics systematically collected and published from 1857 onwards which illustrate a steady decrease in violent crime until the eve of the First World War.[12]

Although forms of public violence declined or were largely eradicated during this period, the same cannot be said for violence in the private sphere, especially that between husbands and wives. Accurate statistics on the rate of domestic violence in the nineteenth century are hard to compile: evidence suggests that the number of unreported assaults within the home remained high as it still does today, and legislative action during the second half of the nineteenth century meant that alternative routes were often taken in the courtroom to deal with such cases which did not result in criminal prosecutions. Even in the absence of solid data, some historians have claimed that violence between husbands and wives may have actually increased during the first half of the century, while others more cautiously have suggested that if marital violence did not become more frequent, it certainly did not demonstrate any notable decline before the First World War. However, in the wider context of the civilising process, historians have not regarded the tenacious hold of violence in the domestic sphere as problematic or contradictory. Some, for example, have drawn our attention to the emergence of a range of methods or strategies through which women could abandon violent husbands or seek redress for their behaviour, the gradual formalisation of such choices the result of a growing attitude among magistrates, judges and MPs that wife beaters were brutish, unmanly and in need of discipline.[13]

Such attitudes have been related to the development of new gender-role definitions from the eighteenth century onwards. While men became perceived as more dangerous and more in need of control, women, characterised as passive, delicate damsels, were increasingly represented as less dangerous and more in need of protection.[14] Yet ideals of masculinity and femininity could also have a very negative impact, especially when expectations clashed with the realities of working people's lives. Women who fought back could be more severely condemned than their violent husbands and even punished. For those with social aspirations, the creed of respectability could work against exposure and the pursuit of remedies. In other words, the same processes responsible for the overall decline in violence in English society seem to have also ensured the persistence of specific types of violence in discreet locations.

Moreover, studies of patterns of actual violence in English society have limits in what they can tell us about the lives of ordinary people, whether they believed they were living in a violent or increasingly orderly society, and whether they supported the efforts of the authorities to stamp out perceived inappropriate behaviours. There are other ways by which a society might be defined as or considered to be violent. Statistics alone cannot confirm or deny the success of the civilising process. Bearing this in mind, we might do well to take a closer look at the cultural imagination in our accounts of social change. The pastimes and amusements that comprised popular culture offer a useful way into the mentalités of their subscribers, by the 1820s, mostly men, women and children of the lower-middle and working classes. And as this book will show, in the case of London, we do not have to look very far before we encounter a wide range of very violent entertainments enjoyed openly by large audiences which suggest that, in a very important sense, things were becoming much *less* civilised.

In spite of an awareness of the existence of such entertainments, the theme of 'taming' or 'civilising' has also undeniably coloured most accounts of the fortunes and character of popular culture in the nineteenth century. In 1973, Robert Malcolmson demonstrated how traditional entertainments from pre-industrial society were eliminated during the first few decades of the nineteenth century as these recreations came to be regarded as a threat to an effective and disciplined industrial workforce. The second quarter of the nineteenth century, Malcolmson argued, represented something of a dark age in which working people had few outlets for pleasure until a new, commercial leisure industry emerged after 1850.[15] By the end of the 1970s, revisionist historians had already begun to challenge Malcolmson's conclusions, highlighting the extent to which leisure opportunities around the turn of the nineteenth century were expanded for all: new recreations emerged, while some older entertainments adapted to and thrived in the new urban environment. However, for the most part, these scholars continued to focus largely on the political dimensions of popular culture; for example, the growing efforts of the authorities to control public spaces and the attempts by middle-class philanthropists to impose a programme of rational recreation on those below them.[16] John Walton and James Walvin have suggested that this historiographical pattern came about because the activities of legal institutions and reforming agencies were well documented during the nineteenth century and thus captured the interest of historians.[17] As a result, popular culture has been identified as an arena of conflict: clashes were evident both between classes and even within classes as pastimes became identified as either respectable or rough. But this tells only half the story.

By drawing attention to the very violent content of a range of prominent genres of entertainment between *c.* 1820 and *c.* 1870, and through exploring their social and economic context, this study challenges the common narrative of reform and pacification so often used to describe nineteenth-century society. And it seeks to balance evidence of both change *and* continuity in popular culture. The amusements and pastimes presented in the following chapters suggest that excess and the carnivalesque spirit were far from eradicated or even substantially marginalised in Victorian society. To dismiss these violent entertainments as mere survivals from pre-industrial culture as a number of historians have simply will not do.[18] Although some had firm roots in the eighteenth or even seventeenth century, these were enlarged and substantially altered at the turn of the nineteenth century, and were joined by several new, innovative amusements. Furthermore, by analysing the reception of these entertainments and charting their progress over the course of the century, this book will highlight the extent to which seemingly unrespectable pastimes remained exempt from programmes of improvement and legal curtailment imposed from above. But most of all, *Violent Victorians* will show that, in many respects, the Victorian popular imagination was bloodier, much more explicit, and more angry and turbulent than historians have thus far been prepared to acknowledge.

Popular culture in pre-industrial English society was vibrant, boisterous and violent. While work and play were closely tied together and were largely based on an agrarian calendar, entertainments encouraged indulgence and celebrated excess. These pastimes could be cruel and dangerous. Animals were frequently used to satisfy spectators' thirst for blood, and social interactions could quickly turn from being amicable to aggressive and back again. Plebeian culture also contained established social rituals which were used to express the relationship of the common people to authority. Swift, but disciplined, riots were staged in order to reinforce the customary rights of the people against encroachments by the rulers.[19] Moreover, wakes, fairs and other public assemblies incorporated important carnivalesque traditions that were used to subvert the social hierarchy. Carnival, according to Douglas Reid, 'was a period of indulgence in food and drink, enhanced sexuality, singing and dancing in the streets, familiarity between strangers, the acting out of aggressiveness, and acceptance of folly and "carnival" madness'.[20] The freedom provided by carnival allowed the people to display a regulated disdain for the dominant powers and dominant values, most evident in rituals of inversion, such as the election of a Lord of Misrule and mock-mayor ceremonies.[21]

Unprecedented social change caused by industrialisation, urbanisation and rapid population growth in London during the eighteenth and early nineteenth centuries cannot be ignored and it is important not to underestimate its impact on the character of popular culture. Some pastimes and festivals that had previously enjoyed tremendous support did disappear, often swallowed up as the metropolis expanded and a formal police force was eventually introduced to clear the streets, enforce public order and regulate behaviour. However, metropolitan popular culture never entered a 'dark age'; the second quarter of the nineteenth century never represented a cultural wasteland. New amusements quickly emerged to entertain the growing populace, especially the working classes, arguably the inheritors of pre-industrial popular culture. Canny entrepreneurs, with a sense of the substantial profits that could be made, promptly took advantage of this situation.

Yet popular culture in the first half of the nineteenth century did display a striking degree of continuity with that of previous centuries. A significant number of entertainments from the pre-industrial world survived and were even expanded. These amusements were reconfigured to meet the new demands of their audiences and accommodate the restrictions of the confined metropolitan environment. Traditional showmen and printers readily took advantage of the new technologies available to them in order to widen the scope of their products and increase their profits. The success of these amusements demonstrates that there never was a wholesale replacement of older cultural forms by new, modern leisure pursuits. Instead, traditional entertainments coexisted alongside, and were incorporated into, the new.

Moreover, continuity is also evident in the actual content of popular culture, notably in the persistence of the theme of violence. The main expression of this theme in pre-industrial culture was in the form of actual violence and these entertainments or mechanisms for managing social relations formed part of that 'customary mentality' referred to earlier. Staged and random combats between men frequently occurred when common people were at leisure. Brutal animal sports such as cockfighting, throwing-at-cocks, bull- and badger-baiting and dogfights regularly attracted large, heterogeneous audiences. Even though these forms of actual violence did face suppression or regulation at the turn of the nineteenth century, the theme of violence continued to be a prominent feature of mainstream, metropolitan entertainment throughout the Victorian period. However, as a result of massive social upheaval from 1780, it was reconfigured, re-emerging in the form of graphic representations of interpersonal violence. Thus, while pastimes involving the display of actual violence were increasingly brought under control, 're-enactments' of high-level violence flourished. By harnessing new technologies and methods of dissemination, these images of interpersonal violence were intensified. Murder, brutal forms of discipline, duels and brawls, to name but a few, were presented to audiences in a more extreme manner than they had ever been in previous centuries.

This process was experienced most intensively in London, where rapid social change combined with a large population base and new structures of authority sparked the transformation in popular culture. Change was both possible and necessary in the metropolis first, and that is why this book focuses on the capital. Moreover, as the primary locus for innovation, the new narratives of violence that filled popular culture tended to be expressive of the experience of life in the metropolis. That is not to say that the provinces did not feature in this crucial socio-cultural process. As we shall see, traditional networks of printers, distributors and showmen ensured that violent narratives, not all originating in the metropolis, circulated throughout the country. Though it is fair to say that the shift from the predominance of actual violence to the represen-tation of violence in popular culture was much more drawn out in other towns and rural areas, and was only completed with the nationalisation of culture from mid-century onwards.

Although all of the entertainments under investigation in this book have formed the basis of discrete individual studies by scholars in history, literature and cultural studies, who have noted the appeal of the bloodthirsty narratives contained within them, few have attempted to delineate the links between them, to see such forms of amusements as part of a 'culture of violence' in Victorian England. There are some notable exceptions to this rule. Recently, Billie Melman drew attention to the use of violence in Victorian presentations of the past, especially the Tudor and late Georgian periods, highlighting a popular desire to encounter history as a location of 'horror', which 'constituted a set of attitudes and sensations in which repulsion, apprehension and fear combined with attraction and delight'.[22] But the even more common use of narratives of violence in the presentation of contemporary society, most notably in the range of dramatisations and publications relating to topical murders, demands investigation. And the only scholar to have seriously attempted this has been Richard Altick in his oft-cited book, *Victorian Studies in Scarlet*, published in 1972. Not content with merely describing the taste for blood amongst the Victorians, Altick sought to explain the attraction to the crude and brutal images in the theatre, popular fiction, broadsides and weekly newspapers. He wrote:

> It does seem likely that the Victorian masses' sustained enthusiasm for murder was in part a product of their intellectually empty and emotionally stunted lives, so tightly confined by economic and social circumstance. In current murder they found a ready channel for the release of such rudimentary passions as horror, morbid sympathy, and vicarious aggression and for the sheer occupation of minds otherwise rendered blank or dull by the absence of anything more pleasing or intellectually more elevated.

And so Altick concluded that many of the amusements explored in this book 'gave the Victorians something to think about, something for their emotions to respond to in however crude a fashion'.[23] Altick's analysis is certainly a product of its time, its purpose being to emphasise the truly destructive impact of the industrial revolution and the growth of capitalism upon the common people. However, research since has shed light on the more complex nature of society during this period, and has demonstrated, through identifying patterns of change and continuity, just how lively and vibrant Victorian society and culture actually were. In other words, the people's intellect has been rescued from obscurity. Any new study must take account of these developments.

The chapters that follow are arranged in a roughly chronological sequence, in part to highlight the ways in which the different genres of violent entertainment fed off and into each other. As this book will show, none of these amusements can be assessed in isolation from the others: the interconnectedness of Victorian popular culture was all-important. Furthermore, the socio-economic context from which these entertainments, and crucially, the theme of violence, sprang is essential to an understanding of their role or function and their appeal to metropolitan audiences. By identifying these phenomena as 'entertainment', I am not suggesting that they were frivolous or trivial; rather that they were encountered by people in their leisure time or were diversionary. Their representations of violence were captivating, therefore entertaining, but their ability to reflect social experiences and tensions, as well as popular taste, formed their raison d'être.

Thus, chapter 1 describes life in London for ordinary people during the first half of the nineteenth century, exploring the social tensions and opportunities created by the industrial revolution and urbanisation. Chapters 2 and 3 demonstrate how such conditions forced traditional amusements left over from the pre-industrial world of leisure, notably travelling entertainments and broadsides, to adapt and change, or, in other words, to increase their overtly violent content to continue to attract paying customers. Entrepreneurs keen to realise large profits followed suit in their efforts to establish relatively new entertainments, such as the theatre, cheap fiction and weekly newspapers: these are the subjects of chapters 4, 5 and 6. Combined, these pastimes served to entertain millions of men, women and children in London between *c.* 1820 and *c.* 1870. They very much show that what we are dealing with in the nineteenth century is an innovative and assertive popular culture. It was not necessarily defensive and it was not always under attack. And, as we shall see, its decline was not inevitable, nor even achievable.

Notes

1 N. Elias, *The Civilising Process*, trans. E. Jephcott (Oxford: Oxford University Press, rev. edn, 2000).

2 See, for example, R. McGowen, 'A powerful sympathy: terror, the prison and humanitarian reform in early nineteenth-century Britain', *Journal of British Studies*, 25 (1986), 312–34, McGowen, 'Civilising punishment: the end of public execution in England', *Journal of British Studies*, 33 (1994), 257–82, McGowen, 'The image of justice and reform of the criminal law in early nineteenth-century England', *Buffalo Law Review*, 32 (1983), 89–125, McGowen, 'Revisiting the Hanging Tree: Gatrell on emotion and history', *British Journal of Criminology*, 40 (2000), 1–13, J. S. Cockburn, 'Punishment and brutalisation in the English Enlightenment', *Law and History Review*, 12 (1994), 155–79, P. Spierenburg, *The Spectacle of Suffering: Executions and the Evolution of Repression: From a Pre-Industrial Metropolis to the European Experience* (Cambridge: Cambridge University Press, 1984), G. T. Smith, 'Civilised people don't want to see that kind of thing: the decline of public physical punishment in London, 1760–1840', in C. Strange (ed.), *Qualities of Mercy: Justice, Punishment and Discretion* (Vancouver: University of British Columbia Press, 1996).

3 R. B. Shoemaker, *The London Mob: Violence and Disorder in Eighteenth-Century London* (London: Hambledon & London, 2004), pp. 290–8, Shoemaker, 'The decline of public insult in London, 1660–1800', *Past & Present*, 169 (2000), 97–131.

4 V. A. C. Gatrell, *The Hanging Tree: Execution and the English People, 1770–1868* (Oxford: Oxford University Press, 1994).

5 V. A. C. Gatrell, *City of Laughter: Sex and Satire in Eighteenth-Century London* (London: Atlantic 2006), p. 425.

6 M. J. Wiener, *Reconstructing the Criminal: Culture, Law and Policy in*

England, 1830–1914 (Cambridge: Cambridge University Press, 1990), p. 11, V. A. C. Gatrell, 'Crime, authority and the policeman state', in F. M. L. Thompson (ed.), *The Cambridge Social History of Britain, 1750–1900. Volume 3: Social Agencies and Institutions* (Cambridge: Cambridge University Press, 1992), R. D. Storch, 'The policeman as domestic missionary: urban discipline and popular culture in northern England, 1850–80', *Journal of Social History*, 9 (1976), 481–509.

7   A. Macfarlane, *The Justice and the Mare's Ale: Law and Disorder in Seventeenth-Century England* (Oxford: Blackwell, 1981).

8   T. R. Gurr, 'Historical trends in violent crime: a critical review of the evidence', *Crime and Justice: An Annual Review of Research*, 3 (1981), 295–393, L. Stone, 'Interpersonal violence in English society, 1300–1980', *Past & Present*, 101 (1983), 22–33, M. Eisner, 'Modernisation, self-control and lethal violence: the long-term dynamics of European homicide rates in theoretical perspective', *British Journal of Criminology*, 41 (2001), 618–38, Eisner, 'Long-term historical trends in violent crime', *Crime and Justice: An Annual Review of Research*, 30 (2003), 83–142, R. Roth, 'Homicide in early modern England, 1549–1800: the need for a quantitative synthesis', *Crime, Histoire et Sociétés*, 5 (2001), 33–67.

9   Gatrell, 'Crime, authority and the policeman state', C. Emsley, *Crime and Society in England, 1750–1900* (London: Longman, 2nd edn, 1996), pp. 21–49.

10 M. J. Wiener, *Men of Blood: Violence, Manliness and Criminal Justice in Victorian England* (Cambridge: Cambridge University Press, 2004).

11 J. C. Wood, *Violence and Crime in Nineteenth-Century England: The Shadow of our Refinement* (London: Routledge, 2004), R. B. Shoemaker, 'Male honour and the decline of public violence in eighteenth-century London', *Social History*, 26 (2001), 190–208, Wiener, *Men of Blood*, C. Emsley, *Hard Men: Violence in England since 1750* (London: Hambledon & London, 2005), P. Spierenburg, *A History of Murder: Personal Violence in Europe from the Middle Ages to the Present* (Cambridge: Polity, 2008), pp. 165–98.

12 V. A. C. Gatrell, 'The decline of theft and violence in Victorian and Edwardian England', in V. A. C. Gatrell, B. Lenman and G. Parker (eds), *Crime and the Law: The Social History of Crime in Western Europe since 1500* (London: Europa, 1980).

13 A. J. Hammerton, *Cruelty and Companionship: Conflict in Nineteenth-Century Married Life* (London: Routledge, 1995), N. Tomes, 'A "torrent of abuse": crimes of violence between working-class men and women in London, 1840–1875', *Journal of Social History*, 11 (1977), 328–45,

A. Clark, *The Struggle for the Breeches: Gender and the Making of the British Working Class* (Berkeley: University of California Press, 1995), Clark, 'Domesticity and the problem of wife-beating in nineteenth-century Britain: working-class culture, law and politics', in S. D'Cruze (ed.), *Everyday Violence in Britain, 1850–1950: Gender and Class* (Harlow: Longman, 2000), pp. 27–37, E. Ross, '"Fierce questions and taunts": married life in working-class London, 1870–1914', *Feminist Studies*, 8 (1982), 575–602, S. D'Cruze, *Crimes of Outrage: Sex, Violence and Victorian Working Women* (De Kalb: Northern Illinois University Press, 1998), E. Foyster, *Marital Violence: An English Family History, 1660–1857* (Cambridge: Cambridge University Press, 2005).

14 M. J. Wiener, 'Alice Arden to Bill Sikes: changing nightmares of intimate violence in England, 1558 to 1869', *Journal of British Studies*, 40 (2001), 184–212.

15 R. Malcolmson, *Popular Recreations in English Society, 1700–1850* (Cambridge: Cambridge University Press, 1973).

16 P. Bailey, *Leisure and Class in Victorian England: Rational Recreation and the Contest for Control, 1830–1885* (London: Routledge & Kegan Paul, 1978), Bailey, *Popular Culture and Performance in the Victorian City* (Cambridge: Cambridge University Press, 1998), J. Walvin, *Leisure and Society, 1830–1950* (London: Longman, 1978), J. K. Walton, *The English Seaside Resort: A Social History, 1750–1914* (Leicester: Leicester University Press, 1983), Walton and Walvin (eds), *Leisure in Britain, 1780–1939* (Manchester: Manchester University Press, 1983), A. P. Donajgrodski (ed.), *Social Control in Nineteenth Century Britain* (London: Croom Helm, 1977), R. D. Storch (ed.), *Popular Culture and Custom in Nineteenth-Century England* (London: Croom Helm, 1982), H. Cunningham, *Leisure in the Industrial Revolution, 1780–1880* (London: Croom Helm, 1980), Cunningham, 'Leisure and culture', in F. M. L. Thompson (ed.), *The Cambridge Social History of Britain, 1750–1950. Volume 2: People and their Environment* (Cambridge: Cambridge University Press, 1992), J. M. Golby and A. W. Purdue, *The Civilisation of the Crowd: Popular Culture in England, 1750–1900* (London: Batsford, 1984).

17 J. K. Walton and J. Walvin, 'Introduction', in Walton and Walvin (eds), *Leisure in Britain*, p. 3.

18 R. Price, *British Society, 1688–1880* (Cambridge: Cambridge University Press, 1999), pp. 7–11, I. McCalman, *Radical Underworld: Prophets, Revolutionaries and Pornographers in London, 1795–1840* (Oxford: Clarendon Press, 2nd edn, 2002), pp. 236–7. See also A. B. Hilton, *A Mad, Bad and Dangerous People? England, 1783–1846* (Oxford: Oxford University Press, 2006), pp. 625–7.

19 E. P. Thompson, *Customs in Common: Studies in Traditional Popular Culture* (New York: New Press, 1993), especially pp. 185–231.

20 D. A. Reid, 'Interpreting the festival calendar: wakes and fairs as carnivals', in Storch, *Popular Culture and Custom*, pp. 125–41.

21 Malcolmson, *Popular Recreations in English Society*, pp. 79–82, Golby and Purdue, *Civilisation of the Crowd*, pp. 37–9.

22 B. Melman, *The Culture of History: English Uses of the Past, 1800–1953* (Oxford: Oxford University Press, 2006), p. 31.

23 R. D. Altick, *Victorian Studies in Scarlet: Murders and Manners in the Age of Victoria* (London: Dent, 1972), p. 10.

London 1800–1850: coping with change, expressing resistance

I N   H I S   A U T O B I O G R A P H Y, which described a life encompassing several turbulent but momentous decades in metropolitan history, the famous Charing Cross tailor, Francis Place, reflected on the changes he had witnessed. In particular, Place sought to emphasise the difference between life in London during the eighteenth century, and life in the nineteenth, identifying 1820 as the key turning point. In sum, he wrote, 'we are a much better people now than we were then, better instructed, more sincere and kind hearted, less gross and brutal, and have fewer of the concomitant vices of a less civilised state'.[1]

Despite his obviously self-interested agenda in emphasising such a change, Place's comments are confirmed by a large number of studies on life in the late eighteenth- and early nineteenth-century metropolis. For the most part, these historians have highlighted the great increase in order and civility that occurred around the turn of the nineteenth century. Robert Shoemaker, for instance, demonstrates how factors such as rapid population growth, economic change and social mobility had altered patterns of social interaction over the course of the eighteenth century so that city dwellers from all ranks were much less likely to take to the streets to express their discontent.[2] Order only increased during the opening decades of the nineteenth century. Fears of potential disorder and popular unrest fanned by events in France and by a perceived rising crime rate led to an official drive to create a more orderly society. From 1820 especially, the authorities sought to regulate public life. While the old 'Bloody Code' was dismantled and many public punishments abolished, ever-tightening restrictions were placed on formerly rowdy entertainments such as fairs, and a new police force was established, the primary function of which was to clear the streets and impose new standards of urban discipline.

At the same time, there was a related push to change the face of the metropolis through a programme of urban improvements. The intention was to revitalise London, as urban growth during the preceding century had placed strain on the existing infrastructure, as well as significantly adding to the dirt and decay that had accumulated in the City and its surrounding neighbourhoods. Early improvements focused largely on the western edge of the City and the fashionable West End, as reformers, planners and architects were concerned with widening streets to relieve congestion while beautifying the main thoroughfares and affluent parishes. Particular attention was paid to old roads that stretched across the metropolis, routes which connected the main centres and provided access both into and out of London. To ensure the smooth and orderly flow of people, traffic and trade, these main arteries were unblocked and new ones were carved into the cityscape. As V. A. C. Gatrell writes, 'visitors returning to London in 1820 would have encountered a city that looked more ordered, planned and controlled than it had been ... Materially, topographically, as well as culturally, we witness the coming of a more socially differentiated, ordered and decorous world.'[3]

Urban regeneration continued after 1820, as planners such as James Pennethorne turned their attention towards the old slums and rookeries that persisted within the City and on its eastern edge. Highways such as New Oxford Street and Commercial Road were designed to drive right through these unhealthy centres of crime and hotbeds of civil disobedience thus removing them from the urban landscape.[4] By 1848, A. H. Hamilton was able to write in his guide to the amusements of London for the provincial excursionist that 'most of the narrow streets of the West End have disappeared, and these crowded districts have been connected into spacious and elegant streets, well-drained, lighted and paved, and in which are erected some of the most magnificent commercial establishments in the kingdom'.[5]

However, this narrative emphasising reform, pacification and increasing order in late Georgian London is in danger of distracting attention away from the fact that this period was, for the majority of Londoners, one of instability, social upheaval and discontentment, especially from c. 1820 onwards. Processes of change, such as urbanisation and industrialisation, already underway in the eighteenth century, greatly intensified during the first half of the nineteenth century. The effects had a substantial impact on the daily lives of many Londoners, dramatically shaping the conditions in which these people were forced to live and work. It is certainly easy to be seduced by the accomplishments of the metropolitan improvements. As one historian has recently reminded us, during the 1820s, while London's 'best circles were agog with excitement about the wave of metropolitan improvements', a 'seamier and more squalid side of urban life' persisted.[6] Although the improvement programme was redirected towards tackling these issues from the late 1830s onwards, by mid-century large parts of London remained untouched, improvements accomplished had often intensified already unbearable conditions in surrounding neighbourhoods, and nothing had prevented the erection of new slums in old and new districts to accommodate an ever-increasing population. Thus the clash between 'old' and 'new' London continued.[7] Such tension was further reflected in the political realm, where reform was also on the agenda. Legislative changes often fell short of expectations generating great disappointment and increasing social divisions. Moreover, the direction of government policy ensured that throughout the first half of the century the battle between traditional values, rights and customs on the one hand, and capitalism, laissez-faire ideology and new middle-class values on the other, continued to rage.

These tensions and feelings of disappointment and loss are explored in depth in this chapter. The experience of life in the metropolis for the large number of ordinary people is central to an understanding of why the theme of violence emerged in a new form in popular entertainment around 1820. The social, economic, political and cultural conditions under which common Londoners laboured ensured the longevity of this theme in addition to its centrality in popular culture. Moreover, this was a period in which much of the culture and entertainment was created by the people, for the people. It is not surprising that many of the social pressures about to be described are constantly referred to in the various narratives of violence utilised in the different genres of amusement explored in the following chapters.

Violent entertainments were largely patronised by the so-called 'lower classes' of the metropolis: those who inherited the plebeian culture of the eighteenth century largely abandoned by the new middle classes, who formed the majority in London, and upon whose shoulders the wealth of the capital and its industry had been built and was sustained. Although a convenient short-hand, the term, 'lower classes' belies the incredible diversity that characterised this audience, reflected in their occupations, living quarters, and even contrasting outlooks. Moreover, to our assessment we must add yet another socio-economic group, the lower-middle class, many members of which also patronised the entertainments described in this book. The presence of men, women and children from this group fragments our audience even further. Different groups certainly had different experiences of life in the city.

However, while it is important to recognise the divisions within the lower classes, it is also crucial to acknowledge that key processes of change such as industrialisation, urbanisation and population growth which intensified during the nineteenth century affected the lives of all, albeit unequally. In addition, we must also remain sensitive to instances of contact between these different groups, which may suggest more cohesion than first glance suggests.

A significant number of recent studies have challenged the application of the terms 'urbanisation' and 'industrialisation' to London during the first half of the century. Not only have historians argued that the most intensive period of population growth and urban expansion in the metropolis actually occurred during the eighteenth century, but they have also been eager to demonstrate that the truly urbanising centres of nineteenth-century Britain were located at quite a distance from London. As the new, industrial towns in the midlands and the north were subjected to a much more rapid pace of growth and experienced a far more distinctive change in character, these historians have argued that if social shock or instability generated from urbanisation is to be found anywhere at this time it would have most likely occurred in cities such as Manchester and Birmingham.[8] Similarly, historians have questioned the extent to which industrialisation affected workers in the metropolis. Factories did not dominate the skyline in London as they did in cities in the north-west. Work within a factory, with new machinery, and on a production line, a pattern of work typically associated with industrialisation, was much less likely for labourers in London.[9]

Yet, both substantial urban growth and changing patterns of work resulting from industrialisation in London cannot be denied. During the opening decades of the nineteenth century, urbanisation and population growth in the capital intensified. Geographically, the expansion of the metropolis overturned the traditional order and structure of the city, pushing its boundaries far beyond those established in the eighteenth century.[10] London's population also continued to increase at an extraordinary rate as people poured into the city seeking work and opportunities. It more than doubled during the first half of the nineteenth century, rising from about 1 million in 1800 to 2½ million by 1851.[11] Similarly, while large factories did not come to dominate the skyline (though, of course, we cannot totally ignore those factories that were constructed on the south bank of the Thames), the capital remained at the very heart of manufacturing in England during this period and retained an important role as a port for receiving raw materials and distributing finished goods to the rest of the world.

Furthermore, the impact of industrialisation was felt at every level of society, and particularly by those who formed the audiences for violent melodramas, graphic broadsides, Sunday newspapers and penny bloods.

London's skilled tradesmen and artisans, a large group situated at the higher end of what came to be described as the lower classes, perhaps experienced the greatest degree of upheaval as a result of industrialisation. Indeed, the nature of change that these men and their families were subjected to demonstrates the peculiar character of industrialisation in the metropolis. During the eighteenth century in particular, as the luxury trades flourished in London, skilled artisans became central to the economy, positioned at the very heart of metropolitan manufacturing. Their tendency to live and work within the same neighbourhood, or even the same residence, meant that different trades came to occupy different parishes spread out across London: weavers in Spitalfields and Bethnal Green, watchmakers in Clerkenwell, tailors and cabinetmakers in Covent Garden, to name but a few. The acquirement of the finely tuned skills necessary to produce well-finished products depended on a system of training through which a worker would progress from apprentice to journeyman and eventually to master craftsman. This system was further bolstered by a shared ethos and culture based on paternalism and a sense of pride in their independence. Artisans also mixed with those of a similar rank and affluence in their neighbourhoods, forming close relationships with shopkeepers and others in the service industry. These men thus acquired a similar outlook, and for a time the occupations were united in the cause of metropolitan radicalism.[12]

However, after 1820 the position of skilled workers in London was frustrated by political developments and the progress of the industrial revolution. The Great Reform Act of 1832 split this group in half. While the more successful master craftsmen and shopkeepers filled the ranks of the new lower-middle class, skilled tradesmen, deprived of citizenship, were pushed into the higher ranks of London's large labouring population. This division was certainly important; it put an end to a valuable political alliance and created a fundamental social distinction.[13] With their middling social aspirations, sense of deference to their social superiors and desire to emulate more affluent lifestyles, the lower-middle class worked hard to distance themselves from the working classes.[14] Yet in spite of their pretensions, the lower-middle class lacked cohesion and also maintained important links with those below. They continued to rub shoulders with the skilled labourers in their work and sometimes living environments. As they were positioned on the border between the middle and lower classes, slippage, in terms of their economic and social position, was always a possibility. Thus, they continued to participate in, enjoy and support entertainments patronised by the lower classes.

What prevented many skilled tradesmen and artisans from rising into this new social group was the depression and even disintegration of many of the traditional trades resulting from the imposition of a system of 'sweating'. While this system ensured that London's industrial character and economic structure were largely distinct from that of the new provincial centres, the effect upon workers was no less devastating. Work formerly completed by skilled artisans was subdivided into a number of piecemeal tasks which could be completed in different stages by semi- or unskilled workers, who could be taught the necessary repetitive skills quickly and were paid at a much lower rate. Factories were unnecessary in London as tasks could be completed in either small, ill-ventilated workshops or within the home as outwork. In the latter case, neighbourhoods became centres of production, as semi-finished goods were passed from house to house for completion. Whole families were recruited for the work, in the hope of increasing the family income. Sweating not only frustrated the traditional system of apprenticeship, prohibiting journeymen from rising to the status of master, but also launched many into poverty. The traditional ethos of paternalism was challenged as new capitalist principles of competition, flexibility and profit encouraged the exploitation of the workforce. Low pay and long hours of work characterised the lives of many.[15]

For the most part, the traditional London artisan 'tended to become just another specialist process worker, using his delicate skills on a narrow basis or was made redundant altogether by mechanisation or cheap labour'.[16] While skilled tradesmen fought to maintain a sort of social exclusivity, their economic and cultural distance from those below can be overemphasised. During the first half of the century, the skilled shared the experience of social precariousness and poverty with the unskilled. Moreover, in many cases they were placed in direct competition with unskilled workers, including women and immigrants, who were able to complete tasks for much lower wages. As a journeyman tailor reflected in his interview with Henry Mayhew during the 1840s, 'since the increase of the ... sweating system, masters and sweaters have searched everywhere for such hands as would do the work below the regular ones. Hence the wife has been made to compete with the husband ... [and] if the man will not reduce the price of his labour to that of the female, why he must remain unemployed.'[17]

Crude rates of pay for both skilled and unskilled workers were typically higher than their provincial equivalents.[18] But any gain was substantially negated by the higher costs of living in London as well as the fact that, in the case of outwork, fees for heating and light also had to be paid from personal finances. Evidence of rates of pay does indicate that real wages experienced long-term growth after the 1820s and prices fell into decline. As a result, historians have long debated whether industrialisation really had such a negative or even devastating impact on the lives of workers. However, taking into account the combined effects of other external factors such as the growing size of families, the decline in relief expenditure after the introduction of the New Poor Law (1834) and the deleterious features of urban life, reflected in the rise in mortality and the decline in nutritional standards, any improvements on paper may not have been experienced in reality. As Charles Feinstein concludes, 'it was only from the late 1850s that the average British worker enjoyed substantial and sustained advances in real wages'.[19] Thus, we could suppose from Feinstein's estimates of 10 to 15 per cent growth that, while skilled and unskilled workers were unable to change unsavoury living conditions or alter unhealthy diets, they would have been able to afford the very minimal outlay required to enjoy the new cheap entertainments described in this book.

Positioned between the skilled and unskilled was a rather distinctive but significant sub-class sometimes identified as semi-skilled: servants. Although there is some dispute over the rate of growth in the industry between the late eighteenth and mid-nineteenth centuries, service, including both live-in positions and outwork (for example by charwomen), remained a crucial sector of employment in the metropolis, especially for women.[20] Servants who lived in the homes of their employers have been regarded as quite distinct and isolated from the working class, and evidence has been presented of their limited engagement with radical working-class movements. But their distance from working-class or popular culture can be overemphasised. Men and women moved in and out of the service industry, entering the profession from mostly lower-class families in which parents were employed in a range of occupations, and many leaving it again to marry and form families of their own. Their role as consumers of the entertainments to be described is important. As we shall see, servants were often identified as readers of broadsides, cheap fiction and Sunday newspapers, and by bringing these 'unrespectable' publications into the homes of the affluent middle and upper classes, and even sharing them with members of the family, breached perceived socio-cultural boundaries.

As Gareth Stedman Jones has written, 'London thrived on its surplus of unskilled labour',[21] its ranks constantly inflated by the influx of immigrants from the rest of Britain, especially the south-east of England and Ireland. This surplus kept wages low and work irregular. Casual labourers not involved in seasonal trades turned their hands to a range of laborious or unsavoury jobs to pay the rent, from coalheaving to scavenging and grave digging. One of the largest places of employment was the London docks, situated along the banks of the Thames in the East End. Every morning, thousands of men struggled for a single day's hire.[22] After the first third of the century, dock labour had been largely 'casualised' in order to increase profits, and labourers were paid just 4d per hour. Competition meant that a full week's work was rare.[23] At a similar socio-economic level, but also distinct in terms of occupation, living quarters and outlook, were the London costermongers or street-sellers, a large number of whom resided in the New Cut in Lambeth, on the south bank of the Thames. Costermongers traded in a wide variety of goods, mainly foodstuffs, and while some successful sellers made a reasonable sum, income for most was very limited, and, moreover, dependent upon the weather. The costermongers were a tight community who strongly asserted their separate identity within the lower classes. Costermongers tended to socialise and form relationships with other costermongers.

They also shared the economic potential of the city streets with those situated on the margins of society, the itinerant sellers of crude literature and entertainment. These men (and sometimes women) suffered from a tremendously precarious lifestyle, as chronicled by Henry Mayhew during the late 1840s and early 1850s, which undoubtedly was reflected in the amusements they offered for sale. Their potential to make a fortune from their skills, or even just a decent income, was severely limited by the greater regulation of street activity by the authorities from 1820 onwards. Yet their persistence in the public sphere through the first half of the century is important, as is their crucial role as producers and distributors of popular culture; in other words, the creators and promoters of narratives of violence.

Finally, according to contemporaries, also perching on the margins was a substantial criminal underclass, feared and despised by the new middle classes and the subject of much debate in the formation of social and penal policy. This 'class' comprised gangs of thieves of the type immortalised by Charles Dickens in *Oliver Twist* (1838), professional beggars, sharpers or tricksters, and prostitutes. Members of this transitory group could be found throughout the metropolis, mostly inhabiting the low-lodging houses prominent in the East End but also scattered around London, in dirty neighbourhoods that emerged in the south or that persisted in the City and the West End. Reports composed by anxious journalists and social investigators suggested that these men and women composed the bulk of the audience for murder melodramas, street performances, executions and cheap fiction, the violent tales contained within these amusements even encouraging their pursuit of lives of crime.[24] Yet the extent to which these men, women and children formed a separate underclass has been called into question by a number of historians who have successfully demonstrated how petty crime and prostitution were used by many as another means of survival, a way in which to supplement meagre incomes and to cope with periods of unemployment, a fate within the realm of possibility for the majority, not just the casual poor.[25]

To these substantial divisions of occupation, earnings and living quarters we must add yet another, that of race or ethnicity, especially noticeable in the large Jewish and Irish populations that had settled in the metropolis, the latter increasing substantially during the 1840s as a result of famine in Ireland. While both groups competed for the various jobs described above, they largely remained socially isolated. Such great diversity within the lower classes thus suggests considerable variation in their experiences of metropolitan life. These differences certainly seem to thwart our attempts at establishing a broad, inclusive and perhaps even cohesive audience for violent entertainments. But it is too easy to overemphasise the importance of economic differentials and social divisions. Commonalities of experience, in terms of hardship, anxiety and frustration, do exist. If the impact of industrialisation on the lower classes was both disparate and uneven, then the process of urbanisation with its attendant problems was much more communally felt, and its impression on the popular imagination more obvious.

Maps of London drawn during the 1830s and 1840s certainly lead us to question the rate of urbanisation and population growth that the capital was subjected to during the first half of the nineteenth century. Not only could one walk from its eastern reaches to the western edge or from its northern to southern boundaries in a matter of hours, but large swathes of green can be identified in the east and west, while open fields persisted to the north of the New Road and on the boundary of Kennington and Southwark. While these superficial maps are in danger of deceiving us, they also point to the main problem of urbanisation in London: overcrowding. As Dr Thomas Southwood Smith explained to the Select Committee on the Health of Towns in 1840:

The district of Bethnal Green contains upwards of 70,000 inhabitants; in the greater part of it, the streets are not close, nor

are the houses crowded; on the contrary, large open spaces of
ground intervene between them, but in one part the population is
as densely crowded as in the closest and most thickly peopled parts
of the city.[26]

During the early nineteenth century, the geographical growth of
London did not keep pace with the increase of population, and the
existing infrastructure was put under severe pressure. This situation
did not occur for want of space; rather it was a question of land value,
especially in the central districts. While the affluent were eager to move
away from the City, resorting to new, exclusive and private residences in
the west, the poorer artisan and labouring classes were tied to enclaves
in the old West End, the City and the East End because of their need
to be within close proximity to their places of work. Low wages, high
rents and profit-hungry landlords combined with increasing numbers
of people seeking employment ensured that these neighbourhoods
degenerated into overcrowded slums. New building did occur in
the east, in particular along the edge of the Thames following the
construction of the new docks. However, many of these new, often
poorly constructed developments also rapidly became unhealthy slums,
not least because of the poverty of their tenants who did not have
the means to improve their dwellings or lifestyle. As space in the
metropolis became such a valuable commodity, multiple families were
forced to share a house, each familial unit confined to a single room.
In the very poorest districts, mid-century social investigators found
multiple families within the same room. Dwellings were extremely
unhealthy, poorly lit and ill-ventilated and disease and mortality were
a fact of life for slum inhabitants.

At this point, we might suppose that the extremes in which the
lower classes were forced to live and work generated a desire for
extremes in the entertainment that they patronised. Living in close
quarters characterised by poverty and hardship meant that these men,
women and children were very familiar with drunkenness, conflict,
violence and death. Thus, it is not surprising that they sought such
a high level of excitement and stimulation in their leisure time.
Violent entertainments popular during the eighteenth century, such
as cockfighting and prizefighting, might well have satisfied this lust.
But these brutal sports had been dramatically restricted and even
outlawed by the authorities who no longer viewed their presence as
possible or desirable in the tightly confined spaces of the metropolis.
Flagrant violations of these laws did occur. Cockfighting, for example,
lived on in slum basements in the back-alleys of Westminster, and

prizefighting persisted simultaneously as a form of entertainment and as a method of dispute resolution.[27] Such high-level, confrontational violence accompanied by mob enthusiasm certainly would have invigorated audiences and quenched their thirst for sensation. However, brutal sports were not only subjected to external pressures that increasingly limited their role and presence, but also were not as socially cohesive as the new entertainments described in this book. Thus graphic images of violence colouring broadsides and gratuitous violence presented in playhouses were a useful alternative. Yet to argue that these amusements merely filled a hole left by the decline of brutal sports is to miss the importance of the narratives which accompanied violent displays. These suggested that although their audiences may have been living unbearably close together, a powerful sense of anomie pervaded the popular imagination.

Recent urban historiography has been eager to emphasise the existence and importance of established communities within the rapidly expanding metropolis during the nineteenth century. Leonard Schwarz, for example, has suggested that we regard London as a kaleidoscope of neighbourhoods set amidst a large, amorphous urban region, each with its own distinct character.[28] Attention has also focused on the close ties of interdependence within lower-class communities, between men and women.[29] Similarly, some historians have demonstrated the methodological integration of newcomers into these communities. Migrants to London did not target the city indiscriminately. If they did not already have family in the metropolis, which they often did, the newly arrived would seek out their kin group. Thus it was with relative ease that migrants developed a sense of belonging within the city.[30] This evidence has led a number of historians to emphasise the social stability of nineteenth-century London. For example, F. M. L. Thompson has argued that these community structures ensured cohesion and orderliness, and indeed were the primary reason why 'the anomie, anarchy and collapse of social order, so much feared by early Victorian observers never materialised ... Anomie and urban alienation were imagined rather than real dragons.'[31]

Violent entertainments could also generate a sense of communal identity. As we shall see, reports of murders in newspapers almost always opened with a declaration of the shock felt by the local community. Melodramas based on crimes of violence that had occurred in the local community provided the opportunity for inhabitants of the neighbourhood to express their disapprobation and participate in a ritual of popular justice. However, it is important not to overemphasise the extent of community interdependence and neighbourhood solidarity in London. As Roy Porter has warned, we must avoid the sense of nostalgia when examining London's various districts: 'village London', he argues, 'conjures a myth of local identity, solid, rooted, stable, duckponds and all; but in reality, London's districts were ever in flux, [as] turbulent eddies of change'.[32] Structures of community in London, especially in lower-class neighbourhoods, did exist. But these were fragile, constantly challenged by the city's growth, population movement and problems resulting from rapid urbanisation. In fact, community solidarity is in part belied by the substantial divisions between different occupational groups outlined above. And these different groups were often forced to reside in close proximity. Local networks and identity mattered a lot less when people ventured outside their own neighbourhood, as they often did. The city could be a strange and frightening environment: becoming lost in the maze of the metropolis was always a possibility.

Historians such as F. M. L. Thompson are right to argue that rapid urbanisation and population growth did not lead to social breakdown, manifested in rising levels of crime and riots. But it might be worth noting here that many men and women in the early nineteenth century did believe that crime, including violent crime, was increasing, a perception confirmed by official statistics and a mounting number of prosecutions in London courts even if this was a result of administrative changes rather than expanding criminality.[33] Moreover, fears about crime and disorder in towns generally provided the rationale for the founding of a metropolitan police force, a group of largely ill-disciplined, young, working-class men, intended to impose order on the very class from which they were drawn. From the 1820s onwards, police powers were continuously extended to include the suppression of previously legitimate behaviours, such as drunkenness, and legitimate uses of public space, from street selling to street games.[34]

Thus unsatisfactory employment, harsh living conditions, dense and potentially hostile neighbourhoods, perceived rising crime rates and new structures of authority created a very real sense of nostalgia, and the sense of 'anomie' or 'urban alienation' found an expression in metropolitan popular culture.[35] Anomie is, of course, nothing new. It was a phenomenon written about by literate city dwellers and visitors since the growth of London took off during the eighteenth century. But this was a new expression, by and for a new audience. For the most part, historians' analysis of community and identity within the city has been largely functional, highlighting the operation of actual networks and the existence of tangible artefacts. However, tactile, neighbourly networks can co-exist with more abstract and even contradictory perceptions of urban life that pervade the popular imagination. Recently, Karl Bell has demonstrated how supernatural folktales, from stories of gruesome murders, the victims of which continued to haunt particular and aptly named sites, to the more famous characters, such as Spring-Heeled Jack, were used by the inhabitants of nineteenth-century Norwich and Manchester as one way of 'mentally mapping the ever-changing urban landscape'. On the one hand, these magical tales helped individuals and communities to adapt to urbanisation. In particular, in the face of perceived fragmentation and the loosening of neighbourhood ties, the folktales helped reinforce local identity through the construction of a 'collective fantastical memory'. Yet, on the other hand, folktales contained an element of resistance to urban change, through their insistence on the significance of the past and their provision of an alternative geography of the city.[36]

Unease, anxiety and fear created by the effects of urbanisation (and even industrialisation) and a narrative of resistance to change were likewise strongly articulated in the representations of violence that became ubiquitous in Victorian popular culture. In this location it was not unusual for such concerns to be exaggerated for the purposes of identification and entertainment. In graphic images and extreme narratives of violence discussed in the following chapters we find a crucial interplay between a number of key binaries, such as the familiar and the unpredictable, community solidarity and urban anonymity.

Interpreting early Victorian entertainments as an expression of 'anomie' is also useful because it hints at yet a further function of representations of violence in nineteenth-century culture. This culture of violence encapsulated and was driven by a reaction against social change, and, at the same time, posed a direct challenge to authority and the establishment.

A climate of political unrest persisted in London throughout our period, from the 1820s until *c.* 1850, as the government was constantly confronted by various forms of radical protest. Radicalism had emerged in the metropolis during the final decades of the eighteenth century, its purpose to lobby for the reform of a corrupt and outdated political system as well as to achieve political representation for all. Success of similar political movements of the people in America and France further encouraged its proponents and it flourished in spite of efforts at suppression by the authorities. During the 1820s, metropolitan radicalism was still enjoying its 'golden age'. Although political change soon came in the form of the Great Reform Act of 1832, it did not live up to the hopes and expectations of many. Most importantly, it split radicalism in half, ending the previously useful alliance between shopkeepers, master craftsmen, skilled workers and the London crowd. While shopkeepers and successful craftsmen swelled the ranks of the new, enfranchised lower-middle class, poorer artisans and skilled tradesmen remained excluded, along with the mass of unskilled workers below them, and experienced further hardship and depression with the onset of 'industrialisation'.[37]

After 1832, tension and hostility came to characterise the relationship between the middle and working classes. This was further increased by the New Poor Law of 1834 which, by reducing the provision of relief for the poor, represented the disintegration of paternalism and heralded the triumph of laissez-faire capitalism and new middle-class values of thrift and respectability. Thus, while the middle classes became increasingly anxious to consolidate their social position and increase their distance from the vulgar crowd, the new working class attempted to form a new political movement, Chartism, in order to continue the cause of old radicalism and secure a system of universal male suffrage. The 'people', however, were now defined as the workers. Yet Chartism was not, arguably, first and foremost a metropolitan movement: its most powerful and thriving centres were actually at quite a distance from London, in the north, the midlands and South Wales. And its expression in the capital, even during significant moments of apparent unity (for example, Kennington Common in 1848), was plagued by fragmentation. For the most part, occupational and social differences between the various groups that comprised the 'working class', or 'the people' as defined by the Chartists, worked against the movement, and thwarted some of the grander attempts at mass protest.[38]

In these conditions, violent entertainments could serve as useful alternatives for the expression of discontentment and as an instrument of protest. As we shall see, their potential was recognised by a number of radical printers and publishers who used the theme of violence, and sensation more generally, to increase the popularity of their products. Some of these men abandoned radical pamphlets altogether in favour of violent stories. Violent entertainments had the potential to unite audiences characterised by such great diversity, to bridge both vertical and horizontal divisions, while providing merriment and fun in the process. Unlike political associations, the theme of violence in popular culture was much more malleable, the entertainments flexible enough to serve particular interests while also expressing common ones. Most of all, this violent culture provided a way through which the lower classes could express their relationship to the establishment: extreme representations of violence became a vehicle of popular resistance. To understand how this state of affairs might have come about, we need to return to an examination of the structures of authority and expressions of resistance that E. P. Thompson located in eighteenth-century society.

In Thompson's view, early modern English society was bipolar: at one end were the gentry and the aristocracy (the patricians) while at the other was the crowd or mob (the plebeians). While middling sorts of people, such as professionals and traders, also existed in the eighteenth century, they were divided between these two poles. For the most part, they were bound by lines of magnetic dependency to the rulers, but on occasion hid their faces in common action with the crowd. Thompson argued that patrician society enjoyed an overarching cultural hegemony, maintained by the self-confidence of the gentry and their control over patronage and the law. Furthermore, this authority was expressed through elaborate theatrical representations, from the grand ornamentation in their dress, homes and mode of travel, to their rehearsed contact with those below, for example their appearances and segregation in the parish churches, and to the larger ceremonial displays in the courtroom. However, hegemony did not equal unqualified dominance as, while it defined the limits within which plebeian culture was free to act and grow, its secular nature meant that it could not determine the character of plebeian culture. Moreover, at the heart of plebeian culture rested a crucial paradox: plebeian society was, at the same time, conservative and rebellious, as the people staged riots in order to reassert their traditional, customary rights.[39] Within eighteenth-century society, therefore, established social rituals existed that encouraged controlled rebellion to protect the culture and lifestyle of the common people. Thompson described in great detail the crowd's capacity for rapid, direct action when they feared encroachments on their rights by the establishment. And he pointed out that, although the actions of the mob could spiral out of control, as did the efforts of the magistrates in suppressing riots, neither side did this very often. Thus, far from being 'blind', 'the crowd was often disciplined, had clear objectives, knew how to negotiate with authority and, above all, brought its strength swiftly to bear'.[40]

Thus, while early modern society was characterised by conflict, acts of rebellion could, in fact, enforce structure and uphold order. But this state of affairs did not last. Through the processes of industrialisation, urbanisation and modernisation, the framework of eighteenth-century society was dismantled. In its wake, a new social system built on class-consciousness emerged during the early nineteenth century. As a result of this tremendous social upheaval, rituals of controlled rebellion were swept away. This dilemma was further complicated by the dramatic restructuring of society in this period: not only had the nature of authority and the exertion of cultural hegemony changed, but also different methods of social control had been developed.

A new idiom of popular resistance, however, may be found in the emergence of representations and narratives of high-level interpersonal violence in entertainment after 1820. As will become clear in the following chapters, entertainments often contained a multi-layered commentary. On the surface, deference and an implied acceptance of new values were displayed (for example, the intolerance of extreme violence and the condemnation of violent offenders). However, underneath, the celebratory presentation of a traditional theme suggested a protest against the imposition of urban discipline, the increasing intolerance for the traditional, popular uses of violence, and the rhetoric of politeness and restraint contained in the emerging ideology of respectability. Violent entertainments were used to assert an alternative, mainstream culture to that promoted by the establishment, which expressed plebeian values, kept alive the 'customary mentality' and directly confronted the growing cultural hegemony of the middle class.

In order to demonstrate that this cultural reading is not far-fetched, in the absence of other historical examples it is perhaps useful to draw upon some relevant studies in social anthropology.[41] Through an examination of Balinese cockfighting, Clifford Geertz has demonstrated how the meaning of specific entertainments can be read on multiple levels. Geertz argued that, on the surface, the cockfight embodied discourses about masculinity and animality. However, it also performed a deeper function: cockfighting was a means of social expression and a dramatisation of status concerns. What holds relevance here is the way in which social tensions that cannot be expressed openly can be articulated and aired through 'play'.[42]

Similarly, in *Domination and the Arts of Resistance*, James C. Scott argued that subordinates in large-scale structures of domination have an extensive social existence outside the immediate control of their rulers, and that in these sequestered settings a critique of domination, or a hidden transcript, emerges. Moreover, subordinates find ways in which to publish the contents of this hidden transcript, articulating a discreet challenge to the control and impositions of their social superiors. Scott described how the subculture of subordinates, which includes songs, rituals, rumours, theatre and folktales, should reflect the smuggling of portions of the hidden transcript onto the public stage. However, the discreet public expression of resistance is complicated: it must be sufficiently indirect and garbled so that it is capable of two readings. When challenged, the innocuous reading provides subordinates with a viable avenue of retreat. Scott concluded that the 'ambiguous polysemic elements of folk culture mark off a relatively autonomous realm of discursive freedom [for subordinates], on the condition that they declare no *direct* opposition to the public transcript as authorised by the dominant'.[43] Much of Scott's evidence for this theory is derived from peasant and slave societies as well as early modern Europe. However, some of these concepts still remain applicable to early nineteenth-century society in London and can assist us in understanding the deeper function of violent entertainments.

Although the English aristocracy and gentry retained large amounts of wealth and power after the disintegration of the ancien régime, over the course of the nineteenth century this power was increasingly challenged by a rising middle class anxious to achieve social status. After 1832, the middle class was able to add a substantial portion of political influence to their increasing financial power. But the main exertion of dominance by this class was in the formation and promotion of an ideology of respectability. Originally a reaction against frivolity and excess of culture above and below, respectability also had firm roots in several eighteenth-century movements, including evangelicalism, politeness, sensibility and humanitarianism.[44] By the early Victorian period it had become the dominant social rhetoric after being embraced by the new Queen and large numbers in the gentry, as well as a significant number of working people, too.

Respectability was a style of living, a creed and code for the practice of personal and family life, ordered by morality and discipline. It enshrined the ideal of the Christian home and shunned displays of luxury, sexual transgressions and activities that were not uplifting and improving.[45] As Geoffrey Best stated, by the early Victorian period there had developed a common cult of respectability and, as an ideology that all could subscribe to, it offered social consensus. A line ran through society, dividing those who were respectable from those who were not.[46] Yet this was, in fact, as much a horizontal division as vertical. Expressions of unrespectability by members of the higher classes were easier to conceal. Moreover, in the name of respectability, the middle classes actively sought to alter what they perceived to be the unrespectable behaviour of the working class. Thus, as respectability became the public transcript, the middle classes achieved cultural hegemony. Patronage and concessions awarded to the lower classes became dependent on displays of respectable behaviour.

Working-class reactions to this cultural hegemony were multifarious. First, we see signs of deference as common people demonstrated an acceptance of this public transcript. Many working people did strive to become respectable, especially as it was not a particularly expensive lifestyle.[47] Its values were not alien to the artisans and skilled tradesmen, whose eighteenth-century outlook had included the promotion of thrift, hard work and independence. However, as Peter Bailey has pointed out, we cannot take displays of respectability at face value. Respectability was 'assumed as a role, or a cluster of roles, as much as it was espoused as an ideology'.[48] It is also important to remember the multifaceted nature of working people's taste in this period. As Patricia Anderson argued, working people's taste 'embraced every conceivable level of cultural expression – literary, lurid, radical, religious, respectable, morbid, moralistic, serious, sensational, salacious, educational [and] escapist'.[49] Thus, a working man or woman might sincerely adhere to some of the central tenets of respectability, yet still be a regular subscriber to a penny blood, or an enthusiastic theatregoer with a passion for gory melodramas.

But patronage of violent entertainments could also be a way in which to express resistance to the cultural hegemony of the middle class. These amusements could be regarded as a method of discreet publication of the hidden transcript: both resisting the imposition of respectable ideology and asserting support for tradition. It is no accident, then, that this new 'culture of violence' emerged and adopted its particular shape during the 1820s, at the very moment when historians claim respectability began to assert its new-found power and other alternative cultures fell into retreat.[50] The 'celebration' of violence, through its excessive representation and the enjoyment audiences derived from it, suggested the continued promotion of a 'customary mentality' which, with roots in a shared culture of pre-industrial England, regarded violence and the physical display of passion as a legitimate form of expression.[51] If actual violence was losing its place in the 'customary mentality', this was substituted by representations of excessive violence. At the same time, violent entertainments invoked a broader social commentary specifically related to life in the early nineteenth-century metropolis and which expressed discomfort and discontent with the effects of industrialisation and urbanisation.

In this context, we might also be able to understand the rather limited offensive launched by the authorities to suppress this rather 'rebellious' culture. Scott argued that the significance of particular social sites which came to represent the location of the hidden transcript is best attested to by 'the unremitting efforts of elites to abolish or penetrate such sites'.[52] But, as we shall see, for the most part violent entertainments were not attacked by the authorities. Except in the case of street amusements, they were largely autonomous and encountered little interference from the law. Their content was questioned by concerned, moralising figures in the middle classes but was never officially tampered with or censored. We might suppose that the authorities were distracted by more obvious and dangerous forms of protest, such as radicalism and Chartism. Or perhaps these entertainments were recognised as something besides resistance. They could, in fact, have operated as a safety valve, providing an outlet for the release of social tensions and frustrations. In other words, these entertainments may have comprised something of a 'Victorian carnivalesque', a useful term recently suggested by Rohan McWilliam, largely assertive rather than subversive, as the world is only momentarily turned upside down, its restoration ultimately proving supportive of the social hierarchy.[53] And as dissatisfaction was expressed in a largely controlled and regulated fashion, with little threat posed to public morality, the role of these entertainments may have even gained tacit approval from the authorities. Violent entertainments could be useful to the establishment. In a very important way, they siphoned off much of the actual violence that had hitherto been expressed in all manner of social and political dealings, thus providing a crucial accompaniment to schemes for the reformation of manners and the taming of the streets.

Finally, a word of caution. By using the concept of cultural hegemony in reference to respectability, we do not want to suggest that violence was necessarily just a counter-culture, or indeed a shadow generated by the majority's adherence to a way of life that had become the accepted norm.[54] 'Cultural hegemony' is a useful term to describe the culture of respectability, because respectability dominated in the seat of social, economic and political power, affording it a currency not shared by early nineteenth-century popular culture. In other words, we do not to want suggest that violence was a culture in decline. Whilst being sensitive to this method of resistance, we might do well to remember that the culture of violence was not always totally antithetical to the culture of respectability. Throughout the following chapters, we will encounter the participation, at times very committed, of the respectable middle and upper classes in some of the entertainments, not to mention their appropriation of particular amusements or features to which they gave new life and impetus.

In sum, this chapter has attempted to come to terms with the questions surrounding the emergence of the theme of violence in popular culture in c. 1820 and suggested some of the key motors that sustained it until c. 1870. We have explored some of the reasons why violence might have taken the distinct shape and expression that it did, as well as the extent to which it actually represented a crucial break from the past as much as, if not more than, a continuation of traditions in pre-industrial popular culture. In addition, we have been given an insight into its malleability. Popular culture can be interpreted on a number of different levels and the theme of violence could incorporate a range of meanings. Thus it had the potential to appeal across the occupational and social divisions that plagued the lower classes and frustrated alternative attempts at protest and representation. And, in addition, the entertainments on offer could also attract a substantial number of lower-middle-class patrons. The chapters that follow turn our attention to the role and presentation of violence in the range of genres that comprised early nineteenth-century popular culture, showing how this theme was put to use, and how much it was enjoyed by audiences. Particular attention is paid to content and narrative, as it is here that we can clearly see how the social and political issues outlined above were invoked by writers, performers and journalists, whether consciously or not.

Notes

1 F. Place, *The Autobiography of Francis Place, 1771–1854*, ed. M. Thale (Cambridge: Cambridge University Press, 1972), p. 82.

2 R. B. Shoemaker, *The London Mob: Violence and Disorder in Eighteenth-Century England* (London: Hambledon & London, 2004), pp. 290–9, Shoemaker, 'Male honour and the decline of public violence in eighteenth-century London', *Social History*, 26 (2001), 190–208, Shoemaker, 'The decline of public insult in London, 1660–1800', *Past & Present*, 169 (2000), 97–131.

3 V. A. C. Gatrell, *City of Laughter: Sex and Satire in Eighteenth-Century London* (London: Atlantic, 2006), p. 595.

4 J. White, *London in the Nineteenth Century: A Human Awful Wonder of God* (London: Jonathan Cape, 2007), pp. 9–35, H. J. Dyos and D. A. Reeder, 'Slums and suburbs', in H. J. Dyos and M. Wolff (eds), *The Victorian City: Images and Realities. Volume 2* (London: Routledge, 1973), p. 365, M. Reed, 'The transformation of urban space, 1700–1840', in P. Clark (ed.), *The Cambridge Urban History of Britain. Volume 2: 1540–1840* (Cambridge: Cambridge University Press, 2000), p. 639.

5 A. H. Hamilton, *The Summer Guide to the Amusements of London and Provincial Excursionist for 1848* (London: Kent & Richards, 1848), p. 11.

6 A. B. Hilton, *A Mad, Bad and Dangerous People? England, 1783–1846* (Oxford: Oxford University Press, 2006), p. 573.

7 White, *London in the Nineteenth Century*, p. 35, L. Nead, *Victorian Babylon: People, Streets and Images in Nineteenth-Century London* (New Haven: Yale University Press, 2000).

8 Shoemaker, *The London Mob*, J. Langton, 'Urban growth and economic change: from the late-seventeenth century to 1841', in Clark, *The Cambridge Urban History of Britain. Volume 2*, p. 487, D. Eastwood, 'The age of uncertainty: Britain in the early nineteenth century', *Transactions of the Royal Historical Society*, 8 (1998), 91–115, J. Stevenson, 'Social aspects of the industrial revolution', in P. O'Brien and R. Quinalt (eds), *The Industrial Revolution and British Society* (Cambridge: Cambridge University Press, 1993), p. 235.

9 L. D. Schwarz, *London in the Age of Industrialisation: Entrepreneurs, Labour Force and Living Conditions, 1750–1850* (Cambridge: Cambridge University Press, 1992), pp. 31–49, 182–4, 227, 231, M. J. Daunton, 'Industry in London: revisions and reflections', *London Journal*, 21 (1996), 1–8.

10 Schwarz, *London in the Age of Industrialisation*, pp. 3–4, 7–9.

11 R. Porter, *London: A Social History* (London: Hamish Hamilton, 1994), pp. 248–9, Hilton, *A Mad, Bad and Dangerous People?*, p. 575.

12 Gatrell, *City of Laughter*, pp. 82–109, M. J. Daunton, *Progress and Poverty: An Economic and Social History of Britain, 1700–1850* (Oxford: Oxford University Press, 1995), pp. 495–7.

13 Gatrell, *City of Laughter*, pp. 576, 586. G. S. Jones, *Outcast London: A Study in the Relationship between Classes in Victorian Society* (Harmondsworth: Penguin, 1976), pp. 340–1.

14 F. M. L. Thompson, 'Town and city', in Thompson (ed.), *The Cambridge Social History of Britain, 1750–1900. Volume 1: Regions and Communities* (Cambridge: Cambridge University Press, 1990), p. 65.

15 Schwarz, *London in the Age of Industrialisation*, pp. 11, 182–227, Jones, *Outcast London*, pp. 32, 106–18, Daunton, *Progress and Poverty*, pp. 495–7.

16 White, *London in the Nineteenth Century*, p. 173.

17 H. Mayhew, *London Labour and the London Poor* (4 vols, London: Griffin, Bohn & Co., 1861–62), II, p. 314.

18 Jones, *Outcast London*, pp. 30–1.

19 C. H. Feinstein, 'Pessimism perpetuated: real wages and the standard of living in Britain during the industrial revolution', *Journal of Economic History*, 58 (1998), 625–58 (quote p. 642). See also S. Szreter and G. Mooney, 'Urbanisation, mortality and the standard of living debate: new estimates of the expectation of life at birth in nineteenth-century British cities', *Economic History Review*, 51 (1998), 84–112, N. F. R. Crafts, 'Some dimensions of the "quality of life" during the British industrial revolution', *Economic History Review*, 50 (1997), 617–39, L. D. Schwarz, 'The standard of living in the long run: London, 1700–1860', *Economic History Review*, 38 (1985), 24–49, and

for the optimistic case, P. H. Lindert and J. G. Williamson, 'English workers' living standards during the industrial revolution: a new look', *Economic History Review*, 36 (1983), 1–25.

20 For example, see L. D. Schwarz, 'English servants and their employers during the eighteenth and nineteenth centuries', *Economic History Review*, 52 (1999), 236–56.

21 Jones, *Outcast London*, pp. 30–1. See also Schwarz, *London in the Age of Industrialisation*, p. 49.

22 Mayhew, *London Labour and the London Poor*, I, pp. 71–2.

23 Jones, *Outcast London*, pp. 111–13, Porter, *London: A Social History*, p. 268.

24 P. Bratlinger, *The Reading Lesson: The Threat of Mass Literacy in Nineteenth-Century British Fiction* (Bloomington: Indiana University Press, 1998), pp. 69–92.

25 For example, see V. A. C. Gatrell, 'The decline of theft and violence in Victorian and Edwardian England', in Gatrell, B. Lenman and G. Parker (eds), *Crime and the Law: The Social History of Crime in Western Europe since 1500* (London: Europa, 1980), Gatrell, 'Crime, authority and the policeman-state', in Thompson, *Cambridge Social History of Britain. Volume 3*, J. Davis, 'Jennings Buildings and the Royal Borough: the construction of an underclass in mid-Victorian England', in D. Feldman and G. S. Jones (eds), *Metropolis London: Histories and Representations since 1800* (London: Routledge, 1989).

26 Report from the Select Committee on the Health of Towns (Parl. Papers, 1840, XI.277) [hereafter SC (1840)], evidence of Dr Thomas Southwood Smith, p. 5.

27 For prizefighting during the nineteenth century, see J. C. Wood, *Violence and Crime in Nineteenth-Century England: The Shadow of our Refinement* (London: Routledge, 2004), pp. 70–94.

28 L. D. Schwarz, 'London, 1700–1840', in Clark, *Cambridge Urban History. Volume 2*, p. 647.

29 Ibid., p. 654, P. Sharpe, 'Population and society, 1700–1840', in Clark, *Cambridge Urban History. Volume 2*, pp. 513–27, White, *London in the Nineteenth Century*, pp. 124–7.

30 Sharpe, 'Population and society, 1700–1840', pp. 513–27, Thompson, 'Town and city', pp. 56–9.

31 Thompson, 'Town and city', p. 57.

32 Porter, *London: A Social History*, p. 252.

33 V. A. C. Gatrell, 'Crime, authority and the policeman-state', in Thompson, *Cambridge Social History of Britain. Volume 3*.

34 D. Taylor, *The New Police: Crime, Conflict and Control in Nineteenth-Century England* (Manchester: Manchester University Press, 1997),

C. Emsley, *The English Police: A Political and Social History* (London: Longman, 2nd edn, 1996), R. D. Storch, 'The policeman as domestic missionary: urban discipline and popular culture in northern England, 1850–80', *Journal of Social History*, 9 (1976), 481–509, Storch, 'Introduction', in Storch (ed.), *Popular Culture and Custom in Nineteenth-Century England* (London: Croom Helm, 1982), pp. 1–14, S. Inwood, 'Policing London's morals: the Metropolitan Police and popular culture, 1829–1850', *London Journal*, 15 (1990), 129–46.

35 Similar sentiments are expressed by these other historians: G. Best, *Mid-Victorian Britain, 1851–1875* (London: Weidenfeld & Nicolson, 1971), p. 9, and P. Garside, 'London and the home counties', in Thompson, *Cambridge Social History of Britain. Volume 1*, p. 489.

36 K. Bell, 'The magical imagination and modern urbanisation' (PhD thesis, University of East Anglia, 2007), ch. 4, passim.

37 Jones, *Outcast London*, pp. 339–41, Hilton, *A Mad, Bad and Dangerous People?*, E. P. Thompson, *The Making of the English Working Class* (London: Gollancz, 1963), Gatrell, *City of Laughter*, pp. 467–546.

38 G. S. Jones, 'Rethinking Chartism', in his *Languages of Class: Studies in English Working-Class History, 1832–1982* (Cambridge: Cambridge University Press, 1983), pp. 90–178, Hilton, *A Mad, Bad and Dangerous People?*, pp. 612–25, D. Goodway, *London Chartism, 1838–1848* (Cambridge: Cambridge University Press, 1982).

39 E. P. Thompson, *Customs in Common: Studies in Traditional Popular Culture* (New York: New Press, 1993), pp. 16–96.

40 Ibid., p. 71.

41 Historians have become very critical of the use of social anthropology. See E. Griffin, 'Popular culture in industrialising England', *Historical Journal*, 45 (2002), 624–6, R. G. Walters, 'Signs of the times: Clifford Geertz and historians', *Social Research*, 47 (1980), 537–56, R. Samuel, 'Reading the signs', *History Workshop Journal*, 32 (1991), 88–109, and Samuel, 'Reading the signs II', *History Workshop Journal*, 33 (1992), 220–51.

42 C. Geertz, 'Deep play: notes on the Balinese cockfight', in his *The Interpretation of Cultures: Selected Essays* (London: Hutchinson, 1975).

43 J. C. Scott, *Domination and the Arts of Resistance: Hidden Transcripts* (New Haven: Yale University Press, 1990), p. 157 (quote). See also Scott, *Weapons of the Weak: Everyday Forms of Peasant Resistance* (New Haven: Yale University Press, 1985).

44 F. M. L. Thompson, *The Rise of Respectable Society: A Social History of Victorian Britain, 1830–1900* (London: Fontana, 1988), pp. 250–1.

45 Ibid., and G. S. R. Kitson Clark, *The Making of Victorian England* (London: Methuen, 1965), pp. 126–8.

46 Best, *Mid-Victorian Britain*, pp. 256–63.

47 Ibid.

48 P. Bailey, *Popular Culture and Performance in the Victorian City* (Cambridge: Cambridge University Press, 1998), pp. 32–40.

49 P. Anderson, *The Printed Image and the Transformation of Popular Culture* (Oxford: Clarendon Press, 1991), p. 180, R. McWilliam, 'The mysteries of G. W. M. Reynolds: radicalism and melodrama in Victorian Britain', in M. Chase and I. Dyck (eds), *Living and Learning: Essays in Honour of J. F. C. Harrison* (Aldershot: Ashgate, 1996), pp. 182–95.

50 In particular, Gatrell, *City of Laughter*. Also Wood, *Violence and Crime in Nineteenth-Century England*.

51 Phrase coined by Wood, *Violence and Crime in Nineteenth-Century England*, pp. 5, 47–68.

52 Scott, *Domination and the Arts of Resistance*, p. 108.

53 R. McWilliam, *The Tichborne Claimant: A Victorian Sensation* (London: Hambledon Continuum, 2007), p. 192.

54 For example, some historians have demonstrated how dominant cultures can create marginal counter-cultures, which a small number of adherents to the dominant culture enjoy participating in because it creates illicit pleasure. K. Halttunen, 'Humanitarianism and the pornography of pain in Anglo-American culture', *American Historical Review*, 100 (1995), 303–34, and H. Berry, 'Rethinking politeness in eighteenth-century England: Moll King's coffee house and the significance of flash talk', *Transactions of the Royal Historical Society*, 6th Ser., 11 (2001), 65–81.

2

About town with Mr Punch

D URING HIS TOUR of England in 1826, the German Prince Puckler-Muskau recorded in his diary the vast array of travelling showmen and their colourful entertainments that crowded the streets below his London lodgings. While he wrote that the barrel organs, in particular, proved 'insufferable', one diversion caught his attention, the English puppet Punch. The Prince provided a long description of the macabre violence mixed with comedy in this puppet show, as Punch beat each opposing character to death with his stick, from his wife, to the doctor, constable, hangman and, finally, the Devil. He concluded that:

> It is not to be denied that Punch is a wild fellow, – no very moral personage, and not made of wood for nothing. No man can be better fitted for a boxer, – other men's hits he feels not, and his own are irresistible. With that, he is a true Turk in his small respect for human life; endures no contradiction, and fears not the devil himself.[1]

From the middle ages, itinerant showmen had followed seasonal circuits around England, including the countryside, provincial towns and the metropolis in their tours, to present to the people a wide range of amusements, from curiosities to theatrical shows and musical performances. Their transitory nature meant that showmen erected their exhibitions in locations where they could attract paying audiences, for example in the fairgrounds and, in the case of smaller shows, in the streets. As urbanisation in particular began to change the character of town life, these entertainments proved to be surprisingly adaptable. Moveable exhibitions found in London during the first half of the nineteenth century were undeniably descended from those which had coloured the pre-industrial world of leisure. However, on closer inspection, it is apparent that most entertainments which did survive were subjected to some form of change, especially in the content that amused audiences.

Using the particularly popular Punch and Judy show as a case study, this chapter demonstrates how vivid and often confronting representations of interpersonal violence were increasingly used by showmen in their portable entertainments in London to capture the attention of passers-by after the turn of the nineteenth century. Although originally occupying a favoured role in early modern popular culture, Punch was radically transformed during the opening decades of the nineteenth century from a comic buffoon into a murderous anti-hero. Despite this change, or even perhaps because of it, the English public continued to adore the puppet. Punch's progress offers a way of understanding the emergence of a new expression of violence in popular culture as well as its specific, functional purpose.

Mirth and merrymaking
in the changing metropolis

The marionette puppet Punchinello, from which the character Punch evolved, first arrived in England during the Restoration period. The overseer's books for the parish of St Martin's in the Fields record several payments in 1666 and 1667 from 'Punchinello, ye Italian papet player, for his booth at Charing Cross', and the famous diarist Samuel Pepys described the pleasure he and his wife derived from the puppet show performed at Covent Garden.[2] Over the course of the eighteenth century, Punch became a popular character in shows presented at fashionable marionette theatres in the West End and in the more popular booths of the fairground. Famous motion masters, such as Powell at the opening of the century and Flockton at its close, attracted audiences which comprised both the sophisticated and the common.[3] Despite his great popularity, Punch did not appear as the central character in their performances, but instead, in the tradition of the English clown, provided a comic interlude, his inappropriate interruptions vocally encouraged by the spectators.[4] In 1728, Jonathan Swift captured the nature of Punch's frequent appearances on stage:

> Observe the audience is in pain,
> While Punch is hid behind the scene;
> But, when they hear his rusty voice,
> With what impatience they rejoice!

...
In doleful scenes that break our heart,
Punch comes, like you, and lets a fart.
There's not a puppet made of wood,
But what would hang him if they could![5]

Far from the murderous scoundrel depicted at the opening of this chapter, Punch played the buffoon. In 1789, Giuseppe Baretti described him as 'a timid and weak fellow, always thrashed about by the other puppet-actors in the show; yet always boasts of victory after they are gone'.[6]

The puppet shows in which Punch appeared embodied many of the themes and characteristics of pre-industrial popular culture. And, in the metropolis, the fairground occupied its very core. Travelling showmen converged at locations such as Smithfield and Greenwich each season and, as the trading function of many London fairs had declined by the eighteenth century, pleasure increasingly provided their main rationale.[7] In addition to the puppet shows, a large variety of entertainments regularly appeared in the fairground, including theatrical booths, exhibitions of freaks and monstrosities, waxworks, menageries, learned pigs and dancing dogs. Excess and spectacle were widely celebrated and amusements incorporated large doses of bawdiness, humour and satire. Moreover, festivities such as fairs where large numbers of pleasure seekers gathered were carnivalesque territories. Controlled rituals which expressed defiance towards authority both amused youths and were largely tolerated by the higher classes who recognised their value as safety valves, providing crucial outlets for the release of tensions in society. Each year, for example, Bartholomew Fair in Smithfield was opened with the rough music rituals of Lady Holland's Mob, a violent gang of youths who, by night, terrorised the local neighbourhood. For the duration of the fair, many entertainments were also permitted to thumb their nose at authority.[8]

Itinerant entertainments of the eighteenth-century fairground also highlight the level of participation of the fashionable in early modern popular culture. In retrospect, Thomas Frost claimed that the fairs 'were resorted to by all classes of people, even by Royalty', and that people of quality took great pleasure in the variety of entertainments on offer.[9] Themes of the fairground were also incorporated in London's fashionable amusements, such as the West End theatres. Dramatic genres such as Italian burlesque and farce were performed with regularity in Covent Garden and Drury Lane, interspersed with circus-type entertainment such as trapeze stunts and mock battles. Moreover, a close relationship was established between travelling theatre booths and the royal theatres from the late seventeenth century. During the period of the fair, London theatres would close and well-known actors from Drury Lane and Covent Garden appeared in the theatrical booths. Some of these men forged business relationships with the travelling theatre industry, becoming pro-term proprietors and managers of the booths. These connections remained strong even after attempts by the authorities to suppress fairs in the mid-eighteenth century. While the reduction of the duration of the fair from fourteen to three days meant that managers of London theatres saw little point in closing for this short period, travelling booths continued as important training grounds for aspiring actors.[10]

However, early modern popular culture was multifaceted. Alongside 'innocent simplicities', such as puppet shows and performing animals, flourished brutalities. As William Boulton concluded in his study of amusements in the two hundred years preceding the reign of Victoria, 'there were never, in modern times, audiences more easily moved to laughter or so easily delighted with the spectacle of bloodshed and suffering as gatherings of Londoners'.[11] Many historians of pre-industrial recreation concur.[12] As well as bawdy and humorous, the people's entertainments were also cruel and bloodthirsty. Violence was an important element of this culture, and its most common expression was in the form of blood sports.

First, Londoners engaged in and enjoyed various types of man-to-man combat, including cudgelling, backsword, singlestick, wrestling and bare-knuckle fighting, the aim of which was to 'break heads', or, to draw blood. Organised matches were held at specific venues in the City or in booths in the fairground. An advertisement in 1743 drew Londoners' attention to a large booth erected at Tottenham Court Fair devoted to wrestling and singlestick. Local participants were presented with the opportunity to win various prizes if they could break the heads of the talented sportsmen from Gloucestershire travelling with this pavilion.[13] On Sundays, common people gathered in the fields surrounding London, where spontaneous matches of cudgelling and singlestick would provide amusement. One newspaper in 1768 recorded a match between two women, who 'fought for a new shift valued at half a crown in Spa Fields, New Islington. The battle was won by a woman called Bruising Peg, who beat her antagonist in a terrible manner.'[14] Londoners also derived much pleasure from blood sports involving animals, such as cockfighting, bull-baiting, bear-baiting, dogfighting, duck-hunting and throwing-at-cocks, which also took place in fairgrounds and in the courts and alleys of Westminster.[15]

Furthermore, re-enactments of high-level interpersonal violence in travelling theatrical entertainments also appear in some accounts of the eighteenth-century fairground. May Fair, held annually on a site near Piccadilly until its abolition in 1760, included a number of booths for prizefighters and cudgelling, but, among these violent diversions, one particularly stood out, the 'Beheading of Puppets', which featured a cast of puppets acting out mock executions. In a coal-shed by the grocers, a shutter was fixed horizontally, on the edge of which, after a series of precious ceremonies, a puppet laid its head which was then instantly chopped off by the other puppet wielding a large axe. The decapitated puppets typically represented well-known figures, for example the Scottish Lords who played a role in the Rebellion of 1745, Charles I, Sidney, Raleigh 'and other martyrs of history'.[16] The violence was incidental rather than central to this performance. The raison d'être of the puppets was carnivalesque, reflecting popular political values.

In accounts of Bartholomew Fair, another entertainment incorporating gross images of interpersonal violence is mentioned. In c. 1721, Lee and Harper's travelling theatre booth staged the play *The Siege of Bethulia, containing the Ancient History of Judith and Holofernes, and the Comical Humours of Rustego and his man Terrible*. Lee and Harper's booth was placed in the centre of a print of the fair (see figure 1). On the outside platform of this booth, where entertainments offered within are advertised, a poster illustrates Judith in the act of decapitating the enemy of the Jews, Holofernes, holding his severed head high while blood spurts from his trunk. This poster suggests that the play may have contained graphic violence in the staging of the biblical story. However, from this limited evidence we cannot assume that representations of high-level violence were a frequent occurrence.[17]

During the last quarter of the eighteenth century and the first decades of the nineteenth, itinerant entertainments in the metropolis began to exhibit grave signs of decline. First, the higher classes, becoming increasingly distanced from the common people, began to desert the fairground. Fairs were thus patronised almost exclusively by the vulgar lower orders. Although the crowds attracted to the fairground grew as the population of London continued to increase rapidly, the receipts of the showmen diminished, as their reduced charges, necessary to attract audiences, failed to produce worthwhile profits.[18] Moreover, the authorities began to launch a full-scale attack on potentially disruptive elements of traditional popular leisure, including the fairground. In a climate of political and social unrest, magistrates were becoming particularly sensitive to possible threats to public order. Metropolitan fairs, with their large public assemblies of people and the exhibition of

Part of Bartholomew Fair, 1721.

1. Lee and Harper's theatrical booth at Bartholomew Fair (*c.* 1721)

boisterous and licentious entertainments, were not only dangerous to public morality, but encouraged heated displays of defiance and riot.[19] As Robert Malcolmson explains, underlying this growing hostility towards popular recreation was the concern for effective labour discipline. Annual holidays and pleasure fairs, impediments to a productive labour force, needed strict regulation.[20] The war waged on the fairground began with the reduction of the duration of the fair. Next, the cost of showmen's permits was raised and various entertainments excluded. Fairs became increasingly unprofitable for showmen. While some fairs died naturally, others were actively suppressed by law. During the 1820s, for example, Shoreditch, Hampstead, Bow, Brook Green, Torhill, Edmonton and Stepney Fairs were prohibited, while the famous fairs of Greenwich and Bartholomew were substantially curtailed.[21]

However, the role of authority and the increasingly hostile upper classes in the suppression of popular entertainments can be overemphasised. In *Memoirs of Bartholomew Fair* (1859), Henry Morley traced its declining fortunes throughout the eighteenth century. Morley acknowledged the increasing restrictions imposed by the Corporation of London, but related these actions, and other declining elements of the fair, to other social processes at work in the metropolis. Rapid population growth meant that each year larger crowds began to descend on the fair, their mass closing important city thoroughfares and threatening public order. Moreover, the increasing rate of urbanisation altered the relationship between the fairground and the city: Smithfield was no longer located in the suburbs but had become a central point in the metropolis.[22] The processes of urbanisation and population growth were further accelerated and intensified during the first decades of the nineteenth century. Space became an increasingly valuable commodity. As Peter Bailey argues, footpaths, public gardens and common land were swallowed up or subjected to an exclusive interpretation of property rights.[23] While a number of smaller fairgrounds on the outskirts of the city were able to survive the attacks of the magistrates and police, recreations that had enjoyed space in the centre of London, however, became endangered.[24]

In 1825, the famous antiquarian William Hone visited Bartholomew Fair and recorded in detail all the shows that appeared that year. The amusements he described, most admitting pleasure seekers for only a penny, included theatrical booths, large and small menageries, waxworks, curiosities from human abnormalities to prodigies, intelligent animals, and circus tents with balancing acts, feats, clowns and tumbling children. These entertainments bear much resemblance to those of the eighteenth century, and the fair itself seems lively, still at the centre of metropolitan life. However, recognising crucial signs of decline, Hone's purpose was to record the dying traditions of the fair for posterity. As he stated in his opening passage, 'I write as regards Bartholomew Fair, rather to amuse the future, than to inform the present, generation.' In his narration of its past and present condition, Hone demonstrated how the authorities, with justification, had become increasingly determined in their efforts to suppress the fair. Moreover, he argued that fairground entertainments were no longer needed, that the people of the metropolis 'are beyond the power of deriving recreation from them'.[25] Whatever the faults and biases inherent in Hone's description of this demise, he did accurately predict the fair's ultimate end. During the 1840s certain amusements were excluded from the fair. In 1849, the civic authorities forcibly moved the remaining showmen to Britannia Fields, alongside the Britannia Theatre in Hoxton. This new fairground was unsuccessful. Old Bartholomew Fair was reduced to a few dozen gingerbread stalls and, in 1855, in the absence of any traders, the fair was officially abolished.

What does become evident in Hone's description of the fairground in the 1820s, however, is the emergence of a new theme in some of the itinerant entertainments which attracted large, enthusiastic crowds. Representations of graphic interpersonal violence were beginning to flourish. No longer patronised by the higher classes, the new travelling theatres of Richardson and Scowton presented performances intended to appeal to working people. Their bills of play reflected the entertainments on offer at the emerging popular playhouses in London (see chapter 4), the main attraction being melodrama. For instance, Hone described the large canvas booth erected by Richardson's troupe of players, its auditorium capable of holding one thousand spectators. Hone purchased a ticket to see the short melodrama entitled 'The Wandering Outlaw; or, the Hour of Retribution', a performance which was much 'enlivened' by the murder in the second act.[26]

Hone also visited the waxworks show, which included, among the various personalities, a portrait of Abraham Thornton who was tried for the murder of Mary Ashford.[27] Finally, Hone was attracted by a peep show at the corner of Hosier-lane, which advertised in bold, black letters, '*Murder of Mr Weare, and Mr Probert's cottage. – The Execution of William Probert*'. He wrote that the show 'consisted of scenes rudely painted, successively let down by strings pulled by the showman; and was viewed through eye-glasses of magnifying power'.[28] Contemporary murders were presented in great detail in nineteenth-century fairground entertainments. Thomas Frost described several peep shows at Bartholomew Fair during the 1830s which featured, as their main attraction, the murder of Maria Marten. In the records of the receipts of the fair for 1827, one show, displaying the head of William Corder, raised 100 pounds.[29] Furthermore, in *Merrie England in the Olden Time* (1842), George Daniel stated that amusements at Smithfield in 1828 included 'the "Red Barn Tragedy", and "Corder's execution done to the life!"'[30]

Popular culture in London during the Regency period demonstrated substantial continuity with that of the eighteenth century. Yet its differences were also significant. J. M. Golby and A. W. Purdue have described early nineteenth-century culture as masculine and gregarious, its hedonism, crudeness and sensationalism matched by a strong undercurrent of violence and disorder.[31] Despite the people's celebration of excess, traditional elements of violence in popular culture, in particular blood sports, sharply declined. With the rise of evangelicalism and humanitarian sentiment, a vicious attack was launched by the authorities and public opinion against sports that involved cruelty to animals. Moreover, changing notions of male honour further facilitated the social marginalisation of staged combats and duels between men.[32] Sports that survived this assault were severely curtailed and, especially after 1820, suffered from the withdrawal of patronage from the higher classes.[33] However, the theme of violence in popular culture did not disappear. Instead, this theme was used to assist pre-industrial amusements in their adaptation to the new environment of the metropolis. In other words, violence could help to ensure their survival and continued popularity.

The travelling showmen did not disappear with the decline of the fairground and other traditional locations of entertainment during the opening decades of the nineteenth century. On the contrary, they displayed remarkable resilience, finding new locations and remoulding their amusements in the cast of changing popular themes and values.[34] With the increasing shortage of open space in the metropolis, the street became a prominent site for showmen to exhibit their wares. Henry Mayhew's interviews with the street entertainers in *London Labour and the London Poor* (1861) illustrate both the extent of the use of the streets as venues for entertainment and the exploitation of the theme of interpersonal violence. Mayhew's account was pessimistic about the future of London street culture, as Mayhew and his interviewees feared that this tradition had begun to lose some of its vibrancy. However, the investigation does offer a crucial snapshot of the character of itinerant entertainments during the first half of the nineteenth century.

According to Mayhew, London's streets were noisy public spaces where images of gross violence were frequently encountered. Broadside sellers stationed at street corners attracted large crowds with their rhyming patter and accompanying graphic sheets which described infamous murders and executions in great detail (this will be explored further in the next chapter). Travelling showmen added yet more colour. First, Mayhew interviewed a peep-show exhibitor. While in previous years he had earned three to four shillings a day, with lower admission prices to the theatres the showman now made barely seven shillings a week. However, he was keenly aware of the subjects which drew crowds: 'People is werry fond of the battles in the country, but a murder wot is well known is worth more than all the fights. There was more took with Rush's murder than there has been even by the Battle of Waterloo itself.'[35] Mayhew also found a young street reciter, who stated that the favourites of his audience were extracts from Shakespeare's tragedies and from current melodramas, such as 'The Gipsy's Revenge', 'The Felon' and 'The Highwayman'. The young boy explained that he and his partner 'take parts in these, and he always performs the villain, and I take the noble characters. He always dies, because he can do a splendid back-fall, and he looks so wicked when he's got the moustaches on.'[36] Although of great interest, it is not our intention to simply list the street shows that regularly featured terrific combats and brutal murders. Violence in popular culture performed a deeper function. But to discover this, we must examine a specific entertainment in depth.

Thus we return to chart the fortunes of our old friend, Mr Punch. During the last quarter of the eighteenth century, the fashionable marionette began to appear in glove-puppet form, mainly as part of a trailer show used to encourage patrons into the larger booths.[37] By the turn of the nineteenth century, however, Punch appeared solely in his new form, now the central character of his own drama. Although Punch continued to make an occasional appearance at the metropolitan fairs, primarily he made himself at home on London's streets.[38] The emergence of Punch as a glove-puppet marked a significant turning point for both the entertainment and his characterisation. In contrast to marionette shows of the eighteenth century, the glove-puppet performance was extremely violent as Punch wielded his deadly stick against any who crossed his path. George Speaight attributes this violence to the mechanics of glove puppetry as, given the limited actions of glove-puppets and the difficulties of dialogue within the showman's box, violent fights provided the lively action necessary to attract an audience.[39] Yet the great success of the puppet show suggests that its violence was related to something much deeper at work in early nineteenth-century society. Although the increasingly common name given to the thuggish puppet was clearly an abbreviation of his formal eighteenth-century appellation, 'Punchinello', 'Punch', in the context of his new role, was also certainly suggestive.

With the development of the glove-puppet show, a cast of characters was introduced to share the stage with Punch, who dealt with each by murdering or otherwise disposing of them. The socially sensitive nature of the drama meant that characters featured regularly changed, reflecting wider contemporary developments. John Payne Collier described the appearance of a number of political characters early in the century, including the MP Sir Francis Burdett and Admiral Nelson.[40] Yet a number of characters were common to all shows, including Punch's wife Judy, a foreigner, blind man, constable, hangman and the Devil. As the showman attempted to attract a casual audience, Punch's encounters with each adversary were performed as self-contained episodes, so that passers-by could join or leave at any time.

Punch's violent dealings with these characters have prompted attempts by antiquarians to decipher the meaning of the Punch and Judy show. George Speaight, for example, argues that to try to extract

2. 'Punch's Puppet Shew' (*c.* 1795)

a meaning from Punch's progress is to seek the impossible. Conversely, Robert Leach asserts that Punch, rebelling against the constraints of various social controls, such as the family, the state and the church, was a working-class hero and in his triumph Leach discovers a subversive and dangerous message.[41] Scenes in which Punch confronts authority figures do seem to invoke the carnivalesque spirit so prominent in early modern popular culture. This evil puppet not only beats the constable to death during an attempted arrest, but also tricks the hangman into placing his own neck into the noose, after which Punch, the felon, joyously completes the execution. The increasing distance between plebeians and the gentry during the 1700s, accompanied by political discontent at the turn of the nineteenth century, meant that the traditional licence for saturnalia in public festivities had been largely revoked.[42] Thus, in the renegotiations of the relationship between the people and authority, the Punch and Judy show may have provided a new outlet for the release of social tension and for the controlled expression of defiance. However, the puppet show contained much more than this. The drama encapsulated *both* subversive *and* conservative undertones. As Punch murdered the various characters who crossed his path, the show presented a kind of mini-revolution, yet, at the same time, mocked this very idea

Doings of Punch and Judy.

3. Robert Cruikshank, 'Doings of Punch and Judy' (1828)

in its exaggerated and outrageous violence. Punch's progress thus becomes a satire.

The double-edged nature of the show helps to explain its appeal to such a diverse audience. In Regency London, Punch enjoyed fame in all classes. The location of the show on the street meant that the performance became popular with those who regularly used this public space, from working people and their families to men of the higher classes. Sketches of Punch and Judy shows from this period illustrate this heterogeneity: working men and women, pausing between errands, congregate at the front of Punch's stage, while higher elements gather round the edges. Adults also far outnumber children (see figures 2 and 3).[43] The desertion of the fairground by the more affluent classes meant that the streets offered Punch showmen the opportunity to collect a larger income from the spectators they attracted. The potential for high earnings was further increased by the practice of 'gentleman's orders', in which Punch showmen would be commissioned by gentlemen at a higher rate to perform on the street corner below their windows.[44]

The content of the Punch and Judy show also presents an important contrast with the theatrical genre of melodrama. Its popularity challenges the presumed ascendency of melodrama in popular culture

during the first half of the nineteenth century. In his study of the
melodramatic genre, Peter Brooks identifies the operation of a 'moral
occult': by presenting the highly dramatic conflict between good and
evil, melodramatic plays sought to demonstrate the existence of a moral
universe. The apparent triumph of villainy in a frightening new world
devoid of moral order presented at the beginning of a melodrama is
shattered with the eventual victory of virtue.[45] With its banal violence
and the ultimate triumph of the immoral murderer, Punch, early
nineteenth-century Punch and Judy shows present a stark opposite to
melodrama, particularly in their debunking of sentimentality.

Furthermore, historians have used melodrama and its presentation of seducer-betrayal narratives to highlight the place of the
'delicate damsel' in the cultural imagination and thus demonstrate the
increasing acceptance of changing definitions of femininity.[46] However,
the dramatic portrait of Punch's marital conduct, in which Punch
typically beats his wife to death, reveals the true complexity at the centre
of this cultural imagination. The regularity with which this scene was
played and its great popularity (to the extent that the colloquial name
of the show became 'Punch and Judy') renders it deserving of further
attention. This episode raises several critical questions about popular
attitudes towards masculinity and femininity as well as the role of
graphic violence as entertainment.

'Wives are an obstinate set'

As Samuel Pepys does not mention a wife accompanying his favourite
puppet, *Polichinello*, in his diaries of 1666–67, we can assume that
Punch's acquisition of a spouse was an eighteenth-century, and English,
development. She was commonly called Joan, an appellation which
was also a colloquialism that described country women. In 1720 a
pamphlet advertising Robert Sheppard's puppet show called particular
attention to the 'comical Humours of the "Italian" PUNCH and his
Country Landlady'.[47] The conjugal life shared by Punch and his wife
was turbulent but not especially violent. Joan nagged and scolded her
henpecked husband, and both characters 'playfully' fought with each
other. Henry Fielding's play *The Author's Farce* (1730) captured the
essence of the comical partnership:

> Punch: Joan you are the plague of my life
> A rope would be welcomer than a wife.
> Joan: Punch, Punch, Punch, prythee think of your hunch,
> Prythee look at your great strutting belly;

Sirrah, if you dare
War with me declare
I will beat your fat guts to jelly.[48]

With the transition of the puppets from marionettes to gloves at the turn of the nineteenth century, some of these aspects of their characterisation remained. Levels of bawdiness, for example, continued to invoke humour. In one pamphlet, *Pug's Visit; or, the Disasters of Mr Punch* (1806), Punch and his wife appeared in a mini-drama described in poetry, its content indicative of the show's popularity with adults rather than children. Punch, bored with his wife's company, decides to invite his friend, Pug the monkey, to a dinner party. After they have scoffed Dame Punch's jellies and pies and had too much to drink, the three end up in one bed. By daybreak, Pug has seduced Punch's wife, and, taking Punch's clothes, they run away together, leaving Punch still snoring in the bed. The naked, cuckolded Punch faces great humiliation when he attempts to retrieve his stolen wife and clothes. Eventually, the sniggering villagers come to his assistance. Pug is punished for the rudeness he displayed towards his host:

While the Dame, on her marrow-bones, pardon implor'd
So Punch kindly forgave her for going astray;
And peace to their mansion once more was restor'd.[49]

Similarly, a correspondent describing a Punch and Judy show in the *Pocket Magazine* claimed that, before Punch appeared on the stage, he was heard in bed with, apparently, Judy. The showman then pretended to watch him dress while introducing the puppet to the audience.[50]

Although, the correspondent continued, when he appeared Punch seemed all affection for his wife and child, soon 'the storm of passion sweeps over his soul', he throws the baby out of the window and 'divorces himself by the summary process of knocking his wife on the head'.[51] Thus, in the opening decades of the nineteenth century, Punch, the henpecked buffoon of the eighteenth century, was transformed into a murderous wife-beater. The new violence of the glove-puppets dramatically altered the tone of the Punches' conjugal life and became the central element in their marriage. Moreover, the humour and commentary embedded in this scene highlight its relationship to a wider social phenomenon.

The characterisation of the conjugal life shared by Punch and Joan during the eighteenth century emerged from a tradition in early modern plebeian culture that, in seeking to enforce marital ideals and expectations, regularly depicted marital conflict as arising from female challenges to the 'natural' patriarchal order. Street ballads and broadsides from the seventeenth and eighteenth centuries presented humorous images of disorderly women or shrews and weak, unmanly husbands in order to ridicule alternatives to patriarchal marriage.[52] One broadside, *The Married Man's Complaint who took a Shrow* [sic] *instead of a Saint*, described the fate of a weak and unmanly 'Hen-peckt Husband' under the authority of his 'Head-Strong wife', with an accompanying illustration of the couple's fight for the breeches.[53] Similarly, *The Woman to the Plow, and The Man to the Hen-Roost* depicted a man and his wife who, finding fault with each other in the fulfilment of their work, decide to swap roles. The result is a disaster. While the man spoils the cooking and cannot complete the household chores, his wife, who goes out to plough the fields, not only destroys the crop but kills the horse. Harmony is only resumed when the couple return to their natural roles.[54]

As a result of shifts in definitions of masculinity and femininity as well as social and economic upheaval during the early industrial period, the traditional theme of the 'struggle for the breeches' was dramatically reshaped. A misogynistic streak emerged in popular culture. Women, rather than men, became primary targets for mockery and images of violence began to feature in representations of marriage.[55] Anna Clark has related the appearance of such songs and caricatures, as well as the increase of domestic violence, to new sources of tension that arose during the late eighteenth and early nineteenth centuries. Libertine pleasures of metropolitan life and the increasing flexibility of plebeian morals could spark flares of jealousy and fanned fears of abandonment. More significantly, traditional bachelor journeyman culture clashed with new realities of married life. The growth of large-scale production and the decreasing reliance on skilled labour had severely disrupted traditional patterns of artisan life. Although many journeymen were now unable to proceed to the status of master, they still chose to marry or cohabit, but at the same time refused to transfer loyalty from their workmates to their wives. Furthermore, journeymen's limited incomes meant that they were dependent on their wives' earnings to support the family economy. Conflict erupted when women's independence gained from wage earning clashed with their husbands' desire to dominate. This problem was further compounded during the 1830s and 1840s as working people found that they could not realistically achieve the domestic ideal of separate spheres. Thus, misogyny and violence inherent in artisan fraternities also emerged in mainstream culture. Clark describes at some length the role of the wife-beating cobbler, the subject of many ballads and jokes.[56] Just as prominent was the brutal puppet Punch, who beat his wife into submission almost daily before large audiences.

Although Punch and Judy made regular appearances on London's streets during the first half of the nineteenth century, John Payne Collier's transcription of Giovanni Piccini's Punch and Judy show, published in 1828, is the only surviving script of a performance. In the autumn of 1827, Piccini performed an exclusive show in the parlour of the King's Arms, Drury Lane, for Collier and George Cruikshank, who had been commissioned by a publisher to transcribe and illustrate a Punch and Judy show. Collier's *Punch and Judy*, complete with script and a note on the history of the show, was a great success and many subsequent editions were released to meet popular demand.[57] Furthermore, the tone of the literary analysis and the script is further testament to Punch's continued appeal to adults, especially men, from all classes.[58]

As evidence of an actual street performance, Collier's script contains inherent problems. First, this is a transcript of a private show for two gentlemen. Moreover, Piccini constantly paused the performance to allow Collier to transcribe and Cruikshank to sketch, thus some of the impact of the live performance may have been lost. Finally, Collier's addition of mock scholarly notes on the history of the show immediately raises some questions about the seriousness of his intentions and suggests that he may have even added some literary flair to the script itself.[59] Despite these reservations, when added to other descriptions of contemporary Punch and Judy shows, Collier's script seems to be quite accurate and, for the most part, the performance seen would have been the performance that was transcribed.[60] The episode between Punch and his wife certainly follows a firmly established pattern, as does the rest of the show, and it is doubtful that the book would have achieved such popularity if the script was too remote from the well-known street performance. In addition, the fact that this script forms an account of how Collier (and Cruikshank) saw and absorbed the show, makes it even more useful for understanding how the Punches' relationship was perceived and interpreted, informing contemporary views on conjugal life.

The marital relationship between Punch and Judy forms a substantial part of the first act of Piccini's show and the nature of conflict between the couple unfolds through song, dialogue and combat. Throughout the scene important lessons on shrew-taming are invoked as the power relationship between the spouses is clearly established. Judy's voice is first heard from below the stage, refusing to comply with Punch's requests to appear with him. When she does finally emerge, the opening moments of the scene establish the nature of their life together. Punch attempts to be affectionate with his 'pretty' wife, but instead receives a slap across the face and Judy's shrewishness or disorderliness is confirmed. Judy then fetches their baby and places it in Punch's care. Punch plays with the child in an inappropriate manner, singing homespun nursery ditties which emphasise the unbearable state of his marriage. For example:

> Oh rest thee, my darling,
> Thy mother will come,
> With a voice like a starling; –
> I wish she was dumb!

The baby soon wakes and, unable to stop it from wailing and screaming, Punch becomes impatient and throws it out of the window.

Judy soon returns and is devastated to learn of the fate of her child. She rushes to fetch a stick and begins a savage assault on her husband. Violence is initiated by Judy as she strikes the first blow, and it is only after pleading with his wife to cease her attack against him that Punch snatches the stick. He begins a murderous assault, attempting to 'tame' his unruly wife, crying, 'How you like my teaching Judy, my pretty dear ... Yes, one littel [sic] more lesson.' Judy soon falls to the floor and becomes silent. Punch, at first, believes she is play-acting: 'There, get up Judy, my dear; I won't hit you anymore ... This is only your fun.' When he finally realises that he has murdered her, Punch shrugs his shoulders, tosses her body from the stage and celebrates her death in song:

> Who'd be plagued with a wife
> That could set himself free
> With a rope or a knife,
> Or a good stick, like me.[61]

The grossly exaggerated violence and Punch's nonchalant attitude about his wife's death make the scene rather humorous and ridiculous. Moreover, Punch's disposal of Judy's body (he tosses it from the stage with his stick) objectifies her. Thus, with the re-establishment of mastery in his household, Punch becomes a hero, while little sympathy is left for his painful and ugly wife.

Extreme violence also characterises Punch's encounters with other puppets in Piccini's show, including the doctor, servant and blind man. When Punch is finally sent to the gallows, he succeeds in tricking the hangman into placing his own neck into the noose and the show closes with Punch's terrific defeat of the Devil. These final conquests create a sense of closure. However, while John Payne Collier transcribed an entire Punch and Judy show, in practice, performances, dependent on audiences and takings, could have been concluded at any point.

Accompanying Collier's transcription of the show are George Cruikshank's illustrations of the puppets in action (see figures 4, 5 and 6). The second illustration depicts Judy in a violent rage, charging with stick in hand towards Punch who cowers in a corner. Finally, we see Punch with the stick while Judy's limp body hangs over the edge of the stage. Judy is presented as the instigator of violence. The physical appearance of the puppets themselves is also significant. Captured in these sketches are the well-known figures of Punch and Judy; these portraits closely resemble illustrations of the show by contemporary artists such as Robert Cruikshank (see figure 3 above). Judy is shabbily dressed with an eighteenth-century mob cap, has a long, crooked, warty nose and is generally quite unattractive. She represents the stereotypical shrew. Although Punch has some similar features (the long nose and red face), he resembles a more comical character, especially with the addition of his jester's hat. George Cruikshank also assumes some artistic licence in his interpretation of Piccini's show: his puppets change expressions – Punch shows fear, while Judy scowls. In performance, the comical and exaggerated features of Punch and Judy, as well as the inability of their wooden faces to express emotion or pain, are crucial as the audience is distanced from the violence and the characters themselves become difficult to identify with.

In addition to her appearance, the new name given to Punch's wife, that of Judy, is symbolic and holds special significance for nineteenth-century culture. In Regency London, the name Judy came to hold negative connotations, used mainly by the lower classes as a label to describe 'tarts', unruly females and unmarried women cohabiting with men.[62] Moreover, the term Judy became even more culturally loaded as its biblical roots were subjected to closer scrutiny. During the siege of Bethulia described in the Old Testament, the heroine Judith saved the Jewish people from the armies of Nebuchadnezzar by slaying his commander-in-chief, Holofernes. This tale clashed with emerging passive and submissive ideals of femininity.[63] Furthermore, the colloquialism 'Judy' gradually began to be used in literature, extending its application and understanding through the respectable classes. Various plays and novels of the period used phrases such as 'to make a Judy of yourself' and the label 'Judy' when referring to women who behaved in a disorderly manner.[64] In these cultural surroundings, the name given to Punch's wife was particularly pertinent. The puppet became a crucial visual reference for the colloquialism and, even more than this, Judy Punch and the term 'Judy' became mutually constitutive.

4, 5, 6. George Cruikshank's
illustrations for John Payne
Collier's *Punch and Judy*
(1828)

Literary men regularly wrote about the Punch and Judy shows they saw, celebrating the triumphant conquests of Punch. In their accounts, they described the Punches' marital conflict with notable pleasure. They isolated these characters from the rest of the show and, while not identifying with the puppets themselves, they used Punch and Judy to symbolise the inevitable clash between the sexes. A correspondent to *Blackwood's Edinburgh Magazine* in 1839 pondered, 'if I were a woman of the lower grade, in which alone men are privileged to beat their wives, I would raise a female mob, and draw the merry ruffian [Punch] from the streets [as there must have been many a husband present who] would see, in the general applause, an excuse for beating his wife'.[65] But this correspondent fundamentally misunderstood the puppet show. Despite the enjoyment of violence, the Punch and Judy show did not expressly condone wife-beating, or indeed wife-murder, for those in the audience. Humour and satire trivialised the beatings administered by Punch to his wife, ridiculing Judy's plight. The 'utility' of violence in marriage was, in part, recognised. After all, in this case violence did provide a solution to Punch's domestic problems. However, its extreme presentation overrode any explicit sanctioning of violence in the domestic sphere. The irony inherent in Punch and Judy is all-important, as the following author recognised.

Charles Molly Westmacott's *The English Spy* (1826) is a satirical portrait of the life of the fictitious Bernard Blackmantle. In seeking to make a profitable marriage, Blackmantle is forced by his father to visit the Alderman, Mr Marigold, and his daughter, Miss Biddy. During his visit a Punch and Judy show begins beneath the window. Westmacott provides an animated description of the audience that gathers at the sound of Punch's trumpet, including the butcher's boy, lamplighter, cook and servant girl, all pausing to enjoy the violent conquests of the heroic puppet. This rather diverse audience is reflected in Robert Cruickshank's accompanying watercolour (see figure 7). Wealthy Londoners, for example the Alderman's family, watch from their windows and balconies. In the top right-hand corner, one affluent lady, captivated by Punch's fear of Judy's ghost, absent-mindedly drops her baby from the window, mirroring Punch's careless disposal of his own child. This image establishes a contrast with the thoughts of the Alderman. As he and Blackmantle delight in Punch's reassertion of authority over his shrewish wife, the Alderman cries, 'what a true picture of the storms of life! – how admirable an essay on matrimonial felicity!' Thus the Alderman ponders, as did other literary gentlemen, about the henpecked working men in the audience who may follow Punch's example. At the same time, Cruikshank suggests that this

7. Robert Cruikshank, 'The Great Actor, or Mr Punch in all his Glory'
(1826)

domestic scene, and the attitudes reflected within it, were not so very
isolated from their own lives.[66]

Thus, Punch, in spite of his unlawful behaviour and murderous
deeds, was welcomed in literature as a hero. As a correspondent to
the *Literary Speculum* exclaimed, 'Oh! Punch! with all thy faults I love
thee still!'[67] In contrast, these literary gentlemen have little sympathy
for Judy, the termagant, who is often held accountable for the Punches'
marital problems. Her unwomanly behaviour and 'provocations' are
used to excuse Punch's violence. Furthermore, comments made in
higher-class journals demonstrate how Judy's character continued to
evolve outside the actual performance. She is frequently portrayed
as an unfaithful wife, even though accounts of performances suggest
no such conclusion.[68] The character of Judy is invoked to describe
other disorderly women. In an article in *Fraser's Magazine*, the author
wrote of an encounter experienced by his travelling companion at a
dinner party. The young gentleman was imposed upon by his host's
cousin, Miss Snooks, whose outspoken nature and physical appearance
reminded him precisely of Mrs Punch from the pages of Collier's *Punch
and Judy*: 'Yes, Miss Snooks, the old maid, was the wife of Mr Punch
… The same weasel eyes, the same sharp voice and hooked chin, and
the same nose.'[69]

The declining fortunes of street entertainments

Despite the great popularity of the Punch and Judy puppet shows with all classes during the first half of the nineteenth century, when Henry Mayhew met with a showman during the early 1850s, a grave sense of pessimism pervaded the interview. It was immediately apparent that business was not as lucrative as it had been in previous decades. The showman explained that twenty years ago he collected five pounds a week on average, earning seven or eight shillings from each street performance. However, 'a good day for us now seldom gets beyond five shillings ... Often we are out all day, and get a mere nuffing [sic]'. In the open street, Punch shows now only gathered around threepence per show.[70] Punch's increasing bad luck on the streets was reflective of a decline in the fortunes of street amusements more generally. In his interviews with other street entertainers, Mayhew found that their earnings had substantially diminished and that the number of showmen had decreased. A peep-show exhibitor claimed that he could make three or four shillings a day before the theatres lowered their ticket prices (1846), while another performer explained that street reciters had become a rare class – only five could now be found in London.[71]

Unlike some of the other entertainments that will be examined in this book, the decline of Punch and Judy street shows can, in part, be attributed to the extension of authority and the increasing regulation of street life during the nineteenth century. The relatively wide powers granted to police by the 1839 Metropolitan Police Act have traditionally been held accountable for the transformation of London's streets, including the removal of many street entertainments, from the opening of the Victorian period onwards. Robert Storch argued that the new police officers were 'domestic missionaries', successfully used by the respectable classes to maintain 'order and decorum in all public spaces' and to impose 'new standards of urban discipline'.[72] Recently, Storch's conclusions have been challenged by historians who have produced evidence demonstrating the resilience of street life and the survival of various amusements conducted in this space. Stephen Inwood, for example, has pointed out that street culture proved relatively resistant to police control, and that the police recognised that noise and indecency were a natural part of everyday life, deeply embedded in working-class culture. Thus, the police force established a practical compromise between middle-class ideals and working-class realities, learning 'to live with the popular culture which some of its advocates had expected [it] to destroy'.[73]

In this situation, both change and continuity can be overemphasised. Perhaps it is more useful to consider the differences between so-called 'rough' and 'respectable' neighbourhoods in nineteenth-century London. Street culture did persist throughout the century; however, it became increasingly confined to single-class districts, for example the East End. And this street culture became largely composed of amusements that did not require financial outlay, such as games and sports. Street performers needed higher-class patronage in order to survive. Henry Mayhew's interview with the Punch showman demonstrates just how crucial it was to attract middle- and upper-class audiences. He explained that, while showmen had largely deserted east London, the West End had become 'the great resort for all; for it is there the money lays [sic]'. Punch showmen began an annual pilgrimage to the more fashionable seaside resorts during the summer months and, for the rest of the year, continued to erect booths on street corners in the hope of encouraging paying gentlemen to their windows.[74]

However, during the second half of the century this practice became substantially curtailed as ideas about the appropriate use of public space were dramatically transformed. Urbanisation and population growth challenged the utility of London's streets as entertainment venues. In commercial and business districts the sheer volume of people squeezed into the narrow streets and the overwhelming increase in traffic both restricted space formerly available for entertainers and generated large amounts of noise which performers were forced to compete with. Moreover, in quieter, middle- and upper-class, notions of respectability shaped new regulations on the use of public space. Punch and Judy shows were excluded from Hyde Park.[75] In addition, during the 1860s, a campaign was launched against street musicians, particularly organ-grinders, by a number of middle-class men who wished to exclude the unrespectable vagabonds from their streets. New legislation resulting from the campaign gave householders powers to regulate the space outside their front doors.[76] While Mayhew's showman claimed Punch was exempt from powers outlined in the Police Act, when asked about interference from the constables he replied, 'some's very good men, and some on' 'em are tyrants'.[77] Thus, law and authority did have some impact on the fortunes of Punch and Judy, as well as other street entertainments. However, equally significant was the rate at which more affluent audiences were abandoning Punch and Judy street shows, despite the tremendous enjoyment these men claimed to experience from watching them.

The beginning of the Victorian period witnessed the emergence of a more domestic culture that was orientated around the family and home.[78] Its location indoors meant that previous outdoor amusements that had benefited from higher-class patronage, such as the Punch and Judy shows, began to suffer. Moreover, pausing to watch a Punch and Judy show had become a dangerous activity: while one's attention was occupied with the pleasures of Punch, one could easily find oneself a victim of crime. Petty street crime was common during the first half of the century. The late eighteenth-century watercolour 'Punch's Puppet Show' illustrates this hazard, as the partner of the Punch showman, while collecting money from the audience, picks the pocket of a distracted gentleman (see figure 2). Pickpockets and other criminals, however, were seen as an inevitable part of metropolitan life. They were certainly an inconvenience, but also contributed to the atmosphere of danger and illicit pleasure that informed Regency culture. By the middle of the nineteenth century, however, greater concerns were expressed about crime and deviancy. The consequences of watching Punch and Judy shows were frequently catalogued in the police-court reports contained in the daily newspaper: respectable men found their valuables stolen and others, their attention distracted, were easily duped by sharpers.[79]

Furthermore, the respectable values of the more affluent section of the audience meant that objections began to be raised about the actual content of the Punch and Judy shows. Despite Regency ease with the graphic portrayal of wife-murder in the show, early Victorians began to express some discomfort with the Punches' violent relationship and especially audiences' enjoyment of the scene. Punch still featured regularly in literature, but his conquests were now approached with a sense of embarrassment, especially as the show represented the disruption of public and moral order, threatening the centrality of the institution of marriage and family to society. Clear attempts were made to emphasise the working-class character of both the audience and even the puppets as respectable writers sought to distance themselves from the themes presented. In *Picturesque Sketches of London* (1852), Thomas Miller described the crowd which derived much pleasure from a Punch show, including a 'ragged woman holding up her dirty child. The little rogue claps his tiny hands, and crows again at every blow Judy receives; [and the poor mother is] delighted with the pleasurable expression of her dirty darling's countenance'. However, Miller also draws attention to the respectable gentleman watching the performance from the edge of the crowd, 'half ashamed of being seen in such a motley assembly'.[80]

Although the respectable attempted to disown him, Punch continued to be quietly celebrated in these circles and it was not long before Punch was actually invited into the very institution he threatened to destroy:

the respectable middle-class family. In 1850, John Leech sketched the puppet show in the new surroundings of a middle-class drawing room and, by 1895, one showman claimed that he regularly performed for the children of the royal household.[81] Punch and Judy street shows declined in favour of the steadier income provided by privately commissioned shows in middle-class homes. Mayhew's Punch showman explained that the greater part of his income was now derived from commissioned shows performed indoors. Midsummer and Christmas were known as 'Punch's season. We do most at hevening [sic] parties in the holiday time, and if there's a pin to choose between them, I should say Christmas holidays was best. For attending hevening parties now we generally get one pound and our refreshments.'[82] But why were the uncouth showmen with their rather undomestic portrayal of family life welcomed into these respectable homes?

Robert Leach and Scott Cutler Shershow have both attempted to explain this process of cultural appropriation. While Leach argues that Punch and Judy were adopted by the middle class as part of a culture of conciliation, Shershow views appropriation as a 'natural' development in the evolution of the show, questioning original lower-class patronage by noting the ease with which Punch's so-called 'rebellion' moves from street to nursery.[83] Yet the adoption of Punch and Judy was much more conscious than either allows. The process of domestication began with the decision of a group of literary men to name their new satirical journal, first published in July 1841 for the bourgeois intelligentsia, *Punch*. Their first issue strongly aligned itself with the 'morals' of Punch's puppet show.[84] It was a sense of nostalgia that prompted early Victorian middle- and upper-class men to invite Punch into their homes. They had found immense joy in the show during their youth as young 'men about town', seeing in the puppet a reflection of the pleasurable elements of Regency culture, including hedonism and misogyny. The process of street clearing and the increasing regulation of public space in respectable neighbourhoods helped to fan this sentimentality, as respectable men feared that Punch and Judy shows were fast becoming a relic of the past. Punch's performances in the drawing room were but a short step from shows set up on street corners by 'gentlemen's orders'. However, in order to be accepted into this new environment, substantial modifications were necessary.

For drawing-room audiences, the Punch showman stated that he adapted his performance according to their tastes. He explained to Mayhew that 'some families where I performs [sic] will have it most sentimental ... They won't have no ghost, no coffin, and no devil; and that's what I call spilling the performance entirely.'[85] Despite the showman's apparent distaste with this 'sanitisation', throughout the interview he repeatedly emphasised the moral value of Punch and Judy to his gentleman interviewer. Like other exhibitors of Punch in London, this showman recognised the financial necessity of injecting some respectability and morality into his performances. The transcript of his show included by Mayhew, when compared to John Payne Collier's script of 1828, reveals some significant changes: puppets receive beatings from Punch, but leave the stage alive, and Punch's triumph over the Devil is repositioned as the defeat of evil (sometimes, the showman substituted the Devil with a topical Russian bear), rather than the downfall of Christian morality.[86] As this transcript was meant to be an example of a surviving street show, it also illustrates the extent to which modifications for the drawing room were also applied when the show was performed in its more traditional location. It also demonstrates the complexities of transition. Violence is not completely eradicated and elements of backsliding are apparent. Moreover, contradictions emerge when the script and showman's commentary are compared. And nowhere is this more obvious than in the portrayal of Punch and Judy's relationship.

In the showman's performance, violent domestic quarrels continue to characterise Punch and Judy's relationship. Judy strikes the first blow against her husband when he shows some affection towards her. The couple then reconcile, only to fight once again when Punch demands that Judy fetch his child. After Punch playfully throws the baby out of the window, Judy finds a stick and beats her husband. Punch snatches the stick in the struggle and brutally beats her.[87] While the violence has been toned down in this script – Punch does not kill his wife – important continuities persist in the use of violence and the development of the characters to which audiences would have been sensitive. Judy remains the instigator of conflict and at the centre of the violent struggles. In her rejection of Punch's affection, she not only neglects her wifely duties, but mocks them. In his comments on the Punches' relationship, the showman justifies the violence through its moral purpose. But there are inherent contradictions in his statements. He explains that Punch is taken to prison at the end of the first act for the murder of his wife and child.[88] However, in performance, Judy leaves the stage alive, and few clues are provided by other puppets about her mortality. When Punch is subsequently arrested, his violent marital conduct is not even mentioned. In addition, although the showman superficially condemns Punch's treatment of his wife, and hopes that the show 'will be a good example to both men and wives, always to be kind and obleeging [sic] to each other … (that's moral)', when he describes the characters themselves, responsibility for the violence is redistributed. Punch did not intend to beat his wife; instead, Judy 'irritated' him so much that he was driven to it. And finally, the showman adds, 'Judy, you see, is very ugly ... a head like that there wouldn't please most people.'[89]

This Punch showman, and even his interviewer, Henry Mayhew, were pessimistic about the present and future fortunes of the Punch and Judy show. However, we already know the end to this story: Punch and Judy were not eradicated. Instead, the show was given new life through commercialisation and an accompanying 'willingness' of showmen, largely through financial necessity, to adapt their performances. For all itinerant showmen, during the middle of the nineteenth century respectability became an important marketing device. For instance, after 1850, fairgrounds located on the outskirts of London experienced a substantial revival, but, as Hugh Cunningham demonstrates, new powers granted to law-enforcement agencies, including the police, cannot explain the increasing tolerance of the authorities. Instead, the values displayed by the showmen changed. From the middle of the century, they became 'respectable and wealthy entrepreneurs of leisure, patronised by royalty'. As the norms of the showmen and authorities converged, fairs became tolerated, safe and eventually a subject for nostalgia and revival. Thus, late nineteenth-century observers 'saw the fair as a routine and legitimate occasion for leisure rather than as one of those "violent delights" of Londoners'.[90]

Similarly, after 1850, Punch showmen gradually came to be regarded as more respectable and appeared with greater frequency in the drawing room. Like the other entertainments described in this book, the growing commercialisation of the leisure industry heavily impacted on the character of the show but also, in contrast, this larger process actually made possible Punch and Judy's survival. Furthermore, although the extreme violence of the show was toned down, and the Punches' relationship was somewhat modified, commercialisation, unusually, also ensured the persistence of some degree of rough treatment in the depiction of Punch and Judy's conjugal life. And, perhaps paradoxically, this was encased in the language of respectability.

During the 1860s, Punch and Judy shows became just one genre of amusement offered by large businesses that specialised in the provision of children's entertainment and which regularly advertised in that respectable organ of news, *The Times*. For example, Addro's Magical Repository in Regent Street issued this notice in January 1866:

Evening Parties. – Mr Henry Novra continues to provide (in town or country) all the newest Entertainments in Conjuring, Juggling,

Ventriloquism, Marionettes, Punch and Judy, Dissolving Views, etc. Terms moderate. *Respectable* artists guaranteed.[91]

With the commissioning of these private drawing-room performances, Punch and Judy shows became increasingly sophisticated in terms of financial agency and the commercial processes involved. On one level, shows were put on for the purpose of amusing children. Thus, the children had to be entertained. And young audiences found the slapstick and knock-about violence appealing. As one journalist pondered in 1872, 'why children *should* be fond of such an *un*domestic drama as portrayed in the representation of Mr Punch's adventures can only be accounted for by that love of the horrible so innate even in infantile nature'.[92] Perhaps 'even' should be replaced with 'especially'. Studies in psychoanalysis and child psychology have revealed the particularly violent, anxious and even sadistic character of a child's imagination. Their irrationality and the frequency with which dark and murderous thoughts pervade their minds do go some way towards explaining children's fascination with gruesome and graphically violent tales.[93]

On another level, however, were the adults: as they paid for the entertainment, they exerted some influence over the style of performance. In the interests of respectability, showmen were required to make some modifications. As Mayhew's showman explained above, new characters were introduced that replaced some of the former controversial puppets. In 1895, one writer declared that 'we are ... softening down even this specimen of "good old" aboriginal humour, and now it more frequently closes with a "nigger" song, or something of that nature, than, as formerly, with the death of the Father of Evil'.[94] Men of the middle and upper classes, familiar with Punch from their youth, noticed considerable change when they stopped to watch performances in the street. Thomas Miller claimed that 'Punch was a different performance in our youthful days: then he went out, got drunk, came home and quarrelled with his wife; ... and sorry we are to say the drunken rascal swore dreadfully.'[95] Moreover, in 1872 the editor of *Punch* recalled the invitation issued to a showman by the gentlemen of the Fielding Club to perform for them. Although 'the room was crowded with a great company of men who knew how to laugh, ... [the show] was a dead failure: the very dreariest night I can remember. We couldn't – and we tried hard – get up the smallest laugh.'[96]

However, at the same time, adults commissioning drawing-room shows also wanted to be entertained. Punch and Judy shows were, therefore, family entertainment, designed to appeal to both children *and* adults. And, as a result, violence did persist. As one showman explained, 'the dolls, you see, get so much knocking about that they only last about six months'.[97] Respectable Victorians adopted a violent entertainment for their children's enjoyment and moral instruction, but when they set about to transform the show, they retained substantial levels of violence, especially in the depiction of marital relations between the two central characters, Punch and Judy. Even though this violence had been slightly subdued for juvenile audiences, beatings administered by Punch to his wife continued to form the purpose and humour of this scene. Furthermore, these beatings were surrounded by yet more violent encounters in the show, as Punch continued to vehemently oppose those who came to share his stage.

However, while in the case of Punch and Judy representations of violence persisted right up to the close of the nineteenth century, the show's appropriation by the respectable classes fundamentally altered the deeper function of entertaining violence. On one hand, the violence of Punch's puppet show presented an ideal opportunity to teach children valuable lessons about outbursts of anger and the control of temper.[98] On the other hand, for respectable adults who attempted to subscribe to the ideals of companionate marriage and separate spheres, Punch and Judy were used to confront the realities of marital breakdown. They became important icons in a society in which marriage could, for many, degenerate into a farce or tragedy, as marital partnerships were so hard, legally and socially, to dissolve. In addition, Punch and Judy also fulfilled important psychological functions. Notions of politeness and civility adhered to by the respectable middle class not only led to the displacement of violence onto the working class, but, more significantly, determined how violence was viewed within their own class.[99] Elements of satire and humour in the Punches' marriage were used to accommodate issues of domestic violence which respectable Victorians found uncomfortable, but were forced to confront. And we can only imagine the level of satisfaction some middle-class spouses would have experienced from this portrayal of violence as it was, after all, behaviour in which the respectable were no longer allowed to participate.

Notes

1 Prince Hermann von Puckler-Muskau, *A Regency Visitor: The English Tour of Prince Puckler-Muskau*, ed. E. M. Butler and trans. S. Austin (London: Collins, 1957), p. 86.

2 T. Frost, *The Old Showmen and the Old London Fairs* (London: Tinsley Brothers, 1874), p. 29 and S. Pepys, *The Diary of Samuel Pepys*, ed. R. Latham and W. Matthews (11 vols, London: Bell, 1970–83), III,

entries 9 May 1662, 8 October 1662, VII, 22 August 1666, 29 August 1666, 1 September 1666, VIII, 20 March 1667, 8 April 1667, 4 September 1667, 24 October 1667.

3 G. Speaight, *Punch and Judy: A History* (London: Studio Vista, 1979), pp. 54–60, S. C. Shershow, *Puppets and 'Popular' Culture* (Ithaca: Cornell University Press, 1995), p. 114, R. Chambers, *Book of Days* (2 vols, London: W. R. Chambers, 1863), II, pp. 167–8, Frost, *Old Showmen*, p. 207, W. Hone, *The Every-Day Book* (2 vols, London: Hunt & Clarke, 1825–26), I, pp. 1246–8, Anon., *A Peep at Bartholomew Fair* (London: R. Macdonald, 1837), p. 7.

4 For example, see the description of the opera, *The Old Creation of the World with the addition of Noah's Flood, to conclude with the merry conceits of Squire Punch and Sir John Spendall*, in the *Tatler*, 14 May 1709, quoted in Hone, *Every-Day Book*, I, p. 1247, advertisement for Robert Sheppard's puppet show in London, c. 1720, 'By His Majesty's Permission. Here is come to this place, and is to be seen a play call'd, Dives and Lazarus' (eighteenth-century microfilm collection, 10389), L. McNally, *The Apotheosis of Punch; a Satirical Masque: with a monody on the death of the late Master Punch* (London, 1779), and advertisement at Tottenham Court Fair, 8 August 1730, for Reynold's Great Theatrical Booth, 'A Comical, Tragical, Farcical Droll, called The Rum Duke and Queer Duke, or a Medley of Mirth and Sorrow. To which will be added a celebrated Operational Puppet Show, called Punch's Oratory, or the Pleasures of the Town' quoted in G. Daniel, *Merrie England in the Olden Time* (2 vols, London: R. Bentley, 1842), I, p. 110.

5 Swift quoted in A. Adams and R. Leach, *The World of Punch and Judy* (London: Harrap, 1978), p. 10.

6 Baretti quoted in Speaight, *Punch and Judy*, p. 66.

7 R. Malcolmson, *Popular Recreations in English Society, 1700–1850* (Cambridge: Cambridge University Press, 1973), p. 20, J. M. Golby and A. W. Purdue, *The Civilisation of the Crowd: Popular Culture in England, 1750–1900* (London: Batsford, 1984), p. 37.

8 W. B. Boulton, *The Amusements of Old London* (2 vols, London: J. C. Nimmo, 1901), I, p. 60, Hone, *Every-Day Book*, I, pp. 1167–252, Malcolmson, *Popular Recreations in English Society*, pp. 80–2, Golby and Purdue, *The Civilisation of the Crowd*, p. 23.

9 Frost, *Old Showmen*, p. 146, H. Morley, *Memoirs of Bartholomew Fair* (London: Chapman & Hall, 1859), p. 335, Hone, *Every-Day Book*, I, pp. 1167–252.

10 Chambers, *Book of Days*, II, pp. 263–7, Frost, *Old Showmen*, p. 146, Hone, *Every-Day Book*, I, pp. 1167–252.

11 Boulton, *Amusements of Old London*, II, pp. 222–3.

12 Malcolmson, *Popular Recreations in English Society*, p. 43, Golby and Purdue, *Civilisation of the Crowd*, pp. 22–3.

13 Frost, *Old Showmen*, p. 157.

14 Quoted in Boulton, *Amusements of Old London*, II, p. 234. See also the evidence of William Lovett, cabinetmaker and manager of the National Hall in High Holburn, in Select Committee on Public Libraries (Parl. Papers, 1849, XVII.1), p. 178 [hereafter SC (1849)], H. Vizetelly, *Glances Back through Seventy Years* (2 vols, London: Kegan Paul, 1893), I, p. 13, and D. Brailsford, *Bareknuckles: A Social History of Prizefighting* (Cambridge: Lutterworth, 1998).

15 [John] Stow's *Survey of London* (1720 edn), quoted in J. Strutt, *The Sports and Pastimes of the People of England* (London: Printed for Thomas Tegg, 1801), p. xxvii, Boulton, *Amusements of Old London*, I, p. 175, and II, p. 249 the evidence of William Lovett, SC (1849), p. 178.

16 Hone, *Every-Day Book*, I, pp. 572–7, Boulton, *Amusements of Old London*, II, p. 66 (quote), and Chambers, *Book of Days*, II, p. 169.

17 While Hone wrote that this print was made in 1721, Frost dates it at 1723. Hone, *Every-Day Book*, I, pp. 1167–252, and Frost, *Old Showmen*, pp. 111–12.

18 Frost, *Old Showmen*, pp. 199–200, 319–20, Strutt, *The Sports and Pastimes of the People of England*, p. 141.

19 Chambers, *Book of Days*, I, pp. 643–5, II, p. 263, Golby and Purdue, *Civilisation of the Crowd*, pp. 89–90, Malcolmson, *Popular Recreations in English Society*, p. 146, H. Cunningham, 'Metropolitan fairs', in A. P. Donajgrodski (ed.), *Social Control in Nineteenth-Century Britain* (London: Croom Helm, 1977), p. 163.

20 Malcolmson, *Popular Recreations in English Society*, pp. 89–98.

21 Daniel, *Merrie England*, I, p. 105–10, Cunningham, 'Metropolitan fairs', p. 165, M. Judd, 'The oddest combination of town and country: popular culture and the London fairs, 1800–1860', in J. K. Walton and J. Walvin (eds), *Leisure in Britain, 1780–1939* (Manchester: Manchester University Press, 1983), p. 15.

22 Morley, *Memoirs of Bartholomew Fair*, pp. 315, 351, 387, 438.

23 P. Bailey, *Leisure and Class in Victorian England: Rational Recreation and the Contest for Control, 1830–1885* (London: Routledge & Kegan Paul 1978), pp. 14–15. See also E. Griffin, *England's Revelry: A History of Popular Sports and Pastimes, 1660–1830* (Oxford: Oxford University Press, 2005), pp. 83, 169, 176–7.

24 Fairs described by Cunningham, 'Metropolitan fairs', pp. 163, 172.

25 Hone, *Every-Day Book*, I, pp. 1167–252.

26 Ibid. See also descriptions of Richardson's and Scowton's theatres and

performances in Frost, *Old Showmen*, pp. 217 and 230, Chambers, *Book of Days*, II, pp. 263–7, Morley, *Memoirs of Bartholomew Fair*, p. 471.

27 Hone, *Every-Day Book*, I, pp. 1167–252, Frost, *Old Showmen*, p. 292.

28 Hone, *Every-Day Book*, I, pp. 1167–252.

29 Frost, *Old Showmen*, pp. 302–3, 305, 307.

30 Daniel, *Merrie England*, I, p. 191.

31 Golby and Purdue, *Civilisation of the Crowd*, pp. 14, 63–5, 80–7.

32 R. B. Shoemaker, 'Male honour and the decline of public violence in eighteenth-century London', *Social History*, 26 (2001), 190–208.

33 H. Cunningham, *Leisure in the Industrial Revolution, 1780–1880* (London: Croom Helm, 1980), pp. 25–6, Hone, *Every-Day Book*, II, pp. 799–801, Strutt, *The Sports and Pastimes of the People of England*, p. 205, Boulton, *Amusements of Old London*, II, pp. 96, 109, 224, 252. For disagreement with this traditional historiography, see Griffin, *England's Revelry*, p. 114.

34 Golby and Purdue, *Civilisation of the Crowd*, pp. 39–40, 65, 80–3, Bailey, *Leisure and Class in Victorian England*, 8–11, Cunningham, *Leisure in the Industrial Revolution*, pp. 9, 15, 38 and Griffin, *England's Revelry*, p. 176.

35 H. Mayhew, *London Labour and the London Poor* (4 vols, London: Griffin, Bohn & Co., 1861–62), III, pp. 88–9. See also G. W. M. Reynolds, *The Mysteries of London* (2 series, 4 vols, London: G. Vickers, 1844–48), first series, I, pp. 158–9: description of the entertainments in the streets of the New Cut.

36 Mayhew, *London Labour and the London Poor*, III, pp. 151–4. See also Mayhew's description of the strolling players, III, pp. 139–44, and the exhibitor of mechanical figures who continued to tell the gory story of Judith and Holofernes, III, pp. 177–9.

37 R. Leach, *The Punch and Judy Show: History, Tradition and Meaning* (London: Batsford, 1985), p. 33, Speaight, *Punch and Judy*, p. 71.

38 Note that Hone does not record a Punch and Judy show in his list of entertainments at Bartholomew Fair in 1825: Hone, *Every-Day Book*, I, pp. 1167–252.

39 Speaight, *Punch and Judy*, p. 76.

40 J. P. Collier, *Punch and Judy, with twenty-four illustrations designed and engraved by George Cruikshank* (London: Printed for S. Prowett, 1828), pp. 50–2.

41 Speaight, *Punch and Judy*, pp. 78–9, Leach, *The Punch and Judy Show*, pp. 35, 54–5.

42 E. P. Thompson, *Customs in Common: Studies in Traditional Popular Culture* (New York: New Press, 1993), pp. 16–96.

43 See audience descriptions in J. Eagles, 'Reflections on Punch: morals

and manners', *Blackwood's Edinburgh Magazine*, 45 (1839), pp. 190–200, Anon., 'The puppet show', *Literary Speculum*, 1 (1821), p. 155, J. T. Smith, *Nollekens and his Times* (London, 1828), p. 114, and C. M. Westmacott, *The English Spy* (2 vols, London: Sherwood, Jones & Co., 1826), II, p. 62.

44 Described by Mayhew's Punch showman in *London Labour and the London Poor*, III, p. 46. See also Westmacott, *The English Spy*, II, p. 59, and figure three.

45 P. Brooks, *The Melodramatic Imagination: Balzac, Henry James, Melodrama and the Mode of Excess* (New Haven: Yale University Press, 1976), pp. 13–17, 20–2.

46 M. J. Wiener, 'Alice Arden to Bill Sikes: changing nightmares of intimate violence in England, 1558 to 1869', *Journal of British Studies*, 40 (2001), 184–212, J. R. Walkowitz, *City of Dreadful Delight: Narratives of Sexual Danger in Late Victorian London* (Chicago: University of Chicago Press, 1992), pp. 85–102, A. Clark, 'Rape or seduction? A controversy over sexual violence in the nineteenth century', in London Feminist History Group (ed.), *Men's Power, Women's Resistance: The Sexual Dynamics of History* (London: Pluto, 1983), pp. 13–27, and M. Vicinus, 'Helpless and unfriended: nineteenth-century domestic melodrama', *New Literary History*, 13 (1981), 127–43.

47 Sheppard, 'Dives and Lazarus'.

48 H. Fielding, *The Author's Farce* (London: Printed for J. Roberts, 1730), Act III, Scene 1. See also advertisement for Reynolds's Great Theatrical Booth at Tottenham Court Fair, 8 August 1730, one of the entertainments including 'several diverting passages, particularly a very elegant dispute between Punch and another great Orator; Punch's Family Lecture, or Joan's Chimes on her tongue to some tune'. Quoted in Daniel, *Merrie England*, I, p. 110.

49 Anon., *Pug's Visit; or, the Disasters of Mr Punch* (London: J. Harris, 1806).

50 Quoted in Leach, *The Punch and Judy Show*, pp. 52–3.

51 Ibid.

52 J. Wiltenburg, *Disorderly Women and Female Power in the Street Literature of Early Modern England and Germany* (Charlottesville: University Press of Virginia, 1992), pp. 7, 9, 28, N. Z. Davis, *Society and Culture in Early modern France* (Stanford: Duckworth, 1975), pp. 124–51, especially pp. 142–3, and F. Dolan, *The Taming of the Shrew: Texts and Contexts* (Basingstoke: Macmillan, 1996), pp. 2–4.

53 *The Married Man's Complaint Who took a Shrow instead of a Saint*, Oxford, Bodleian Library (Bod.), Francis Douce Collection, vol. II. See also *Advice to Bachelors, Or, A Caution to be Careful in Their Choice*, Bod., Francis Douce Collection, I.

54 *The Woman to the Plow and The Man to the Hen-Roost*, Bod., Francis Douce Collection, II.

55 V. A. C. Gatrell, *City of Laughter: Sex and Satire in Eighteenth-Century London* (London: Atlantic, 2006), pp. 345–87.

56 A. Clark, *The Struggle for the Breeches: Gender and the Making of the British Working Class* (Berkeley: University of California Press, 1995), pp. 5–7, 31–4, 64, 87, 248, 260–3.

57 P. McPharlin, 'The Collier-Cruikshank Punch and Judy', *Colophon*, 1 (1936), 371–87.

58 Collier's book was also advertised in *The Times*, demonstrating its appeal to men of the higher classes. *The Times*, 3 December 1831, p. 4.

59 Speaight, *Punch and Judy*, p. 81.

60 For example, the show described above in the *Pocket Magazine*, von Puckler-Muskau, *A Regency Visitor*, pp. 85–7, and Anon., *Punch's Pleasantries: The Tragical Comedy of Punch and Judy* (London, 1838?).

61 Collier, *Punch and Judy*, pp. 69–76.

62 Anon., 'The Punch and Judy men of England', *Pall Mall Gazette*, 45 (15 June 1887), 1–2, Speaight, *Punch and Judy*, p. 85. See also report from police courts in *The Times*, 14 November 1850, p. 7: 'Southwark. – Peter Bent, alias Lewis, a well-dressed man, and Emma Barber, nicknamed "Judy", a woman of the town with who he cohabits, were placed at the bar before Mr A'Beckett, charged with stealing a hat, pocketbook, knife and snuff-box, from William Arnold, in the Equestrian Coffee-house, near the Surrey Theatre. Both prisoners were committed.' Antiquarians place the change of name to Judy for the glove-puppet around 1820, once the show became more violent and Judy's character further developed. See Speaight, *Punch and Judy*, p. 85.

63 M. Stocker, *Judith, Sexual Warrior: Women and Power in Western Culture* (New Haven: Yale University Press, 1998), pp. 1–2, 135, 137–42.

64 G. Colman, *The Review; or, the Wags of Windsor* (London: J. Cawthorne, 1808), Act I, Scene II, J. P. Pirsson, *The Discarded Daughter; A Comedy in Five Acts* (New York: W. Stodart, 1832), Act I, Scene IV, G. Eliot, *Scenes from Clerical Life* (London: Blackwood, 1858), ch. 1, and Eliot, *The Mill on the Floss* (London: Blackwood, 1860), ch. 6.

65 Eagles, 'Reflections on Punch: morals and manners', p. 190. The German Prince Puckler-Muskau similarly questioned what effect the Punch and Judy show had on the morality of the lower classes. See von Puckler-Muskau, *A Regency Visitor*, p. 87.

66 Westmacott, *The English Spy*, II, pp. 59–62. See also Anon., 'Stanzas to Punchinello', *New Monthly Magazine*, 10 (1824), 441–2.

67 Anon., 'The puppet show', p. 156.

68 Anon., *Pug's Visit*, and von Puckler-Muskau, *A Regency Visitor*, pp. 85–7.

69 Anon., 'Punch and Judy', *Fraser's Magazine for Town and Country*, 3 (April 1831), 350–4.

70 Mayhew, *London Labour and the London Poor*, III, pp. 45–6.

71 Ibid., pp. 88–9, 151–4.

72 R. D. Storch, 'The policeman as domestic missionary: urban discipline and popular culture in northern England, 1850–80', *Journal of Social History*, 9 (1976), 481–509, Storch, 'Introduction', in Storch (ed.), *Popular Culture and Custom in Nineteenth-Century England* (London: Croom Helm, 1982), pp. 1–14, and Storch, 'Police control of street prostitution in Victorian London: a study in the contexts of police action', in D. H. Bayley (ed.), *Police and Society* (London: Sage Publications, 1977), pp. 49–72.

73 S. Inwood, 'Policing London's morals: the Metropolitan Police and popular culture, 1829–1850', *London Journal*, 15 (1990), 129–46. See also J. Winter, *London's Teeming Streets, 1830–1914* (London: Routledge, 1993), pp. 66–8.

74 Mayhew, *London Labour and the London Poor*, III, pp. 46–7.

75 See, for example, editorial in *The Times*, 6 October 1862, p. 6.

76 B. Assael, 'Music in the air: noise, performance and the contest over the streets of the mid-nineteenth-century metropolis', in T. Hitchcock and H. Shore (eds), *The Streets of London: From the Great Fire to the Great Stink* (London: Rivers Oram, 2003), pp. 183–97.

77 Mayhew, *London Labour and the London Poor*, III, pp. 46–7.

78 F. M. L. Thompson, *The Rise of Respectable Society: A Social History of Victorian Britain, 1830–1900* (London: Fontana, 1988), pp. 254, 256–7, and J. Walvin, *Leisure and Society, 1830–1950* (London: Longman, 1978), pp. 9–16.

79 See for example, *The Times*, 10 June 1858, p. 11, 18 October 1859, p. 9, 31 January 1860, p. 11, 4 December 1861, p. 11.

80 T. Miller, *Picturesque Sketches of London, Past and Present* (London: Office of the National Illustrated Library, 1852), p. 256. See also A. G. Bowie, 'The story of Punch and Judy', *The Theatre: A Monthly Review*, N.S. 3 (1 January 1884), 18, and C. Dickens, *The Old Curiosity Shop* (London: Chapman & Hall, 1841), ch. 26: Dickens parodies this duality of embarrassment and enjoyment.

81 A. T. Story, 'Punch and Judy', *Strand Magazine*, October 1895, p. 463.

82 Mayhew, *London Labour and the London Poor*, III, pp. 45–7, 50.

83 Leach, *The Punch and Judy Show*, pp. 76–7, 80, 85, 91, Shershow, *Puppets and 'Popular' Culture*, pp. 162–70, 173–4, S. C. Shershow, 'Punch and Judy and cultural appropriation', *Cultural Studies*, 8 (1994), 541–6.

84 'The moral of Punch', *Punch*, 1 (1841), 1.

85 Mayhew, *London Labour and the London Poor*, III, p. 43.

86 Ibid., pp. 53–60, especially p. 59.

87 Ibid., pp. 54–5.

88 Ibid., pp. 45, 58.

89 Ibid., pp. 48, 50–1.

90 Cunningham, 'Metropolitan fairs', pp. 163–4, 170, 180.

91 *The Times*, 13 January 1866, p. 1, my emphasis. See also: 14 December 1864, p. 1, 30 December 1864, p. 1, 28 January 1865, p. 1, 13 January 1866, p. 1, 24 January 1866, p. 1; *W. G. Sylvester's royal high class drawing room entertainments for evening parties* ... [advertisement] (London, n.d. [1870–1900]), p. 2, Bodleian Library, Oxford, John Johnson Collection, Actors, Actresses and Entertainers, IX.

92 *Harper's Weekly*, 6 January 1872, p. 5.

93 B. Bettelheim, *The Uses of Enchantment: The Meaning and Importance of Fairy Tales* (Harmondsworth: Penguin, 1978), pp. 120–2. See also P. M. Pickard, *I Could A Tale Unfold: Violence, Horror and Sensationalism in Stories for Children* (London: Tavistock Publications, 1961).

94 Story, 'Punch and Judy', p. 463. See also M. Beerbohm's comments in R. Thorndike and R. Arkell, *The Tragedy of Mr Punch: A Fantastic Play and Prologue in One Act, with an introductory essay by Max Beerbohm* (London: Duckworth, 1923), p. 7.

95 Miller, *Picturesque Sketches of London*, p. 255.

96 B. Jerrold and G. Doré, *London: A Pilgrimage* (London: Grant & Co., 1872), p. 177. See also 'A Modern Frankenstein', *All the Year Round*, N.S. 1 (1868–69), 202.

97 Story, 'Punch and Judy', p. 463.

98 See parallels discussed in P. N. Stearns, 'Men, boys and anger in American society, 1860–1940', in J. A. Mangan and J. Walvin (eds), *Manliness and Morality: Middle-Class Masculinity in Britain and America, 1800–1940* (Manchester: Manchester University Press, 1987), pp. 77–82, Stearns, 'Girls, boys and emotions: redefinitions and historical change', *Journal of American History*, 80 (1993), 36–74, and E. Foyster, 'Boys will be boys? Manhood and aggression, 1660–1800', in T. Hitchcock and M. Cohen (eds), *English Masculinities, 1660–1800* (London: Longman, 1999), pp. 151–66.

99 E. Foyster, 'Creating a veil of silence? Politeness and marital violence in the English household', *Transactions of the Royal Historical Society*, 6th Ser., 12 (2002), 395–415, M. Hunt, 'Wife-beating, domesticity and women's independence in eighteenth-century London', *Gender and History*, 4 (1992), 10–33.

3

From scaffold culture to the cult of the murderer

PORTABLE THEATRES AND PUPPET SHOWS were not the only entertainments from the pre-industrial world to survive and flourish in the nineteenth-century metropolis. As long as public execution persisted in London so did scaffold culture. However, changes in penal law, the shifting interests, motivations and abilities of audiences, and the development of new technologies meant that while some expressions of this culture fell into decline, others received new life, and more still came into existence. Although the scaffold remained an important element, over time it ceased to loom so large in depictions of crime. As we shall see, it was replaced by the theme of violence. Actual narratives of violence, especially those about brutal murders, whether or not the offender was hanged for his or her crimes, now attracted the great interest, though it must be added that the completion of the tale on the scaffold did enhance this attention. And in these representations of violent crime, the theme of violence was intensified.

The transformation of the early modern popular literature of crime

In eighteenth-century England, the public nature of criminal behaviour and its punishment meant that every level of society became intimately acquainted with and almost obsessively interested in crime. After all, with over two hundred capital offences listed in the statutes, hangings in the metropolis were a common occurrence and, at this time, social niceties did not preclude the attendance of so-called polite observers at these events. It is not surprising then, that such widespread interest in crime encouraged the emergence of a popular literature which intricately explored its commission and punishment. During the closing decades of the seventeenth century, this formerly marginal literature experienced tremendous proliferation and, by the middle of the eighteenth century, both its genres and audience had become diverse.

The texts were truly popular: their range and prices as well as the scale of publication suggested that purchasers came from all ranks of society. For instance, Gertrude Savile, sister to the Seventh Baronet Savile, Lord of Rufford, mundanely recorded reading '"The Life, Robberies etc. of [James] Dalton", and evidence against several of the Robers [sic] which are to be hanged' in her diary of 1728.[1] However, some historians have argued that the more detailed and prominent genres were, for the most part, largely consumed by the middling sorts, from professionals and merchants to small landholding farmers. These were mostly amusing and lively pamphlets and multivolume biographies on the lives of criminals who perished on the scaffold, including common thieves and pickpockets as well as notorious highwaymen and murderers. More official reports and narratives of crime were also sold in great numbers to these subscribers, such as the *Old Bailey Sessions Papers*, *Select Trials* and the *Ordinary's Account*.[2] While these genres were substantial and durable, there also existed more ephemeral publications. At the foot of the scaffold on the days of execution, hawkers sold crude broadsheets at rock-bottom prices which contained little detail except for the briefest outline of the malefactors' offences, perhaps a short sorrowful lamentation and, very occasionally, a rough woodcut of the gallows. These sheets provided some sort of access to the popular literature of crime for the lowest and poorest ranks of society, representing a kind of souvenir, a way of prolonging the experience of their day at Tyburn.[3]

As many of these vulgar, cheap sheets have not survived, historians have chosen to devote much of their attention to the more 'sophisticated' genres of the popular literature of crime and have found that each performed different functions. The detailed proceedings of trials in the *Old Bailey Sessions Papers*, for example, offered the public 'objective facts' about crime to ponder. Conversely, although based on official accounts, the composition of biographies of felons was greatly influenced by popular taste and the imaginations of their anonymous authors. On one level, criminal lives were cautionary tales, designed to deter audiences from the path of temptation and crime. However, on another level, shrewd publishers also recognised the necessity of entertainment and, as a result, pamphlets and multivolume biographies were extremely sensational. Descriptions of outrageous violence and sexual scandal were woven into narratives of the exploits of highwaymen, footpads and prostitutes. Many of these tales were, of course, fabricated. Fact was regularly embellished with absurd fiction in the hope of creating a 'deep and lasting impression' on the minds of readers.[4]

In these lewd and often titillating tales, historians have uncovered a number of recurring themes. These texts shed light on popular notions of criminal responsibility and the place of crime in early modern society. Lincoln B. Faller, for example, highlights the operation of two distinct types of narrative in the pamphlet literature. The first, that of the 'familial murderer', contained a serious description of the felon's fall from grace, the crime, and the resulting sorrow and regret. By smoothing over the disruptive effects of his or her behaviour, these pamphlets were intended to reintegrate the offender into society. The second, however, refused to acknowledge any social threat posed by the offender, instead presenting the tale of the picaresque rogue, typically a romantic highwayman, and mostly concerned with the details of his fantastic and improbable adventures. At the same time, authors would amplify his cruelties in order to justify his end on the scaffold.[5] As Andrea McKenzie states, both narratives hinted at wider preconceptions about crime and punishment in early modern society. All men and women were perceived to be inherently sinful and thus at least potentially criminal. The murderer, highwayman or common pickpocket had 'tempted fate by indulging in those vicious tendencies to which all men and women are prone'. Therefore, the eighteenth-century murderer 'served as a metaphor for the frailty and inherent depravity of human nature'.[6]

During the last decades of the eighteenth century and first decades of the nineteenth century, while key genres of the early modern popular literature of crime fell into decline, other peripheral elements were transformed. Change was first apparent in the purchasing patterns of the middling sorts, who were fast becoming the new metropolitan middle class, whose new values had a decisive impact on the content of the literature they chose to purchase. Based largely on Captain Alexander Smith's *Lives of Highway-men*, the *Old Bailey Sessions Papers* and the *Ordinary's Account*, the *Newgate Calendar* was one publication that aimed to keep abreast of these social developments. *Newgate Calendars* were lavish collections, often illustrated with fine engravings featuring the criminal, his or her trial, and his or her execution. However, the content of the *Newgate Calendars* was indicative of an important change in the composition of biographies of criminals. *Newgate Calendars* were increasingly moralistic publications. Elements of sensationalism, from detailed accounts of barbarity to salaciousness and scatology, were largely removed from their pages. Thus, the popular literature of crime, or at least those genres dependent on middle-class patronage, had become subjected to a process of taming.[7]

Although *Newgate Calendars* remained in press from their first appearance in the 1770s until the early twentieth century, they remained fairly marginal publications for much of the nineteenth century, attracting a relatively tiny audience in comparison with their eighteenth-century success, a process indicative of the fortunes of criminal biographies in general. General themes in this literature had ceased to be of relevance to the lives of readers. For example, the new shape of the city, the increasingly urban character of people's lives and improvements in cross-country travel meant that the figure of the highwayman, so central to the genre, was no longer of such contemporary relevance. The last breath of this tradition was felt in the emergence of the genre of Newgate Novels which flourished during the 1830s. Written mainly by William Harrison Ainsworth and Edward Bulwer-Lytton, these were fictional and often romantic accounts of the lives of highwaymen and criminals which many contemporaries feared glamorised the commission of crime. First published as serials in highbrow periodicals, Newgate novels undoubtedly enjoyed popularity with middle-class readers. But this was largely fleeting, as loud sections of the community began to voice their great disapproval.[8]

As the genre became increasingly 'unrespectable', the tales were kept alive and in circulation by young men and boys of the lower classes. Their particular delight in Ainsworth's *Jack Sheppard*, the story of the infamous housebreaker of the 1720s who repeatedly thwarted attempts of the authorities to incarcerate him, generated much concern among social investigators who feared Sheppard's exploits would serve as a great encouragement for youths.[9] In reality, however, the popularity of Jack Sheppard was derived from a tradition as old as Robin Hood: the fascination with outlaws and the tendency to create heroes out of figures who thumb their nose at authority has long been common among the disenfranchised and adolescent boys.[10] This readership also continued to support the large number of cheap, romantic criminal biographies of eighteenth-century highwaymen and *Newgate Calendar* plagiarisms that were produced throughout the nineteenth century, first as a lucrative sideline of the penny-blood publishers and later by the marginal publishers of juvenile penny dreadfuls.[11]

As the deeds of criminals were now regarded by the respectable as inappropriate subjects for literature, the image of Tyburn was retreating into the distant past and began to be seen by many as quaint. But public executions in the capital persisted, and so did a culture that surrounded the scaffold. The dismantling of the Bloody Code during the 1820s, which saw the repeal of many of the capital statutes, meant that murder became one of the few capital crimes and, throughout the first two-thirds of the century, increasingly the only crime for which Londoners watched felons hang. As the highwayman drifted into the romantic past, the stage was left to the character of the murderer. The theme of violence, therefore, became central to scaffold culture during the early nineteenth century. Yet the change was even more significant than this. The enthusiasm for narratives of murder which ended at the gallows dovetailed into a wider, more general interest in representations of violent crime.

In spite of the narrative of decline and the withdrawal of the middling sorts provided above, this continued to be a culture in which both high and low participated. Actual hangings were regarded by many as a form of entertainment and certainly held out attractions as a part of a narrative of violence in which keen spectators could participate. Scaffold audiences sustained a healthy dose of diversity, but increasingly the lower orders dominated the proceedings. Perhaps more important, however, was the material production derived from this culture, its purpose to assist in the re-enactment of narratives of extreme violence. Figures of infamous murderers and their victims were cast in wax to be placed in museums for the elite and the humble, exhibitions that persisted into the twentieth century (and even into the twenty-first century). Moreover, the obsession with tales of murder encouraged the production of 'tat', cheap souvenirs and mementoes that were sold for display within the home and were designed to assist individuals and their families in the commemoration of particularly notable crimes.

In addition, while criminal biographies were subjected to a process of marginalisation, other genres of the popular literature of crime, mainly supported by the lower orders, both persisted and expanded during the nineteenth century. Both traditional printers and emerging commercial publishers eagerly exploited new technologies and were quick to take advantage of a rapidly growing and increasingly literate working- and lower-middle-class population who were in need of entertainments suited to the constrictions of the urban environment. Thus, on the one hand, the half-penny broadside trade, which specialised in sensational crimes and executions, exploded during the opening decades of the nineteenth century. Printers flocked to London to open workshops, especially in the famous district of the Seven Dials, and produced and sold sheets at an unprecedented rate. And, on the other hand, ambitious entrepreneurs, drawing heavily on traditions in the popular literature of crime, used methods of violent crime reporting to attract subscribers to their new cheap weekly newspapers, which first appeared in the marketplace during the 1840s and that form the subject of our sixth chapter. Both genres came to occupy a crucial place in mainstream culture.

Legendary murderers and material culture

During the nineteenth century, the fascination with murderers and the intricate details of their crimes was, undeniably, an interest shared by high and low. In *Victorian Studies in Scarlet* (1972), Richard Altick claimed that this common enthusiasm was evidence of a cultural consensus. While the passion for murder 'was most unapologetically manifest among the working class', it also prevailed 'by the firesides of the middle class and sometimes, though rather covertly, in the stately halls of the aristocracy'. For Altick, entertainment derived from murder was 'a great social leveller': 'when the gentleman and the working man found a common interest in the most sanguinary deed related in the newspapers … this helped ease the social tensions of the time'.[12]

But on closer inspection, it becomes clear that both the presence of the polite and respectable at hangings and their patronage of entertainments featuring infamous murderers were far more complicated than this. Far from being a social leveller, participation by the elite in the popular culture of violence could, if anything, reinforce the divisions between high and low. Yet, as we shall see, at certain points the 'respectable' unavoidably rubbed shoulders with the apparently rowdier plebeians, both actually and metaphorically. These intersections are important because through them we can begin to understand how the more affluent and polite could, during the second half of the century, begin to appropriate elements of the popular culture of violence, transporting them with a substantial degree of comfort into respectable culture, and largely unaware of (or at least unashamedly avoiding) the contradictions in this process.

The old punishment of public execution continued throughout the period under analysis in this book. Despite the increasingly vocal objections raised by critics, the question of its abolition was successfully evaded or defeated until 1868, when the spectacle was finally removed from public view. Its prominent and visible place within the metropolis before this date has often led contemporaries, antiquarians and historians to describe executions as one of the great entertainments of the Victorians, especially of the unwashed masses. Particularly large crowds of Londoners gathered to watch hangings by the debtor's door at Newgate and on the roof of Horsemonger Lane gaol in Surrey. The decline of the Bloody Code and the restriction of the death penalty almost solely to the crime of murder meant that the relative rarity of executions during the nineteenth century intensified interest. Crowds swelled to even greater numbers when noteworthy murderers who had excited substantial public interest were hanged. The executions of Francois Courvoisier (1840) and Frederick and Maria Manning (1849) were attended by 30,000 spectators, while Franz Muller (1864) attracted an audience of around 50,000.[13] Furthermore, Londoners were also known to travel in significant numbers to attend executions of infamous murderers in other towns, for example that of William Corder in Bury St Edmunds in 1828 and of poisoner William Palmer in Stafford in 1856.

In an age when, through the acquisition of an increasingly civilised sensibility, at least the middle and higher classes had become largely squeamish about and sensitive to the suffering of human beings, the composition of the execution crowd, its behaviour and even the desire of the people within it to view such a spectacle, are difficult questions for us, as historians, to tackle. Many middle-class writers and journalists emphasised the overwhelming presence and unruliness of the lower classes at these events. In *The Great Metropolis* (1837), James Grant wrote that 'they are, with very few exceptions, the most depraved and most criminal of the population. Their uproarious conduct, their shouts of laughter, their vile expressions, their imprecations at themselves and on each other, all show that in the scale of morals they are but a few removes from the brute creation.'[14] Similarly, J. Ewing Ritchie wrote of the type of crowd that gathered over the course of Sunday night in preparation for the execution at Newgate on Monday morning: 'the public houses had been closed, decent people had gone to bed; but already the crowd had become denser, already had the thief and the bully from all the slums and stews of the metropolis been collected together'.[15]

The levity, jokes, humour, rowdiness and apparent thirst for executions displayed by the lower orders provoked great concern among the higher classes, especially as growing numbers of the respectable lobbied for the abolition of public executions.[16] There is certainly no denying that the bulk of the crowd was composed of those chiefly of the lower classes, from tradesmen to unskilled labourers and coster-mongers, and even perhaps a large minority of the criminal class. And they were indeed a boisterous lot when awaiting the arrival of the condemned convict. But these accounts need to be balanced with those that describe the solemnity of the audience at the moment of justice, which could be expressed either in the form of silence and awe or, in the case of particularly heinous murderers, as loud shouts of disapprobation.[17] Both sets of behaviour suggest the display of some kind of respect for the punishment.

On the one hand, this solemnity may have derived from the deep psychic meaning of the gallows as identified by V. A. C. Gatrell, which, as a hangover from the eighteenth century, was bound up tightly with long-held superstitions about its role and power. While the majority of people left Newgate after life had left the body of the criminal, a large number stayed to watch the dismantling of the gallows and then stand on the very spot of the execution, a practice that had also been common at Tyburn.[18] As Gatrell writes, 'it was as if people needed to assimilate the aura of the crime and punishment within themselves – through their feet, into their bones, as it were'.[19]

On the other hand, solemnity might have also been related to something new in the nineteenth century, brought about by changes in the ritual of execution and the emergent fascination with violent crime. Simon Devereaux has revisited the question of the removal of execution from Tyburn to Newgate in 1783, demonstrating that the new location and features of the scaffold were designed to increase the solemnity of the occasion, 'to make the display itself more shocking to the individual observer's psyche, and thus hopefully more effective as a deterrent'. Crucially, reformers sought to achieve this by increasing the theatricality of the event: black cloth enclosed the foot of the scaffold, the platform was raised, not only to ensure security, but to afford to all in the street a better view, and the gallows was designed as a portable apparatus that could be both rapidly erected and packed away.[20]

Attention to the enhanced theatricality of execution in London perhaps helps us to understand the cause of the numerous theatrical metaphors and the common parallels made by contemporaries between hanging and theatre audiences. For instance, Thomas Kittle, an inspector in the metropolitan police, explained to the Royal Commission on Capital Punishment in 1866 that he mixed 'frequently with crowds, at theatres and different places ... it appears to me that they look upon a theatrical scene precisely in the same way as upon an execution'. An execution, Kittle added, produced the same effect upon the spectators as a tragic scene in a play.[21] These comments become yet more comprehensible when we consider the expanding interest in narratives of violence in popular culture more generally. In the case of extreme violence such as murder, the execution of the offender represented the final chapter in the story. Witnessing the punishment of the murderer offered a chance of participation in the story. And, the narrative of violence was contained within the body of the convicted felon on display, providing spectators with an opportunity to revisit that tale.[22]

In addition, the theatricality of the event, the presentation of this final chapter upon a stage, may have further increased the distance between the crowd and the felon, making the occasion at once both confronting and entertaining. As we shall see in chapter 4, melodramas, both fictional and those based on actual events, almost always featured a final act of justice in which murderers were punished for their crimes. Perhaps it is also appropriate to mention here the similarities between murder and execution broadsides and playbills that developed during the first half of the nineteenth century, evident in their layout and design especially when images became increasingly central to both. It is little wonder then that some of the same responses came into play in both locations.

Although the majority, the lower classes were not the only voluntary spectators at executions in London. The so-called respectable classes were also in attendance. John Haynes, former superintendent of the metropolitan police, stated emphatically to the Select Committee on Capital Punishment in 1856, 'there are many persons of a more respectable class of life who witness executions, perhaps more than your Lordships might imagine'.[23] For the most part though, the respectable tried to separate themselves from the noisy and potentially dangerous rabble by hiring rooms with windows that overlooked the scaffold. Observing the gathering of the execution crowd in the few hours before the fatal drop, Thomas Miller described the cries that 'rang upon the ear' of '"Comfortable room!" "Excellent situation!" "Beautiful prospect!" "Splendid view!" as each in turn recommended what may be termed the box-places at the windows, or the open and airy gallery on the roofs; for the pit lay dark and crowded below, and there the audience had free entry'.[24] For these views, the respectable could be charged quite large sums of money; Thomas Kittle claimed as much as twenty-five pounds for a single room (see figure 8).[25]

When pressed for a reason for the attendance of the respectable, many contemporaries sought to reinforce this distance between the polite observers and the large crowd. Charles George Hudson, superintendent of the City of London police, claimed that 'mere curiosity brings them there, while the others, who form the mass of the people present, seem positively to enjoy the sight'.[26] They were right to emphasise some distinction in the type of participation and even the level of commitment of the middle and upper classes. But perhaps this marks an appropriate moment to suggest some commonalities and shared interests. For these higher classes were also fascinated by narratives of violent crime and demonstrated a matched or even greater eagerness to witness first-hand some of the unfolding chapters in the saga. Ladies in

AN ELIGIBLE INVESTMENT.

8. *Punch* satirises
rooms let out to
watch executions
(1849)

particular crowded the benches at the Old Bailey to snatch a glimpse
of the accused and to hear for themselves the sensational evidence
presented to the court. Barrister William Ballantine, in his account
of the trial of Francois Courvoisier, who had murdered Lord William
Russell in 1840, remembered that:

> The court was crowded with ladies dressed up to the eyes, and
> furnished with lorgnettes, fans, and bouquets; the sheriffs and
> under-sheriffs, excited and perspiring, were rushing here and there,
> offering them what they deemed to be delicate attentions... the
> presiding judge, was so hemmed in by the extensive draperies of the
> surrounding ladies that he had scarcely room to move, and looked
> disgusted at the indecency of the spectacle.[27]

During the 1840s, the satirical journalists of *Punch* lost no time in
ridiculing the polite audiences of sensational presentations of crime and
its punishment. One journalist went so far as to liken the practice of
attending Old Bailey trials to that of popular theatregoing, suggesting
that 'every accommodation should be afforded to the frequenters of
the galleries, and an usher going round with "Apples, Oranges, Nuts,
Bills of Indictment, Ginger Beer" would be a great convenience to
the audience'[28] (see figures 9 and 10). On one level, these articles and

9. *Punch* compares the fashionable observation of criminal trials with popular theatregoing (1849)

10. Again, *Punch* ridicules the 'respectable' who attend the trials of notorious criminals (1849).

cartoons appeared to dismantle boundaries in society by demonstrating the similarities in the taste of the uncouth and respectable, while at the same time expressing a degree of nostalgia and sentimentality for former 'unrespectable' Regency London. However, on another level, the use of humour and parody actually served to reinforce difference by highlighting the unrespectable nature of such behaviour. And, we may ask, how serious were these polite participants about their involvement in spectacles of crime and punishment? Going to trials and executions was perhaps so exciting because they served as rituals of inversion. Ladies and gentlemen smugly flirted with the boundaries, indulging base instincts which they claimed to have tamed and so felt they could easily control. Perhaps nowhere was this clearer than in the establishment of Madame Tussaud's Chamber of Horrors, a perceived safe and respectable location for such indulgence and enjoyment.

Metropolitan audiences already had a long familiarity with waxworks exhibitions. Wax models were often popular amusements in fairgrounds. They were displayed in travelling open-air shows and were exhibited in more permanent museums from the seventeenth century onwards. As we saw with the entertainments described in the last chapter, strong connections were forged between the different types of exhibition and audiences came from all levels of society. One particularly famous show during the eighteenth century clearly illustrates the role of waxworks in early modern popular culture. Mrs Salmon, a canny impresario, maintained a permanent waxworks museum, first in St Martin's le-Grand and later in Fleet Street. The museum was exceptionally popular and attracted a number of famous visitors, including James Boswell, who wrote in his journal that it was 'excellent in its kind, and amused me very well for a quarter of an hour'.[29] Like its competitors, Mrs Salmon's waxworks included effigies of kings and queens, famous characters from folktales and fiction, beasts and freaks. The very last display was a figure of 'Old Mother Shipton, the witch, who kicked the astonished visitor as he left'.[30] Mrs Salmon also exhibited her waxworks at Bartholomew and Southwark fairs.[31]

Although Mrs Salmon has often been cast as the 'Madame Tussaud' of the eighteenth century, crucial differences exist between the two personalities and the nature of their exhibitions. Waxworks remained popular with both high and low during the nineteenth century. However, exhibitions were increasingly enjoyed within socially segregated spaces, as was particularly evident in the flourishing of Madame Tussaud's waxworks in Baker Street from 1835.[32] Madame Tussaud was a shrewd businesswoman. She used her former close relationship with the French royal family, her skill in wax-modelling and her keen social awareness to transform an entertainment which had begun to fall into decline into a respectable form of leisure to which the affluent classes would flock. As Billie Melman writes, 'unlike older wax collections which displayed nude and wax erotica, Madame Tussaud's determinedly guarded the rules of respectability, shunning the display of the naked body. And unlike these older establishments it was deemed safe, and catered for, women and children'.[33] Education, rather than novelty or cheap thrills, was proclaimed to be at the centre of this entertainment, as patrons were introduced to important historical and contemporary figures with the aid of detailed guidebooks. This was aptly summarised by a letter 'from a lady in London to her niece in the country', published in *Chambers's Edinburgh Journal* in 1842:

> This, my dear Jane, closes my rambling account of Madame Tussaud's famed exhibition, which you must not allow yourself to associate in your mind with those tawdry and tinselled spectacles which are often seen in provincial towns; there is nothing paltry, or mean, or got-up looking about it, but, on the contrary, everything bears evidence of the excellent judgement and liberality of the indefatigable conductor, Madame Tussaud, who, I believe, changes the linen, laces, etc, every week or two, so that they are all beautifully clean and neat.[34]

The author of the letter also mentioned to her niece the separate room at Baker Street which contained the figures of Burke, Robespierre and Courvoisier. But, the respectable spectator continued, 'I thought it a pity to destroy the pleasing impression which was left by the more interesting exhibition in the large saloon, and so I passed over them.'[35] Most visitors, however, did not. Madame Tussaud's famous Chamber of Horrors was a waxworks novelty in the nineteenth century. Eighteenth-century exhibitions may, from time to time, have included the effigy of a famous criminal who had expired at infamous Tyburn. But in terms of the quantity of figures and their display and permanency, the Chamber of Horrors was original. At the very opening of the century, the 'separate room' contained just the severed heads of victims of the French guillotine which Madame Tussaud had been forced to model while resident in Paris during the Revolution. In England, both on tour and later in her new permanent London exhibition, Madame Tussaud began to add the figures of domestic murderers with whom her audiences were well acquainted (see figure 11). These murderers added considerably to her (and later her sons') profits. For example, in 1849 an editor of *Lloyd's Weekly Newspaper* claimed that the hangman Calcraft had 'received seventy guineas from Madame Tussaud, for the suit in

11. Madame Tussaud's waxworks parodied by *Punch* (1849)

which Rush was executed. The speculation has proved a successful one, she having realised, it is stated, upwards of £1,500 by her wax work model of the murderer.'[36]

In her recent study, Billie Melman draws a line of continuity from the eighteenth century deep into the nineteenth, linking the early modern popular literature of crime, the practice of attending executions and the entertainment on offer at Madame Tussaud's within a broad gallows culture.[37] But attention to more subtle nuances is also important. The Chamber of Horrors was related to a new, more specific interest in narratives of extreme violence. It did not contain the images of past highwaymen and housebreakers celebrated in criminal biographies and Newgate novels. And the interest in violence, especially the fascination with the personality of the murderer, ensured that the Chamber would continue long past the abolition of public execution in 1868.

Displaying waxen images of infamous murderers, as well as relics collected from the scenes of their crimes, paradoxically did not compromise the respectability of the exhibition. Although motivated by curiosity and sensationalism, patronage of the 'civilised' was justified through the language of respectability. For example, successive proprietors of the exhibition were always careful to insert the following passage into guidebooks directing visitors around the Chamber: 'they [Madame Tussaud & Sons] assure the public that so far from the exhibition of the likeness of criminals creating a desire to imitate them, Experience teaches them it has a direct tendency to the contrary'.[38] As Melman states, the 'presence of women and families in shows and exhibitions reproducing the horrors and crimes of past and present was sanctioned and deemed beneficial to the public at large'.[39] Indeed, the very label – 'Chamber of Horrors' – might also provide some useful clues here. In *Murder Most Foul* (1998), Karen Halttunen asks why apparently 'civilised' nineteenth-century American readers were so attracted to graphic tales of extreme violence and did not avert their newly sensitised eyes. Cast in the gothic genre and using the convention of horror, she suggests that this literature '[presented] images of the culturally forbidden and [invited] readers to give free play to their illicit desires in the realm of imagination. In doing so, it permits readers to triumph over forbidden impulses by suppressing them again.' Pleasure was derived through the repetition of this process, as readers proved their mastery over the 'dark forces which constantly threaten to seize the upper hand'.[40]

In principle, Madame Tussaud's was open to all. However, in practice, working-class patronage was alternately prevented, discouraged or made awkward.[41] Waxworks exhibitions continued to appear in the metropolitan fairgrounds during the early decades of the nineteenth century, their cheap, limited displays featuring effigies of one or two of the very latest murderers to make news headlines.[42] As the fairgrounds declined during the 1820s and 1830s, new waxworks exhibitions quickly became established in locations in the metropolis to supply the demand. Most were semi-permanent, either attached to travelling shows that had rented a temporary shop in the capital as part of their circuit, or crude, budget displays that survived as long as they received some meagre custom. Effigies of murderers came to form an important part of their attraction for lower-class patrons. Names such as Corder, Burke, Hare, Courvoisier and Greenacre, to name a few, appeared on almost all their advertisements. Proprietors promised a lifelike and gruesome display, often without any pretensions to moral purpose or respectability. The advertisement for Mrs Pollard's moving waxworks in Pentonville Hill, for which admission was just twopence, included a description of:

A Beautiful Cyclorama of the mysterious MURDER OF MARIA

MARTEN, by WILLIAM CORDER, at the Red Barn, Polstead, Suffolk. Showing the moment at which he decoyed her from her Father's cottage to the Red Barn where he Murdered Her: concealing her remains in the Barn, where they were Discovered after a lapse of Eleven months, by HER MOTHER'S DREAM. The Mother represented in bed asleep – the Clouds gradually and beautifully Opening – the form of Maria Marten comes forth to her Mother's Bedside, with one hand pointing to her Breast, where there is a large wound, from which the *Blood is Flowing*; with her other hand she points to the Red Barn, then gradually disappears through the clouds.[43]

Examiner of Plays William Bodham Donne was asked by the Lord Chamberlain to attend one of these performances in early 1859 in response to concerns about competition raised by local popular theatre managers. Although Donne's personal mission was the elevation of drama and the theatre in mid-nineteenth-century London, he found nothing offensive about this mute re-enactment of love, murder and punishment, and in his report drew attention to the orderliness and even respectable behaviour of the working men (seemingly artisan), females, boys and girls who made up the audience. He wrote, in the 'corner of the gallery was a fruit and cake stall, with a few bottles of lemonade and ginger beer, … [there was] no appearance of excisable liquors on sale, nor any drunkenness in the audience'.[44]

Where Madame Tussaud provided just the waxen images of the murderers and perhaps a relic or two from their crimes labelled beside them, allowing patrons to reconstruct the narrative of their violence from memory and the excerpt provided in the guidebook, lowbrow shows supplied many more visual accompaniments. There seemed to be a real concern to recreate the scene of the crime in tableaux. The result may appear to us rather vulgar and distasteful, but perhaps for their patrons this gave the entertainment extra appeal and purpose. Charles Dickens described one such exhibition in an old tumbledown house in the New Cut in 1866, for which admission was just one penny. In addition to his stereotypical working man, Mr Whelks, boys, young girls and domestic servants pausing between errands gathered in the shed to listen to a 'gloomy lad' (in place of a guidebook) give an account of the crimes with which the figures were associated. 'A dirtier, or a more wretched, ragged and in the last degree mean and miserable exhibition, it is impossible to conceive', wrote Dickens. Not only did the heads bear little or no resemblance to the persons represented, but most of them were also broken.

But perhaps the finer details, including accuracy, were not so important to this audience. The representation of the actual violence may have mattered more. Earnest Southey, while not at all like the original, was displayed in the very 'act of murdering his wife, in the same room where his children (all of the same age) lay side by side in bed, poisoned'.[45] Miserable gaffs of this type persisted throughout the century. For example, around 1890, an exhibition in Whitechapel featured the recent victims of Jack the Ripper: 'the heads were represented as being nearly severed from the bodies, and in each case there were shown, in red paint, three terrible gashes reaching from the abdomen to the ribs'. But while their tendency to illustrate in wax the extreme violence with which their figures were associated continued, their audiences became more marginal and select as time progressed. Moreover, their distasteful character and the collection of people that seemed to gather at their doors offended others within the neighbourhoods, including those who might have patronised such entertainments fifty years earlier, and attracted the grave attention of the authorities.[46]

Despite the avoidance of such venues and displays by the respectable, a fascination with the actual scene of the crime was another element of the culture of violence shared by high and low during the first half of the nineteenth century. Not only did thousands of the fashionable and the vulgar gather to gaze upon the site, but many also insisted on taking home relics or souvenirs. Profit-hungry businessmen were quick to see valuable opportunities in this market. The hedge through which William Weare's murdered body was dragged was sold to punters

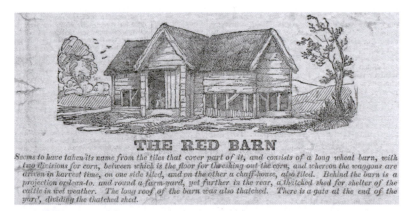

THE RED BARN

Seems to have taken its name from the tiles that cover part of it, and consists of a long wheat barn, with two divisions for corn, between which is the floor for threshing out the corn, and whereon the waggons are driven in harvest time, on one side tiled, and on the other a chaff-house, also tiled. Behind the barn is a projection or lean-to, and round a farm-yard, yet further in the rear, a thatched shed for shelter of the cattle in wet weather. The long roof of the barn was also thatched. There is a gate at the end of the yard, dividing the thatched shed.

12. Sketch of the Red Barn printed in the *Essex Herald* at the time of the trial of William Corder which shows most of the wooden cladding missing from the lower walls

by the inch. The Red Barn in which William Corder murdered his sweetheart Maria Marten was almost torn to pieces by souvenir-hunters.[47] One man, the *Suffolk Herald* reported, 'had been seen passing through Polstead with a bundle of boards from the barn … it was his intention to take them to London to make a variety of articles for sale as curiosities'[48] (see figure 12).

Madame Tussaud at times bargained for particular relics alongside managers of popular theatres who hoped to use them as props in their melodramatic re-enactments of the violent crimes. As we shall see in chapter 4, audiences for these plays were mostly composed of the lower orders. But there were moments when the polite participated and gazed in a manner similar to that of the common. For example, in 1834, after German whip-maker Steinberg murdered his mistress and her four children before committing suicide, a wax exhibition of the murder was set up in his house in Pentonville: 'wax figures of the woman and her children [were] placed in the various rooms, in the postures in which they had been found. The victims' clothes were bought for £25, and nearly £50 was taken for admission in one day.'[49] Such profits would have not been possible without the patronage of at least some members of the more affluent classes. Thus, we can understand the concern of Charles Hudson, superintendent of the City of London police, about returning the bodies of hanged convicts to their families. 'I should rather fear that they would be inclined to exhibit it,' he told the Select Committee in 1856.[50]

However, perhaps more interesting in the material culture of murder was the manufacture in large quantities of cheap souvenirs of violent crime, in particular the earthenware figurines of murderers and models of sites associated with their crimes by the Staffordshire potters. During the nineteenth century, aided by new techniques in production and the expanding domestic market, the Staffordshire potters turned their attention to the production of pottery commemorating famous figures, including royalty, historical personalities, characters from fiction and the stage, and sporting heroes. While some artefacts served functional purposes, such as plates, mugs or chamber pots, the vast majority were purely decorative, mainly in the form of portrait figures, which, as P. D. Gordon Pugh states, had 'a "Madame Tussaud" fascination' about them.[51] And, as Madame Tussaud cast murderers in wax, so too did the Staffordshire potters in earthenware.

The craze for commemorating famous murders in pottery seems to have flourished during two distinct periods. During the 1820s, John Thurtell's infamous murder of William Weare in Hertfordshire inspired the production of a mug featuring Thurtell's face (see figure 13).

13. Creamware mug with the portrait of murderer John Thurtell, *c.* 1824

14, 15. Earthenware figurines: William Corder and Maria Marten, *c.* 1828, and Pearlware model of the Red Barn at Polstead *c.* 1830

Only four years later, the potters again saw an opportunity for profit in William Corder's murder of Maria Marten. Not only were figurines of the main characters in the drama moulded, but also a model of the Red Barn in which Corder killed his sweetheart (see figures 14 and 15). Despite the great possibilities offered by noteworthy murderers during the 1830s and early 1840s, for example James Greenacre, Francois

16, 17, 18.
Earthenware portrait
figurines: James
Blomfield Rush, c. 1849,
and Emily Sandford,
c. 1848; Earthenware
model of Potash Farm,
c. 1848

Courvoisier and Daniel Good, none seem to have been produced in earthenware until 1849, the year in which James Blomfield Rush and Frederick and Maria Manning were executed for murder in April and November respectively.[52] Rush's murder of Isaac Jermy and his son at Stanfield Hall in Norfolk, in particular, created a frenzy of activity among the potters. In addition to portraits of Rush and his mistress Emily Sandford, key locations in the narrative of murder were also modelled, including Rush's residence, Potash Farm, at the centre of his dispute with Jermy, Stanfield Hall, the site of the murders, and

Norwich Castle, where Rush was executed (see figures 16, 17 and 18). Over the next couple of decades just two more murderers were deemed fit subjects for earthenware: William Palmer, the Rugeley poisoner, and William Collier, who killed Thomas Smith, a poacher on his land.

In his assessment of the popularity and inherent meaning of the figurine of Arthur Orton, the Tichborne Claimant, Rohan McWilliam stated that the Staffordshire figurines 'served a growing world of working-class consumerism and were a vehicle of identity construction'.[53] Although exact prices are lost to us, we know that the cheapness of the figurines was one of their primary attractions, the other being their vibrant colours.[54] They were mostly sold by itinerant sellers in the streets, outside theatres (and later music halls), at fairgrounds and at seaside resorts. Thus, we have some idea about who might have purchased them. Men and women of the higher ranks of the working class and the lower-middle class who used the streets in their daily lives and who had a small, disposable income, probably purchased the characters on impulse, attracted by the vivid colours which promised to brighten their dwellings as well as motivated by a desire to commemorate the event that the figurine represented. At home, buyers placed these nostalgic treasures in safe zones designed for display, for example the mantelpiece, 'a place for the celebration of beauty and repository of memory'.[55] As McWilliam writes, the figurines represented a 'conjunction of narrative and portraiture', and thus possessed an 'inherent theatricality': 'people bought representations of contemporary or historical figures because they knew their stories and saw those stories enacted in the figure'. And, their miniature size meant that public events could be transported into and enjoyed within the domestic sphere.[56]

But this begs the question: why murderers? The answer already lies within the pages of this book: the new preoccupation with narratives of extreme interpersonal violence that emerged around 1820 ensured that murderers predominated within the criminal genre and meant that there were men and women eager to purchase them for display within their homes.

Apart from the figurines of the Mannings, all the other murderers featured both committed their crimes and were executed outside the capital. This might have increased their value and role for London audiences, as the figures and accompanying models helped to provide some of the visual aspects of the narratives that purchasers otherwise would have missed. They supplied a cheap alternative to visiting the key locations featured in the tale of the murder and attending the execution. Figurines and models were also part of the expanding

pictorial world of the lower classes.[57] Except for the figure of William
Collier, which represents him in the act of murdering poacher Thomas
Smith, the portraits give no clues about the reasons for the subjects'
fame. McWilliam relates this to the Victorian concern with character
and the teaching of virtue, that the figurines were intended to be
emblems of virtue or character. This may be so, but the result, surely,
was to give a great deal of free reign to the imagination.

Murder and execution broadsides

While the more respectable classes maintained an interest in murderers
and their punishment during the nineteenth century, their separation
from the lower classes and their withdrawal from the popular literature of
crime are most evident in the growth and character of the metropolitan
broadside trade. During the first half of the nineteenth century, the
broadside trade dramatically expanded to become a dominant method
of crime reporting for the common people and a central feature of
life in London.[58] The price of broadsides and the scale of publication
ensured their accessibility. The sheets, with their unreserved exploitation of the imaginative, became a crucial form of entertainment. In
addition, broadsides had firm roots in plebeian culture, their literal
vulgarity and independence of patronage offending polite society.[59]
Although, traditionally, broadsides had been concerned with a wide
variety of subjects, including radical politics, upper-class scandal and
supernatural happenings, crime and its fatal punishment dominated
a large part of the trade. And from 1820, this section was not only
significantly enlarged, but the theme of violence featured within it,
especially murder, was intensified. V. A. C. Gatrell has drawn attention
to the paradox inherent in this development: the trade expanded as the
number of executions actually declined. He suggests that as attention
was focused on fewer cases since only murderers now hanged, the rarity
value of an execution heavily boosted sales.[60] Furthermore, Philippe
Chassaigne has argued that the increasing focus on violent offences in
crime broadsides encouraged the propagation of a subculture in which
violence played a prominent part.[61]

While changes in the penal law during the 1820s helped focus
attention on violent crime, simultaneous advances in printing
technology both generated the massive expansion of the broadside
trade and further intensified the theme of violence. The invention of the
Stanhope iron-frame press in 1815 both increased the speed of printing
and reduced cost. As David Vincent has pointed out, while elsewhere
machinery destroyed the artisan workshop, the printing trade was

opened to anyone who could purchase a £30 press and hire a small room. Consequently, a large number of printing establishments were opened across England.[62] As London's large and expanding population suggested that substantial profits could be made in street literature, the metropolitan trade exploded. Several printers enjoyed unprecedented success. James Catnach, for example, was said to have amassed a fortune of £10,000 by the time of his death in the middle of the century.[63] Businesses were opened in several neighbourhoods, but the most popular was the Seven Dials. As a correspondent to *Chambers' Journal* wrote in 1856, 'The Seven Dials press is in good keeping with its vulgar surroundings ... seeing that its literature is decidedly tattered, that three-fourths of its productions are stolen property, that both its verse and prose are crippled and mangled beyond cure, and that its philosophy is principally of the tipsy and staggering sort.'[64]

Although printers devoted their resources to a wide range of sensational topics and, when resources of information were unfruitful, published fictional 'cocks', they soon found that significant profits were derived from reports on murders and executions. James Catnach's coverage of John Thurtell's murder of William Weare in 1823 first demonstrated just how lucrative representations of extreme violence could be. To meet the seemingly insatiable demand on the street, Catnach printed over 250,000 copies of the 'Full and True Account of the Murder of Weare by Thurtell and His Companions'. Catnach's biographer Charles Hindley later wrote that while this sale surprised 'the establishment' and put their rapid printing process to the test, the trial of Thurtell in early 1824 'out-did it tenfold'. Nearly 500,000 sheets were printed and Catnach made a substantial profit of £500.[65]

Inspired by such success, printers soon developed a specific procedure for reporting 'good' murders and executions. Earliest reports of the murder first appeared on quarter-sheets. These were soon followed by a series of half-sheets which contained the latest particulars, discoveries or examinations. Next, whole- or broadsheets were printed for the day of execution. Execution broadsides were especially decorative productions, often featuring a woodcut of the gallows and portraits of the felon, as well as textual accounts of the crime, trial and execution. In the case of particularly notorious murders, a 'book', consisting of four or eight pages folded from the broadsheet, was released for sale after the execution. 'Books' were popular as they formed a durable record of the event. As one seller explained, 'people who loves such reading likes to keep a good account of them; and so, when I've sold Manning's bills, I've often shoved off Rush's books'.[66] Murder and execution broadsides continued to be sold in ever increasing numbers. One journalist stated that 'the sale of these gloomy sheets far exceeds that of any other publication of the press throughout the world', estimating that £12,000 was spent each year on sheets, half-sheets and quarter-sheets.[67] Biographers of printers and mid-century social investigators claimed that sales of broadsheets at executions often reached millions. When James Greenacre was executed in 1838, approximately 1,650,000 sheets were sold, a figure that rose to 2,500,000 for the execution of Maria and Frederick George Manning in 1849.[68]

In his interviews with the sellers of street literature during the 1850s, Henry Mayhew found that murders and executions were the most profitable subjects. As one patterer commented, 'there's nothing beats a stunning murder, after all'.[69] Descriptions of violence were frequently incorporated into selling techniques. Patterers were street performers and active participants in the creative process. As David Vincent stated, the success or failure of a broadside depended on how well it could be sung or recited.[70] Several different types of patterers were regular features on London's streets. First, running patterers sold broadsides while continuously on the move. 'Mobs' or 'schools' of men ran through the streets, their urgent cries designed to attract purchasers. Most of their patter was inaudible, but several key words, such as 'murder', 'horrible', 'barbarous', 'love' and 'former crimes' were intended to be heard and induce sales.[71] In contrast, the standing patterers selected fixed pitches on prominent street corners, gathering large crowds either by means of brightly coloured illustrative boards or by 'giving a lively or horrible description of the papers or books they are "working"'.[72] Finally, chaunters used music and rhyme to sell their printed verses.[73] All these street-sellers could also be found selling their wares at the foot of the scaffold on execution days: in this location, they made some of their largest profits.

Philippe Chassaigne has argued that broadsides were aimed at a wide market, as evident from the variety of styles and semantic fields in their composition.[74] However, the vast majority of purchasers in London were from the lower classes. In this, London may have been an exceptional case. Evidence suggests that in the provinces farmers, tradesmen, professionals and even gentlefolk often bought murder and execution sheets. In contrast to the literature printed in the metropolis, these sheets were often moral, undecorated homilies and were perhaps used by heads of households to educate servants and other dependents.[75] London sellers who toured the provinces distributing their wares found that the middle and higher classes might become purchasers. One patterer told Henry Mayhew that when he sold sheets at the execution of William Corder in Bury St Edmunds in 1828, a footman was sent out by his master to buy half a dozen.[76] But, as another patterer explained, in London 'the murders are bought by men, women and children. Many of the tradespeople bought a great many of the affair of the Mannings ... [But] Gentlefolks won't have anything to do with murders sold in the street; they've got other ways of seeing all about it.'[77] Gatrell concluded that most broadsides in London were unambiguously directed at humble people and thus 'we are safe in presuming that their ethical and sentimental messages accorded with plebeian expectations'.[78]

But what messages did these often grossly decorated broadsheets contain? And what was their fundamental role in nineteenth-century popular culture? These are questions historians have already attempted to tackle. Beth Kalikoff, for example, has discerned key shifts in the common themes of murder and execution broadsides that interacted with changing fears and anxieties about violence. While sheets of the 1830s and 1840s expressed great concern about personal betrayal in human relationships, broadsides of the 1850s and 1860s reflected a growing insecurity about the nature of public life in the technologically advanced, modern city.[79] In a rather different vein, Chassaigne has drawn attention to the 'moralising' and 'socialising' function of violent broadsides. He argued that unlawful violence was presented in the crudest way for the purposes of deterrence. At the same time, these sheets brought people together and gave them a sense of belonging through entertainment and collectively experienced feelings of revulsion and horror. Broadsides, Chassaigne concluded, marked the only moment when the whole community could unite together against the criminal.[80] Gatrell has also highlighted the morality of broadsides. Based on their largely conservative language, he demonstrated that the sheets were never as dangerously or tacitly subversive as the increasingly obsolete flash ballads. Broadsides 'either described the trials and executions with emotions well-guarded, or else they moralised unashamedly'. At most, Gatrell suggests execution sheets were some kind of souvenir, perhaps 'symbolic substitutes for experiences signified or the experiences watched, ... mementoes of events whose psychic significance was somehow worth reifying'.[81]

Murder and execution broadsides were primarily a form of entertainment. These sheets contained so many features, from sensational descriptions of crime and accounts of executions, to musical verses and graphic woodcuts, that they could amuse purchasers for hours. But broadsides also contained messages for their subscribers. On the surface, they were largely moral, as both Gatrell and Chassaigne have argued, and they certainly did not reflect the outrageously subversive character of the flash ballads. However, in their characterisation of violent offenders, in their comments about society's management of extreme forms of violence and in their ability to entertain through the use of graphic images of interpersonal violence, nineteenth-century broadsides were much more complicated and confusing than historians have yet allowed. The printing industry expanded at a time of significant social upheaval and turbulence, when new forms of community were emerging in the metropolis and traditional popular values and preconceptions had become shaken and dislocated. Authors and publishers incorporated these pressures and confusions into their especially violent broadsheets. Outwardly, they argued that murder was a terrible crime that demanded appropriate punishment. Yet underneath, a significant degree of murkiness persisted.

The following analysis of the characteristics and social functions of murder and execution broadsides is based on a sample of 124 sheets contained in collections held by the British Library in London and the Bodleian Library in Oxford. All these broadsheets were published during the nineteenth century, from its opening to the abolition of public execution in 1868. Although the sample unmistakably suggests that the 1840s represented a peak in the broadside trade by the very large number of sheets comparatively printed in that decade, an in-depth statistical discussion is not very helpful or reliable due to the essentially ephemeral nature of the broadsheets. Approximately ten sheets in this sample were either printed in the provinces or concerned the punishment of a murderer outside the metropolis. Despite this, the great majority of these broadsides were published by London printers and were sold to eager purchasers on the city streets. Contained in this sample are quarter-sheets, half-sheets and whole-sheets providing a detailed coverage of each stage in the printing process, from reports on the discovery of a murder to the trial and execution of the felon. Most, however, are large broadsheets which, sold both on and after the day of execution, described in detail the 'Life, Trial and Execution' of the murderer. Finally, with few exceptions, each sheet contained at least a mixture, if not all, of the characteristics about to be described.

First, murder and execution broadsheets contained a large portion of text or prose, often occupying as much as half the sheet in space. Text was typically divided into portions describing different aspects of the case. A smaller handbill (or quarter-sheet), breaking the news of a recent murder, may have included several separate but small reports in order to accommodate the latest particulars before going to press. Similarly, large broadsides printed for sale at the scaffold often incorporated reports issued in earlier quarter- and half-sheets, such as the first report of the crime, the apprehension of the offender and his trial. These were pasted alongside the account of the execution and the felon's life history. Long passages of text were designed not only to inform readers on the details of the crime, but, by using often graphic narratives, to entertain them. From 1820 onwards, with the decline in the number of felons executed and the increasing focus on violent crime, accounts of murder became especially graphic.

Either directly through detailed narratives of the violent act, or indirectly through descriptions of the discoveries of victims' bodies, the horrific brutality of murder was communicated to audiences. James Catnach's broadsheet printed for the execution of John Thurtell in 1824 suggested the extremity of Thurtell's violence towards his victim, William Weare, in this statement: 'On Saturday morning, October 25th, before it was quite daylight, some labourers went to work in Gill's Hill Lane and found a pistol and a pen-knife, the former of which was covered with blood, and bits of hair on the outside, and some particles of human brains were lodged in the barrel.'[82] Another example is that of William Lees, executed in 1839 for the murder of his wife. One sheet not only described the discovery of Mrs Lees's body by relatives, but also attempted a reconstruction of the murder itself:

> On entering the shop they found the Young Woman lying stretched on the ground, which was covered with Blood. There were several gashes on her face, and a deep wound on the throat separating the jugular vein, there was also a bruise on the right eyebrow, which appeared to have been inflicted by the same blunt instrument from which it appears that the murderer, after striking his hapless victim with a stick or piece of wood and rendering her perfectly senseless, completed by cutting her throat, and that in her struggles he cut her about the face.[83]

No details of violent crimes were considered too shocking or distasteful for publication. Indeed, extra brutalities were a bonus: they helped to sell more sheets. And this was especially evident in the many broadsheets printed on the murder of Hannah Brown by James Greenacre in 1837. After murdering Hannah by a sharp blow to the head, Greenacre then dismembered his victim and scattered the body parts throughout London, details that were lavishly elaborated by authors in every sheet.[84]

Summaries of the trials of murderers provided yet more space to describe his or her violent acts, not least in the evidence of the surgeon. As the professional who examined the victim's injuries and determined the cause of death, the surgeon's testimony was crucial to the trial. What is noteworthy, however, is the frequency with which this evidence appears in the popular literature, sometimes to the exclusion of other witnesses' statements. For the most part, the surgeon's statement augmented the descriptions of violence already included in the text, though in some instances his words became a substitute for other lengthy discussions. Moreover, the medical testimony was graphic, demonstrating the public interest and thirst for detail. T. Birt's broadside on the apprehension of Eliza Grimwood's murderer in 1838 is fairly typical. The surgeon's statement before the police-court magistrate was included in the sheets as he had described the two deep gashes in Grimwood's neck that had severed her windpipe as well as wounds that had penetrated the abdomen and the right cavity of her chest.[85] Likewise, during the trial of Francois Courvoisier for the murder of Lord William Russell, the surgeon was reported as having said that the fatal wound 'was so deep as to penetrate the vertebrae of the neck'.[86]

Especially graphic, however, was the surgeon's evidence quoted in a London broadsheet providing a report on the trial of Thomas Drory, accused of strangling his sweetheart, Jael Denny, in a field near Doddinghurst. The surgeon stated to the court, 'I found the eyes of the deceased much distorted and effused with blood, the pupils much dilated and tongue protruding, with swelling of the face. There was a laceration of the skin covering the throat and marks of two cords having been tied tightly around the neck.' As if such detail was not enough, the printer could not resist adding the testimony of a second surgeon who provided yet further, more intimate and titillating evidence: in seeking to emphasise the great force used by Drory, the surgeon drew the court's attention to the quantity of blood present on the victim's small clothes.[87]

Broadsheets printed for sale on the day of execution also contained an often brief account of the felon's last moments and fatal punishment. It mattered little to purchasers that at the time of printing the final act of justice had not yet taken place. Generally, the execution of a convicted murderer was viewed by authors and publishers of broadsides as just and necessary. Some sheets even referred to that famous maxim, that 'blood will have blood', as well as other similar biblical quotes. However, discomfort was evident in the words chosen to describe the judicial death of a murderer. Euphemisms were overwhelmingly used: convicts either were 'launched into eternity' or simply 'ceased to live'. This sense of unease on the part of both authors and purchasers perhaps resulted from the tenacious place that the gallows continued to occupy in the popular imagination. These awkward phrases may have been an acknowledgement of the power of the gallows as well as a product of the popular superstition that continued to surround it. There is at least one exception to this rule in the sample. Sheets printed by H. Paul of the Seven Dials for the execution of Robert Blakesley not only stated that the murderer of James Burdon was 'launched into eternity', but also described the 'few convulsive struggles' that were perceptible before he 'ceased to exist'.[88] Furthermore, while the general punishment for murderers was approved of, its public nature increasingly attracted mutterings of disapproval from the authors of execution broadsides, especially during the 1860s. For example, 'The Life, Character and Execution of William Godfrey' (1860) described the unfortunate behaviour of the execution crowd, drawing attention to their melancholy songs and ribald jokes.[89]

Within various parts of the text, authors of murder and execution broadsides also remembered former violent crimes of relevance or significance. This practice offered an opportunity to re-characterise murders of the past by comparing them with those of the present, weaving together a culture of violence in the popular imagination. Moreover, comments could also raise fears in the community about the prevalence of violent crime, increasing interest in its accompanying popular literature and thus generating further business. For example, James Catnach linked a 'crime passionel' of times past with the seemingly unrelated murder of William Weare by John Thurtell. He wrote:

> After the decision of the Coroner's inquest, the body of the unfortunate man [Weare] was interred in the Elstre church-yard, near the chancel window, where a Miss Ray was buried fifty years ago. Miss Ray was a tradesman's daughter in the parish of Elstre, and was courted by a Rev. Mr Hackman. She was CherAmie to Lord Sandwich, and used to accompany him to public places. This was more than the jealousy of her rev. lover could bear, and he accordingly shot her under the piazza of Covent Garden, as she came out of that theatre. Her remains were carried to Elstre and her rev. Lover was tried, found guilty and executed within twelve days of her funeral.[90]

When news broke of the discovery of a horribly dismembered and burnt corpse in a Surrey barn in 1842, broadside printers immediately compared the events to those of the Greenacre–Brown tragedy of 1837. One author stated that this appalling murder 'in the annals of crime, has only been equalled in atrocity by that of Hannah Brown, by Greenacre, and that of Mr Paas, at Leicester'.[91] Connections between past and present murders could also be used to illustrate the didactic value of crime. Eliza Grimwood, for example, did not take warning from the murder of Maria Marten by William Corder, despite being 'on a visit at a friend's in the neighbourhood and the first person who entered the Red Barn and saw the mangled corpse of that ill-fated girl'. Instead, Grimwood went on to lead a reckless, immoral life and hence suffered a similar fate.[92]

Broadsheets printed for murderers' executions often contained short, fictional letters supposedly written by the felon in the condemned cell. As the time between conviction and execution lengthened over the course of the century, these letters also began to appear on sheets printed during that interim, designed to sustain public interest in his or her fate. Letters were typically addressed to a loved one, often a family member, and each usually contained a confession, expressions of great remorse, an acknowledgement of the justness of the awaited punishment and appeals to heaven. One early exception is that of James Abbott, convicted in 1828 for cutting the throat of his wife with murderous intent. While Abbott expressed guilt and sorrow for his crime, the letter also passed judgement on the conduct of his wife, Hannah. Abbott wrote, 'Only consider, my dear wife, what my feelings must be; see what disgrace you have been the cause of bringing on our dear babes.' The author of this broadside also mentioned that Hannah refused to see her husband, denied him access to their children before his death and took no notice of his penitent letter.[93]

Most letters, however, followed a rigid formula and little distinction was made between levels of barbarity of different murders. For example, Daniel Good, executed in 1842 for butchering his sweetheart, was granted a letter by the author of this execution sheet:

> A few more hours and your unhappy father will have ceased to breathe in this world. Oh, how can I face the multitudes that flock to see my fatal exit from this world? How can I meet my heavenly Father with the horrid crimes I have committed on my head! … take warning by your father's untimely fate, and guard from the effects of drink, passion and dishonesty, for they have been the downfall and fatal end of your unfortunate father.[94]

Many letters concluded with words of warning addressed to readers, suggesting that, at least on the surface, some kind of didactic purpose might have been intended. However, Beth Kalikoff argues that they may have performed a deeper function. Remorse and contrition not only provided satisfying religious symmetry for readers, but words of atonement mended the moral fabric that the murder had ripped.[95]

If remorseful letters of confession were designed to placate and soothe purchasers, the large images that dominated the murder and execution sheets achieved very different results. Woodcuts of the gallows and murder scenes did encourage sales. As one contemporary wrote, these large cuts 'may be described in one word – abominable; when covered with flashy watercolours they are gorgeous to the uneducated eye, and, being retailed at a low price, sell by the thousands'.[96] In comparison to the crude sheets printed during the eighteenth century, broadsides of the early nineteenth century were often extravagantly decorated. Important technological innovations contributed to this development. Cast-iron presses began to be used which produced cheaper and more finely detailed prints.[97] Although these illustrations were, therefore, somewhat advanced, they were still, to the more sophisticated eye, rather rough and ready. As Thomas Gretton has pointed out, these images were enjoyed by people whose access to other pictorial forms was limited. Moreover, the images came to represent another way of seeing, not only affording an understanding of what the less privileged expected from illustrations, but reflecting their perceptions of the kind of world that they lived in.[98] The role played by these illustrations was, at the same time, both entertaining and symbolic. Special cuts were made for specific executions or notorious murders, but in many cases illustrations used bore little direct relation to the crime they were meant to capture.

The most common illustration found in the execution broadsides was that of the gallows, the image capturing the very moment at which the felon was 'launched into eternity'. In fact, the inclusion of the gallows was almost mandatory. It was also very repetitive. London printers had only one or two representations of Newgate or Horsemonger Lane, typically made with gaps to allow for the insertion of multiple convicts. These were used and reused for decades. Yet the very power of the image was derived from its crudeness and repetition. In the popular cheap serial *The Mysteries of the Court of London* (1848), G. W. M. Reynolds included a chapter describing the fictional execution of the murderers Martin and Ramsey, during which he referred to the loud hawkers who sold their Last Dying Speeches and Confessions under the scaffold:

> And these printed lies were easily caught up by those who had a halfpenny to give for them, although the purchasers knew that no Dying Speeches had been made at all, and had read the Confessions in the newspapers the preceding day. But then those narratives had a rough and rudely executed woodcut of a scaffold at the top – and *this* was the main attraction.[99]

Gatrell has argued that execution sheets were 'totemic artefacts', purchased needfully by the common people. And at the heart of this

Savage and Inhuman
MURDER
OF ANN TAPE
In George Street St. Giles's.

Last night, shortly before 11, o'clock, one of the most ferocious and deliberate murders which have been perpetrated for many years was committed upon the body of a woman named Ann Tape, at a house of ill fame, 11, George-street St Giles's.

It appears that the deceased, who was a married woman, who had separated from her husband, and was well known to the neighbourhood as an abandoned character, had about the hour mentioned, accompanied a man (whose person is unknown but his name the neighbours are unacquainted with) to a back parlour on the ground-floor of the house in question. After they had been there for some short time the man took his departure without exciting any particular attention. Not hearing the female move for some time, the servant of the house proceeded to the room, when she was horror stricken on discovering the unfortunate female lying on the bed, welting in her blood from no less than six deep and desperate stabs in the throat, neck and breast. The hands of the unfortunate victim had also been much cut in her struggles to escape from the hands of her assassin; and the knife with which the wounds had been inflicted was still left sticking in her throat.

Information of the circumstance was immediately forwarded to Mr. Greenwood, of the E division of police, who, accompanied by Inspectors Bird and Campbell, repaired to the house, and Mr. Fitzgerland and Mr. Simpson, two Surgeons re-

siding in the immediate neighbourhood, were sent for, and promptly attended. They pronounced life to have been extinct for some time. The house in which the murder has been perpetrated is remarkable as having been that in which the celebrated Mr. Justice Byot resided and died. As soon as the circumstance became known in the neighbourhood, immense crowds of persons assembled around the house, and several of the inhabitants were permitted by the police to view the body, which presented a most appalling spectacle.

It is stated in the neighbourhood that the murderer and the deceased for some time cohabited together, and that a threat on the part of the woman to return and live with her husband was the man's motive to the dreadful act. Other motives are assigned, but little that can be depended upon is at present known.

As soon as the murder became known, the most active measures were promptly taken by the police in order to discover the retreat of the murderer and written descriptions of his person and dress have been forwarded for circulation throughout the various divisions of the force in order that his escape from justice may be prevented. Several persons were, in the course of this afternoon, taken into custody on suspicion of being implicated in the transaction but they were speedily liberated on their satisfying the police that they were in no way concerned in the matter.

The following is a description of the murderer:—He is a man of middle stature, of dark and pale countenance. He wore a rough hair or fur cap, dark velveteen jacket and light trousers. His hair is dark and short, and his whiskers somewhat closely shaven. His person is known to the police & others in the neighbourhood of the murder but not his name.

The deliberation with which the murder was contemplated, planned, and carried into execution, will appear from the fact, that at ten o'clock last night he purchased a knife at the shop of Mr. Oldham, of High Street, St. Giles's. It is a carving knife sharply pointed, as usual, and a portion of the point is broken off, no doubt, by coming in contact with the bones of his victim.

The Street in which this atrocious and savage act has been committed runs parallel with that portion of Bloomsbury Street which previously to the improvements in that neighbourhood, was called Plumtree-street, and the house in which the ill-fated woman lost her life is almost close to the back of charlotte-street chapel. George Street forms a portion of what is well known as the "Rookery," and is thickly inhabited by persons of the poorest, lowest, most abandoned, profligate and squalid population,

Paul, Printer 8, Great St. Andrew Street, 7 Dials, and 52, Fashion St Spitalfields.

19. Half-sheet printed after the discovery of Ann Tape's body the previous evening (1845)

need were the woodcuts of the gallows. These simple and undeveloped images, he suggested, should be regarded as ideograms, rather than clumsy representations, as they drew on an 'image magic' which had 'fuelled the imagination for centuries'. These woodcuts did not contain any messages. Instead, Gatrell concludes, as souvenirs they materialised a way of experiencing.[100]

The growing variety of illustrations on murder and execution broadsides also suggests a simple function: entertainment. Images helped to make broadsides accessible to the illiterate. Moreover, they substantially increased working people's experience of the printed image. Woodcuts also satisfied the curiosity of readers of broadsides, satiating their thirst for details about the crime and violent offender. Especially after 1820, in addition to images of the gallows, printers increasingly included portraits of murderers and victims and illustrations of prisoners confined in the condemned cell, either bidding farewell to their families or writing their letters of confession. Sheets printed to report on murderers' trials sometimes featured a woodcut of the courtroom's interior. And it became more and more common for half-sheets and whole-sheets, from those that contained reports of the crime to those printed for execution, to present an image of the crime scene itself. Some of these images bore little resemblance to the facts, but their accuracy did not concern purchasers. Their importance lay in their representation of violence, particularly the extent to which the image could invoke a range of emotional responses from the spectator.

Woodcuts of brutal murders were extremely detailed, usually capturing the actual moment of violence or presenting to viewers the most heinous aspects of the crime. These graphic images shocked and horrified purchasers. In fact, they still do so today, despite their crudeness, exaggerations and the often ridiculous theatrical poses of both felons and victims. At the same time, woodcuts titillated spectators. Illustrations placed great emphasis on the blood that flowed from the victim's fatal wounds. Often crime scenes were drenched in it. In some cases, blood spurted in an accusatory manner from the victim, splattering the murderer. Especially horrendous were the woodcuts made for a number of cases in which female victims were dismembered by their assailants. Broadsides printed for the apprehension, trial and execution of James Greenacre depicted him in the very act of sawing the head, arms and legs from the body of Hannah Brown. Similarly, Daniel Good was shown cutting the throat of his lover, Jane Jones, and then attempting to conceal the crime by shoving her severed limbs into an oven (see figures 19, 20 and 21).

20. Broadsheet printed after the inquest on the body of Jane Jones and the apprehension of her murderer, Daniel Good (1842)

21. *opposite*: Broadsheet printed for sale at and after James Greenacre's execution in 1838

The EDGEWARE-ROAD TRAGEDY.

LIFE, TRIAL, AND EXECUTION OF JAMES GREENACRE.

CALL me not to a strict
account,
How I have lived here:
For then I know right well,
O Lord,
Most vile I shall appear,
I need not to confess my life
For surely thou canst tell,
What I have been and what I
Thou knowest very well.(am
O Lord, thou knowest what
things be past,
Also the things that be:
Thou know'st also what is to
come,
Nothing is hid from thee.
Before the heavens and earth
were made; (were then,
Thou know'st what thing
As all things else that have
been done,
Among the sons of men.
And can the things that I have
done,
Be hidden from thee then?
No, no, thou know'st them all,
O Lord, (when.
Where they were done and

MY hour is come, my glass is run, now
by the law's decree, (tal tree,
On Tuesday next condemn'd to die upon a fa-
All for a cruel murder as all do understand
Which has caused great sensation and horror
thro' the land.
In vain I sought to cloak my crime, & stead-
fastly deny'd, (I try'd,
That I had been her murderer & many schemes
Thinking thereby to save my life, but vain was
ev'ry plan, (guilty man.
For in the minds of all mankind I stood a
When I review my wicked life, I shudder with
dismay (way;
No consolation cheers me- a wretched casta-
No ray of hope revives my soul, to look be-
yond the sky, (now you must die."
While ev'ry moment seems to say, "To-mor-
The sacred law of GOD and man I spurned
with disdain (to gain,
Left no dishonest means untried my purposes
But now my crimes have found me out,—the
blood my hands have shed, (head,
Now cries aloud for vengeance on my devoted
O could I for one moment a list'ning world ad-
dress (happiness;
If in this world or that to come,they hope for
The ranks of factious traitors, as from destruc-
tion run! (sands has undone,
Flee from those hellish counsels, which thou-
For had I been but timely wise, and kept the
honest way, (this day;
I might have been a prosperous and happy man
But mark the sad alternative—I die by law's
decree
A wretched malefactor upon a fatal tree.

On Wednesday the Recorder made his report to his Majesty of the prisoners under sentence of death. To all of whom his Majesty was graciously pleased to extend his royal mercy except to James Greenacre who was left for execution on Tuesday, May 2nd.

THE trial of Greenacre, for the murder commonly called, 'the Edgeware-road Murder,' having been specially fixed for Monday, the 10th April, the court was crowded at an early hour. About 10 o'clock the prisoners were put to the bar and arraigned—Greenacre for the wilful murder of Hannah Brown, and the latter with having a guilty knowledge of the matter after the act, and with continuing to aid, assist, and comfort the murderer.

Samuel Pegler, policeman.—On the 28th Dec. I was in the Edgeware-road with a person named Bond. I went to a place pointed out by Bond, and found a sack containing the trunk of a human body. The arms were tied with a part of the cord now produced. The sack had a mark, as if it had been recently tied. I found some pieces of rag lying near, and upon the bag. There was a flag-stone partly covering it. On examining the bag I found some mahogany shavings.

Mathias Rolfe, lock-keeper at Johnston's lock, Regent's canal.—About half-past 8 on the morning of the 6th Jan., I was called by a bargeman, who said there was something prevented the gates closing. I procured a hitcher, and raised something which I thought was a dead dog, but which turned out to be the head of a human being. The water was about 5 feet in depth. On examining the head, which was taken up by the hair, I found that the right eye had been knocked out by a stick or some other weapon. The left jaw-bone had been broken, and the bone protruded through the skin. The left ear had a seam, as if the ear ring had been torn out in the youth of the person, and that it had grown up again. The hole in the other ear was perfect. The head seemed to have been some days in the water. I fetched a cloth, and put the head in it, and took it home.

James Page.—I am a labourer, and on the 2d Feb. I was working at an osier bed in Coldharbour-lane, near Camberwell. I found a sack among some bushes, and found in it the legs and thighs of a human body. A man who was with me pulled the sack open. They were taken to the station house, and the police took charge of them.

Evan Davis—I am a cabinet maker of 45, Bartholomew-close. I knew the deceased Hannah Brown for about five years. I heard shortly before Christmas last that she was going to be married. About nine days before Christmas I was called down from my workshop, and found Mrs. Brown and her beau. The prisoner at the bar is the man. Mrs. Brown introduced him to me. They remained about three quarters of an hour, and the prisoner and myself adjourned to a public house where we had some drink. He had a deal to say about America, and said he had a large farm of about 1,000 acres at Hudson's Bay—that he had returned from it 4 months previous, and was returning a few weeks after Christmas.

Catharine Glass—I live in Windsor-street, Tottenham-court-road. I knew the deceased Hannah Brown. She was with me on Christmas Eve, about 12 o'clock in the day. I knew she was about to be married on the following day. She was to sleep with me that night, and she promised to be with me at 9 o'clock at night. She remained about half an hour that day. She had no marks of black eye or bruise on her face at that time. I never saw her alive again.

William Gay—I live in Goodge-street, and am a broker. I am shopman to my mistress. The deceased was my sister. Just before her death we were not on friendly terms. I saw her the Thursday before her death. I saw Greenacre on the Tuesday night following. He came to our shop. My mistress was in the shop when he came. I heard him tell her the wedding was put off, and that Mrs Brown had no property. He said that she had *run* him in debt at a tally-shop; that they had a few words, and were not going to be married; and that he was going to take a shop instead of going to America. I never saw Greenacre before to my knowledge. My sister had a mark on her ear. I *have seen a head at Paddington workhouse*. The ear, eye, and hair resembled that of my sister's. I told the overseer of the poorhouse that I believed it was the head of my sister.

A number of other witnesses were then examined, after which Mr Price made an eloquent speech in behalf of the prisoners. The Lord Chief Justice the summed up the evidence, and the Jury returned a Verdict—GUILTY against both prisoners.

The trial lasted two days, and was not concluded till 10 o'clock on Tuesday night.

Greenacre's Confession.

After receiving sentence, Greenacre appeared very depressed, and begged an interview of the Sheriffs, who immediately visited him in his cell. Greenacre addressed them in a clear, firm voice, the substance of which is as follows:—

After his arrivel with his unfortunate victim at Carpenter's-place, on Christmas-eve a quarrel arose between them on the subject of the property each had reppresented themselves to possess, when the deceased (Mrs. Brown) using strong language towards him for deceiving her, so exasperated him that he took up a piece of wood resembling the roller of a jack towel, or for a piece of silk, which at the moment was lying near him, and struck her violently over the right eye, which blow inflicted the injury that as been so ably described by Mr. Girdwood and the other surgeons at the different examinations, and at the trials. The blow instantly stunned her, but he prevented her falling to the ground by seizing hold of the chair. He then placed a pail which was standing in the room by the side of the chair, and holding her neck over it, he, with a common table knife, cut her throat, and held her in that position until the blood had ceased to flow. After dissevering the head and limbs from the trunk he put the former in a bag, and placing it under his arm he proceeded to Stepney, when taking the head out of the bag, he threw it in the Regent's canal, not far from the spot where it was afterwards discovered.

The Ordinary as soon as the order for the execution of Greenacre was received at Newgate, went, accompanied by the Governor, to the room in which the prisoner is confined, for the purpose of communicating the result. Greenacre was writing at the time at the table, at which he had been sitting placidly most of the day. Upon seeing the Ordinary with a paper in his hand, with the black seal attached, he rose from his seat, but without appearing *to be at all agitated or disturbed.*

The Ordinary said, as is the custom on occasions of the kind, 'The Recorder has made his report to the King, and I am sorry to inform you that it is unfavourable to you."

Greenacre.—It cannot be helped—I am sacrificed through prejudice and falsehood.

The Ordinary expressed a hope that Greenacre would occupy that period between the moment the communication was made and the time of execution, in earnest and hearty prayer.

The Ordinary then handed a book of prayer to him, and called his attention most earnestly to it.

About thirty years ago Greenacre' mother was married to a respectable farmer in Norfolk of the name of Towler; two families immediately came to reside together. Of the Greenacres there were seven, and Mr. Towler had but a son and a daughter. Old Towler, as he was commonly called was a very conscientious man, and took as much care of the Greenacres as if they were his own family, and on James Greenacre being about 19 years of age about 25 years since, he wrote to a friend who was a respectable tailor in the west end of the town, and to whom his son was apprenticed, to look out for a business that he might purchase for young Greenacre. His friend promised compliance; at the same time he observed that he thought him too young. The old man said, "Oh, by no means; you will find he is sharp enough." It was not long until an opportunity presented itself in the goodwill of a house in the grocery line at Westminster, quite close to Astley's Theatre. Old Towler's friend immediately entered into a negociation for the purchase of it, and having agreed upon the terms he wrote to Old Towler to come up to town, and perfect the agreement. After the negociation was concluded Greenacre was heard to say, that if he could get the lease moderate in his own name he would snap his fingers at the old man. *His friend, on hearing this, took* care to get the assignment made out in old Towler's name. The old man subsequently arrived in town and the agreement was perfected, and young Greenacre was put into possession. He succeeded very well. Being unmarried and in want of a housekeeper, old Towler sent his only daughter, a girl about 16, to keep his house. In a short time Greenacre began to make overtures to her of a base kind; she, however spurned them. Finding that no persuasion would do, he made a forcible attempt on Miss Towler, who successfully resisted, and fled to the house of her father's friend, where her brother was apprenticed.—Old Towler was so incensed at the conduct of Greenacre, that he sold off the stock, and sent him adrift. Attributing the frustration of his villany to old Towler's friend, and the master of his son-Tom Towler, then a very fine lad, he ingratiated himself into the youth's confidence, for the purpose of indulging his revenge, and he prevailed on the unfortunate lad to summon his master to Bow-street office, for not teaching him his trade. The youth being sworn, stated thot he was not sufficienty instructed in his trade; when his master produced a pair of small clothes made by the lad, and every gentlemen on the beuch declared nothing could be better executed Sir Richard Birnie asked the youth (who admitted that he made the small clothes) what could have induced him to summon his master, the poor boy hung down his head and made no reply. His master turned round and said to Sir Richard that he could account for it, as it was owing to the scoundrel that stood at his elbow (Greenacre) a better lad never was. The unfortunate young lad was taken home by his master, and as usual treated as one of the family. When on the subsequent Sunday in the evening, he went to hear a sermon at a chapel in Great Queen-street. On his return home he rushed into the presence of his master and family, and threw himself on his knees and solicited their forgiveness for the perjury which he had committed at Bow-street. He feared that God would not, as the sermon which he had heard at the chapel gave him but little hopes. His master and family did every thing in their power to tranquilise his mind, but all was in vain; such was the impression the circumstance made on his mind, that reason fled, and he was obliged te be put under controul until his father was written to, who came up to town and removed his son, who did not survive, and died a maniac.

THE EXECUTION.

On Tuesday morning the above unhappy malefactor paid the forfeit of hia life to the offended laws of his country, in front of the debtor's door, Newgate. No execution of late years has attracted so large an assemblage of spectators, some thousands being present. About seven o'clock be partook of some refreshment, and shortly afterwards the Sheriffs arrived at the prison, and immediately proceeded to the condemned cell. The usual melancholy preparations having been completed, Greenacre was brought from the cell to the room where he was te be pinioned. He appeared quite calm and collected, and walked with a firm step. The melancholy procession then proceeded towards the scaffold, which he mounted without any assistance, and in less than a minute the drop fell, and he soon ceased to exist.

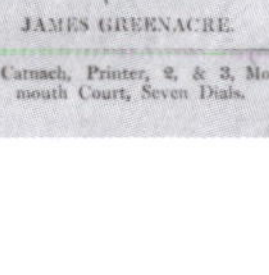

JAMES GREENACRE.

J. Catnach, Printer, 2, & 3, Monmouth Court, Seven Dials.

That these illustrations entertained purchasers is evident not only from their inclusion on the sheets, but also in their presentation. Over the course of century, methods of presentation became increasingly sophisticated: for example, sequences of cuts began to appear, each separate image capturing different moments or events in the crime, combining to offer a pictorial narrative. Captions were soon added, providing a literary reference. But most of all, the ability of these vivid and disturbing woodcuts to entertain suggests the operation of more complex emotions and social discourses that formed part of the popular imagination. V. A. C. Gatrell has established an important contrast between eighteenth-century flash ballads and nineteenth-century execution broadsides. While ballads were knowing, sardonic and half-comic celebrations that ignored conventional morality, conversely, broadsides were sentimental, warning readers about error and focusing on the felon's repentance, thus paying lip service to conventional morality.[101] However, in their gross illustrations and accompanying lengthy textual accounts of murder, broadsides also performed a celebratory function.[102] If anything, the intensification of the theme of violence in broadsides, especially evident in vulgar and outrageous images of brutal murders, posed a direct challenge to conventional morality and was certainly an obstruction to those who sought to tame popular culture.

Verses, perhaps the most important feature on murder and execution broadsheets, were songs or ballads that provided catchy, rhyming narratives summarising the drama of crime and its punishment. Their composition often adhered to a rigid formula, the stanzas sickly moralistic and final judgements on the actions of felons typically harsh. However, beneath this conservative, even deferential exterior, can be found a complex and multi-layered commentary on violence and a critique of contemporary social change. Verses were often repetitive, evidence of the rampant plagiarism that plagued the unregulated printing industry. Despite this, they performed a crucial role in the sale and consumption of broadside literature. Standing patterers and chaunters would gather potential customers by singing or chanting these ballads, their successful sale dependent on the effectiveness of the performance.[103] Moreover, it is likely that the songs were sung again by purchasers. Their rhyming attributes and repetitive features meant that they were especially easy to memorise, thus providing access for the illiterate as well as the newly literate.

Like the textual and illustrative accounts of murder described above, verses were also graphic in their presentation of violent crime. As the publication and distribution of broadsides steadily increased, narratives of violence in the verses became more dramatic and elaborate. Verses became detailed stories, capturing the life of the criminal, the moment he or she decided to commit the crime, the murder and his or her subsequent capture and punishment. Crucially, the act of violence itself was given much attention. For example, on the capture of Richard Gould and Mary Ann Jarvis for the murder of John Templeman, one poet provided a harrowing account of the discovery of the crime by Templeman's charwoman:

> She gave the alarm, the door was forc'd
> And then all stood aghast
> In a pool of crimson gore he lay
> And his hands were tied fast
> His skull was near to atoms dash'd
> A bloody stocking round his head
> His teeth were scattered on the floor
> And his blood had dyed the bed.
>
> Such a mangled corpse none e'er had seen
> Before in all their life
> With his murder it does appear
> He had a mortal strife
> When pinioned like a Murderer
> They did their victim slay
> Oh, take my money, the old man cried,
> But spare my life I pray.
>
> His appeal for life was all in vain
> No feeling they had got
> Remorseless of the law of God
> They slew him on the spot
> Only to gain his little wealth
> With his blood their hands were dyed
> And for this horrid deed of blood
> They shortly will be tried.[104]

Likewise, in sheets printed in London reporting the conviction of Thomas Drory for the murder of Jael Denny, the voice of the felon was used to describe his diabolical deed:

> Beneath a tree I threw her down
> A rope around her neck I wound
> She gave one scream so shrill and clear
> Oh God, that cry I can still hear

> Her lovely neck so white and pure
> With the rope both cut and tore
> Upon her snowy tender breast
> My cruel knee I basely press'd
>
> Her face turned black, bloodshot and red,
> Her eyes protruding from her head
> My love I with deceit beguiled
> Then murdered her and unborn child.[105]

As well as providing readers with amusing, rhyming accounts of bloodthirsty acts of murder, verses also contained crucial layers of comment on the motivations behind violent crime. And the poets did not necessarily agree on what that comment should be, or even the direction of their moral judgements. Two distinct styles of verses existed in nineteenth-century broadsides: the subjective and the objective. When verses were composed in the subjective voice, they allowed the murderer to directly address his or her audience. While he or she provided an account of their crime, the murderer also used the opportunity to express great sorrow and remorse, and to endorse the justness of his or her punishment. However, at the same time, he or she went to great lengths to emphasise the didactic purpose of his or her execution, hoping to deter others from life choices that had led to the murder. For example, verses featured in one sheet distributed at the execution of James Greenacre in 1837 adopted the subjective tone. After describing his mutilation of Hannah Brown, Greenacre appealed to purchasers:

> Now all young men that hear these lines
> Pray think upon my sad state
> Reflect upon your evil ways
> Before it is too late
> Your vicious ways may lead you on
> To commit a heinous crime
> Which may lead you to a fatal tree
> And cut off in their prime.[106]

A slightly longer plea was supposedly made by Samuel Adams, executed in 1859 for the murder of his sister-in-law. His verses emphasised how a man with a Christian upbringing could easily stray if tempted by passion and jealousy:

> Farewell vain world my time is come
> I must bid a long adieu

> May all good Christians now take a warning
> And never have cause their lives to rue
> Vain passion and jealousy did tempt me
> My sister in law, alas! did slay
> Alas! what demon then could tempt me
> To take her precious life away
>
> ...
>
> Do not condemn before you listen
> None is without their crimes on earth
> None without some stain upon him
> We all are sinners from our birth
>
> ...
>
> Remember me, keep from transgressing
> Look, before you, at this blight.[107]

What is evident in these verses is some measure of continuity with sentiments contained in the early modern popular literature of crime. Appeals of these murderers did not mitigate their guilt. However, they reminded readers and listeners that everyone has the potential for criminal activity, in this case murder. Audiences were invited to identify with the violent criminal and were warned of the consequences of indulging too heavily in passion and excess.

In contrast, verses written in the objective voice both highlighted the horror of the crime and proceeded to demonise the murderer, casting him or her outside of society. An anonymous narrator's voice was usually adopted, allowing sweeping judgements to be passed.[108] The verses were also very rigid and formulaic. Many opened with a passage like the following emphasising the inhuman nature of the crime:

> From dire revenge and deadly hate
> What mischief doth arise
> The mournful tale I now relate
> Will plainly testify;
> A tragic scene here is display'd
> Most frightening to behold
> Your hearts will ache, as it will make
> Your very blood run cold.[109]

In this case, the very next verse introduces Emanuel Barthelemy to the audience, the murderer of Mr Moore and Mr Collard. In order to prevent identification, the narrator usually drew attention to abnormal aspects of the convict's life. More often than not, these claims were totally fabricated. Emanuel Barthelemy, for example, was described as a drunken Frenchman. Loaded adjectives were also employed by the poets. Murders were characterised as monsters or demons. For example, one broadsheet printed after the confession of James Greenacre contained the following verse:

> He with a saw cut off each limb, as you have heard it said,
> And the *monster*, full of sin, did sever off her head.
> To a separate place each part he took – what fiend of deadly
>   spite!
> And then foul conscience pierc'd his soul with anguish day and
>   night.[110]

Joseph Connor was similarly labelled a monster in the verses compiled for his execution in 1845:

> What force he must have struck the blow
> To make his victims blood to flow
> Such vengeance he the deed had done
> The knife he broke against the bone
>
> Then to escape the *monster* tried
> Tho' deep in blood his hands where [sic] dyed
> But God's alseeing [sic] Eye did heed
> And frown'd in vengeance on the deed.[111]

Verses composed in the third person rarely contained a warning for listeners. There are, however, several exceptions, as in some verses the victim's voice was allowed to speak from the grave, warning others who could potentially suffer the same fate. In this way, the voice of Jane Mew was heard in 1842. As the victim of the seduction, betrayal and murderous assault of Captain Henry Smyth, Mew declared:

> Come all true lovers lend an ear
> Unto this tale of woe
> I hope you will a warning take
> By my sad overthrow[112]

Curiously, neither the subjective tone nor the objective tone dominated the method of writing verses for murder and execution broadsides over the course of the nineteenth century. While the objective did rise in prominence throughout the 1830s and 1840s, it never replaced the subjective, which persisted until the disappearance of this genre of street literature after 1870. In some isolated cases, the two styles were fused together: in his composition a poet could swing from first-person to third-person narration and back again.

Superficially, this clash presents a rather confusing picture. However, these verses and the broadsides more generally might actually offer a rare glimpse behind the scenes, exposing overlap between old and new, or rather revealing the process of evolution at work in popular culture, something that remains largely hidden from view in other entertainments. For example, the use of the subjective in these verses links the broadsides to an older, pre-industrial popular literature of crime described at the opening of this chapter, which drew upon popular notions of criminality centred on the potential sinfulness of 'everyman'. Undoubtedly, this formed part of the customary mentality before 1780, when actual violence was much more a part of everyday life. We have already seen how, during the late eighteenth and early nineteenth centuries, as a result of the changing urban environment as well as efforts of law-enforcement agencies, actual violence was becoming less of a feature of everyday life for the majority, which might have helped to challenge the relevance of 'everyman's' guilt.

As the experience of violence was largely transferred from the streets to the imagination, the 'monster' murderer replaced 'everyman'. His violence was more extreme and socially disruptive, but was equally real. Thus he was able both to invoke fears and anxieties associated with the modern, and mostly urban, environment because he, himself, was often a product of that environment; and, within the context of this restrictive environment, to provide a new outlet for the enjoyment of violence, the extremity of his representation assisting with that transfer of the expression of violence. Murder and execution broadsides therefore reveal, in popular culture, a process of remaking at work with respect to the customary mentality.

Despite the tremendous sales of broadsides during the 1840s and 1850s, and the substantial profits made by some prominent London printers, murder and execution sheets suffered a serious decline after 1860. Charles Hindley recorded that Catnach's firm only managed to sell 280,000 broadsheets detailing the execution of Franz Muller for the murder of Thomas Briggs in 1864.[113] After the abolition of public execution in 1868, the market basically collapsed. It could be argued that this was a logical progression: that the removal of this public spectacle severed the dramatic narrative of crime and its punishment. No longer so highly visible to the common people, interest in crime and violence thus began to dwindle and broadsheets were increasingly marginalised. However, this explanation has limits. It certainly does not fit with the process described above, namely, the intensification of graphic representations of violence and the massive expansion of the broadside trade during a period of declining executions after 1820.

Similarly, it cannot be argued that the decline of broadsides represented a triumph of the civilising process, a result of concerted efforts to tame popular culture. In the absence of authority and the imposition of strict regulations, we must consider whether there is a more functional explanation for this unusually rapid demise, a question that will be considered further in chapter 6.

Notes

1 Entry for 18 May 1728. G. Savile, *Secret Comment: The Diaries of Gertrude Savile, 1721–1757*, ed. A. Saville (1997), p. 115, http://www. open.ac.uk/Arts/reading/UK/record_details.php?id=486, accessed 28 August 2007.

2 L. B. Faller, *Turned to Account: The Forms and Functions of Criminal Biography in Late Seventeenth and Early Eighteenth Century England* (Cambridge: Cambridge University Press, 1987), p. x, Faller, 'Criminal opportunities in the eighteenth century: the "ready-made" contexts of the popular literature of crime', *Comparative Literature Studies*, 24 (1987), 121, P. Rawlings, *Drunks, Whores and Idle Apprentices: Criminal Biographies of the Eighteenth Century* (London: Routledge, 1992), pp. 1–3, A. McKenzie, *Tyburn's Martyrs: Execution in England, 1675–1775* (London: Hambledon Continuum, 2007), pp. 31–54.

3 V. A. C. Gatrell, *The Hanging Tree: Execution and the English People, 1770–1868* (Oxford: Oxford University Press, 1994), pp. 156–96.

4 See particularly A. McKenzie, 'Making crime pay: motives, marketing strategies and the printed literature of crime in England, 1670–1770', in S. Devereaux, A. May and G. T. Smith (eds), *Criminal Justice in the Old World and the New: Essays in Honour of J. M. Beattie* (Toronto: Centre of Criminology, University of Toronto, 1998), pp. 234–7. See also J. Wiltenburg, 'True crime: the origins of modern sensationalism', *American Historical Review*, 109 (2004), 1377–404.

5 Faller, *Turned to Account*, pp. 193, 124, and Rawlings, *Drunks, Whores and Idle Apprentices*, pp. 4, 10–11, 17.

6 McKenzie, *Tyburn's Martyrs*, ch. 3. See also V. McMahon, *Murder in Shakespeare's England* (London: Hambledon & London, 2004), pp. 225–6.

7 McKenzie, *Tyburn's Martyrs*, pp. 154–5, 252–4, and Gatrell, *The Hanging Tree*, pp. 114–17.

8 K. Hollingsworth, *The Newgate Novel, 1830–1847: Bulwer, Ainsworth, Dickens and Thackeray* (Detroit: Wayne State University Press, 1963).

9 See, in particular, H. Mayhew, *London Labour and the London Poor* (4 vols, London: Griffin, Bohn & Co., 1861–62), I, p. 416, and Select

Committee on Criminal and Destitute Juveniles (Parl. Papers, 1852, VII.1), Appendix 2: Juvenile delinquency, Liverpool: Extract from the sixth report of the Inspectors of Prisons, Northern and Eastern district.

10 G. Spraggs, *Outlaws and Highwaymen: The Cult of the Robber in England from the Middle Ages to the Nineteenth Century* (London: Pimlico, 2001). See also comments of a South Wales miner who was raised in an orphanage from the late nineteenth century: 'Robin Hood was our patron saint or ideal. We sincerely believed in robbing the rich to help the poor.' J. H. Howard, *Winding Lanes* (Caernarvon: Calvinistic Methodist Printing Works, 1938), pp. 27–30.

11 For example, *History of the Pirates of All Nations* (London: Lloyd, Purkess, Strange, 1836–39), *Lives of the Most Notorious Highwaymen, Footpads and Murderers* (London: Lloyd, 1836–37), *Remarkable Trials, Including Amongst Others, the Celebrated Cases of Eugene Aram, Marchioness Brinvilliers, Jonathan Bradford, etc.* (London: George Vickers, 1851), *Tales of Brigands and Bandetti* (London: E. Harrison, 1865–68), *Tales of Highwaymen; or, Life on the Road* [periodical] (London, 1865–66), *Famous Crimes Past and Present. Police Budget Edition* [periodical] (London: Harold Furniss, 1903–5). British Library, London, Barry Ono Collection.

12 R. D. Altick, *Victorian Studies in Scarlet: Murders and Manners in the Age of Victoria* (London: Dent, 1972), pp. 41–2.

13 Gatrell, *The Hanging Tree*, p. 57.

14 J. Grant, *The Great Metropolis*, 2nd Ser. (2 vols, London: Saunders & Otley, 1837), II, p. 263.

15 J. E. Ritchie, *The Night Side of London* (London: W. Tweedie, 1857), p. 27. See also T. Miller, *Picturesque Sketches of London, Past and Present* (London: Office of the National Illustrated Library, 1852), pp. 183–90.

16 For example, the execution of Daniel Good reported in *The Times*, 24 May 1842, p. 8 (loud shouts) compared with the execution of Francois Courvoisier, *The Times*, 7 July 1840, p. 6 (silence).

17 Evidence of Rev. John Davis Ordinary of Newgate, and evidence of Thomas Kittle, police inspector, Royal Commission on Capital Punishment (Parl. Papers, 1866, XXI.1) [hereafter RC (1866)], pp. 150 and 166 respectively, report on the 'Execution of Greenacre', *The Times*, 3 May 1837, p. 4.

18 For example, evidence of Adam Sparry, Inspector of the Reserve in the City of London Police, Select Committee of the House of Lords to Consider the Present Mode of Capital Punishments (Parl. Papers, 1856, VII.9) [hereafter SC (1856)], p. 30.

19 Gatrell, *The Hanging Tree*, pp. 73 (quote), 81–3.

20 S. Devereaux, 'Recasting the theatre of execution in London: the end of Tyburn', *Past & Present*, 202 (2009), 127–74.

21 Thomas Kittle, RC (1866), pp. 112–13. See also Grant, *The Great Metropolis*, II, p. 263 and Ritchie, *The Night Side of London*, p. 30.

22 Gatrell goes one step further, that the crowds' excitement 'suggests a perverse celebration as much as a disavowal of the crime, a vicarious participation in the licence which the outrage signified'. *The Hanging Tree*, p. 70.

23 SC (1856), p. 36.

24 Miller, *Picturesque Sketches of London*, p. 183.

25 Thomas Kittle, RC (1866), p. 110.

26 Charles George Hudson, SC (1856), p. 24.

27 W. Ballantine, *Some Experiences of a Barrister's life* (2 vols, London: R. Bentley, 5th edn, 1882), I, pp. 89–90.

28 *Punch*, 16 (1849), 122.

29 J. Boswell, *Boswell's London Journal, 1762–1763*, ed. F. A. Pottle (London: W. Heinemann, 1952), p. 280. See also the numerous references to Mrs Salmon's in *The Spectator*: 2 April 1711, p. 117, 4 April 1711, p. 129, 20 October 1714, p. 82.

30 W. Thornbury and E. Walford, *Old and New London* (2 vols, London: Cassell, 1878), I, ch. 4.

31 For further descriptions of eighteenth-century waxworks, see P. Pilbeam, *Madame Tussaud and the History of Waxworks* (London: Hambledon & London, 2003), pp. 9–15 and R. D. Altick, *The Shows of London* (London: Belknap Press, 1978), pp. 332–49. Waxworks exhibitions at fairs: T. Frost, *The Old Showmen and the Old London Fairs* (London: Tinsley Brothers, 1874), p. 123.

32 Note that Madame Tussaud had arrived in Britain with her touring waxwork exhibition in 1802, the success of which encouraged her to establish a permanent base in London by the mid-1830s.

33 B. Melman, *The Culture of History: English Uses of the Past, 1800–1953* (Oxford: Oxford University Press, 2006), p. 43.

34 'Letters from a lady in London to her niece in the country: Madame Tussaud's Exhibition', *Chambers's Edinburgh Journal*, 22 January 1842, pp. 4–5.

35 Ibid.

36 *Lloyd's Weekly Newspaper*, 9 December 1849, p. 6.

37 Melman, *The Culture of History*, pp. 38–9.

38 Anon., *Madame Tussaud & Sons Catalogue, Bazaar, Baker Street. Portman Square* (London, 1869).

39 Melman, *The Culture of History*, p. 43.

40 K. Halttunen, *Murder Most Foul: The Killer and the American Gothic Imagination* (Cambridge, Mass.: Harvard University Press, 1998), p. 82.

41 Melman, *The Culture of History*, pp. 60–1.

42 Waxworks in fairgrounds in nineteenth-century London: Frost, *Old Showmen*, p. 292, W. Hone, *The Every-Day Book* (2 vols, London: Hunt & Clarke, 1825–26), I, pp. 1167–252.

43 *An Entire New Exhibition, at 16 Pleasant Row, Pentonville Hill, Near Battle Bridge ... Museum of Moving Wax Work* (London, 1855), Bodleian Library, Oxford (Bod.), John Johnson Collection (JJ), Waxworks 3 (6). See also *Mother Brownrigg who was executed at the Old Bailey ... Ferguson's Grand Oriental Promenade and Exhibition Rooms London* (London, c. 1839), Bod. JJ, Waxworks 4 (5), Mrs Hoyos's Royal Exhibition of Wax Work ... 182 Fleet Street, Bod. JJ, Waxworks 1 (12).

44 Report from William Bodham Donne regarding performances at Mrs Pollard's Wax Works Rooms, 3 January 1859, London, The National Archives (TNA), Public Record Office (PRO), Lord Chamberlain's Papers, LC1/ 70. See also the Report from the Inspector of D Division (Metropolitan Police), 30 December 1858, on the same venue, also in LC1/ 70. For an extended analysis of Donne, see chapter 4.

45 [C. Dickens] 'Mr Whelks over the water', *All the Year Round*, 15 (1866), pp. 591–2.

46 M. Williams, *Round London: Down East and Up West* (London: Macmillan, 1892), pp. 6–8. See also [J. Law], 'Penny Gaffs', *Pall Mall Gazette*, 18 October 1883, p. 3.

47 A. Fonblanque, *England Under Seven Administrations* (3 vols, London: R. Bentley, 1837), II, p. 194. See also C. Hindley, *The Life and Times of James Catnach (Late of the Seven Dials), Ballad Monger* (London: Reeves & Turner, 1878), p. 237.

48 Reprinted in *The Times*, 31 July 1828, p. 3.

49 Thornbury and Walford, *Old and New London*, II, pp. 287–9. For collecting relics of famous murders, see also J. Pope-Hennessy, *Monckton Milnes. Volume 1: The Years of Promise* (London: Constable, 1949), p. 130.

50 Charles George Hudson, SC (1856), p. 25. See also similar concern expressed by Fonblanque in *England under Seven Administrations*, II, p. 194.

51 P. D. G. Pugh, *Staffordshire Portrait Figures and Allied Subjects of the Victorian Era* (London: Barrie & Jenkins, 1970), p. 9.

52 That is, if they were, none of these figures survived and none are recorded in the available lists of products distributed to salesmen by the manufacturers.

53 R. McWilliam, 'The theatricality of the Staffordshire figurine', *Journal of Victorian Culture*, 10 (2005), 109.

54 A. Briggs, *Victorian Things* (London: Batsford, 1988), p. 153.

55 McWilliam, 'The theatricality of the Staffordshire figurine', p. 109.

56 Ibid., pp. 110 and 112 (quote). See also S. Stewart, *On Longing: Narratives of the Miniature, the Gigantic, the Souvenir, the Collection* (Baltimore: Johns Hopkins University Press, 1984), especially pp. 135–6.

57 P. Anderson, *The Printed Image and the Transformation of Popular Culture* (Oxford: Clarendon Press, 1991).

58 A number of historians have previously addressed the broadside trade in early nineteenth-century London. For example, see Gatrell, *The Hanging Tree*, D. Vincent, *Literacy and Popular Culture: England, 1750–1914* (Cambridge: Cambridge University Press, 1989), B. Kalikoff, *Murder and Moral Decay in Victorian Popular Literature* (Michigan: UMI Research Press, 1986), M. Vicinus, *The Industrial Muse: A Study of Nineteenth-Century British Working-Class Literature* (New York: Croom Helm, 1974), R. D. Altick, *The English Common Reader: A Social History of the Mass Reading Public, 1800–1900* (Chicago: University of Chicago Press, 1957), V. E. Neuburg, *Popular Literature: A History and Guide* (Harmondsworth: Penguin, 1977), Neuburg, 'The literature of the streets', in H. J. Dyos and M. Wolff (eds), *The Victorian City: Images and Realities. Volume 1* (London: Routledge, 1973), pp. 191–209, L. Shepard, *The History of Street Literature* (Newton Abbott: David & Charles, 1973), C. Elkins, 'The voice of the poor: the broadside as a medium of popular culture and dissent in Victorian England', *Journal of Popular Culture*, 14 (1980), 262–74.

59 Gatrell, *The Hanging Tree*, p. 161.

60 Ibid., p. 159.

61 P. Chassaigne, 'Popular representations of crime: the crime broadside – a subculture of violence in Victorian Britain?', *Crime, Histoire et Sociétés*, 3 (1999), 40.

62 Vincent, *Literacy and Popular Culture*, p. 201.

63 Mayhew, *London Labour and the London Poor*, I, p. 220.

64 'The Press of the Seven Dials', *Chambers' Journal of Popular Literature*, 2 (28 June 1856), 401.

65 Hindley, *The Life and Times of James Catnach*, pp. 142–3, and C. Hindley, *The History of the Catnach Press* (London: C. Hindley, 1886), pp. 69–70.

66 Mayhew, *London Labour and the London Poor*, I, pp. 280–1, 284 (quote).

67 'The Press of the Seven Dials', p. 403.

68 Hindley, *History of the Catnach Press*, p. 92 and Mayhew, *London Labour and the London Poor*, I, p. 284.

69 Mayhew, *London Labour and the London Poor*, I, p. 222. See also pp. 221, 235.
70 Vincent, *Literacy and Popular Culture*, pp. 201–2.
71 Mayhew, *London Labour and the London Poor*, I, pp. 214, 221–5. See also H. Vizetelly, *Glances Back through Seventy Years* (2 vols, London: Kegan Paul, 1893), I, p. 10.
72 Mayhew, *London Labour and the London Poor*, I, pp. 214–15, 232–5.
73 Ibid., p. 226.
74 Chassaigne, 'Popular representations of crime', p. 25.
75 Gatrell, *The Hanging Tree*, p. 169.
76 Mayhew, *London Labour and the London Poor*, I, p. 222.
77 Ibid., p. 234. See also G. Simmons, *The Working Classes: Their Moral, Social and Intellectual Condition; with Practical Suggestions for their Improvement* (London: Partridge & Oakey, 1849), p. 13.
78 Gatrell, *The Hanging Tree*, p. 171.
79 Kalikoff, *Murder and Moral Decay*, pp. 17, 71.
80 Chassaigne, 'Popular representations of crime', pp. 29–30, 37–40.
81 Gatrell, *The Hanging Tree*, pp. 156–7, 161–6, 175.
82 *A Full and Impartial Account of the Life, Trial and Execution of Mr John Thurtell, Executed in the County of Hertford, for the Murder of Mr Weare* (London, 1824), London, British Library (BL) 1881.d.8.
83 *Sorrowful Lamentation of William Lees, Now Under Sentence of Death at Newgate* (London, 1839), BL.1881.d.8.
84 For example, see *Apprehension of the Murderer of the Female Whose Body was Found in the Edgware Road in December Last, and Attempted Suicide of the Murderer, with the Prisoner's Confession!!* (London, 1837), Bod., JJ., Murder and Execution Broadsides, 6 (5), *Awful Confession of Greenacre to the Murder of Hannah Brown* (London, 1837), Bod., JJ., Murder and Execution Broadsides, 6 (6), and *Particulars of the Confession and Execution of James Greenacre, Who was Executed this Morning, at the Old Bailey, for the Wilful Murder of Mrs Hannah Brown* (London, 1837), Bod., JJ., Murder and Execution Broadsides, 6 (7).
85 *Apprehension of Hubbard on Monday Morning. Examination at Union Hall, charged with the Wilful Murder of Eliza Grimwood, Who was Murdered at No. 12 Wellington Terrace, Waterloo Road, On Saturday May 26, 1838* (London, 1838), Bod., JJ., Murder and Execution Broadsides, 6 (25).
86 *Life, Trial, Confession and Execution of F. B. Courvoisier for the Murder of Lord William Russell* (London, 1840), BL.1881.d.8.
87 *Trial and Sentence of Thomas Drory for the Murder of Jael Denny at Doddinghurst* (London, 1850), Bod., JJ., Murder and Execution Broadsides, 10 (35).

88 *Life, Trial and Execution of Robert Blakesley for the Murder of James Burdon* (London, 1841), Bod., JJ., Murder and Execution Broadsides, 10 (13).

89 *Life, Character and Execution of William Godfrey Youngman, For the Murder of his Mother, Brothers and Sweetheart in Manor Place, Walworth* (London, 1860), Bod., JJ., Murder and Execution Broadsides, 9 (21). This might have been because the broadside authors sometimes copied stock narratives from the newspapers – see chapter 6.

90 *A Full and Impartial Account of the Life, Trial and Execution of Mr John Thurtell, Executed in the County of Hertford, for the Murder of Mr Weare* (London, 1824), BL.1881.d.8. For further detail on the murder of Martha Ray by James Hackman, see J. Brewer, *Sentimental Murder: Love and Madness in the Eighteenth Century* (London: HarperCollins, 2004).

91 *The Full Account and Latest Particulars of the Awful, Inhuman and Barbarous Murder of a Female, by Cutting off her head, arms, and legs, and burning them, with the proceedings of the Coroner's Inquest* (London, 1842), Bod., JJ., Murder and Execution Broadsides, 5 (39).

92 *Apprehension of Hubbard on Monday Morning. Examination at Union Hall, charged with the Willful Murder of Eliza Grimwood, Who was Murdered at No. 12 Wellington Terrace, Waterloo Road, On Saturday May 26, 1838* (London, 1838), Bod., JJ., Murder and Execution Broadsides, 6 (25).

93 *Particulars of the Trial and Execution of Joseph Hunton, the Quaker, with a Copy of a Letter he sent to a Friend, and an extract from a Prayer he composed the Night before his Execution; J. James, J. Mahoney and J. Abbott, who were Executed on Monday at Newgate, with Abbott's Letter to his Wife and James's Speech at the Place of Execution* (London, 1828), Bod., JJ., Murder and Execution Broadsides, 6 (27).

94 *Life, Trial, Sentence and Execution of Daniel Good for the Willful Murder of Jane Jones, at the Stables of Mr Shiell, near Roehampton, on Sunday April 3, 1842* (London, 1842), BL.1881.d.8.

95 Kalikoff, *Murder and Moral Decay*, p. 15.

96 'The Press of the Seven Dials', p. 404. See also Hindley, *History of the Catnach Press*, pp. 257–8.

97 T. Gretton, *Murders and Moralities: English Catchpenny Prints, 1800–1860* (London: British Museum, 1980), p. 8.

98 Ibid., pp. 7, 13.

99 G. W. M. Reynolds, *The Mysteries of the Court of London* (4th series, 8 vols, London: J. Dicks, 1848), 1st series, I, p. 227.

100 Gatrell, *The Hanging Tree*, pp. 175–8.

101 Ibid., p. 156.

102 Gatrell acknowledges this sentiment in the response of the execution crowd to particularly brutal murderers: ibid., pp. 70–1.

103 Vincent, *Literacy and Popular Culture*, pp. 201–2.

104 *The Committal to Newgate of Richard Gould and Mary Ann Jarvis, for the Murder of Mr John Templeman* (London, 1840), BL.1881.d.8.

105 *Trial and Sentence of Thomas Drory, for the Murder of Jael Denny at Doddinghurst* (London, 1850), Bod., JJ., Murder and Execution Broadsides, 10 (35).

106 *Particulars of the Confession and Execution of James Greenacre, Who was Executed this Morning at the Old Bailey, for the Wilful Murder of Mrs Hannah Brown* (London, 1837), Bod., JJ., Murder and Execution Broadsides, 6 (7).

107 *The Life, Trial, Sentence and Execution of S. Adams for the Murder of his Sister-in-Law, Martha Page* (London, 1859), Bod., JJ., Murder and Execution Broadsides, 10 (1).

108 One exception in the sample is the sheet printed after the sentencing of Job Joseph Ward who murdered a child, Timothy Easthead, in 1841. Instead, verses are written in the voice of the boy's mother, soliciting great sympathy and condemning the murderer. *Trial and Sentence of Job Joseph Ward for the Murder of a Little Boy named Timothy Easthead* (London, 1841), BL.1881.d.8.

109 *Trial, Sentence and Execution of Emanuel Barthelemy, who was Executed at the Old Bailey this Morning for the Murder of Mr Collard and Mr Moore of Warren Street, Tottenham Court Road, on the evening of the 8th of December last* (London, 1855), Bod., JJ., Murder and Execution Broadsides, 10 (7).

110 *Awful Confession of Greenacre to the Murder of Hannah Brown* (London, 1837), Bod., JJ., Murder and Execution Broadsides, 6 (6). My emphasis.

111 *Life, Trial, Confession and Execution of Joseph Connor, For the Dreadful Murder of Mary Brothers in Bloomsbury* (London, 1845), Bod., JJ., Murder and Execution Broadsides, 10 (25). My emphasis.

112 *Full and True Account of a Most Inhuman and Cruel Murder, Committed by Capt. Henry Smyth upon the Body of Jane Mew, whom he Basely Betrayed* (London, 1842), Bod., JJ., Murder and Execution Broadsides, 8 (17). See also *The Trial, Sentence and Execution of Joseph Connor, who was executed at the Old Bailey this Morning for the Wilful Murder of Mary Brothers, on Monday March 31st* (London, 1845), Bod., JJ., Murder and Execution Broadsides, 5 (7).

113 Hindley, *History of the Catnach Press*, p. 92.

4

The 'Blood-Stained Stage' revisited

JEMMY CATNACH and the Staffordshire potters were not the only businessmen to make a substantial profit from the murder of William Weare by John Thurtell near Watford in October 1823. Even before the outcome of Thurtell's trial, the Surrey Theatre on London's south bank advertised the production of a new melodrama based on the tragedy, 'The Gamblers', to be performed nightly from 17 November. Playbills drew in enthusiastic audiences with the promise of 'Fac-similes of those Scenes, now so much the object of general interest, on an EXTENSIVE SCALE PECULIAR TO THE LIMITS OF THE STAGE', as well as 'THE IDENTICAL HORSE AND GIG Alluded to by the Daily Press in the Accounts of the Murder'.[1] Thurtell's lawyers immediately applied for an injunction to prevent further performances of the melodrama, arguing that it would prejudice the outcome of Thurtell's trial and was fundamentally immoral. But the magistrates were not convinced, and after a short period performances recommenced, only by this time a rival playhouse in the neighbourhood, the Coburg, had begun to advertise a competing spin-off, 'Hertfordshire Tragedy; or, the Victims of Gaming!'[2] From the second decade of the nineteenth century onwards, the popular theatre formed another site for representation of contemporary topical murders, but in this location the re-enactment of actual murders was accompanied and overwhelmed by a virtual tidal wave of melodramas featuring fictional, but equally bloody combats and assassinations.

Of course murder was not new to plots presented in English theatre generally, but there was something quite distinct about its quantity and quality in nineteenth-century drama as historians and literary historians have noted in previous studies. As early as 1970 Richard Altick included a long description of the delight Victorian theatregoers experienced through watching their favourite murders dramatized, aptly titled, 'The Blood-Stained Stage'. But the sticking point for Altick and writers since has been the interpretation of this phenomenon, the inherent meaning or function of these violent plays. Altick, Martha Vicinus and, most recently, David Worrall have argued that murder melodramas, in particular those derived from real life, served as a meditation on real violence in society, a way of understanding, coping and coming to terms with gruesome murders which strained the social fabric, and offered an opportunity for the expression of popular justice.[3]

But, as this chapter will show, these plays, especially when viewed in the context of the other violent entertainments described in this book, were more than just a meditation on real violence. We need to be aware that plays based on real murders actually comprised the minority of the murder plays produced. The location of their performance, in the new, large popular playhouses opened outside the traditional theatrical heartland in increasingly populous districts to the south and east of the City, and their presentation within the framework of the new theatrical style of melodrama, suggest that deeper and perhaps more important meanings and functions were also operational. Even though a number of very brutal and well-publicised murders characterised the first half of the nineteenth century, we must not forget that at this time actual violence was most likely declining and public orderliness increasing. Murder melodramas offered ordinary people a space for voicing their disapproval of various forms of violence in society. But this very literal response to the plays was also determined by the rigid framework of melodrama, something we need to examine much more closely, in particular for the ease with which extreme violence could be comfortably slotted within it. Previous research has alerted us to the operation of the sub-genre as a coping mechanism, a tool of social pacification. But, as we shall see, by using gross violence, it could also act as a form of cultural assertion against the establishment, not about politics, but on a far more unifying level, about the content and role of popular culture.

Mapping theatrical London

At the turn of the nineteenth century, London witnessed a dramatic, unprecedented phase of theatre construction. New theatres were established in the West End just a stone's throw from the Theatres Royal (or Patent Theatres), Drury Lane and Covent Garden, for example the Sans Pareil (later renamed the Adelphi) and the Olympic in 1806, and the Lyceum and the Prince of Wales in 1809. More particularly, encouraged by the success of eighteenth-century playhouses situated outside the traditional theatrical heartland (such as Sadler's Wells and Astley's), a large number of theatres were built in neighbourhoods on the edge of the City and Westminster which, as a result of urbanisation and population growth, had begun to expand. On London's south bank, the Surrey in Southwark opened in 1805 and the Coburg (later renamed the Victoria), situated on the edge of the New Cut, began to stage plays in 1818. The fast-expanding districts to the east of the City also attracted theatrical speculators: the Pavilion and Effingham were established in Whitechapel (1828 and 1834 respectively), the City Theatre in Cripplegate (1831), the Garrick in Leman Street (1831), the Standard in Shoreditch (1835) and the City of London in Norton Folgate (1837). An alteration in licensing laws also encouraged the emergence of theatrical saloons in these neighbourhoods, such as the Grecian, Albert and Britannia in Hoxton, founded between 1838 and 1841. By 1866, the Select Committee on Theatrical Licences listed twenty-five metropolitan theatres with a total audience capacity of just over 48,000, the majority of which had been founded before 1845.[4]

Styles of theatre construction and management during the early nineteenth century marked a significant departure from that of the pre-industrial period. Unlike the Patent Theatres (Drury Lane and Covent Garden) which, relying on an established tradition of cultural patronage, were dependent upon rich aristocratic subscribers, new theatres were largely built and managed by local entrepreneurs with amateur theatrical connections who recognised their commercial potential. Furthermore, the new playhouses reflected the rapidly transforming urban structure that surrounded them. Whether theatres were converted buildings or new structures, a particular level of grandeur was adopted in their construction.[5] Their splendid decorations matched those of the Patent Theatres while their design surpassed that of Drury Lane and Covent Garden, as managers promised every patron a view of the stage. Moreover, their auditoriums were constructed to accommodate larger audiences. Although each of the Patent Theatres could hold 3,000 patrons, the gallery of the Coburg alone could hold over 2,000 people.[6] During the first decades of the nineteenth century, these audiences had become almost 'democratic' in their composition. For example, despite the location of the Patent Theatres in so-called 'high culture', James Grant noted that 'many a hungry belly and ragged back is there among a host of the unwashed in the upper shilling galleries of Drury Lane and Covent Garden'.[7] As one theatre historian has written, 'at a time of extraordinary social and political upheaval, the theatre represented one of the few kinds of leisure patronised by all social classes'.[8]

Yet the cultural politics and snobbish rivalry which dictated the character of the early nineteenth-century theatre boom and had, at first, encouraged such mixed patronage would soon engender crucial divisions. An important distinction existed between the Patent Theatres and the new playhouses established both in and outside the West End. In 1662, Charles II had granted theatrical patents to his favoured courtier playwrights, Thomas Killigrew and William Davenant, with instructions to found two theatres in London for the production and promotion of legitimate drama. Drury Lane and Covent Garden were thus erected in 1663 and 1732 respectively and held an exclusive licence for the performance of tragedy and comedy, or, more simply, spoken drama. There were, of course, some minor exceptions to the rule. In 1720 a licence was granted to the newly built Haymarket Theatre for the performance of drama during the summer months, and we have already noted in chapter 2 the close relationship that developed between the Patent Theatres and the theatrical booths at the London fairs whereby Drury Lane and Covent Garden would close for the period of the fair, their most favoured actors sometimes appearing in the dramas staged there.

However, for the most part, and especially by the early nineteenth century, the Theatres Royal jealously guarded their monopoly over the spoken drama. Thus the new theatres which opened at precisely this time were forced to adopt new dramatic sub-genres or styles, such as pantomime, burlesque, burletta, farce and melodrama, which many considered to be popular and plebeian. An illegitimate culture emerged which drew heavily on the fairground and the circus, and, to the horror of many higher- and middle-class critics, the new so-called minor theatres began to overshadow the Theatres Royal.[9] The 'demise of the drama' became a popular theme in dramatic publications. Alfred Bunn, late lessee of Covent Garden and Drury Lane, wrote in his memoirs that the English 'are an untheatrical people' who supported theatrical establishments 'not through any love of the art or profession practised within them, but from the extraneous excitement held out to us as a temptation to enter them'.[10] An anti-theatrical bias began to surface among the new, so-called respectable classes which became especially pronounced by the early Victorian period as emphasis was increasingly placed on rational recreations and leisure within the domestic sphere.

Although, as we shall see, large numbers of middle-class men and women recovered their love of the theatre during the latter decades of the nineteenth century, their strong dislike of early nineteenth-century illegitimate culture was replicated in traditional literary criticism during the twentieth century. The prodigious output of the minor theatres was mostly overlooked, often regarded as an unfortunate blip in the development of the dramatic canon. Recently, however, theatre historians have embarked on a process of rehabilitation and exploration. Jane Moody's *Illegitimate Theatre in London* (2000) has done much to recover the vibrancy of illegitimate theatrical culture and demonstrate its importance as a site of political, moral and generic transgression. Plays produced and consumed in minor theatres, she argued, 'defied cherished assumptions about cultural and social hierarchy'. The monopoly of the Patent Theatres provoked a crucial debate over dramatic free trade which became deeply political as dramatic genres were used as potent cultural weapons. Moreover, the success and popularity of illegitimate drama meant that it profoundly shaped modern British drama. As a vigorous illegitimate culture flourished, legitimate dramatic culture and style languished. Thus, when the privileges of the Patent Theatres were finally abolished in the 1843 Theatres Act, and all licensed playhouses in London were granted the freedom to perform legitimate drama, the illegitimate continued to heavily influence performance styles and audiences' tastes.[11]

For Moody and other theatre historians, the primary division in London's theatrical map during the early nineteenth century was that between the Patent and minor theatres. However, other important distinctions in theatrical culture also emerged during these years and persisted long after the destruction of the theatrical monopoly. Theatres established outside the West End, particularly in the new expanding districts of south and east London, afforded a distinctive theatregoing experience in terms of the composition of their audiences and the content of their plays.[12] They were mostly local entertainment venues, within easy walking distance for patrons, and were well suited to new constrictions on urban space while able to accommodate large numbers of people. For instance, Samuel Lane's application for a renewal of his licence for the Britannia Saloon in 1843 stated that his theatre had been opened 'at the request of the inhabitants of the neighbourhood' due to the lack of theatrical entertainments in the vicinity 'and the expense, inconvenience and long walk to see such entertainments'.[13] The social demographics of the locality, then, often determined the theatres' audiences, mostly lower-middle and working class. A report from the Lord Chamberlain's office in 1843 described the audience of the Pavilion Theatre in Whitechapel as 'persons in the neighbourhood and many from the docks, many sailors', and that of the Standard Theatre in Shoreditch as 'tradesmen, mechanics [and] their children'.[14]

But it is important to note that some evidence does suggest that theatres in the south and east did attract higher-class patrons, or were at least supported by wealthier members of the community, from time to time.[15] A survey conducted by the Lord Chamberlain's department in 1843 revealed that, while a large local audience regularly attended the Surrey Theatre, the nobility and gentry also occasionally visited the playhouse.[16] Similarly, Thomas Rouse's petition for a licence for the Grecian Saloon was supported by overseers of the Parish, merchants, solicitors and a gentleman.[17] Also, some patrons were prepared to travel to see the entertainments promised at various theatres around the metropolis. London's rapid growth at this time was relative. One could walk from east to west, or north to south, across the city within a few hours and many Londoners chose to travel this way. P. P. Hanley wrote in his memoirs that he walked from his home in Camden Town to the Surrey Theatre to see Douglas Jerrold's 'Martha Willis'.[18] Public transport continued to improve throughout the first half of the nineteenth century and some theatres in outlying districts advertised omnibus services for theatre patrons from locations in the City and the West End.[19] But these tended to be used by the few rather than the majority. If anything, methods of transport and Londoners' predilection for walking tended to increase competition between playhouses and generate some conformity in the theatregoing experience.

Competition and managers' dependence on the patronage of the lower classes are reflected in the pricing strategies of theatres located in London's hinterlands. The new minor theatres nearly always sold tickets at prices which undercut the Theatres Royal. Edward Wedlake Brayley's guide to the metropolitan theatres in 1826 listed these box-office prices: Drury Lane and Covent Garden each charged seven shillings for the boxes, three shillings for the pit, two shillings for the lower gallery and one shilling for the upper gallery, while, in contrast, the Coburg, Adelphi, Olympic and Surrey sold box tickets for three shillings, the pit for two shillings and the gallery for one shilling.[20] The growth of competition among theatres in the south and east meant that these prices dropped even further. Sixpence became a standard ticket price for the gallery and during the price war that erupted in 1846, tickets were as cheap as one shilling for the boxes, sixpence for the pit and threepence for the gallery. In their correspondence with the Lord Chamberlain's office, managers argued that such prices were necessary to compete with similar theatres in the neighbourhood and in other districts across London.[21]

Advertised prices also usually disguised strategies adopted by theatre managers to accommodate an audience with little expendable income.

For example, family tickets, or free orders, would admit two people for the price of one. In a report for the Lord Chamberlain on the City of London Theatre in 1845, the author wrote that although he could not obtain a family ticket to the boxes or gallery, he supposed that such tickets were available if one applied immediately when the doors of the theatre opened, especially as 'there appeared to be many in the gallery, that I should say could not afford to pay sixpence, the regular charge published on the bills'.[22] On a playbill of November 1846, the manager of the Victoria Theatre declared that his prices placed the theatre 'within the means of all classes of society', but were adopted with the working man in mind:

> The industrious Mechanic, in too many instances, is unable to afford to take his Wife and Family their usual pleasure trips as formerly, the demand upon his pocket and loss of time rendering the EXPENSE almost more than he can retrieve by the remainder of the week's hard toil; but HERE for a small amount saved from his earnings, he can witness an excellent and superior Entertainment and go cheerfully to his work on the morrow, with the consciousness that he has not purchased a too-dearly-bought gratification.[23]

Cheap tickets attracted large crowds, and with large crowds came the need for control. In their study of theatre audiences, Jim Davis and Victor Emeljanow, relying on accounts provided by theatre managers, concluded that violent disturbances among patrons were relatively rare, arguing that accounts of rough behaviour in the press contained an inherent anti-theatrical bias.[24] But theatre managers were always in danger of losing their licences, and would frequently describe the orderly conduct of their patrons in correspondence with the Lord Chamberlain when the reality was often quite different.[25] The posting of police constables in theatres demonstrates that disorderly conduct was always at least a possibility. Many theatrical managers, without pressure from the authorities, initiated some sort of system of control and law enforcement, from the employment of security personnel (including retired police officers) to the establishment of informal relationships with local police divisions. By 1847 the Lord Chamberlain had formalised this arrangement, a policy which theatre managers unanimously supported.[26]

Police-court reports provide us with some clues about the types of violence or disorderly behaviour that managers and the authorities sought to prevent. On the one hand, forms of low-level violence were used by patrons to amuse themselves in the auditorium. Theatre reviewers made reference to the 'pugilistic encounters' that occurred both before and even during performances, one reporter writing that, at the Victoria, 'invitations to drink – never refused when acceptance was possible – invitations to fight, received with almost equal cordiality – flew about the house and afforded amusement alike to participants and spectators'.[27] Gallery patrons often entertained themselves by throwing objects around the auditorium, sometimes causing serious injury. As a result, some theatres placed signs at the box office announcing the prohibition of certain articles.[28] Bottles, for example, could be dangerous projectiles and commonly feature in police-court trials. During a performance at the Coburg in July 1824 one man threw a large stoneware beer bottle from the gallery which struck an elderly woman in the pit. When her friends removed her bonnet, they found that 'her cap was deluged with blood'.[29]

Violence was also used by patrons to solve disputes and against authority figures stationed in the playhouses. Injuries sustained could be extreme, and in the case of attacks against police officers, magistrates increasingly imposed serious penalties against the perpetrators. Most arguments between patrons were the result of the jostling and discomfort caused by a large crowd in a confined space and were encouraged by a ticketing system which did not pre-allocate seats and impose order. In March 1847 such a dispute arose between John and Jane Moore and Eliza Allen. The Moores had gone to the Britannia Saloon with friends to celebrate their nuptials and had found an agreeable spot in the pit when Allen attempted to squeeze past them to join her friends at the front of the stage. Witnesses described how Jane Moore had 'assailed her with most opprobrious epithets, and commenced an outrageous attack upon her, in which she was assisted by her husband and several other persons'. The Moores were detained by the constables of the theatre and appeared before the magistrate at Worship Street the very next day, still attired in their 'wedding dresses'.[30] Constables interfering in these disputes put themselves at risk. When constable Kain attempted to arrest John Simmonds for assaulting a fellow patron at the City of London Theatre in 1855, Simmonds assisted by several other audience members launched an attack on Kain, the blows he received permanently disfiguring him.[31]

I do not want to overemphasise the prevalence of violence among theatre patrons in London's popular theatres, but nor do I want to create a myth of orderliness which might obscure the degree of popular control which continued to be exerted in these spaces. A degree of disorderly behaviour was encouraged by the particulars of the theatrical space. Audiences were not provided with regular seats and at this time auditorium lights were not dimmed at the commencement of the performance. Thus no division was created between audience and stage. As we shall see, audiences participated in the performance and the drama in the auditorium created by patrons could be as important as that on the stage. Attempts to impose order were always under challenge. The significance of such activity should become clearer as we turn to examine the high emotions generated by the murder melodramas so frequently staged in these venues.

Murder melodramas

Illegitimate theatrical culture encouraged variety in the bills of play across London. As in the theatres of the West End, London's more popular theatres presented enthusiastic audiences with pantomimes, burletta, farce, burlesque, ballet, dancing acts, acrobatics and melodrama. This diversity draws our attention to the operation of multiple but simultaneous cultural levels, or to the multifaceted nature of working people's taste, where the dividing lines between respectable and unrespectable, and educational and sensational, were often blurred and insignificant.[32] We can also take this assessment outside the theatre. A significant number of working men and women did not attend theatres, perhaps sharing the anti-theatrical bias exhibited by the so-called respectable classes. But more significant are the gradations and range of taste found within single performances, as these should draw our attention to the function of especially prominent themes. And in the playbills, accounts of performances and scripts of plays one theme does emerge as particularly prominent: violence.

From the early 1820s when a significant number of theatres had been established in south and east London journalists and dramatic critics began to use the graphic presentations of violence exhibited in performances to distance this 'new' theatrical culture from that of the West End. In 1824, a reviewer for the *Theatrical Magazine* wrote that whenever he felt inclined to 'sup upon horrors' he would direct his steps to the Coburg, as 'there murder "bares her red arm" with most appalling vividness'.[33] Similarly, the theatrical correspondent for *New Monthly Magazine* remarked that at the Pavilion, under the management of Mr Farell, 'should a very atrocious murder be committed, the assassination is, in a few days, represented in a manner very little short of the original horror'. When the Garrick Theatre opened but a few streets away, Mr Farell, 'trembling for his monopoly of absurdity and horror, tried every means to destroy it'. And, he added, at the Surrey Theatre, 'murder there has been the staple article', the playwrights of the theatre commanded by the manager 'to their work, in the language of the prompt direction of an old play, that all might die, leaving the stage as bloody as it might be'.[34] In 1820, when both Covent Garden and the Coburg gave representations of Shakespeare's *Richard III*, the primary scene distinguishing them was the murder of the children in the Tower: at Covent Garden, this scene took place off stage, but at the Coburg the murders were dramatised in full view of the audience and accompanied by music designed 'to drown the cries'.[35]

And it was not just snobbery which drove these comments. In their interviews with Henry Mayhew, the costermongers of the New Cut declared that they enjoyed most the Shakespearian tragedies which contained violent scenes. As one explained, 'of *Hamlet* we can make neither end nor side; and nine out of ten of us – ay, far more than that – would like it to be confined to the ghost scenes, and the funeral, and the killing off at the last. *Macbeth* would be better liked if it was only the witches and fighting.'[36] Scanning the titles of plays submitted for licensing to the Lord Chamberlain we can see that murder especially featured also in farce, burletta and pantomime, but most often in melodrama, which, during the first decades of the nineteenth century, rapidly rose to become the most popular sub-genre or dramatic style in London's popular theatres. The largest audiences were drawn by melodramas that promised dramatic scenes of high-level violence. Henry Mayhew observed that the long, zig-zag staircase leading to the pay-box of the Victoria Theatre was often crowded to suffocation at least an hour before the theatre opened. But, 'on the occasion of a piece with a good murder in it, the crowd will collect as early as three o'clock in the afternoon' (see figure 22). Similarly, the East End dustmen he interviewed frequented the Pavilion and the City of London theatres where 'they are always to be found in the gallery, and greatly enjoy the melodramas … especially if there be plenty of murdering scenes in them'.[37]

Playbills printed for these theatres further confirm this common taste. As Jane Moody states, the playbill represented 'the most important form of publicity for managers at the minor houses'.[38] Early nineteenth-century advances in printing technology meant that playbills could be printed rapidly en masse and dispersed throughout the neighbourhood and even the metropolis. Networks of distribution were of crucial importance. First, playbills were displayed in the windows of local businesses. Mr Brading, manager of the Albert Saloon, claimed that around 2,000 shops in the neighbourhood exhibited his bills. While some shopkeepers were paid for this service, many instead accepted free theatre tickets for the 'slack nights'.[39] In his memoirs, John Hollingshead described running to the tobacco-shop or the pastry-cook's as a child

THE NEW CUT. —EVENING.

22. Enthusiastic crowds gather to view the playbills at the Victoria Theatre

to examine the long playbills advertising performances at the various London theatres.[40] Second, playbills were posted on walls around the city at night by bill-stickers.[41] And third, playbills were sold by large numbers of street-sellers in the thoroughfares and lanes surrounding the theatres. In 1851, Henry Mayhew suggested that there were approximately 200 sellers in London, the majority of whom were based around the more lucrative theatres in the south and east.[42]

Playbills had a variety of functions. Managers relied on the sheets to communicate with their patrons, providing notices about the future intentions of the theatre, the employment of new actors and the theatre's role in the local community. Playbills not only advertised the week's entertainment, but also served as a programme and a general review. A great deal of information was provided on the individual plays, and aspects of the performances that were known to be popular with audiences were prominently highlighted.

Violence was one of these features. Words such as 'horror', 'fatal', 'blood', 'crimson', 'death', 'crime', 'assassination', 'hanging' and 'gallows' frequently coloured the bills. Descriptions of scenes and action highlight the centrality of violence to the plots of melodramas, especially as words promising violent action were enlarged or placed in bold, contrasting fonts. For example, in 1827 the Coburg advertised the production of 'The Prodigal; or, the Horrors of Extravagance', the intricate account of the plot promising, in bold type larger than the play's title, a scene depicting the prodigal father 'MURDERING HIS WIFE AND CHILDREN'.[43] Some years later the same theatre announced the production of 'Old Man's Bride; or, the Murder at Norwood Villa', the playbill for the melodrama advertising these scenes: 'The Assignation! – and – The Murder!', 'MURDER AT NORWOOD VILLA', 'Distant Portal Opening to the Place of Execution' and the 'Awful Retributive Death'.[44]

As printing technology improved throughout the first half of the century, more and more became expected of the playbills. From the late 1820s, simple but eye-catching colours were sometimes added. During the 1840s, woodcuts illustrating climactic scenes from advertised plays began to appear. Again, violence was a prominent theme in the illustrations. In September 1857, the Britannia Saloon's production of 'Belinda Seagrave; or, the Tempter and the Betrayer' was advertised with the use of a sequence of woodcuts, including 'The Suicide', which showed Belinda's body falling through the air to meet a painful end on the pavement, and 'The Grave', in which Belinda's seducer meets his 'Awful End' as her vengeful father stabs him to death.[45] In 1862, the Grecian Theatre used a graphic illustration of the murder of several men for the playbill announcing the production of 'The Devil's Gap; or, Time Tells Tales' (see figures 23 and 24).[46] During the 1850s, a number of theatres capitalised on the popularity of performing animals. Trained dogs filled a novel role, often saving the hero whilst savagely punishing the villain. Large graphic pictures of these scenes were placed on the bills. For 'The Cattle Stealers! or, the Drover and his Dogs!', the climactic scene of the 'Death of the Villain by the Fangs of the Noble Dog' was used to draw audiences to the theatre.[47]

These illustrated playbills especially had features in common with the murder and execution broadsides discussed in chapter 3, for instance the central positioning of illustrations surrounded on all sides with text, the large, bold masthead and the contrasting subheadings, as well as summaries of the main action in the play or crime. Playbills and broadsides were displayed alongside each other on street corners or on the walls of the public house, blurring the distinction between fact and fiction in the stories they told.

As Jane Moody writes, nineteenth-century playbills (like the crime broadsides) were 'designed to surprise and captivate audiences amidst the sheer razzmatazz of urban typography'.[48] Evidence suggests that the language and visual prominence of violence certainly did attract the attention of city dwellers. Thomas Wright recalled that, as a child, he

BRITANNIA

PROPRIETOR · Mr. S. LANE. HOXTON. 188, High Street, Hoxton.
LICENSED BY THE LORD CHAMBERLAIN.

STAGE BOXES 1s. 6d. BOXES & STALLS 1s. BOX SLIPS, AND FRONT PIT, 6d. GALLERY, equal to the Boxes of any other Theatre, 4d. BACK PIT, 3d
Children under Seven Years of Age, Half-Price to Boxes and Pit. No Person admitted to the Boxes unless suitably attired. Omnibuses
from all parts of London, stop within Two Minutes Walk of the Britannia every Quarter of an Hour. Performance to commence at half-past Six.
Private Entrance, Open at Half-past Five, no extra charge to the Boxes,
HALF-PRICE AT EIGHT TO BOXES AND STALLS, TO PIT AT HALF-PAST.

RE-PRODUCTION of AMBITION

IN ALL ITS ORIGINAL SPLENDOUR! Never was there a more GLORIOUS HIT than this Revival—Nothing could by possibility exceed the

ENTHUSIASTIC WELCOME of MRS. S. LANE

On her Re-appearance; of the HEARTY APPROBATION bestowed on the other Principal Performers, as well as on the Brilliant Scenic and Dramatic Effects of the Piece. In compliance with the Universal Desire for its
Repetition, the Management respectfully announce this Popular Drama, with

Mrs. S. LANE - In her Original Character of - **Nelly! Every Evening this Week.**

On MONDAY, SEPTEMBER 22nd, 1856, and all the Week, will be presented,
The Domestic, Interesting and Epigrammatical Drama by the Author of the ' Beggar's Petition ' entitled

AMBITION!
OR, POVERTY! COMPETENCE! & RICHES!

The Hon. Captain Carlton........in the 1st Act aged 30 , in the 2nd, a Colonel, 44, then killed in a duel.........Mr. PARRY
Dr. Fear ... the Four Pastes of Witham, in 1st Act, 51 ; in the 2nd, 67 ; in the 3rd, 71... Mr. F. WILTON
John Trafford.....in the 1st Act a Parish Labourer, aged 44 ; in the 2nd, a Wealthy Farmer, aged 54 ; in the 3rd,
Nobleman, aged 64 ... Mr. J. REYNOLDS
Robert Trafford ...his Son, in the 1st Act enlisting in the Army , in the 2nd, a rising Soldier, aged 19 ; in the
3rd, a Commissioned Officer, aged 23 ... Mr. C.J. BIRD
Farmer Grey.....in the 1st Act a substantial Yeoman, aged 52 ; in the 2nd, a Decayed Farmer, aged 62 ; in the
3rd, blind to Lord Trafford, aged 72 ... Mr. C. WILLIAMS
William S'ection ... called Sweet William, a Pun of the Meadow, in the 1st Act, a Lacquey, aged 28 ; in the 2nd,
Valet to the Colonel, aged 38 ; in the 3rd, major Domo to My Lord ... Mr. W. D. NEWHAM
Roger Bunny ... in 1st Act aged 44, Servant to Farmer Grey ; in the 2nd Act, 54, out of employ ; in the 3rd,
aged 64, Landlord of the "Dancing Pig" ... Mr. W. ROGERS

Quid Grey.... Son of Farmer Grey, in the 2nd Act a Colour Sergeant, aged 27 ; in the 3rd, a Major, aged 37...Mr. C. PITT
Charles Trafford ....youngest Son of his Father, in the 3rd Act, a hopeful youth ; in the 3rd, a Baronet, very
tart indeed ... Mr. W.R. CRAWFORD
John Bull ... Mr. LUCAS Mons. Do-re-mi ... a French Valet ... Mr. WILSON Mr. Beaufort ... Mr. M. PAUL
Callender and Black Barnsley...Messrs. BUG-BEE & DAVISON Dr. Dobbs ... a Crusty Proctor...Mr. W. SMITH
Sergeant Tike... Mr. JOHNSON Soldiers, Recruits, Farm Servants, &c.
Mary Trafford ... Wife to John Trafford, in the 1st Act aged 44 ; in the 2nd, 54 ; in the 3rd a Titled Lady... Mrs. N. COWLE
Kate Trafford...her Daughter, in the 1st Act, 19 ; in the 2nd, 29 ; in the 3rd, Wife to the Major...Miss C. BORSON
Nelly (in the 1st Act, 19, a Servant and Guardian to Kate ; in the 3rd, **Mrs. S. LANE**)
reduced to feel the sting of ingratitude, in the 3rd, Married to Hodge
Miss Precious ... a Fashionable Milliner ... Mrs GREEN Sapro ... a Gipsy Fortune Teller... Mrs E.S. GASTON
Mademoiselle De L'Esprituos ... French Lady, holding a dubious position in the family of Lord John ...Mrs PETTIFER

ACT I—POVERTY.		ACT III.—RICHES.
HOME of the PARISH LABOURER		**THE MANSION OF LORD JOHN !**
The Stone Breaker going to his Work		The Landlady of the Dancing Pig in a New Character !
THE HUSBAND		**The Wife Confronts the Mistress !**
Confronts the Seducer !		**THE SPENDTHRIFT SON AND HEIR !**
JOHN FINDS A GOLDEN TREASURE !		**THE MASKED BALL !**
The First Step on Fortune's Ladder !		**Lord Trafford signs the Forged Will**
Ten Years are supposed to elapse between each Act.		The Sky clears—The Discovery ! The
ACT II.—COMPETENCE.		**ECLAIRCISSEMENT !**
Farmer John Trafford a Gentleman !		The Millionaire performs an Act of Justice !
JOHN TRAFFORD		Not forgetting honest Hodge and faithful Nelly –Their termination our Lesson on
The Richest Man in the Country		**Poverty ! Competence !**
He Curses his own Children !		**and Riches !**

A GRAND PAS DE DEUX - **Mlle. CELESTE STEPHAN & Mr.W. Smith**

To conclude with (Wednesday excepted) the unprecedentedly successful Rustic Drama, by the Author of " Kathleen," "Charlotte Hayden," " The Corporal's Daughter," &c., &c., entitled the

BEGGAR'S PETITION!
Or, a Father's Love & a Mother's Care !

Ten Years or supposed to elapse between the Acts. Ten Years more elapse between the Acts.

On Wednesday, for the Benefit of Miss Pettifer

23. Playbill advertising 'Ambition! Or, Poverty, Competence & Riches!' at
the Britannia Saloon, 22 September 1856

24. *opposite*: Playbill advertising 'Devil's Gap! Or, Time Tells Tales', at the
Grecian Theatre, 6 October 1862

ROYAL GRECIAN THEATRE

Proprietor . . . . . Mr. B. O. CONQUEST, Eagle Tavern, City Road.

The Public are respectfully informed that there is no Re-admission after Nine o'Clock, except by Re-payment.

The Magnificent Grounds, Corridors, Halls, &c., are Open for Refreshments & Promenading, every Sunday evening, between the hours of 5 and 11 o'Clock.

☞ **POSTPONEMENT OF THE OPENING OF THE NEW HALL,**
IN CONSEQUENCE OF THE NON-FULFILMENT OF THE BUILDER'S CONTRACT:
DUE NOTICE of THE OPENING NIGHT WILL BE GIVEN
ON WEDNESDAY—"THE DEVIL'S GAP,"—INCIDENTALS.—AND "THE OSTLER'S VISION."

ON MONDAY, OCTOBER 6th, 1862, AND DURING THE WEEK,

The Performance in the Theatre will commence with a New and Original Drama, in Three Acts, written expressly for this Theatre, by Mr GEORGE CONQUEST, embracing Powerful Domestic and Splendid scenic effects, entitled THE

DEVIL'S GAP!

OR, TIME TELLS TALES.

PROLOGUE. TIME—Present.

PLACE.—COAST OF CORNWALL

George Clayton — (a Fisherman) — Mr. T. MEAD
Bowen — First Mate of the "Sea Gull" — Mr. H. GRANT
Lewis—Second Mate of the "Sea Gull"(. — Mr. SMITHSON
Phil Phinings—a Half-witted Lad—Mr. GEO. CONQUEST
Captain Boden — Mr. W. HOLLAND
Sarah — Wife of George Clayton— Miss JANE DAWSON
Alice — (her Child) — Miss SMITHERS

WRECK of the "SEA GULL."
THE FISHERMAN'S HOME!

Desertion of the Vessel by the Crew.—The 3 Officers.—Disappearance of the Wreck. The Swim for Life.

Remnants of the Wreck
BY MOONLIGHT.

Discontent.—Arrival of the Two Mates.—Departure of George Clayton, in search of Captain Boden.—The Assassination of Captain Boden.—Phil's Plunge and Rescue.

A LAPSE OF EIGHTEEN YEARS.

VILLAGE, NEAR YORK

Alfred Clayton — (a Rich Banker) — Mr. T. MEAD
George Clayton — (his Son)
Ben Bigby—(a young Lieutenant in the Navy)—Mr. W. JAMES
Charles Rixley — (his Friend) — Mr. SHIRLEY
Dudley — (Friend of Alfred) — Mr. COOK
Phil Phinings—Rogue & Vagabond—Mr. G. CONQUEST
Bob & Rich—his Associates—Messrs. BARNES & TILBROOK
Tavern Keeper — Mr. SLOAN
Walter — Mr. H. POWER
Mary Boden — Mrs. CHARLES DILLON
Alice Rick — Miss MARIE BREWER

The Sailor's Return.—The Poor Sempstress.—Cigars and Champagne.—The Wager.—Conspiracy of Alice Rick.

MARY'S CHAMBER

The GARDENS OF THE BANKER'S HOUSE!

THE OFFICE!

ROBBERY, DISCOVERY, & RECOGNITION.
Act 3.—Interview Between Ben Bigby and Mary! The Concealment.—Departure of Ben.

A STREET IN YORK.

THE DIAMOND STUD!
The Promised Reward, & Appointed Meeting Mary Boden's Resolve!—Revelations.

THE DEVIL'S GAP

DESCENDING TO
THE LOVER's LAKE.

The Mechanical Arrangements by ... Mr C. SMITHERS, Sen.

☞ TIME TELLS TALES.

DANCING

ON THE MONSTRE
PLATFORM

Weather permitting. To Commence at Eight o'Clock, Each Evening.
BAND OF 25 PERFORMERS.
Conductor ... Mr. EDROFF. M.C. ... Mr. T. TRIPP.

To be followed by the highly Successful BALLET, in One Act, and THREE TABLEAUX, entitled, THE

SLEEP WALKER

A SELECTION FROM THE OPERA OF "LA SONNAMBULA."

The Entertainments will conclude with, (Wednesday excepted), a New Drama, in Three Acts, by Mr G. CONQUEST, entitled THE

HANGED MAN

FOR CHARACTERS—SEE SMALL BILLS.

Each Evening, (Saturdays Excepted), at the permission of the Dramatic Performances, A CONCERT in the ASSEMBLY ROOM, to which there will be No Charge for Admission.
Mr B. HOFFMAN (the Blind Tenor), Mr WOOD and his SON, in their Celebrated Negro Characters. Miss EMMA KERRIDGE & Miss ELLEN HALE.
Managing Director ...... Mr. C. SLOMAN. Mr. FITCHETT will preside at the Piano.

DOORS OPEN AT SIX O'CLOCK, TO COMMENCE AT HALF-PAST SIX.
Private Boxes, 10s. 6d., or 2s. each Person. Stalls, 1s. 6d., Second Price at Nine o'Clock, 1s. Boxes, 1s. Pit, 6d. Gallery, 4d.
ACTING & STAGE MANAGER ...... MR. GEORGE CONQUEST.
All Applications respecting the Bills, to be made to Mr. CHARLES OLIVER, at the Theatre.—Enclose a Stamped Envelope, if an answer required. E. J. BATH, (late POWELL), Steam Printer, 43, Leman-st., Whitechapel.

would walk home from school with friends pausing along the way 'to read, admire, and compare the playbills of the different theatres'. On one occasion, they were drawn to a particular bill which announced the production of 'The Guilty Banker; or, the Convict's Return'. It was 'very large, very highly coloured, and very profusely illustrated', featuring the terrific combat between the 'tar' and the 'black-hearted pirates'. 'As the tar was represented surrounded by heaps of the slain, the pirates were evidently getting much the worse of it.' Wright and his friends, excited by the playbill, purchased tickets for the performance.[49] But the increasing prevalence of the use of graphic violence on playbills displayed in public places, beyond the boundaries of containment offered by the space of the popular theatre, did provoke some concern in the respectable press. An article in *The Times* complained of the display of 'a hideous "death's head" of monstrous size' by a playhouse in Whitechapel, the journalist arguing that while 'people who go to theatres have a right to their pennyworth of excitement … the right of theatrical horror-mongers to offer gratuitous outrage to the people disposed to avoid horror is not so clear'.[50] As will become clear, this report provides an example of moments when violence was regarded by the establishment as less of a useful safety valve and more of a cultural threat.

Inside the popular theatres, audiences were rarely disappointed with the scenes of violence that unfolded in the melodramas, as these were often very graphic and extreme. This extremity was encouraged by the development of sub-genres and the theatrical styles within illegitimate theatre. As spoken dialogue was permitted only in the Patent Theatres before 1843, acting conventions in the minor houses were forced to place great weight on spectacle and gesture. The illegitimate became a drama based on a physical rather than a mental aesthetic. Actions were exaggerated to compensate for the lack of speech, and were designed to provoke similarly inflated responses from both characters and audiences. Actors used their entire bodies to convey emotions and a highly codified system emerged in which specific attitudes symbolised specific sentiments.[51] As the century progressed, minor theatres gradually became more daring in their protests against the monopoly on legitimate drama and regularly breached the law by including spoken dialogue in plays. Indeed, by the 1830s, melodrama was only distinguished, in this sense, by the inclusion of a musical note, and restrictions on speech were finally abolished in the 1843 Theatres Act. However, these early conventions continued to have a profound influence on performances for the remainder of the century.

The peculiarities which developed in the sub-genre of melodrama were to have an even greater impact on the presentation of violence on the popular stage. Melodrama was a repetitive and spectacular theatrical style, reliant on broad physical action and emotional extremism. Subtlety was never intended, and as theatre historians have noted, acting in theatres patronised by the lower classes was generally cruder and more exaggerated than later performances in fashionable playhouses.[52] Stock characters supplied the cast of the play. These superficial character types, such as hero, heroine, villain and buffoon, were instantly recognisable by their costumes and highly specified actions. Villains spoke in deep voices, wore black wigs and their brows were furrowed with burnt cork, while comic characters, ludicrously dressed, would appear in grossly farcical scenes at routinely set intervals.[53] Gesture was also codified. Emotions were expressed by characters in a very visual manner which employed the entire body. A number of nineteenth-century theatre handbooks instructed actors on how to convey crucial feelings to audiences. For example, one stated that despair, which could seldom be overacted, 'rolls the eyes and sometimes bites the lips and gnashes with the teeth', while the whole body must be 'strained and violently agitated. Groans, expressive of inward torture, accompany the words.'[54]

Movement was also incredibly overdrawn and extravagant. Outstretched arms and pointed fingers were used to accuse the guilty. Stage directions encouraging excess were littered throughout prompt copies of scripts, including 'trembles violently', 'exhibits the most violent agitation' and 'exits wildly'.[55] Melodramatic speech was also distinctive. Not only were the words of early melodramas accompanied by music, but the genre also quickly developed a set of peculiar pronunciations as well as a special rhythm.[56] Charles Dickens captured the essence of this speech style in his review of a play at the Victoria Theatre: [a character exclaims] 'I ster-ruck him down and fel-ed in er'orror! ... I have liveder as a beggar – a roadersider vaigerant, but no ker-rime since then has stained these hands!'[57]

Within these melodramatic conventions, violence could not be presented in a manner other than extreme and spectacular. Combats and dying scenes were particularly drawn out as characters struggled to display the very violent nature of their actions while alternately expressing key emotions such as pain, triumph and despair. Moreover, lifelike effects were employed and often overused to exaggerate the violence performed on stage. George Augustus Sala described the grand melodramas at the Victoria which featured 'real horses, real armour, real blood, almost real water! These were the days of "Ginevra the Impaled One" and "Manfroni the One-Handed Monk".'[58] Great quantities of red ochre were used in murder scenes to imitate blood.

F. G. Tomlins claimed that as Dick Turpin cut his horse's throat on the stage red ochre flowed freely onto the boards.[59] In the quest to present tremendous spectacles of violence, accidents were always a possibility. In 1842, actor Charles Alworthy from the Garrick Theatre was rushed to hospital with severe facial injuries after a pistol was discharged too close to him during a performance, the powder and wadding burning his face.[60]

These conventions and aspects of the melodramatic style were brought together in very rigid and formulaic plots. For the most part, the authors of these plays were irrelevant. With the exception of a few famous names, including George Dibdin Pitt, playwrights were typically anonymous theatrical hacks employed, at times by several theatres, to churn out 'new' plays at a rapid pace. They were at the mercy of the genre and the audience: the playwright was a 'handyman to the company; he existed to make performance possible, rather than they [the actors] to interpret his work'.[61] Melodramatic plays were concerned with the articulation of the moral occult. Tales opened with the apparent triumph of villainy in a frightening new world that had lost the traditional patterns of moral order, but, through an intense, dramatic struggle, which included sinister plottings and great suspense, virtue always emerged victorious. As plays featured a simple and idealised world, and used uncomplicated binaries of good and evil, rich and poor, town and country, questions of morality were judged by inflexible standards and life's complexities were reduced to black and white answers.[62]

The strict narrative framework of melodrama meant that while character and place names might have changed from play to play, and new, minor, semi-original subplots included, the main story never did. There was no mystery in melodrama: for every play, audiences knew what to expect, from their experience with previous melodramas, from the outline of the entire story provided on the playbills and from the immediately identifiable, one-dimensional characters that appeared in the opening scenes. Rich, mostly aristocratic villains either seduced innocent village maidens or stole the rightful inheritances of sincere and homely country families. But noble and typically beautiful or handsome heroines and heroes would uncover the dastardly plots and effect the restoration of morality. Ultimately, melodramas told the story of the oppression of the poor by the rich. While seductions did not feature in all plays, a love plot was nearly always incorporated into the tale, as a crowd pleaser if for no other reason. As a set number of themes or locations became popular among audiences, a number of superficial sub-forms became identifiable, such as nautical melodrama, gothic melodrama and domestic melodrama, though all of these continued to use the same narrative structures. In particular, plays often centred on the lives of common, almost recognisable people, allowing audiences to see aspects of their lives dramatised on the stage. Most importantly, melodrama presented a nostalgic story, its plots looking back to a perceived golden age, in which the simplicities and innocence of rural or village life were preferred to the corrupting, anonymous city.[63]

Within this set framework, murder and other forms of high-level violence could easily be slotted, as this type of action, with its emotional and spectacular value, created a perfect climax. Real murders which had attained notoriety through broadside and press coverage provided ideal material for melodramas as playwrights liberally manipulated the specifics of the story to fit within inherited plot structures. The magistrates presiding over the case of the representation of Thurtell's murder of Weare in the Surrey Theatre's 'The Gamblers', mentioned at the opening of this chapter, had to acknowledge that the play was concluded 'in a manner very different from what might be supposed'.[64] Just five years later, the murder of Maria Marten by her lover, William Corder, near Polstead in Suffolk provided theatrical hacks around the country with ample material for a range of plays and other dramatic entertainments.[65] The facts of the case meant that this murder was ideally suitable for melodrama and hardly any dramatic licence needed to be taken. Corder was the son of a prosperous yeoman farmer, while Maria was the daughter of a humble molecatcher. In 1826 Corder became romantically involved with Maria, and when she fell pregnant the pair apparently made plans to elope and marry. However, when Maria met Corder at the Red Barn near her home for this purpose, Corder murdered her, burying her body in the floor of the barn. Corder went alone to Ealing where he married a respectable schoolteacher who had answered his advertisement for a wife in *The Times*, while, anxious to avoid suspicion, he wrote to Maria's family describing his new, happy life with Maria. But, in time, his foul crime was uncovered through the prophetic dreams of Maria's stepmother.

The story of Corder and Maria was, therefore, the ideal seducer-betrayal narrative. In London, versions of the play entertained audiences at the Pavilion Theatre and the Bower Saloon, and it soon became one of the most popular melodramas of the century, finding regular audiences at all playhouses.[66] Spin-offs also appeared, such as 'Ruth Martin, The Fatal Dreamer' at the Royal Albert Saloon in 1846 and 'The Red Farm; or, the Well of St Marie' at the more fashionable Sadler's Wells Theatre in 1842, from their scripts obviously clear attempts to create some novelty whilst relying on the draw-card of an old favourite.[67]

The rural setting of the murder and its basis in fact meant that it was one of the few melodramas that travelled well: audiences at playhouses throughout England were treated to a version of the play. And as the melodrama(s) was often performed at the Theatres Royal in provincial towns, the audiences at the venues probably extended beyond the skilled workers to include the more polite town dwellers and local farmers.[68] Moreover, these plays were not isolated cultural products; that they were enmeshed within a wider, supportive culture is evident in the waxwork exhibitions and travelling peep shows and theatrical representations found at fairs and in the centres of large towns which also exploited the Maria Marten story (see chapters 2 and 3).

Original scripts from the early Maria Marten plays are almost impossible to find. Their composition before the 1843 Theatres Act, when the jurisdiction of the Lord Chamberlain in terms of licensing and censorship was extended beyond the city of Westminster, might explain their absence from the Lord Chamberlain's collection of plays in the British Library's Additional Manuscripts, while being advertised on bills of play each decade. But one script that does survive, 'Maria Marten; or, the Murder in the Red Barn', performed at the Star Theatre in Swansea during the 1870s, might provide us with some clues. It is possible that, given the typical title used by this theatre for the play, the same as that in general use by the London playhouses, that elements of the melodrama, from characterisation to action, might have become standardised.[69]

For example, as we would expect, the characters of both Maria and Corder have been simplified and moulded into the necessary one-dimensional heroine and villain. In the press reports and trial it became clear that Maria had been sexually involved with a number of men before Corder, affairs which had involved illegitimate children, but this sexual past was eliminated in the dramatic representation of her story. Corder is her only lover and although she has lost her innocence with him, she intends to recover her morality through marriage. But the villain clearly has no intention of marrying her. From the opening we are warned by other characters that he is 'a nasty, mean, ugly, sulky fellow'.[70] The murder, which forms the climax of the play, is cold-hearted and brutal as Corder experiences no internal conflict about the deed he is to commit: as he waits in the shadows of the Red Barn he is eager to get rid of the burden he has acquired. When Maria begs for mercy, Corder replies, 'Nay, shrink not, 'tis in vain, for I am desperate in my thoughts, and thirst for blood'. He struggles with his victim, attempting to stab her with his knife, the final stage directions stating that '*He again tries to stab her. She clings round his neck. He*

dashes her to the earth and stabs her. She shrieks and falls. He stands
motionless till the curtain falls.[71]

Protracted murder scenes were also used for the crucial climax
in fictional plays which formed the majority of output in theatrical
melodrama. In 'Grace Clairville; or, the Crime at the Symon's Yat'
(Surrey, 1843) the villain, Hubert Edgecombe, eager to disguise his early
crimes and immorality and secure a marriage with an heiress, murders
his lover, the village beauty Mabel Humphreys. It is a long-drawn-out
scene, highly wired with emotion, in which Hubert beats then strangles
Mabel, before finally throwing her from the edge of the Yat into the
rough-flowing river below.[72] Victims of violent villains are not always
unfortunate, duped lovers. In George Dibdin Pitt's 'Charlotte Hayden,
the Victim of Circumstance; or, the Maid, the Master, and the Murderer!'
(Britannia Saloon, 1844), the audience is introduced to the particularly
nasty Mr Gifford and his son Enoch, fortune hunters, who have already
murdered the heroine's father, Mr Hayden, disinheriting her family
who are forced into a horrific workhouse owned by the Giffords. But it
soon becomes clear to Enoch that Charlotte Hayden's grandmother has
discovered his heinous crime. And so we come to a climactic scene, in
which Enoch murders the grandmother in a protracted and extreme
manner. The prompt directions provide us with clues as to exactly
how the scene was presented to audiences. Enoch attempts to strangle
grandmother, but the old woman fights against him, and so he 'draws a
knife and stabs her repeatedly – the knife falls on the ground as he gives
the last blow, and throws her back upon the bed – old man [Mr Gifford]
stands horror struck'. Throughout the scene, large pools of blood collect
on the floor. In her last moment, grandmother raises her head and
proclaims 'Men of wretchedness – the blood you have shed be on you
and on your souls.' Charlotte, our heroine, is framed for the crime.[73]

Until now we have looked to the scripts for guidance on the
presentation of violence in the theatre. Contemporary accounts of
performances are also useful. One of the most famous Victorian
murder scenes, in literature and on the stage, was that of Nancy by
the thieving villain, Bill Sikes, in Charles Dickens's *Oliver Twist*. This
was how one playgoer remembered the performance of the scene at the
Victoria Theatre:

Nancy was always dragged round the stage by her hair, and after
this effort Sikes always looked up defiantly at the gallery ... He
was always answered by one loud and fearful curse, yelled by the
whole mass like a Handel Festival chorus. The curse was answered
by Sikes dragging Nancy twice round the stage, and then, like

Ajax, defying the lightning … Finally, when Sikes, working up to a well-rehearsed climax, smeared Nancy with red ochre, and taking her by the hair seemed to dash her brains out on the stage, no expression of dynamite invented by the modern anarchist, no language ever dreamt of in Bedlam, could equal the outburst.[74]

Audiences showed no sympathy towards violent villains. They fervently condemned acts of extreme violence performed before them and loudly demanded justice. Occasional playwright and author Thomas Frost stated that an 'outburst of indignation against the villain of the play … brings together every rough pair of hands in the gallery to endorse it'. Thus bringing plays to a satisfying conclusion became all-important. As melodrama demanded the destruction of evil and the triumph of morality, murderer-villains needed to be punished, preferably with equal violence. As George Augustus Sala wrote, 'blood-and-murder' pieces at the Victoria 'always ended with the detection of the assassin and his condign punishment'.[75] To deviate from the formula risked great audience disapprobation and as one playwright explained, 'their dislikes [are] very violently expressed. I do not know anything more terrible than an outraged audience.'[76] Scripts of plays were littered with popular maxims forecasting the decline of the villain, such as 'blood will have blood', and 'the scaffold must claim its own guilty'. In some versions of 'Maria Martin; or, the Murder in the Red Barn', William Corder was executed in full view of the audience.[77] When the facts of real murders dramatised on the stage did not conform to this pattern, a new ending was substituted. Although Abraham Thornton was acquitted of the rape and murder of Mary Ashford, plays based on the tragedy ended with his (or Baron Falconbridge's) fatal punishment during a 'Grand Combat' as he is slain by the protectors of Ashford's (or Geralda's) honour.[78]

But we must not take this show of morality at face value. At a deeper level, extreme punishments for these villains were used as a form of closure that would ensure that other climactic scenes of violence in the plays would be entertaining. While repetitive, graphic violence built layer upon layer of tension and expectation in audiences, the brutal punishment of the offenders at the conclusion generated cathartic pleasure.[79] Audiences both expected and sought this cathartic pleasure. In Hollingshead's account of Sikes's murder of Nancy at the Victoria Theatre above, we can see how the gallery, through their expression of rage at the villain, encouraged him to yet further, more dramatic violence, which in turn increased the satisfaction, sense of relief and emotional release felt by the audience on his punishment.

Moreover, historians and literary critics have found in these tales of the destruction of villainy by ordinary people an articulation of anxieties about such themes as class, gender, urbanisation, industrialisation and so on. Martha Vicinus, for example, has argued that melodrama 'served as a cultural touchstone for large sections of society that felt both in awe of and unclear about the benefits of the new society being built around them'.[80] In seducer-betrayal narratives, Anna Clark has found both an expression of unease at the growth of sexual immorality and illegitimacy caused by disruptions to traditional plebeian work patterns, and a protest against the exploitation of the poor by the rich.[81] In the idealisation of country life and in the use of wealth, title and privilege in the characterisation of villains, it is not difficult to identify the rhetoric of class war. Thus some historians have seen melodrama as an authentic political voice of the new urban working classes. And others have shown how the 'melodramatic mode' was subsequently taken outside the theatre and used in political and social campaigns to enlist support by appealing to the emotions.[82]

But the overt political content of melodrama, especially melodramatic plays, can be, and has often been, overemphasised. Plots were inherently conservative. Despite their nostalgic undertones and obvious class themes, the plays offered audiences no solutions, but in the destruction of villainy insisted on the preservation of the status quo. As Rohan McWilliam has written, 'whilst it [melodrama] featured evil aristocrats, the preferred solution to their machinations was a more benevolent aristocracy'.[83] Melodramas were a useful coping mechanism for ordinary people. They allowed audiences to give vent to social frustrations while providing comfort and certainty through narrative closure.[84] Melodramas assisted in the process of assimilation in a time of social upheaval and disruption by demonstrating 'how difficult circumstances could be endured and even turned to victory'.[85] The plays in popular theatres posed no political threat. Instead they were a useful, conservative articulation of popular culture.

The conservative outlook of melodramatic plays meant that scripts easily slid past censors in the Lord Chamberlain's office who were responsible for licensing performances. From the mid-eighteenth century, stage drama had been 'the only literary form continuously under government regulation', and this censorship played a key role in defining and shaping drama.[86] Successive Examiners of Plays appointed by the Lord Chamberlain were not only on the look out for plays which challenged the monopoly of the Patent Theatres, but especially in the years of radicalism and Chartism, were also very sensitive to overt political content which threatened the social hierarchy. Despite the emergence of respectability during the opening decades of the nineteenth century, the violent content of many melodramas did not trouble these men either. In 1832 before the Select Committee on Dramatic Literature, Examiner of Plays George Colman acknowledged the frequency with which murders were portrayed, but explained that such plays were rarely excluded, except where they seemed to justify murder.[87] In other words, the censors' sole concern was with the romanticisation of crime, especially property crime. For this reason Colman's successors John Kemble (1840–49) and William Bodham Donne (1849–74) placed a ban on dramatisations of William Harrison Ainsworth's *Jack Sheppard* and Charles Dickens's *Oliver Twist*.[88] Similarly, Donne's marginal comments and underlinings on scripts for 'The Thieves' House! or the Murder Cellar of Fleet Ditch' and 'The Murder House; or, the Cheats of Chick Lane', submitted by the Albert and Britannia Saloons respectively in August 1844, show little attention was paid to the sequences of murders and cellars full of the bodies of victims contained in both, but that the plays were refused a licence based on their references to Jack Sheppard and Jonathan Wild.[89]

But this does not mean that violence had no role to play beyond providing dramatic climaxes and generating cathartic pleasure. Murder melodramas in popular theatres served another purpose which the censors may well have been aware of but generally unconcerned about. This function lay in their graphic portrayal of bloodshed, as such scenes, with the response they encouraged, posed a direct challenge to the values of respectability and restraint promoted by the establishment. Violence did not, in any way, constitute a form of political protest, though it may have filled a void left by the absence of politics in these plays. As a theme, it seemed to have the ability to appeal to or unite working- and even lower-middle-class men and women across occupational divides. Gruesome violence was a very visual form of cultural assertion.

If we look again at the responses of audiences to the combats and murders they were presented with in the popular theatres, this additional function of violence might become clearer. As some historians have noted, these audiences were much more sophisticated than we would imagine from the surviving scripts, and were able to respond to plays on multiple levels: 'they believed and did not believe', or as Rohan McWilliam has argued, they were 'able to laugh at the absurd plots and yet feel thrilled by them at the same time'.[90] Melodramas operated at a high emotional level. Loud indignation towards villains was expressed alongside roaring laughter at the regular comic interludes designed to provide outlets for release. This structure, combined with the overdrawn nature of the action, could encourage among audiences moments of detachment. In *Some Habits and Customs of the Working Classes* (1867), Thomas Wright described in great length the reaction of an audience in a south London theatre to the murder of a character played by 'Bricks', a very popular actor, in an exciting melodrama. After losing the 'terrific combat', Bricks, 'in doing the dying business', crawled about the stage and groaned in the most exaggerated fashion. This 'hard dying' pleased the audience in the gallery immensely: 'they applauded him most lustily, and when they had finished cheering, one of them, led away by his enthusiasm, stood upon his seat, and ... roared out at the topmost pitch of a very strong voice, "Die again, my bold Bricks! Die again!"' The cry was answered by the rest of the gallery and Bricks enthusiastically rose to his feet and did 'die again'.[91]

'Catherine Howard; or Woman's Ambition', performed at several theatres from the 1850s onwards, was later used by critic H. Chance Newton as an example of the extreme realism with which executions were performed on stage.[92] However, T. W. Erle's description of the Royal Grecian Saloon production in 1860 alerts us to the very ridiculous and pantomimic style with which violence could be portrayed, the ways in which peculiar conventions of melodrama outlined above, such as speech patterns, encouraged this and the audience's good-humoured response. Catherine Howard, eager to become queen, murders her husband with a large dose of poison. She marries Henry VIII, but, just when she believes her ambitions are fulfilled, the 'pisoned one' appears and 'bores her horribly by continuing to upbraid her with the impropriety of her conduct towards him'. The injured husband proclaims to the guilty queen, 'You shall wear the ker-rown, but it will scorch your brain', to which the audience reacted with 'a general chorus of Brayvo Smithers!' In fact, Erle continued, throughout the entire play, 'any intense tragic effect was received with tumultuous approbation and cries of "Yoiks!", "Horray!", "Tally-ho!", "Go it again!", and shouts of laughter'.

The audience continued to express their approval in this manner during the final act as Catherine's designs were thwarted and she was rightfully punished. As Erle explained, the annoying husband succeeds in making the king savagely jealous so that he is forced to sentence his queen to death. But Catherine handsomely bribes the executioner to leave town so that she might have time to escape. The executioner 'honourably fulfils his engagement by retiring to the wing, where he could be seen in conversation with the injured husband'. When the hour of her execution arrives, Catherine's plan rapidly falls apart:

An amateur Jack Ketch comes forward and volunteers to do the job. Just as she kneels down to receive the fatal stroke, he raises his mask, and discloses himself to be her injured and now avenging husband. Here, however, his pluck fails him, so instead of cutting off his wife's head as he intended, he slides about eighteen inches of lath and tinfoil under his left armpit, and falls, this time really, as dead as a doornail. Meanwhile, the professional executioner has been caught, and is now brought back just in the nick of time, so that a blow from his axe puts a conclusive end to Catherine – and the drama.[93]

Violence, then, was not always taken seriously by theatre patrons, and nor was it meant to be.

The decline of the popular theatres

We opened this chapter with an account of the dramatisation of John Thurtell's murder of William Weare in 1823 in plays staged at the Surrey and Coburg theatres. After a gap of more than thirty-five years, the Marylebone Theatre, a playhouse located on the edge of the West End but with a 'low' reputation, attempted a revival of the tragedy. In August 1862 the theatre's manager submitted the script of a melodrama entitled 'The Gipsy of Edgware; or, the Crime in Gill's Hill Lane' which made very little attempt to disguise the event on which it was based. And for this reason, the play was refused a licence for performance. The censor's red underlining and marginal notes highlighted, as the most objectionable parts, those which drew too closely on the facts of the real case, and when the script was referred to the attention of the Lord Chamberlain, Viscount Sydney, he declared in his response to William Bodham Donne, 'all such representations of recent murders on the stage appears to me to be very undesirable. It only gives the Public a morbid feeling and encourages mischievous thoughts in their minds.'[94]

Yet just the previous year, a play based on an actual, and truly recent, murder had received a licence for performance from the same office. In August 1861 the City of London Theatre had submitted a script dramatising the events surrounding the case of Roberts and Murray, a money lender and solicitor who had fought to the death at Murray's law chambers near the Strand. At first, William Bodham Donne refused to approve 'The Usurer; or A Struggle for Life', as, he wrote to the Lord Chamberlain, he did not think the subject was 'fit for theatrical representation for some time to come'.[95] However, after discussions with the theatre's manager, Nelson Lee, and with his assistance pruning the manuscript of the most offensive content and changing its title to 'The Usurer; or, the Life of a Vagrant', Donne gave the play a licence for performance, justifying his actions to the Lord Chamberlain on account of the distressed state of the City of London Theatre.[96]

This brief glimpse at the censorship records of the Lord Chamberlain's office alerts us to some important changes that had begun to occur around 1860. First, we become aware of a gradual change in the attitudes of the dramatic censors from that described above. While it is true that the theme of violence was still approved, there was a clear move to curb the representation of violent crime, including recent and past events. To crack down on violence in the popular theatre per se would have been almost impossible, although Donne did toy with the idea in 1858: censors could not ban murder from plots, and to regulate the presentation of violence would have required a virtual army of spies.[97] But the refusal to licence plays based on factual murders was a solid policy which demonstrated at least some concern about the effects of gruesome violence on the sensibilities of theatregoers. It also matches another clear policy formulation of the department. From his appointment as Examiner of Plays in 1849, William Bodham Donne began to work towards the moral and social improvement of metropolitan drama, his aim to attract a more elevated class of patron to the theatre. Donne wanted to turn the theatre into a respectable leisure pursuit.[98]

Before long, Donne's policy coincided with a decline in popular theatregoing, the second trend we can identify from the censorship records above. The fortunes of the City of London Theatre were reflective of the fortunes of theatres located on the eastern and southern boundaries of the city more generally. Regular audiences began to disappear, attracted to a bright, novel form of entertainment, music hall. Although the halls had roots in the early nineteenth-century free-and-easies and song-and-supper rooms, they were part of a new, commercial mass-entertainment industry which began to rise to dominance in London from around 1850. In that decade, several important halls were established in the metropolis, including the Canterbury in Lambeth and the Middlesex in Drury Lane, and in 1861 Charles Morton opened the Oxford in the West End, the first purpose-built music hall. By 1870 the number of halls in London had exceeded forty. As Peter Bailey argues, these large and elaborate music halls displayed 'all the elements of a prototype modern entertainment industry in terms of scale, investment and ethos'.[99]

As working- and lower-middle-class patrons deserted the theatres for the halls, theatre managers recognised that the new halls posed a

serious threat to their businesses. Letters on the subject flooded into
the Lord Chamberlain's office. Theatre managers demanded that some
sort of licensing restrictions be introduced to prevent the rise of the
halls, but with their lack of strictly dramatic entertainments, without a
change in the law the Lord Chamberlain was powerless to act.[100] At the
Select Committee on Theatrical Licences in 1866 the managers argued
that they were put in a severe disadvantage by the laws regulating
metropolitan theatres. Theatre patrons were attracted to the halls,
they argued, because there they could smoke, drink and socialise in
the auditorium while watching the entertainment, activities largely
prohibited in the theatres.[101] But, what the theatre managers probably
did not fully understand, was that the movement of audiences away
from the theatres was fundamentally indicative of a change in taste.
Murder melodramas were no longer pulling in the crowds.

And so we can see in the dramatic submissions of the City of London
and Marylebone theatres a last-ditch attempt to draw the audiences
back in, through the revival of an old crowd-pleaser, the dramatisation of real murders. Yet this move may have only compounded
their problems. As the regular audience began to desert these theatres,
managers attempted to hold on to the patrons by lowering prices. As their
profits rapidly decreased, the galleries instead became filled with young
adolescents, often troublemaking boys. A local resident complaining to
the Lord Chamberlain about the Garrick Theatre in 1868 wrote that the
playhouse had become a 'penny gaff', 'a source of great annoyance to
the residents of Leman Street and the neighbourhood as no respectable
person can pass without being annoyed by boys and girls of the lowest
order, who congregate in crowds round and near the building'.[102] In
cultural terms, popular theatres were being pushed to the margins.
Although there were always links with and parallels between the
popular theatres and the illegal, theatrical underworld, characterised by
the penny theatres or 'gaffs', now they began to share an audience and
repertoire. The dramatisation of the Roberts and Murray combat would
probably not have attracted new music hall attendees back to the City
of London Theatre, but instead would have encouraged the patronage of
audiences who were regulars at the local gaffs, where the representation
of real murders had always been much more frequent.[103]

The process of commercialisation would also deal a death blow to
the popular theatre from another angle as it combined with the new
policies of reform and revival being pursued by the Lord Chamberlain's office. During the second half of the nineteenth century, theatre
construction in the metropolis experienced a second boom, although
this time the effects were mostly limited to the city of Westminster.

As Jim Davis and Victor Emeljanow have argued, new strategies based on commercial imperatives, rather than cultural expectations, were developed in order to reassert the centrality of the West End and attract a new type of audience to the theatre. A theatrical 'theme park' was created, designed to lure middle-class patrons from the suburbs and wealthier visitors from the provinces.[104]

This was largely achieved through the radical transformation of the character of the nineteenth-century theatre. The tradition of half-price tickets at nine o'clock was abolished, excluding those whose employment prevented them from attending earlier performances as well as those who could not afford the full price. Prices were also increased.[105] Furthermore, the auditorium was significantly modified. Stalls replaced the pit, and the new practice of darkening the auditorium during performances meant full attention was directed towards the stage and silence among patrons was enforced. Finally, the character of melodrama changed. The theatrical style became much more subtle: the acting became quieter and certain peculiarities vanished. Dramas now reflected the lives of the new audiences, the action set in drawing rooms or at grand balls.[106] Thus, by the last decades of the century, theatregoing had been transformed into a 'middle-class and fashion-conscious leisure activity'.[107]

In this climate, the traditional popular theatres were given two options: to adapt or to close. For many, the financial pressure was just too much. In the East End, the City of London closed in 1868, followed by the Garrick in 1875 and the Effingham in 1879. Others attempted to stay afloat by mirroring the example of the West End. These managers made serious efforts to attract a higher class of theatre patron. In 1859, the Victoria Theatre introduced tickets for their new pit-stalls at one shilling sixpence each. By 1868, lessee J. A. Cave had inserted this notice on the playbills: 'Any person whistling or making any other disturbance will be expelled by the police. No encores will be allowed during the pantomime.' And in 1870, Cave further increased his endeavours by selling programmes for a penny and including on his list of interval refreshments, champagne at one shilling a bottle, a gesture that not so much excluded working people from the theatre, but rather offered a greater range of drinks for those affluent enough to afford them, while also attempting to align the establishment with a new, hedonistic mass culture largely celebrated in the music hall, the rising star of which was the increasingly popular Champagne Charlie.[108] In an interesting twist of fate, murder melodramas did not become extinct in these playhouses. Rather, the change in theatre patron combined with common knowledge of the history of the theatres meant that a select number of favourites became subjects for revival in a process of nostalgic appropriation, in other words, quaint, melodramatic knee tremblers.

Notes

1 Playbill for the Surrey Theatre, Monday 17 November 1823, Harvard Theatre Collection/ Playbills/ Surrey Theatre.

2 E. Fitzball, *Thirty-five Years of a Dramatic Author's Life* (London: T. C. Newby, 1859), pp. 402–3, *The Drama; or, Theatrical Pocket Magazine*, 5 (November 1823), 191–3, *The Times*, 20 November 1823, p. 3 and 26 November 1823, p. 3, *The Morning Chronicle*, 18 November 1823, p. 4, Playbills from Surrey Theatre, Monday 24 November 1823 and Monday 26 January 1824, Harvard Theatre Collection/ Playbills/ Surrey Theatre, and playbill for the Royal Coburg Theatre, Monday 12 January 1824, Harvard Theatre Collection/ Playbills/ Coburg Theatre.

3 R. D. Altick, *Victorian Studies in Scarlet: Murders and Manners in the Age of Victoria* (London: Dent, 1972), ch. 4, *passim*, M. Vicinus, *The Industrial Muse: A Study of Nineteenth-Century British Working-Class Literature* (New York: Croom Helm, 1974), p. 16, D. Worrall, *Theatric Revolution: Drama, Censorship and Romantic Period Subcultures, 1773–1832* (Oxford: Oxford University Press, 2006), pp. 314–33. See also C. Pedley, 'Maria Marten, or the Murder in the Red Barn: the theatricality of provincial life', *Nineteenth-Century Theatre and Film*, 31 (2004), 26–40, who also suggests, like Worrall, that such dramas performed in London and the provinces represented a unification of taste between the centre and the periphery.

4 Select Committee on Theatrical Licences and Regulations (Parl. Papers, 1866, XVI.1), appendix 1. [Hereafter SC (1866)].

5 J. Moody, *Illegitimate Theatre in London, 1770–1840* (Cambridge: Cambridge University Press, 2000), pp. 148–51.

6 E. W. Brayley, *Historical and Descriptive Accounts of the Theatres of London* (London: Printed for J. Taylor, 1826), pp. 11, 20, 55, 75, 91, J. Grant, *The Great Metropolis* (1st series, 2 vols, London: Saunders & Otley, 3rd edn, 1838), I, p. 75, H. Mayhew, *London Labour and the London Poor* (4 vols, London: Griffin, Bohn & Co., 1861–62), I, p. 18.

7 Grant, *The Great Metropolis*, I, pp. 21–2. See also J. Davis and V. Emeljanow, *Reflecting the Audience: London Theatregoing, 1840–1880* (Hatfield: University of Hertfordshire Press, 2001), pp. 112–36.

8 Moody, *Illegitimate Theatre*, p. 4.

9 Ibid., pp. 6–7, 54, 242, H. Cunningham, *Leisure in the Industrial Revolution, 1780–1880* (London: Croom Helm, 1980), p. 28, J. M. Golby

and A. W. Purdue, *The Civilisation of the Crowd: Popular Culture in England, 1750–1900* (London: Batsford, 1984), pp. 69–72.

10 A. Bunn, *The Stage* (3 vols, London: R. Bentley, 1840), I, p. 33. See also H. Morley, *Journal of a London Playgoer* (London: Routledge, 1866), and C. Scott, *The Drama of Yesterday and Today* (London: Macmillan, 1899).

11 Moody, *Illegitimate Theatre*, pp. 2 (quote), 5, 46–7, 243. See also Worrall, *Theatric Revolution*.

12 A number of theatre historians have also been sensitive to the distinctive theatrical culture of south and east London. For example, see: A. E. Wilson, *East End Entertainment* (London: A. Barker, 1954), M. Booth, 'East End and West End: class and audience in Victorian London', *Theatre Research International*, 2 (1977), 98–103, C. Barker, 'A theatre for the people', in K. Richards and P. Thompson (eds), *Essays on Nineteenth-Century British Theatre* (London: Methuen, 1971), Barker, 'The audiences of the Britannia Theatre, Hoxton', *Theatre Quarterly*, 9 (1979), 27–41, J. Davis and T. C. Davis, 'The people of the "People's Theatre": the social demography of the Britannia Theatre (Hoxton)', *Theatre Survey*, 32 (1991), 137–65, J. Davis and V. Emeljanow, 'New views of cheap theatres: reconstructing the nineteenth-century theatre audiences', *Theatre Survey*, 39 (1998), 53–72, and Davis and Emeljanow, *Reflecting the Audience*.

13 Humble Memorial of Samuel Lane, seeking a licence for the Britannia Saloon under the new Theatres Acts, 1843, London, The National Archives (TNA), Public Record Office (PRO), Lord Chamberlain's Papers, LC7/5.

14 Lord Chamberlain's Report on new theatres under his jurisdiction, 1843, TNA, PRO, LC7/5. See also Mayhew, *London Labour and the London Poor*, I, p. 15, and evidence of playwright Thomas James Serle, Select Committee on Dramatic Literature (Parl. Papers, 1831–32, VII.1), p. 118 [hereafter SC (1832)].

15 Theatre historians remain particularly eager to emphasise the diversity of these theatre audiences: Davis and Emeljanow, *Reflecting the Audience*, preface, Davis and Emeljanow, 'New views of cheap theatres', pp. 53–72, M. R. Booth, *Theatre in the Victorian Age* (Cambridge: Cambridge University Press, 1991), pp. 5–6, Moody, *Illegitimate Theatre*, pp. 171–4.

16 Lord Chamberlain's Report on new theatres under his jurisdiction, 1843, TNA, PRO, LC7/5.

17 Humble Memorial of Thomas Rouse seeking a licence for the Grecian Saloon under the new Theatres Act, 1843, TNA, PRO, LC7/5. See also Humble Memorial of Samuel Lane seeking a licence for the

Britannia Saloon under the new Theatres Act, 1843, TNA, PRO, LC7/5, the signatories of which included various merchants and other professionals.

18 P. P. Hanley, *Some Recollections of the Stage by an Old Playgoer* (1883), quoted in Davis and Emeljanow, 'New views of cheap theatres', p. 60.

19 Moody, *Illegitimate Theatre*, pp. 172–3, Davis and Emeljanow, 'New views of cheap theatres', pp. 58–60.

20 Brayley, *Historical and Descriptive Accounts*, pp. 11, 20, 75, 86, 91.

21 Prices listed in the Lord Chamberlain's Report on new theatres under his jurisdiction, 1843, TNA, PRO, LC7/5, and Report on the present reduction of prices, December 1846, TNA, PRO, LC7/6. See also managers' statements on playbills about the price war: playbill from the City of London Theatre, Monday 28 September 1846, London, British Library (BL), BL.370.

22 Report on the City of London Theatre, 28 July 1845, TNA, PRO, LC7/6.

23 Playbill from the Victoria Theatre, Monday 23 November and Monday 26 June 1848, Harvard Theatre Collection/ Playbills/ Royal Coburg. See also playbills from the Britannia Theatre with the use of the theme of the 'Battle of Life', Monday 23 November 1846 and Monday 11 January 1847, BL.376, J. E. Ritchie, *The Night Side of London* (London: W. Tweedie, 1857), pp. 211–12, C. Dickens, 'The amusements of the people', *Household Words*, 1 (1850), 58.

24 Davis and Emeljanow, *Reflecting the Audience*, p. 79.

25 For example, see the case of the Royal Albert Saloon; a dispute over disturbances in the theatre arose between theatre manager Henry Brading and the Lord Chamberlain's office. Letter from Brading to Lord Chamberlain, 28 September 1844, and report from Superintendent Johnstone for the Lord Chamberlain, both LC7/6.

26 For example, see the following correspondence: letter from William Martins on behalf of the Lord Chamberlain to Superintendent Mayne, 10 October 1844, LC7/5, Report from Superintendent Johnstone on Britannia Saloon, 12 July 1847, LC7/7, Report from Superintendent Medlicott on Effingham Saloon, 12 July 1847, LC7/7, Circular from Lord Chamberlain to London theatre managers, 25 January 1847, and replies received from Britannia Saloon (26 January 1847), Bower Saloon (26 January 1847), Royal Pavilion (27 January 1847), Lyceum Theatre (27 January 1847), Standard Theatre (27 January 1847), Victoria Theatre (27 January 1847), Marylebone Theatre (28 January 1847), Queen's Theatre (28 January 1847), Haymarket Theatre (28 January 1847), Olympic Theatre (29 January 1847), Effingham Saloon (30 January 1847), City of London Theatre (1 February 1847), all LC7/7.

27 *The Times*, 25 March 1857, p. 8, *The Times*, 28 December 1857, p. 8, and Mayhew, *London Labour and the London Poor*, I, p. 19.

28 *The Times*, 3 June 1857, p. 7.

29 *The Times*, 28 July 1824, p. 2. See also *The Times*, 15 October 1845, p. 8, and *The Times*, 5 November 1864, p. 11.

30 *The Times*, 18 March 1846, p. 8. See also *The Times*, 4 November 1829, p. 4, and *The Times*, 13 September 1869, p. 11.

31 *The Times*, 13 February 1855, p. 9. See also *The Times*, 23 September 1845, p. 8, *The Times*, 7 April 1853, p. 8, and *The Times*, 26 November 1859, p. 11.

32 P. Anderson, *The Printed Image and the Transformation of Popular Culture* (Oxford: Clarendon Press, 1991), p. 180.

33 *The Drama; or, Theatrical Magazine*, 6 (July 1824), 249. See also G. A. Sala, *Twice Round the Clock; or the Hours of Day and Night in London* (London: John & Robert Maxwell, 1858), p. 269.

34 'The playhouses and their prospects', *New Monthly Magazine*, 48 (October 1836), 169–71. See also F. G. Tomlins, *A Brief View of the English Drama from the Earliest Period to the Present Time* (London: C. Mitchell, 1840), p. 65, E. P. Roswell, 'A story about an execution', *Ainsworth's Magazine*, 16 (July 1849), 30–40.

35 Testimony of Doobey, an assistant in Covent Garden box office, reported in *British Stage*, May 1820, quoted in Moody, *Illegitimate Theatre*, p. 119.

36 Mayhew, *London Labour and the London Poor*, I, p. 15. See also evidence of Charles Kemble, proprietor of Covent Garden, SC (1832), p. 55, and T. Martin, 'Shakespeare and his latest stage interpreters', *Fraser's Magazine*, 64 (1861), 772–86, especially 783.

37 Mayhew, *London Labour and the London Poor*, I, p. 18, II, p. 176, and IV, p. 278.

38 Moody, *Illegitimate Theatre*, p. 154.

39 Report on the present reduction of prices, December 1846, TNA, PRO, LC7/6.

40 J. Hollingshead, *My Lifetime* (2 vols, London, 2nd edn, 1895), I, p. 3.

41 J. D. Burn, *The Language of the Walls: And a Voice from the Shop Windows* (London: Abel Heywood, 1855), p. 11.

42 Mayhew, *London Labour and the London Poor*, I, pp. 287–9.

43 Playbill from the Royal Coburg Theatre, Monday 19 February 1827, Harvard Theatre Collection/ Playbills/ Coburg Theatre.

44 Playbill from the Royal Victoria Theatre, Monday 22 April 1844, Harvard Theatre Collection/ Playbills/ Coburg Theatre.

45 Playbills from the Britannia Saloon, Monday 28 September 1857 and Monday 5 October 1857, BL.376. See also playbill for 'Ambition!

Or, Poverty! Competence! & Riches!', Britannia Saloon, Monday 22 September 1856, BL.376.

46 Playbill for the Grecian Theatre, Monday 6 October 1862, Harvard Theatre Collection/ Playbills/ Grecian Theatre.

47 Playbill from the Grecian Saloon, Wednesday 9 May 1855, Harvard Theatre Collection/ Playbills/ Grecian Theatre. See also playbill from the Royal Bower Saloon, Thursday 13 April 1848, BL.376, playbill from the Britannia Saloon, Monday 14 September 1857, BL.376, and playbill from the Royal Victoria Theatre, Monday 12 August 1850, Harvard Theatre Collection/ Playbills/ Coburg Theatre.

48 Moody, *Illegitimate Theatre*, p. 156.

49 T. Wright, *Some Habits and Customs of the Working Classes* (London: Tinsley Brothers, 1867), pp. 155–6.

50 *Pall Mall Gazette* report, reprinted in *The Times*, 16 October 1868, p. 10.

51 Moody, *Illegitimate Theatre*, pp. 83–6, M. R. Booth, *English Melodrama* (London: H. Jenkins, 1965), p. 206.

52 Booth, *English Melodrama*, p. 202.

53 Ibid., pp. 198–9.

54 *The Thespian Preceptor; or, A Full Display of the Scientific Art* (1811), quoted in Booth, *English Melodrama*, p. 205. See also Moody, *Illegitimate Theatre*, p. 84 and E. Mayhew, *Stage Effect: or, the Principles which Command Dramatic Success* (London: C. Mitchell, 1840), pp. 74–5.

55 Booth, *English Melodrama*, pp. 190–4.

56 Ibid., p. 200, Moody, *Illegitimate Theatre*, p. 87.

57 Dickens, 'The amusements of the people', 13–15.

58 Sala, *Twice Round the Clock*, p. 269.

59 Tomlins, *A Brief View of the English Drama*, p. 59.

60 *The Times*, 24 January 1842, p. 7.

61 Booth, *English Melodrama*, pp. 47–8. See also H. B. Baker, *The London Stage* (London: W. H. Allen & Co., 1889), p. 242.

62 P. Brooks, *The Melodramatic Imagination: Balzac, Henry James, Melodrama and the Mode of Excess* (New Haven: Yale University Press, 1976), pp. 13–17, 20–2, Booth, *English Melodrama*, p. 13, R. B. Heilman, *Tragedy and Melodrama: Versions of Experience* (Seattle: University of Washington Press, 1968), pp. 79–81, R. McWilliam, 'Melodrama and the historians', *Radical History Review*, 78 (2000), 57–84.

63 McWilliam, 'Melodrama and the historians', p. 59, M. Vicinus, 'Helpless and unfriended: nineteenth-century domestic melodrama', *New Literary History*, 13 (1981), 129–32.

64 *The Morning Chronicle*, 18 November 1823.

65 For itinerant entertainments based on this murder, see chapter 2.

66 *The Stage; or, Theatrical Inquisitor*, 1 (October 1828), 85–6, Baker, *The London Stage*, p. 241, *The Era*, 24 March 1844, p. 4, *The Era*, 5 August 1855, p. 4.

67 C. Z. Barnett, 'Ruth Martin, The Fatal Dreamer', February to April 1846, London, British Library (BL), Add. Mss 42992, pp. 403–17, W. T. Moncrieff, *The Red Farm; or, the Well of St Marie. A Domestic Drama in Two Acts* (London: J. Dicks, 1842).

68 Playbill from the Lincoln Theatre, 18 October 1830, Bodleian Library, Oxford, John Johnson Collection, Provincial Playbills 3 (110d), Pedley, 'Maria Marten, or, the Murder in the Red Barn', 26–40.

69 Anon., 'Maria Martin; or, the Murder in the Red Barn', reprinted in M. Kilgarriff (ed.), *The Golden Age of Melodrama: Twelve Nineteenth-Century Melodramas* (London: Wolfe, 1974), pp. 203–35. See also B. Kalikoff, *Murder and Moral Decay in Victorian Popular Literature* (Michigan: UMI Research Press, 1986), p. 24.

70 'Maria Martin', Act 1, Scene 1.

71 'Maria Martin', Act 1, Scene 5.

72 A. Lewis, *Grace Clairville; or, the Crime at the Symon's Yat* (London: J. Dicks, 1883). See also W. Rogers, 'The Farmer of Inglewood Forest; or, the Seducer! the Murderer! and the Suicide!', January to February 1846, BL, Add. Mss 42991, pp. 678–712, G. D. Pitt, 'Mary Livingstone; or, the Maiden's Murderer', BL, Add. Mss 42997, pp. 52–108.

73 G. D. Pitt, 'Charlotte Hayden, the Victim of Circumstance; or, the Maid, the Master, and the Murderer!', June to August 1844, BL, Add. Mss 42796, pp. 385–465.

74 Hollingshead, *My Lifetime*, I, pp. 188–9.

75 Sala, *Twice Round the Clock*, p. 269.

76 Evidence of playwright Thomas Morton, SC (1832), p. 219. See also Grant, *The Great Metropolis*, I, p. 84 and review of 'Father and Son' (Covent Garden, 1824), *The Times*, 1 March 1824, p. 4.

77 H. G. Hibbert, *A Playgoers Memories* (London: G. Richards, 1920), p. 86.

78 W. Barrymore, *Trial by Battle; or, Heaven Defend the Right* (London: J. Duncombe, n.d.), performed at the Coburg Theatre, 1818.

79 Kalikoff, *Murder and Moral Decay*, p. 28

80 Vicinus, 'Helpless and unfriended', p. 128, L. James, 'Taking melodrama seriously: theatre and nineteenth-century studies', *History Workshop Journal*, 3 (1977), 154.

81 A. Clark, 'The politics of seduction in English popular culture, 1748–1848', in J. Radford (ed.), *The Progress of Romance: The Politics of Popular Fiction* (London: Routledge & Kegan Paul, 1986), pp. 47–59,

Clark, 'Rape or seduction? A controversy over sexual violence in the nineteenth century', in London Feminist History Group (ed.), *Men's Power, Women's Resistance: The Sexual Dynamics of History* (London: Pluto, 1983), pp. 13–27.

82 For example, see E. Hadley, *Melodramatic Tactics: Theatricalised Dissent in the English Marketplace, 1800–1885* (Stanford: Stanford University Press, 1995), J. R. Walkowitz, *City of Dreadful Delight: Narratives of Sexual Danger in Late Victorian London* (Chicago: University of Chicago Press, 1992).

83 R. McWilliam, *The Tichborne Claimant: A Victorian Sensation* (London: Hambledon Continuum, 2007), pp. 259–60. See also James, 'Taking melodrama seriously', pp. 155–6.

84 McWilliam, 'Melodrama and the historians', p. 61.

85 Vicinus, 'Helpless and unfriended', p. 131.

86 Worrall, *Theatric Revolution*, p. 2. See also J. R. Stephens, *The Censorship of English Drama, 1824–1901* (Cambridge: Cambridge University Press, 1980).

87 SC (1832), pp. 65–6.

88 SC (1866), pp. 83, 88–9, Stephens, *The Censorship of English Drama*, pp. 61–77, Stephens, 'Jack Sheppard and the licensers: the case against the Newgate plays', *Nineteenth-Century Theatre Research*, 1 (1973), 1–13, K. Hollingsworth, *The Newgate Novel, 1830–1847: Bulwer, Ainsworth, Dickens and Thackeray* (Detroit: Wayne State University Press, 1963), p. 145, evidence of John Clay, Select Committee on Criminal and Destitute Juveniles (Parl. Papers, 1852, VII.1), p. 185 and appendix 'Extract from the sixth report of the Inspector of Prisons, Northern and Eastern Districts, 1841', H. Mayhew, *London's Underworld*, ed. P. Quennell (London: Bracken, 1950), pp. 270–8, T. Wontner, *Old Bailey Experience* (London: J. Fraser, 1833), p. 312.

89 S. Atkyns, 'The Thieves' House! or, the Murder Cellar of Fleet Ditch', August 1844, BL, Add. Mss 42977, G. D. Pitt, 'The Murder House; or, the Cheats of Chick Lane', August 1844, BL, Add. Mss 42977, pp. 216–58.

90 James, 'Taking melodrama seriously', p. 156, McWilliam, 'Melodrama and the historians', p. 60.

91 Wright, *Some Habits and Customs of the Working Classes*, p. 165.

92 H. Chance Newton, *Crime and the Drama: or Dark Deeds Dramatized* (London, 1927), p. 269.

93 T. W. Erle, *Letters from a Theatrical Scene Painter* (London: Printed for private circulation, 1880), pp. 22–4.

94 H. Young, 'The Gipsy of Edgware; or, the Crime in Gill's Hill Lane', July to August 1862, BL, Add. Mss 53015, fo. o, Letter from the Lord

Chamberlain to William Bodham Donne, 20 August 1862 (quote), TNA, PRO, LC1/112, letters from William Bodham Donne to Lord Chamberlain, 19 August 1862 and 21 August 1862 both LC1/113.

95 Letter from Donne to Lord Chamberlain, 7 August 1861, TNA, PRO, LC1/98.

96 Letter from Donne to Lord Chamberlain, 10 August 1861, TNA, PRO, LC1/98. See also letter from Donne to Lord Chamberlain regarding the prohibition of 'The Blood Spot; or, the Maiden, the Mirror and the Murderer', 20 May 1858, LC1/58.

97 Report from Examiner of Plays on licensing during previous year, 1 January 1859, LC1/70.

98 Davis and Emeljanow, *Reflecting the Audience*, pp. 105–6.

99 P. Bailey, *Popular Culture and Performance in the Victorian City* (Cambridge: Cambridge University Press, 1991), pp. 80–5, Booth, *Theatre in the Victorian Age*, p. 11.

100 For example, see Lord Chamberlain's notes in relation to the law regulating theatres and music halls, n.d., LC1/168.

101 For example, see evidence of Nelson Lee, SC (1866), p. 179.

102 Letter to Lord Chamberlain, 21 May 1868, LC1/200.

103 For penny gaffs, their repertoire and audience, see J. Grant, *Sketches in London* (London: W. S. Orr & Co., 1838), Mayhew, *London Labour and the London Poor*, I, pp. 40–2, G. Godwin, *Town Swamps and Social Bridges* (London: Routledge, 1859), pp. 94–6, J. Greenwood, *The Seven Curses of London* (London: Rivers, 1869), pp. 44–6, C. Dickens, 'Mr Whelks over the water', *All the Year Round*, 15 (1866), 592. For an account of the decline of the popular theatre, see Dickens, 'Mr Whelks revived' and 'Mr Whelks at the play', *All the Year Round*, 15 (1866), 548–52, 563–6.

104 Davis and Emeljanow, *Reflecting the Audience*, pp. 168–73.

105 Ibid., pp. 187, 192.

106 Booth, *English Melodrama*, p. 202.

107 Davis and Emeljanow, *Reflecting the Audience*, p. 225, G. Weightman, *Bright Lights, Big City: London Entertained, 1830–1850* (London: Collins & Brown, 1992), pp. 110–13, 130–4, P. Horn, *Pleasures and Pastimes in Victorian Britain* (Stroud: Sutton, 1999), pp. 200–6.

108 Davis and Emeljanow, *Reflecting the Audience*, pp. 38–9. See also Dickens, 'Mr Whelks at the play', p. 564, and Bailey, *Popular Culture and Performance*.

5

Selling Sweeney Todd to the masses

THOSE CONTEMPORARIES and theatre historians who have argued that 'Maria Marten; or, the Murder in the Red Barn' was one of the most popular and long-running melodramas in the nineteenth century have almost never failed to mention its competitor, a melodrama staged at nearly every fringe theatre described in the previous chapter and which has enjoyed an even longer run and legacy than 'Maria Marten'. The play was first advertised by the Britannia Theatre in March 1847 under the title, 'The String of Pearls; or, the Fiend of Fleet Street', and was attributed to the theatre's resident playwright, George Dibdin Pitt (see figure 25).[1] Soon rival versions proliferated throughout the East End and south London, rescripted by theatrical hacks servicing the Pavilion, Effingham, Victoria and Bower Saloon, and the melodrama was revived regularly by theatre managers through the 1850s and 1860s.[2]

But the stage was not the only, or indeed the first, location for the telling of this tale. 'The String of Pearls' originally appeared as a serial romance in the *People's Periodical and Family Library*, a weekly miscellany of fiction, oddities and advisory articles produced by emerging publishing giant Edward Lloyd. The *People's Periodical* was intended for young and old, for men and women, and to be shared among family members if not read aloud within that circle. It was 'The String of Pearls' that introduced a new, fictional but frightening celebrity to metropolitan popular culture: the bloodthirsty barber, Sweeney Todd.

Although mingled with some pretty romance, blood and gore dominated the serial from the very opening number. 'The String of Pearls' opens with a description of Mr Thornhill's efforts to find the house of Johanna Oakley in order to break the news of the death of her lover, his friend Mark Ingestrie. Spying a small barber's shop near

Royal Britannia Saloon

Proprietor . . . Mr. Samuel Lane, 188, Hoxton, near Shoreditch Church. Licensed by the Lord Chamberlain.

Facts speak for themselves ! **Good Management !** **Good Business ! !**

LOOK AT THE PRICES !

Boxes 6d Stalls 4d Gal. 2d

Lower Stalls 6d. Half-price to Ditto & Boxes 3d. Ditto to Upper Stalls 2d.

At Half-past 8. **NO HALF-PRICE TO GALLERY.**

☞ Children in arms not Chargeable ; but all Ch'ldren under Ten years of age, will be charged half-price to the Boxes and Stalls.
N.B.---No Persons admitted to the Boxes or Lower Stalls unless suitably attired.

FIRST NOTICE !

MR. HUDSON KIRBY

Having been nightly called before the Curtain, with RINGING CHEERS, to receive the applause of the Audience at the conclusion of his arduous character, it is imperative on the Management to announce

THE LEAR OF PRIVATE LIFE !

For FIVE NIGHTS MORE, after which it must positively be withdrawn to make room for other Novelties which have been long in preparation

SECOND NOTICE !

The Proprietor anxious in catering for the Public, has the pleasure of announcing

THE FIRST NIGHT OF ANOTHER NEW PIECE (from the Pen of DIBDIN PITT) called The STRING OF PEARLS !

THIRD NOTICE ! ! !

On MONDAY, March 8th, will be produced a New Drama, in which Mr. HUDSON KIRBY & Mr. M. HOWARD will perform, to be called The Fate of Xavier, the Prussian Brother; A Tale of the Wars of Napoleon.

Another Romantic Drama called " **The Demon of the Drachenfels,** " is also fast progressing, and will be brought forward as soon as its stupendous Scenic and Machinic effects can be completed.

ON MONDAY, MARCH the 1st, 1847, AND ALL THE WEEK,

Will be presented an entirely New Drama, full of extraordinary Incidents, and creative of the most soul-thrilling situations, entitled THE

STRING OF PEARLS

Or the Fiend of Fleet Street !

Taken from the much admired Tale of that name (founded on fact) in " Lloyd's People's Periodical " For Dramatic effect, and to adapt the Story to general taste, some alterations have been judiciously made, enhancing its interest, The Comic Characters are rich and varied; the laughable voraciousness of the hungry " Jarvis," the bluff humour of the " Beef-eater," the expose of the fanatical Maw-worm, " Dr. Lupin," and the canting " Mrs. Oakley," serve to lighten and relieve the more serious portion of the subject and afford a strong and excellent MORAL LESSON ! The whole is indeed a picture of human nature replete, as human nature is, with LIGHT and SHADE ! and cannot fail both to amuse and instruct.

Lear of Private Life

THERESE!

THE ORPHAN OF GENEVA ! !

THE PRINCE OF PEKIN

Stage Manager . . . Mr. F. WILTON. Prompter . . . Mr. MORDAUNT.

25. Playbill advertising the production of 'The String of Pearls' at the
Britannia Saloon, 1 March 1847

St Dunstan's Church in Fleet Street, Thornhill decides to delay his awkward task and steps inside for a shave. He is promptly seated in the chair by the enthusiastic, if slightly strange barber, Sweeney Todd. During the course of their conversation, Thornhill reveals that he has a valuable string of pearls in his possession which he intends to give to Johanna. Todd becomes excited at this news and makes some inconsequential excuse to leave the room. Thornhill then mysteriously disappears.[3] With the aid of a specially constructed machine, Sweeney Todd routinely murders his customers. After placing the gentlemen in the barber's chair, Todd pulls a lever which causes the chair to spin, casting the unsuspecting victims into the stone vaults below. At a convenient moment, Todd enters the vaults, robs the customer of his valuables, and then slices the body into bite-sized chunks.

Todd's diabolical deeds do not end there. Because of its high value, the string of pearls proves troublesome to sell. Throughout the serial, the true extent of Todd's murder machine is slowly revealed as the barber begins to panic and arouse suspicion. Within weeks of Thornhill's disappearance, Mr Wrankley, the local tobacconist, drops into Todd's shop for a shave. He is eager to tell the barber about a valuable string of pearls sold to his cousin who, anxious to discover its origin, has enlisted Wrankley's assistance. The dangerous information convinces the barber to 'polish him off'. That evening, Todd pays a visit to his friend, Mrs Lovett, the famous pie-shop owner in Bell-yard. As he leaves, Mrs Wrankley enters the shop to ask a favour of Mrs Lovett. She explains that her husband has been missing since the morning and wishes to place a poster in the pie-shop window to draw attention to him. In her distress, Mrs Wrankley claims that she has not eaten since last seeing her husband:

> 'Then buy a pie, madam,' said Todd, as he held one out close to her. 'Look up Mrs Wrankley, lift off the top crust, madam, and you may take my word for it you will see *something* of Mr Wrankley.'
>
> The hideous face that Todd made during the utterance of those words quite alarmed the disconsolate widow, but she did partake of the pie for all that. It was certainly very tempting – a veal one, full of coagulated gravy – who could resist? Not she, certainly, and besides, did not Todd say she should see something of Wrankley? There was hope in his words, at all events, if nothing else.[4]

Mrs Lovett, then, is not only Todd's friend, but his business partner. The chunks of meat from Todd's victims are passed through the vaults under Fleet Street, from his cellar to her bakehouse, which services her famous pie shop.

'The String of Pearls' certainly seems to have been an imaginative tale, its subsequent editions and life in the popular theatre demonstrating the expertise of its author, Thomas Peckett Prest, to strike a special chord with his audiences.[5] But, a brief exploration of the genre in which it was originally launched suggests that, although successful, the story was not all that exceptional. Instead, it serves as a useful example of that great quantity of violent (hence the name 'penny bloods') and sometimes titillating cheap instalment fiction which flooded popular print culture between 1830 and 1860. Very little scholarly attention has focused on the role of cheap fiction in popular culture during the early Victorian period. Many literary historians have dismissed these penny packets as ephemeral junk, preferring instead to chart the impact of canonical texts on self-made men. For the most part, detailed study has been left to the committed antiquarian.[6] Yet the sheer number of penny bloods printed combined with their impressive circulation rates and their relationship to other forms of entertainment in popular culture described in this book alert us to their very important role during the first half of the nineteenth century, precisely what this chapter aims to explore. As an exemplary serial, 'The String of Pearls' offers a useful entry point: this penny blood draws our attention to important inheritances but also key innovations, demonstrates how the theme of violence was used to attract and fulfil readers, and points to crucial intersections with other forms of entertainment further exposing the wider functions of early Victorian popular culture.

Production and dissemination

The publication of 'The String of Pearls' in 1846 was certainly no epoch-making moment. Prest's new serial was launched into an already vibrant market that boasted a large and committed audience, using a tried and tested formula. It was a literary market that had been for the most part shaped by the publisher of 'The String of Pearls', Edward Lloyd, just fifteen years before. Lloyd, and indeed other publishers of cheap literature from the turn of the nineteenth century, took advantage of a peculiar set of preconditions that encouraged the development and ensured the success of cheap publications for lower-class audiences. In the case of cheap fiction, the result was the evolution of a literary genre with no clear precedent. To better understand this great innovation, and the emergence of the theme of violence within it, we must begin by exploring what was there before.

Eighteenth-century England was not devoid of print culture, and we might even be surprised to learn that poor country families had access to a range of texts. Historians have often described a robust trade in crudely coloured chapbooks containing highly imaginative stories which typically sat alongside copies of the Bible or Common Prayer Book in family libraries, though it must be remembered that, especially in rural areas, such collections were mostly very small and single items were intended to provide amusement over long periods of time. Broadsheets containing popular ballads, prophecies or accounts of executions were similarly sold by passing hawkers or displayed on the walls of the local alehouse for customers to enjoy and share.[7] Those who lived in major centres, especially London, were provided with further access to the printed word, as, for example, during the eighteenth century men frequenting coffee houses were provided with a range of newspapers and periodicals to peruse while taking refreshment. In London, the coffee house became an important part of artisanal culture.[8] However, the high cost of paper and printing, and restrictions on access to elementary education for the lower orders limited many benefits of the growth in print to the middling sorts, including merchants and professionals.

But, by the conclusion of the Napoleonic Wars, advances in printing technology, such as the invention of the rotary steam press, and falling prices in paper manufacture meant that some forms of print became much cheaper and quicker to produce. Larger quantities of broadsheets, pamphlets and periodicals which would cater for a burgeoning population became economically viable and desirable. In chapter 3, we described how such developments encouraged the rapid expansion of the broadside trade in London and filled the pockets of a number of traditional printers, such as the famous Jemmy Catnach of the Seven Dials. At the same time, there was another, equally important process underway which we have not yet referred to: the increase in the number of readers in English society. For traditional broadside printers who had been in the business of supplying print to illiterate customers over the course of the previous two centuries, the growth of the reading public was largely incidental. Sheets became more sophisticated during the early nineteenth century, but they still contained a range of features, from illustrations to songs, and small quantities of predictable prose designed to appeal to illiterates and readers alike. While broadside printers capitalised on the population increase to swell their purchasers, the actual growth of readers stimulated the development of new forms of print in popular culture.

On the face of it, the rates of literacy on the eve of the publication of 'The String of Pearls' do not look very impressive. In 1840, around 60 per cent of the national population were considered to be literate by the test of the marriage register, the ability to sign one's name, a figure that had shown very little and mostly uneven progress over the previous one hundred years.[9] In practice, the figures suggest that almost the entire upper and middle classes had achieved full literacy, while a significant proportion of the skilled working class could boast a similar accomplishment. But these rates tell us very little about the numbers of those who could read in English society. Literacy was composed of two skills, the ability to read and the ability to write, which had long been taught sequentially, reading before writing, the former outweighing the latter in importance. At the turn of the nineteenth century, the evangelical movement and, independently, working-class demand, meant that access to elementary education for the lower orders improved. Working-class parents were presented with a range of semi-formal and formal options for the instruction of their children, from the Sunday Schools, British and Foreign Schools, and National Schools run by establishment and dissenting religious authorities to the semi-formal dame schools which were more firmly rooted within the community. But the success of these institutions is difficult to measure through national or even regional rates of literacy. Many children only spent enough time in these schools to acquire the ability to read; in a large number of Sunday Schools this was in fact the only skill taught at all.[10]

Early Victorian society then was composed of a large number of semi-literates or readers. Not only did this encourage the expansion of print culture as entrepreneurs realised the potential profits to be made, but the development of new forms of print also helped to sustain and increase the number of readers, further fuelling the growth of the market. This was not because lower-class men and women were tempted to learn the skill in order to enjoy these new publications (though some undoubtedly were), but rather that the greater availability of a range of reading matter militated against the loss of early learnt skills as life progressed, a problem which had plagued earlier generations.[11] The exact number of readers, or the size of this market, is very difficult to calculate and has so far eluded most historians. Robert K. Webb's endlessly quoted estimate, that the number of readers can be obtained by multiplying the literacy rate by 2.5, might provide some clues, but fails to take account of crucial changes in the provision of elementary education throughout the nineteenth century which would have a substantial impact on gradations of literacy within the lower classes. More work is certainly needed.[12] But despite this, we can say that London, with the highest rates of literacy in England and with a long legacy of print within the public sphere, probably had an especially

large number of semi-literates whose skills had been more finely tuned
with the increase in access to forms of education.

And from the closing decades of the eighteenth century, there was a
great rush from several quarters to take advantage of this market. The
first concerted effort came from the political radicals who sought to
mobilise old and new forms of print in order to rally the people against
Old Corruption and publicise the democratic cause. Men such as
William Cobbett, Richard Carlisle and Thomas Wooler, to name a few,
distributed a range of pamphlets and periodicals among working men
and women in both town and country.[13] Their audience responded with
enthusiasm. In his autobiography, journeyman tailor Thomas Carter
remembered how the men in his London workshop clubbed their pence
together to buy a copy of Cobbett's *Political Register*, which Carter
read aloud to them as they worked.[14] Similarly, in 1816, apprentice
shipbuilder Christopher Thomson read both Cobbett's *Political Register*
and Wooler's *Black Dwarf*: 'it was my custom every Saturday evening,
after work was over, to go to the Market Place and from a stall there, to
purchase the breathings of those men of mind'.[15]

As radicals sought to win hearts and minds, evangelicals and
conservatives responded in kind to preserve the status quo and to
moralise the disorderly lower classes. They, too, utilised both traditional
and emergent forms of print and lines of dissemination. Hannah More
founded the Cheap Repository of Moral and Religious Tracts in 1795,
through which she printed and distributed to institutions, hawkers and
individuals a variety of moral stories.[16] Although the Cheap Repository
closed in 1798, its work was maintained and extended by the Religious
Tract Society (RTS) through the nineteenth century. Concern about
the lack of decent, serious literature for working men also inspired
the efforts of Henry Brougham and Charles Knight, two leading
figures of the Society for the Diffusion of Useful Knowledge (SDUK),
launched during the 1820s. Cheap print, they believed, could be utilised
to educate the masses, a means of imparting 'useful knowledge',
a highly contentious term, and facilitating self-improvement.[17] The
Society's most famous and successful publication, Charles Knight's
weekly *Penny Magazine*, presented readers with a range of articles on
history, science, fine art and economics, the elaborate wood engravings
on the front cover no doubt attracting the attention of purchasers.
By the end of 1832, its circulation had grown to 200,000, while
Knight estimated a readership of close to 1 million.[18] Evidence from
the memoirs of working men also confirms the popularity of the
periodical. For example, Christopher Thomson, delighted with the
contents of the first number which he borrowed from a friend,

decided to forgo sugar in his tea in order to afford to purchase the periodical each week.[19]

Despite some short-term successes, the efforts of radicals, evangelicals and utilitarians were relative failures. The *Penny Magazine*, for example, could not maintain its initially high circulation and by 1845 Charles Knight was only able to sell 40,000 copies weekly.[20] Collet Dobson Collet, Secretary to the Newspaper Stamp Abolition Society, later explained its decline in these terms: '[the magazine] did not reach the class for whom it was intended ... the working classes considered themselves insulted by the *Penny Magazine* because they were told to take it instead of the unstamped press'.[21] Collet placed his finger on something very important here. Organisations and individuals who attempted to impose a literary diet on working men and women fundamentally misunderstood the character and intricacies of the popular culture into which they launched their publications. As already mentioned, the tastes of working people were diverse and encompassing, were never exclusive, and embraced several cultural levels simultaneously. Even autodidacts committed to the goal of self-improvement exhibit such multiplicity in their reading habits. As we saw above, Christopher Thomson read radical and educational publications alike. Similarly, while many working people read the *Penny Magazine* and similar publications, they also sought light entertainment, something which organisations such as the RTS and the SDUK refused to supply.

Radical publishers, on the other hand, were slightly more sensitive to the desires and needs of the common reader. However, from the late eighteenth century they were presented with several crucial obstacles. First, inevitable fractures within the radical movement meant that publications were tied to particular factions and potential audiences were divided. Competing ideals meant that a lowest common denominator to attract large, occupationally and regionally diverse audiences could be difficult to locate. The problem was compounded by the imposition of the stamp duty, a government initiative to contain and eventually eradicate the radical press by placing a tax on the publication of news hence prohibiting the emergence of cheap newspapers. Access to news was certainly something that working people craved. As Thomas Carter explained, the apprentice and journeymen tailors in his London workshop soon tired of William Cobbett's *Political Register* as 'the only news it contained was that which related to the naval and military operations of the British forces ... [and was] thought to be deficient in matters of general interest. It was therefore exchanged for the *Courier*.'[22] Political suppressions during the 1820s put further pressure on radical printers, and some London print shops were forced to close. Yet by the 1830s, a new generation of radical pressmen were keen to employ a different strategy. John Cleave and Henry Hetherington, inspired by the contemporaneous broadside trade, such as stories of disasters, human tragedies and crimes, actively combined radical politics with entertainment material in their periodicals, *Cleave's Weekly Police Gazette* and Hetherington's *Destructive*. These became two of the most successful radical publications of the decade.[23] Thus entertainment, or sensation, could successfully bridge divides within potential audiences.

Moreover, in order to increase profits, many radical pressmen also sought to diversify the range of publications they offered to purchasers. Iain McCalman has provided a detailed account of the way in which ultra radicals and radicals alike dabbled in the production of pornographic, bawdy and obscene works, the former becoming legends in the pornographic trade, the latter continuing to combine titillation with radicalism in the hope of attracting more subscribers.[24] Again, this was certainly no new development as bawdiness was an important characteristic of eighteenth-century plebeian culture.[25] But at the same time, a number of new pressmen also began to extend their business into a new genre which had just begun to emerge: cheap instalment fiction. If we take a moment to glance through the list of publishers in the largest surviving archive of penny bloods, the Barry Ono Collection in the British Library, their presence becomes especially apparent. During the 1830s, several publishers stand out: John Cleave, George Purkess, William Strange, John Clements and George Vickers. Penny instalment fiction was certainly profitable and made commercial sense. And so it encouraged new printers and publishers into the trade, for whom money was the primary or even sole motive. Among these men, two names are particularly notable: Edward Lloyd and G. W. M. Reynolds.

Of the two, George William Macarthur Reynolds has certainly attracted the most attention from historians and literary scholars. Born into an upper-middle-class family in 1814, Reynolds squandered his inheritance in France, returning, bankrupt, to England in 1836. He moved to London where he embarked on a career as a novelist, publisher and journalist, his most famous publications including *Pickwick Abroad; or, the Tour in France* (1837–38), a cheap weekly magazine along the same lines as Lloyd's *People's Periodical*, entitled *Reynolds's Miscellany* (1846–69), the long-running serial *The Mysteries of London* (1844–48) and *The Mysteries of the Court of London* (1848–55), which, with more than 40,000 regular subscribers, has been proclaimed as the most popular novel in nineteenth-century England, and finally a weekly newspaper, *Reynolds's Newspaper* (1850–1967), which will be referred to again in the next chapter. Reynolds's background, commitment to radicalism, diverse range of publications and long-term commercial success have captured the imagination of scholars, many seeing him as the embodiment of the heterogeneous and often contradictory character of Victorian popular culture. Reynolds and his publications were at once respectable, radical and bawdy. At the same time as publishing escapist romantic fiction for servant girls, he was continuing the radical tradition of combining politics with low-level pornography in his long-running serial *The Mysteries*.[26] But Reynolds was not necessarily a great innovator. In many ways he was following trends set by a larger and even more successful publisher-printer, Edward Lloyd.

Unlike Reynolds, Lloyd's socio-economic background generally reflected that of the audience he sought to attract for his range of publications. He was the son of a Welsh labourer and was born just outside London in Thornton Heath in 1815. He enjoyed only a brief elementary education, obtained a position in a solicitor's office, and in the evenings studied shorthand at the Mechanics' Institute in London. By his late teens, Lloyd had moved into the print trade, first selling comic valentines before publishing *Lloyd's Stenography* in 1833.[27] It is fair to claim that Lloyd pioneered the cheap entertaining miscellany of the early Victorian period with the publication of *The Calendar of Horrors* between 1835 and 1836, an eight-page weekly magazine sold for a penny which included a mixture of gothic fiction, accounts of unusual and often violent events, and descriptions of past crimes. By the early 1840s, Lloyd had developed a successful formula for the weekly miscellany: sixteen pages of close print, a front page illustration, a combination of instalment fiction, short stories, advisory articles and various oddities, and a back page partly reserved for advertisements for other publications and readers' feedback. In 1842 he began *Lloyd's Penny Weekly Miscellany* (1842–47), though he soon found he had enough material for several other simultaneous magazines: *Lloyd's Penny Atlas* (1842–45), *Lloyd's Penny Sunday Times* (1840–49?), a spoof newspaper that became devoted to fiction after Lloyd commenced *Lloyd's Weekly News* in 1843, and the *People's Periodical and Family Library* (1846–47), in which 'The String of Pearls' was first published.

In addition, Lloyd soon began to publish penny novelettes, single stories which were often republications of successful tales from the miscellanies, issued in weekly instalments, each containing sixteen pages and a woodcut illustration on the front cover. Thus 'The String of Pearls', like many other serials, received new life in 1850 when Lloyd republished it with the addition of several hundred pages. The weekly issue of the novelettes and miscellanies was a defining feature of this genre of cheap fiction. Unlike seventeenth- and eighteenth-century chapbooks which were collected and cherished by readers, penny fiction was much more ephemeral. Individual publications, especially miscellanies, were designed to provide amusement for a reader over the course of the week. But then they were meant to be discarded, either passed on to another reader or thrown away, as the next issue replaced the former. Their rock-bottom price ensured that this was a possibility for all but the very poorest subscribers.

The vast number of publications in print, their potential short lives and the commercial imperatives of the publishers put a tremendous amount of pressure on the authors who supplied the prose. From the correspondence columns of the weekly miscellanies, it is clear that Lloyd welcomed and encouraged contributions of stories and poems from his readers. For instance, in the *People's Periodical and Family Library*, Lloyd announced: 'We must decline the following – "The Dying Wife"; "Lines to a Youth"; "Sonnet to a Redbreast"; "Ambition"; and the "The Cold Water Cure".'[28] And, to 'A Constant Reader', several issues later: 'Cannot say exactly when "The Divorce" will be published in the "Journal". Should like to see the MS for the "Everyday Book".'[29] Tiny snippets of evidence contained in correspondence columns and even some autobiographies suggest that these unsolicited, irregular contributions were not paid for by Lloyd, a cunning business strategy which exploited the vanity of amateur writers and helped to sustain the large quantity of literary material at such low prices.[30]

However, for the most part, authors of cheap serials were literary hacks who were paid low wages to supply great quantities of fiction at a rapid pace to meet the voracious consumer demand. Despite the tendency to anonymise the contributors, several authors rose to become celebrities in the trade as they were prolific in their output and Lloyd realised that recurring names could foster a devoted following among readers. Two of these 'celebrities' have been credited, at different times, with the authorship of 'The String of Pearls': Thomas Peckett Prest and James Malcolm Rymer. Both came from relatively humble backgrounds, their lives probably reflecting those of their readers, suggesting that they were tuned in to the tastes of the audience for penny fiction. Prest, like several other authors, also wrote melodramas for popular theatres, further nurturing that close relationship between the two genres that we see reflected in the content of the stories told in both locations. In sum, Prest and Rymer were fairly representative of the regular authors Lloyd and other publishers of cheap fiction used. Thus debates about the authorship of particular works within this canon matter very little, apart from further highlighting the uniformity of much of the fiction produced.

With the wide choice of fiction available, Prest, Rymer and others in Lloyd's stable of writers were clearly at the mercy of their audience. The life of any serial depended on the number of purchasers it attracted. Tight profit margins demanded a sale of at least 20,000 copies each week.[31] Serials which achieved more than the baseline were prolonged as far as possible as authors inserted multiple, often irrelevant, subplots into the main narrative. Those which attracted fewer purchasers were brought to an abrupt end. In such a competitive industry, the penny-blood trade was, in a very important sense, market driven, as readers expressed their likes and dislikes through their decision to buy. Moreover, the sheer size of the readership of miscellanies and novelettes was unprecedented. Based on a survey of co-current publications and minimum circulations, Richard Altick estimates that, in 1845, Lloyd's publishing house in Salisbury Square, Fleet Street, sold, weekly, more than half a million copies of penny parts and cheap miscellanies.[32] These figures only record cash transactions. We must not forget the well-used sharing networks in working-class families, neighbourhoods and workplaces. One copy was probably often read, or even listened to, by a number of different people. In real terms, the audience for Lloyd's penny fiction must be expressed in the millions.

From the beginning, Edward Lloyd was committed to providing cheap and entertaining literature for a very specific group of readers, the lower-middle and working classes. In the preface to the first completed volume of his *Penny Weekly Miscellany*, Lloyd wrote that although he intended the periodical to be 'a rational companion for all classes', he claimed 'the merit … of laying before a large and intelligent class of readers, at a charge comparatively insignificant, the same pleasures of imagination which have, hitherto, to a great extent, only graced the polished leisure of the wealthy'.[33] The small literary contributions probably sent in by readers and described above certainly suggest a substantial lower-middle-class following. While the range of short stories and poems are not necessarily indicative of any special talent, these readers obviously had a level of skill beyond basic familiarity with a pen, had some time to use it and money to purchase writing materials. Yet their participation in this cultural production further emphasises the fuzziness and permeability of the perceived boundary between the lower rungs of the middle class and the upper echelons of the working class, especially as Lloyd was particularly keen to publish material which appealed to the more economically marginal. The oft-cited passage from Thomas Frost's autobiography explains how Lloyd would place unpublished manuscripts in the 'hands of an illiterate person – a servant, or a machine boy, for instance. If they pronounce favourably upon it, we think it will do.'[34] Slivers of evidence relating to actual reading experiences, much harder to come by, show that penny bloods were eagerly devoured by the costermongers and their families in the New Cut, Lambeth, the casual inmates of the low-lodging houses and workhouses of the East End, city-crossing sweeps and the rough boys of Spitalfields.[35]

Such accounts also provide us with very brief glimpses at practices of reading, helping to move us one step beyond supposition. In *London Labour and the London Poor* (1861), Henry Mayhew described the role of instalment fiction in the lives of the Lambeth costermongers: 'on a fine summer's evening a costermonger, or any neighbour who has the advantage of being a "schollard", reads aloud to them in the courts they inhabit'. He interviewed an 'intelligent costermonger' who was in the habit of reading aloud to one particular group, the account given by the man drawing attention to the heated reactions of the listeners to contentious subjects, such as aristocratic privilege and police authority, demonstrating how group readings could be important forums at which values and ideals were hotly debated and disseminated throughout the community. By the time of the interview, Henry Mayhew wrote that this particular group of costermongers had shifted their allegiance from Edward Lloyd to G. W. M. Reynolds. However, he added, only a few years back the same men, women and children had 'found great delight' in 'tales of robbery and bloodshed, or heroic, eloquent and gentlemanly highwaymen, or of gipsies turning out to be noblemen'.[36] Precisely how and why they found such entertainment in these publications are crucial questions which we will now turn to consider.

Gore between the covers

T. P. Prest's 'String of Pearls' certainly provides us with a very good example of what a penny blood was like between the covers – the ebb and flow of the plot, the incorporation of multiple subplots and the depth (or rather the lack of) of characterisation, and common themes. Indeed, it is fair to say that to read one penny blood is to read them all. Repetition was commonplace. At times only the briefest details of the plot and character names were changed between serials. And tales were typically filled with the two-dimensional stock characters of villain, hero and heroine. Once Edward Lloyd and his authors had discovered a winning formula, over the next two decades they demonstrated extreme reluctance to stray too far away from it. 'The String of Pearls' also shows how Lloyd's penny fiction was a combination of various styles, narrative frameworks and genres, a mixture of old and new, a melting pot, if you like, in which two crucial ingredients were always prominent: romance and violence. To understand how this came about, and the reasons for its popularity, we need to tease out and explore the range of styles Lloyd blended together.

The first such influence was derived from the *Newgate Calendar* tradition. We have already discussed the rise and fall of this school of literature in chapter 3. From the late seventeenth century onwards, there was a proliferation of pamphlets and multi-volume biographies which focused on the lives of criminals, from murderers and highwaymen at one end, to footpads and prostitutes at the other. During the late eighteenth century, this genre fell into decline as its primary audience deserted. *Newgate Calendars* continued to be published, but in very short print runs, their relatively expensive price tag recommending them to collectors rather than common readers. However, some of this content was also emptied into emergent low print culture and was freely exploited by radical and new commercial printers. Edward Lloyd, George Purkess and William Strange joined forces from 1836 to 1839 to publish a cheap imitation of Captain Alexander Smith's infamous work, *The History of the Pirates of all Nations*. Money made from this venture encouraged Lloyd to produce single-handedly *Lives of the Most Notorious Highwaymen, Footpads and Murderers* between 1836 and 1837. Even more successful and long-lasting were the highwaymen romances published throughout the 1830s, 1840s and 1850s, which were probably intended to appeal to an audience not unlike that described in the previous chapter which filled the galleries of popular theatres to see plays based on the tale of Jack Sheppard.[37]

More importantly, in addition to these imitations, in Lloyd's miscellanies and novelettes we can trace a number of stories originally presented in the popular literature of crime being repeated and slowly updated for nineteenth-century audiences to sustain their popularity. In particular, there emerges a common story about serial murder told repeatedly during the eighteenth century and from which, it is possible to argue, the tale of Sweeney Todd evolved. In post-Restoration popular literature of crime and fiction, we are often told about the sad misfortunes of travellers who, in the absence of alternative choices, find shelter at isolated country inns. Although they take various precautions, such as locking doors and sleeping with their valuables under their pillows, these unfortunate men (and sometimes women) are invariably murdered, and the large purses they have with them to conduct their business are stolen. The typically secluded setting of the murderers' inns ensures that the families and friends of victims are unable to trace their loved ones and identify those responsible.[38] The narrative undoubtedly found its most famous articulation in the tale of Sawney Beane, a frightful cannibal who lived with his meat-loving family in a cave on the Scottish coast, who supported themselves by robbing, murdering and eating travellers passing by.[39]

On the one hand, during the 1830s, 1840s and 1850s we can see how Lloyd and his authors directly copied and republished these tales, almost unchanged, as serials and short stories in novelettes and miscellanies. The stories of the wrongly accused innkeeper Jonathan Bradford and the Scottish cannibal Sawney Beane were given new life as Thomas Peckett Prest extended former pamphlet-sized biographies to several hundred pages.[40] Multiple short stories in *Lloyd's Penny Atlas* and *Lloyd's Penny Miscellany* repeated eighteenth-century stories of murderous innkeepers preying on solitary, naïve travellers, to new audiences. For instance, one author transported readers back in time to a late eighteenth-century cottage situated on a large heath in Devonshire, a building that had 'since been destroyed, owing to the discovery that it was inhabited by a couple of desperate and abandoned characters, simply for the purpose of entrapping the innocent and unsuspecting travellers that perchance happened to take refuge there from a variety of accidental circum-stances'. The closure of this story with the discovery, by the authorities, of a bloody knife beside one of the victim's bodies with the name of the murderer engraved on its handle, directly reflected that of the tale of *The Bloody Innkeeper, or Sad and Barbarous News from Gloucester-shire* (1675), in which a blacksmith, who had recently purchased a former inn for his workshop, unearthed the bodies of seven men and women, and found in the breast of one man a knife with the name of the innkeeper engraved on its handle.[41] This plagiarism, by an author who was not a regular writer for Lloyd and may even have been a reader-contributor to the magazine, is suggestive of the extent to which such tales from the popular literature of crime were still in circulation.

On the other hand, we can trace a process of adaptation, whereby older narratives appeared in an updated form, placed within the structure of the penny blood which, after all, was intended to be a sentimental and fictional story dealing with adventure rather than a criminal biography. Heroes and heroines were the central characters in cheap fiction and the story centred on their troubles. Villains, including dastardly murderers, entered the plot as characters who caused multiple obstructions for the heroes and needed to be brought to justice. Thomas Peckett Prest's *Retribution; or, the Murder at the Old Dyke* (1846), therefore, primarily focuses on the plight of the noble Sir Anthony Wyvill and his wife, Emily, victims of his jealous half-sister, Margaret Wyvill, who seeks to secure the wealth of the Wyvill estate for herself. To achieve this, she enlists the services of the Foster family, local inn-keepers who run an establishment situated by the Old Dyke on the road from London.

Caught in a storm on the return to his estate with his young daughter, Sir Anthony seeks shelter at the Fosters' inn. Like his sister, he has been acquainted with the family for many years, but he entertains no suspicions about them. In his room, Sir Anthony puts the sleeping child to bed. His own sleep, however, is much disturbed. Pacing the room, he finds a note that provides a dire warning: it states that he has taken shelter in the house of murderers. Anthony searches for evidence and, under his bed, finds numerous articles of rich clothing which he drags out. Immediately he is struck by their horrible smell, and on further examination discovers that the different articles are caked together with blood. In panic, his eyes wander, fast resting upon the crimson hue colouring the floor and bed sheets. Anthony rushes to lift the child from the bed, and:

> Scarcely had he done so, when a strange, cracking noise came upon his ear, as if marching of some sort was suddenly set into action, and, to his astonishment, there shot up, right through the bed from beneath, a sanguinary looking blade, of a double-edged sword, but much thicker, which had he or the child been lying on the spot, must have pierced them through.[42]

The traditional serial-killer narrative was incorporated into the plot of this gruesome penny blood, but also crucially updated with the addition of a ghastly murder machine. With their homemade apparatus, the Fosters frequently murder guests who seek shelter from the regular storms that plague the valley. Travellers are placed in a room that contains a bed, slackly laced so that the sleeper would be sure to lie in its centre. On hearing the snores of the victim, Mr Foster and his burly sons would retire to a room below where they would turn the handles of a wooden box, sending a brutal-looking sword between the floorboards of the guest room and into the body of their victim. Their motive is, of course, to acquire the heavy purses of solitary travellers (see figure 26).[43]

Striking parallels, most notably the common murder machines and serial-killer villains, suggest a relatively short step from *Retribution* to 'The String of Pearls'. In fact, the two serials were almost published simultaneously. But before we continue to explore important innovations in the content of cheap fiction, we must make a note of one more significant influence: the late eighteenth-century gothic. Gothic novels were originally published for and mostly read by middle- and upper-class readers. At the top end were the more canonical works which captured

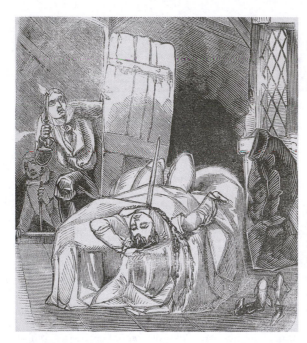

26. The Fosters' brutal murder machine in action. Prest, *Retribution, or the Murder at the Old Dyke* (1846)

the attention of the literati by authors such as Ann Radcliffe, Matthew G. Lewis and Horace Walpole, but at the turn of the nineteenth century these were joined by a small flood of shilling shockers by more obscure writers, a large number of which were published by the famous Minerva Press in London and dispersed among many readers via circulating libraries. Price and distribution networks placed these works beyond the reach of the labouring classes.

Until around 1820 polite readers were entertained by stock narratives typically set in antiquated locations, including castles, foreign lands, abbeys and dungeons, in which spaces past secrets would psychologically or physically haunt the principal characters. The use of the supernatural, often in the form of ghosts, spectres or other beings, suspended these stories in the world of dreams. Violence was pervasive, used to create a mood of morbidity, darkness and fear, and a number of authors were tempted to include rather titillating scenes of tabooed or predatory sexuality. It was no wonder then, with the march of respectability in the early decades of the nineteenth century, that the genre fell into decline through loss of patronage.[44]

Recognising its potential popularity with new readers, publishers of cheap fiction breathed new life into this sub-genre. Not only did

27. Self-
flagellating
nuns on
the cover of
*Reynolds's
Miscellany*,
26 December
1846

they republish in part form some of the more popular novels of
the Minerva Press, but, more importantly, they also used the basic
formula of the gothic tale to create new serials more suited to the
readers they aimed to attract. In analysing this trend, historians and
literary scholars have tended to focus on the output of author-publisher
G. W. M. Reynolds. In 1846, Reynolds used his 'original' gothic tale,
'Wagner the Wehr-Wolf', to launch *Reynolds's Miscellany*, a competitor
to Edward Lloyd's magazines and other new penny journals, such as the
London Journal and the highly respectable *Family Herald*. Littered with
sexual innuendoes and rather racy content, 'Wagner the Wehr-Wolf'
certainly attracted a great deal of attention, not least because of its
depiction of a Carmelite convent in which new novices, often confined
within the walls for past, minor sexual indiscretions, whip themselves
before an altar while half naked (see figure 27).

Reynolds further exploited the gothic genre in his most famous
instalment novel, *The Mysteries of London* (1844–48), continued by *The
Mysteries of the Court of London* (1848–56), after a dispute with his first
publisher, George Vickers. The 'mysteries' tradition of fiction, in which
the criminal and often violent underworld was exposed to the gaze of
wide-ranging audiences, had already been made popular in the work

of Eugene Sue in his serial *Les Mystères de Paris*, published in France in 1842 and translated into English just two years later. Reynolds's *Mysteries* was in many ways a throwback to old turn-of-the-century radicalism, in his demonisation of the upper classes as opposed to the newly emergent middle-class industrial magnates, and in his use of sexual innuendo and titillation to extend his exploration of the exploitation of the labouring classes.[45]

Yet the scholarly focus on G. W. M. Reynolds's use of the gothic has disguised and marginalised Edward Lloyd's similar appropriation which had, in fact, a longer pedigree. Lloyd recognised the potential of the gothic very early on, especially its easy use of horrific violence, a feature which from the very beginning he extended and capitalised on. Lloyd's gothic stories were always exceptionally bloody and must bear at least part of the responsibility for the imposition of the label 'penny blood' to his fictional publications of the period. Lloyd's venture into fiction publishing began with the production of the weekly penny journal *The Calendar of Horrors* with new business partner Thomas Peckett Prest. Short gothic serials comprised the majority of its content and the stories were certainly not short of blood. 'The Tribunal of Blood; or, the Skeleton Arm' is typical. On a stormy night the hero, Don Felix Firardos, is kidnapped by a band of hideous supernatural beings who demand his membership or death. Firardos chooses the former, and in his initiation the beings drink his blood while his arm is stripped to the bone as a mark of distinction.[46] Perhaps Lloyd's most successful gothic serial was the penny novelette *Varney the Vampyre; or, the Feast of Blood* (1846–47), probably written by James Malcom Rymer, which, as a result of popular demand, stretched to 868 pages. Each weekly issue entertained readers with accounts of the blood-sucking activities of a whole community of vampires as well as stories of villagers' attempts to destroy these supernatural pests (see figures 28 and 29).

Much more typical, however, in terms of its plot and even sexual innocence was Elizabeth Caroline Grey's *Villeroy; or, the Horrors of Zindorf Castle* (1844), which contained a very liberal mixture of romance and supernatural hauntings. Caroline Mecklenburg, the heroine, is sent to the castle of Baron Zindorf, her aunt's husband, and during her stay begins to uncover a sequence of frightful secrets, evidence of the past crimes of the wicked Baron, whose castle is plagued by the spectres of

28. *opposite*: Varney sucks the blood from his female victim. Rymer, *Varney the Vampyre* (1846–47)

VARNEY, THE VAMPYRE;

OR,

THE FEAST OF BLOOD

A Romance.

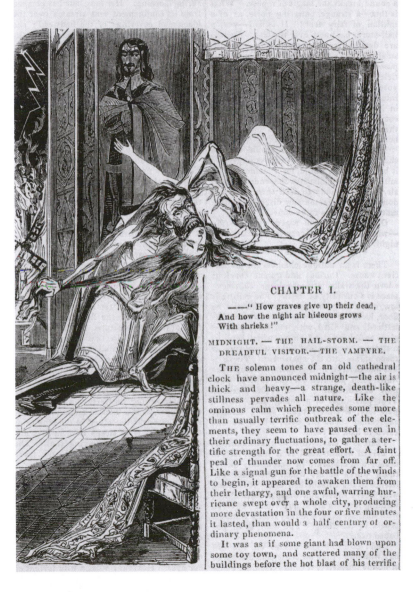

CHAPTER I.

> ——" How graves give up their dead,
> And how the night air hideous grows
> With shrieks !"

MIDNIGHT. — THE HAIL-STORM. — THE
DREADFUL VISITOR.—THE VAMPYRE.

THE solemn tones of an old cathedral clock have announced midnight—the air is thick and heavy—a strange, death-like stillness pervades all nature. Like the ominous calm which precedes some more than usually terrific outbreak of the elements, they seem to have paused even in their ordinary fluctuations, to gather a terrific strength for the great effort. A faint peal of thunder now comes from far off. Like a signal gun for the battle of the winds to begin, it appeared to awaken them from their lethargy, and one awful, warring hurricane swept over a whole city, producing more devastation in the four or five minutes it lasted, than would a half century of ordinary phenomena.

It was as if some giant had blown upon some toy town, and scattered many of the buildings before the hot blast of his terrific

"Well, it may be so." cried the blacksmith, "but still it's good advice, and as I said before it comes to this—is we to be afraid ot lay down in our beds at night, or isn't we?"

Before any reply could be made to this interrogatory, the old clock that was in the public-house parlour struck the hour of eleven, and another peal of thunder seemed to be answering to the tinkling sounds.

"It's a rough night," said one, "I thought there would be a storm before morning by the look of the sun at setting—it went down with a strange fiery redness behind a bank of clouds. I move for going home."

"Who talks of going home," cried the blacksmith, "when vampires are abroad? hasn't old Timothy said, that a stormy night was the very one to settle the thing in."

"No," cried another, "he did not say night at all."

A great many efforts were made to get him to say more, particularly with reference to the case under consideration, as being no common one, but the octogenarian had made his effort, and he only replied to the remonstrances of those who, alternately by coaxing and bullying, strove to get information from him, by a vacant stare.

"It's of no use," said the butcher, "you'll get nothing more now from old Timothy; he's done up now, that's quite clear, and ten to one if the excitement of to-night won't go a good way towards slaughtering him before his time."

"I don't care whether he said night or day; I've made up my mind to do something; there's no doubt about it but that a vampyre is about the old church. Who'll come with me and ferret it out? it will be good service done to everybody's fireside."

29. The villagers plunge a stake into the heart of Clara Crofton's body to ensure the vampire does not strike again. Rymer, *Varney the Vampyre* (1846–47)

his murdered victims. Predictably, Caroline falls in love with the hero of the tale, Claudio, the deprived heir of the castle who has returned to claim his rightful inheritance. The Baron's attempt to wed Caroline to his henchman, the evil Count Durlack, encourages Claudio into the castle to rescue her, the violent encounters of this feat forming the climax of the serial.[47]

The romantic plot provided the narrative glue and also inner satisfaction for readers. However, it was the elaborate illustrations and descriptions of gruesome violence which attracted them in the first place and informed lasting memories of the story. William Edwin Adams may have been too poor to buy Lloyd's penny bloods, but remembered 'the "fearful joy" I used to snatch from them every week through the window of a small newsvendor's shop in the town' where he lived. Adams borrowed a copy of *Villeroy* from a friend and when he later recalled his experience of reading the tale he made no mention of the romantic sentiment, referring instead to 'the villainous personages that passed through [secret] doors, the crimes that were committed in [secret] passages, and the sufferings that were endured in [secret] dungeons, [which] were depicted and combined in such a manner as to make the reader … dream dreadful dreams'.[48] Thus *Villeroy* evoked horror in the breasts of its readers. Horror is, for the most part, a response to the violence of supernatural beings which interact with the world of nightmares. Such beings can never be eradicated or even punished, and hence any success in containing or suspending their violence is only temporary. However, the ability of rational human beings to recognise their essential unreality means that horror experienced by readers is ultimately pleasurable and typically addictive.

But gothic fiction and horrific violence did not form the bulk of the output from Edward Lloyd's publishing house in Salisbury Square. The far larger proportion of serials were 'sentimental domestic stories', yet certainly no less violent or less gruesome. After all, it is in this category that we can place Prest's frightful 'String of Pearls'. The sentimental domestic romance was not a set genre, but rather a melting pot of various styles and influences, including elements of the popular literature of crime, with the common insertion of a murder or even random highwayman character, and elements of the gothic, with the use of the discovery of various secrets inside cupboards or beneath floorboards. Who could not see some gothic influence in the concealment of a murder machine and cannibalistic production line underneath Fleet Street in 'The String of Pearls'? Yet, unlike the traditional gothic narrative, the sentimental domestic romance was set in the present, or the very near past, populated with recognisable

characters facing exaggerated everyday problems. As David Vincent
has written, the 'achievement of the new era was the infusion of the
fabulous with a particular sense of everyday reality'.[49] Penny fiction
provided a 'dramatic working out of moral dilemmas' which the urban
working classes and the precariously positioned lower-middle class
were confronted with.[50] In other words, 'primal fears were clothed in
everyday dress', and made manageable through simple, unambiguous
and morally sound conclusions.[51]

This analysis should sound rather familiar, perhaps reminiscent
of that in the last chapter regarding the popular theatre. For the past
two decades at least scholars of the Victorian period have been eager
to draw our attention to the ways in which stage melodrama became
diffused throughout nineteenth-century culture and society, appearing
in almost every social and cultural arena outside the playhouse,
including parliament, courtrooms, journalism, social investigation
studies and of course fiction, to name just a few. In this chapter, or this
book, I do not intend to contribute to this literature especially as the
free use of the label of 'melodrama' has emptied the term of much of
its meaning and value. But it is logical, helpful and necessary to view
melodrama as one of, if not the, main influence in the production of
penny instalment fiction. Literary hacks working for Edward Lloyd
and theatrical hacks employed in the popular theatres were often the
same people. Plagiarism was rife. Successful plays were issued in penny
instalments only weeks after appearing on stage, and popular serials
were rapidly turned into scripts sometimes even before the story's
conclusion in print. This is precisely what happened in the case of 'The
String of Pearls'. The conversion from stage to print and vice versa was
effortless as tales were told to audiences in almost exactly the same
format, only lengthened or shortened accordingly.

Thus, much of the analysis of the character and function of
melodrama in the previous chapter applies here. Serials were concerned
with simplistic binaries of good and evil. They contained characters
who were easily identifiable as heroes, heroines and villains. A sense
of nostalgia expressed through a preference for the country over the
town, for past values over the present, pervades the narrative. Familial
and personal conflicts and tragedies form the basis of the plot, but
usually conclude happily. Pure and innocent romance is all-important.
And, like theatrical melodrama, extreme violence is expertly woven
into the storyline. Serial domestic romances were almost always very
bloody romances. Murders occur with almost unbelievable frequency.
Seducers murder their victims, villains murder those who obstruct
their paths to fortune, heroes and villains clash in life-changing

combats, disappointed lovers commit suicide; people are variously stabbed, bludgeoned, chocked, suffocated, shot, set fire to, thrown from extreme heights or murdered by machines. In sum, cheap serials were about the elaborate disposal of lots of people in as many different ways as could be imagined. But they always concluded with the romantic and moral union of the lovers and the detection and just punishment of the violent villain(s).

It might be useful at this stage to add another layer to the analysis. Whereas gothic fiction used violence to evoke horror in readers, sentimental domestic romances created a feeling of terror through the use of essentially recognisable, everyday villains. The triumph of good over evil which brought a decisive end to the violence made such feelings of terror pleasurable and addictive for readers. Like stage melodramas, cheap serials were meant to comfort audiences, to restore a sense of community among them, in the process of entertaining them. Despite the overwhelming similarity in the general plot structure of sentimental domestic romances published by Edward Lloyd, close reading of one particular serial might assist in the identification of the particular anxieties authors sought first to expose and second to appease or domesticate. The success of T. P. Prest's 'String of Pearls' makes it an ideal place to begin.

Literary scholar Sally Powell has already explored in some depth the social context of 'The String of Pearls', particularly in relation to other penny bloods containing plots about cadavers. For Powell, the story gave voice to profound social anxiety about aggressive commercial forces generated by the industrial city, and this theme became embodied in Sweeney Todd's murder machine, at the beginning of a sophisticated production line, which transformed unsuspecting customers into a highly marketable product: meat pies.[52] The sale of bodies, even though in disguised form, highlighted the commoditisation of the corpse in urban society, a theme regularly used in other penny bloods that contained the character of the bodysnatcher, a figure who had long occupied an important place in the public nightmare, but whose notoriety had deepened with the expansion of the trade in the early nineteenth century as demand increased from the anatomy schools.[53] Furthermore, Powell argued that Mrs Lovett's pies drew on concerns about the use of diseased meat in products for human consumption, and, even more particularly, fears about the vulnerability of urban foodstuffs to corporeal contamination as a result of badly maintained sewage systems and overcrowded burial grounds.[54] In an environment in which the labouring classes had become isolated from the original source of their food and, due to a lack of adequate cooking facilities, were forced to rely on ready-made meals, it was easy to fan fears about the content of popular foods such as pies, especially as the working classes were far from ignorant.[55]

Powell, usefully, went further still. Through the characters of Lovett's bakers, who are sequentially imprisoned in the pie manufactory, she explored the exploitation of the urban industrial worker. Not only is the baker's entire existence subsumed by his employment, but his place on the production line, involving him only in the assembly of the pies, alienates him from the product. Moreover, his employers, Todd and Lovett, relieve themselves of responsibility for his welfare.[56] Again, we could extend this discussion, strengthening Powell's arguments about the context of the tale. For example, the choice of a bakery and the production of pies might have been quite deliberate. While many skilled, semi-skilled and unskilled labourers in London had direct experience of the production line through the disintegration of the traditional trades, the baking trade had become especially notorious. The long hours, low pay and unsavoury working conditions had prompted a government inquiry around the same time as the publication of the serial, in which attention focused on the reduced life expectancy of the large number of apprentices and journeymen who were forced to work and sleep in dark, suffocating cellars.[57] Those who became too ill for work were replaced with young recruits coming to London for the purpose, a situation replicated in 'The String of Pearls'.

Although important, we should not dwell for too long upon the theme of industrial capitalism in 'The String of Pearls'. After all, it was nothing new. Melodrama on the stage and in print often gave voice to the 'fear and disorientation brought about by the rise of a market economy that disregarded traditional morality, in which the poor were allowed to suffer'.[58] We must not let this theme distract our attention from the basic plot which made this tale stand out: the creation of a sophisticated machine for the murder of urban dwellers and its concealment. As we shall see, the extreme violence at the centre of this tale is vital for understanding its appeal and its place within a very violent early Victorian popular culture. Prest provided readers with a bloody description of the machine in operation and the ease of its concealment:

> There was a piece of flooring turning upon a centre and the weight of the chair when a bolt was withdrawn, by means of a simple leverage from the inner room, weighed down one end of the top, which, by a little apparatus, was to swing completely round, there being another chair on the under surface, which thus became the

30. Sweeney
Todd's murder
machine in action.
Prest, *The String of
Pearls* (1850)

upper chair, exactly resembling the one in which the unhappy customer was supposed to be 'polished off'.[59]

The provision of such intricate details matches that in *Retribution* described above. In both serials, Prest and Lloyd were also sensitive to the desire of their barely literate audiences to see the murder machines in action, satisfying them with very graphic illustrations. While one image could tell the whole story in *Retribution*, in *The String of Pearls* readers were presented with a sequence of woodcuts representing different parts of the machine and production line, one of which was, of course, Todd's lethal barber's chair (see figure 30).

The tale of Sweeney Todd, therefore, demonstrated the potential for gross, unrestrained violence, actual, visual and metaphorical, under the cloak of an expanding and unregulated metropolis. Melodramatic penny bloods and plays, as we saw in the previous chapter, were dominated by a sense of nostalgia and promulgated myths of a past golden age. This theme was central to the inherently conservative outlook of early Victorian popular culture as the simplicities of past or village life were 'preferred to the city where order was overturned and custom replaced by lawlessness'.[60]

Therefore, accounts of criminal activity in cheap fiction typically emphasised the ease of concealment in the dense, anonymous metropolis. G. W. M. Reynolds's *Mysteries of London* presented to readers gloomy labyrinths of dark, frightening streets and alleys. As Reynolds writes of one infamous district, the Mint, 'the houses ... give one the idea of those dens in which murder may be committed without the least chance of detection ... yet that district swarms with population'.[61] In *Ada the Betrayed; or the Murder at the Old Smithy*, by James Malcolm Rymer, murders frequently occur in the dark corners of public streets in London. Moreover, a contrast is established between the illicit and sometimes violent activities of the Thames watermen and the villains, Jacob Grey and Squire Learmont, whose cold-blooded murders alarm the fragile community.[62] The theme is replicated in 'factual' accounts of violent crime presented to the very same audience in the broadsides we examined in chapter 3 and in the new Sunday press, the subject of our next chapter. Reports of horrendous murders routinely opened with a declaration of the terrible nature of the crime and the shock experienced in the neighbourhood on its discovery. These statements were followed by accounts of witnesses who either revealed that the murder might have been prevented if members of the community had not turned a blind eye, or highlighted significant gaps in local knowledge that allowed such a horrid crime to occur.

In 'The String of Pearls', the social evil of anonymity is successfully encapsulated in the character of the villain, Sweeney Todd, who, under the dark cloak of the metropolis, and by taking advantage of the fragility of modern urban communities, could continue to operate his murder machine for years without raising the suspicions of his neighbours. Although some thought the barber was 'a little cracked', the people in the local community genuinely respected this seemingly well-to-do businessman.[63] His portrait on the first number of the 1850 novelette further emphasises his external normality. The illustration suggests that Todd is obviously the villain of the tale, but readers accustomed to stock characters would have understood that others in the story were easily deceived (see figure 31).

Anonymity and community instability again arise in the selection of the serial killer's victims. On the one hand, Sweeney Todd and Mrs Lovett prey upon strangers, new arrivals to the metropolis, without family or friends to track their movements. Todd pulls the frightful

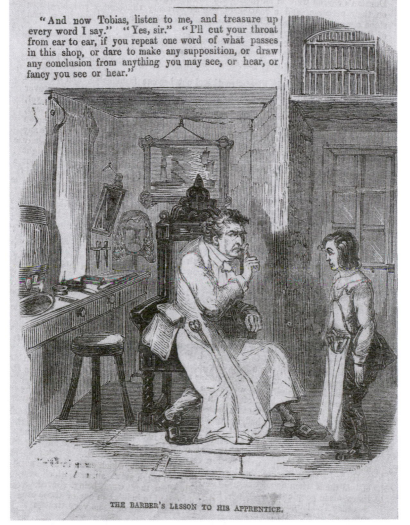

THE
STRING OF PEARLS:
OR,
THE SAILOR'S GIFT.

A ROMANCE OF PECULIAR INTEREST.

"And now Tobias, listen to me, and treasure up every word I say." "Yes, sir." "I'll cut your throat from ear to ear, if you repeat one word of what passes in this shop, or dare to make any supposition, or draw any conclusion from anything you may see, or hear, or fancy you see or hear."

THE BARBER'S LESSON TO HIS APPRENTICE.

31. Portrait of Sweeney Todd, on the first number of Prest's *The String of Pearls* (1850)

lever to dispose of Captain Thornhill, a gentleman recently returned from sea, and Mrs Lovett imprisons a new baker in the ghastly vaults, the self-proclaimed orphaned and friendless Jarvis Williams.[64] On the other hand, opportunity dictates that Todd and Lovett must sometimes select their victims from within the community. While Mrs Lovett uses her charm to encourage the local law students who dine at her shop to visit her friend, the barber, for a shave, local men with family and even substantial connections who visit Todd's shop also vanish without trace, their loved ones appearing at various points in the narrative to question their mysterious disappearance.[65]

As an increasing number of Londoners, from the 'born and bred' to the recently arrived, fall victim to Todd's murder machine, we can see how it acts as a particularly potent metaphor for the early nineteenth-century metropolis, touching upon a range of fears about death in the city. Urban mortality remained a critical problem in the nineteenth century and had been intensified by the accelerated growth of the city. London's population remained incapable of reproducing itself let alone furnishing any natural increase during the first half of the century. The rising population was, in large part, sustained by the influx of immigrants from the countryside of south-east England.[66] The 1830s and 1840s, when penny bloods flourished and the tale of Sweeney Todd was conceived, were also two especially bad decades for life expectancy. Poor nutrition and squalid living conditions encouraged the spread of disease and increased morality rates.[67] Thus, like the mid-nineteenth-century metropolis, Todd's machine sucked in newcomers, shattering their hopes and expectations, while also voraciously devouring the local population. The large number of victims, their anonymity and the mechanical nature of their deaths formed a frightening parallel with the condition of the faceless, poor, urban mass.

Hence the specific setting of the tale of Sweeney Todd in Fleet Street, the very heart of old London, and its popularity and resonance with its intended audience, as well as the persistent confusion and significance of the year in which the story is placed (sometimes c. 1785, sometimes a year early in the nineteenth century). The narrative invoked their particular fears about urban change as it directly reflected contemporary debates about modern urban governance and regulation, or, more accurately, the lack of it. Programmes of metropolitan improvement and beautification centred mainly on the fashionable West End, and when these plans did encroach on the old City, street widening and slum clearance tended to exacerbate problems in neighbouring slums as no provisions were made for the newly homeless poor. Certainly little effort was made by the authorities to upgrade old infrastructure to support the growing population. Such problems were replicated in the expanding districts to the south and especially to the east of the City, where the combination of jerry-building, high rents and overcrowding created new slums. Without serious government intervention and regulation, old London hung like a yoke around the necks of nineteenth-century lower-class Londoners, restrictive and strangling.

Population growth combined with high urban mortality had led to overcrowding in both old, confined inner-city churchyards and new burial grounds in the East End and south London, locations that the labouring poor were forced to use and reside next to through lack of money. Outrageous sights often confronted those attending funerals and those whose windows overlooked churchyards. To make room for new interments, gravediggers were often forced to unearth relatively fresh graves and chop up bodies for alternative disposal.[68] And those who did not witness these scenes read about them in the popular press.[69] Mutilations of corpses by gravediggers and by Sweeney Todd clashed unambiguously with popular ideas and beliefs about death and the body. As a strong tie was perceived to exist between the body and the soul for an undefined period of time after death, the preservation and totality of the corpse was of paramount importance in preparing the dead for their journey into and life in the next world.[70] However, where the gravediggers inadequately disposed of the body parts they chopped up, Sweeney Todd turned his victims into a valuable commodity. Todd's murder machine could, therefore, be regarded as a macabre solution to the mounting dead in the city.

Furthermore, although the resurrection man continued to occupy a central place in the public nightmare, the Anatomy Act of 1832 had transformed these traditional, inherited fears into very modern ones. Through this legislation, the government effectively legalised a branch of the trade in bodies by bequeathing the unclaimed workhouse dead to the anatomy schools, thus placing this horrid and offensive fate within the realm of possibility for all of limited or unstable incomes.[71] The factory-like construction and discipline of the Victorian workhouse could only have made matters worse, and perhaps served as an inspiration for Thomas Prest as he wrote 'The String of Pearls'. Here was a murder machine designed to deal with the urban masses and ensure that their remains would be put to good use. Popular fears even generated rumours that 'children in workhouses were killed to make pies with', and that the bodies of aged paupers 'were employed to manure the guardians' fields to save the expense of coffins'.[72]

While as many bodies as possible continued to be crammed beneath the soil of the churchyards, other more enterprising sextons and private individuals tried other methods to cope with the large numbers of urban dead, including the use of vaults or cellars directly beneath places of human use and habitation.[73] What horrified the public most about these interments was that the bodies, within such close proximity to the living and without adequate protection, posed a real danger to human life. The belief that decaying bodies emitted noxious gases which made people sick and, with enough exposure, could kill, had become fairly widespread in London society.[74] Stories about new and old vaults being opened and workmen suffering disease and death from the dreadful odours which poured into the air circulated in society and fed into urban myths that pervaded popular culture, such as that of Sweeney Todd. Congregations throughout nineteenth-century London, it would seem, were frequently disturbed by the stench of the dead who lay beneath the floor or in the yard outside.[75]

St Dunstan's Church in Fleet Street, under which Todd stored the bodies of his victims until they could be put into pies, had been the centre of a controversy just a decade earlier when the vaults of the church were opened as part of the renovations. Because of the danger, the labourers employed for the job were supplied with brandy and were only able to complete the removal of bodies 'under the influence of a half-drunken excitement'. Within just a few hours, one labourer, William Mutton, 'complained of a nauseous taste in the mouth and throat, severe pain in the chest, accompanied with a cough'. His skin soon turned yellow, and when removing his last body he 'was rendered unconscious for a considerable period'. Mutton's death soon after this was attributed to the effect of the effluvium.[76] This tale may well have been part of the inspiration for the story of Sweeney Todd and perhaps the memory of bodies being removed from vaults underneath that church lent some credibility to 'The String of Pearls', which, after all, was often advertised to have been 'founded on fact'.[77]

Although 'The String of Pearls', like many other serials, used violence combined with recognisable situations to play upon the anxieties of the labouring classes derived at times from very specific aspects of urban life, they also comforted their readers, and ensured feelings of terror were both pleasurable and addictive, by always including a happy, or, at the very least, a morally resolved, ending. In 'The String of Pearls', Sweeney Todd and Mrs Lovett's enterprise is discovered and eradicated, and the villains are destroyed. The lovers, Mark Ingestrie and Johanna Oakley, are reunited, as Lovett's cook masquerading as Jarvis Williams is discovered to be the long-lost sailor on his liberation from the bakehouse. Readers were therefore appeased in the palatable reassurances about everyday life provided by penny-blood authors. But crucially, these resolutions offered no solutions to the social problems experienced by readers touched upon in the stories. Penny bloods presented a useful mechanism for venting social frustrations; they did not suggest readers should protest against the established order or seek change, but instead aimed at gently assimilating readers into their new environment.

The comforting, steadfast belief in the existence of a larger moral order despite the perceived disintegration of society is also reinforced by penny bloods through the frequent use of characters who have knowledge of the villain's crimes and haunt him until justice prevails. In 'The String of Pearls', Captain Thornhill's loyal dog pesters the barber and draws attention to the Fleet Street shop by refusing to leave without his master. More often though, villains are harangued by women driven mad through violence experienced in their youth, at times at the hands of the villain himself. Not only do these characters add to the morbid atmosphere of the serials, they also remind readers constantly of the overarching operation of the moral occult. In *Ben Bolt; or the Perils of a Sailor* (1850), the Weird Woman of the Ruins torments the villain, Sir Raymond, rambling on about his violent crimes:

> 'Ask thine own conscience, where the dark deeds of the past are written in the characters of blood! – aye, blood! – the blood of the good and innocent. Remember the ill-starred Emeline, who, in all the pride of youth and beauty, perished by thy remorseless hands!'[78]

Mad Maud, deranged as a result of the murder of her fiancé on their wedding day by the evil blacksmith Andrew Britton, sees it as her personal mission to expose his multiple crimes in J. M. Rymer's bestselling *Ada the Betrayed; or, the Murder at the Old Smithy* (Lloyd, 1843). Despite Britton's long journey to London and his attempts to hide in the many corners of the vast metropolis, Mad Maud seeks him out and raves very publicly about the blood that stains his hands. Justice is realised and the moral order restored in the final chapter when Britton falls to his death during a police chase and Mad Maud, watching the event, recovers her senses.[79]

It is very tempting to close our analysis at this point, but we still need to reconcile these comforting and even communally bonding messages with the very lurid not to mention almost limitless descriptions and images of violence contained in the penny bloods. Violence in penny bloods was as confronting as in the popular theatres. Every single detail of a murder was provided for readers to ponder, in order to bring the scene to life as far as possible. We have already provided a taste of the relish with which Sweeney Todd's customers were polished off,

32. Andrew
Britton the
blacksmith
murders Jacob
Grey with a meat
cleaver in *Ada the
Betrayed; or, the
Murder at the Old
Smithy* (1843)

including the many accounts of throat-cutting used by the barber in
more challenging situations. Todd's machine may have been somewhat
unique, but the quantity of gore provided for readers was typical. For
instance, the murder of Jacob Grey by his former associate, Andrew
Britton, and former employer, Squire Learmont, in *Ada, the Betrayed*,
although more mundane or standard, is described with at least equal
vivacity:

> Grey then suddenly pushed a chair between himself and Britton
> and fled to the window. Learmont turned his eyes away as he saw
> Britton step over the obstruction with the cleaver uplifted. Scream
> after scream burst from Jacob Grey as he stood with the back of
> his head against the window. There was then an awful crashing
> sound, one gurgling shriek, and a noise of broken glass. 'Kill him!
> Kill him!' gasped Learmont. 'Keep him not in agony!' The cleaver
> descended again, a heavy fall succeeded, and then all was still.

While blood sprayed upon Learmont's hands, 'crimson spots of human
gore' clung to the excited countenance of the blacksmith.[80]

This stomach-churning scene was accompanied by a very graphic illustration, though this was not placed beside the text (see figure 32). Woodcut illustrations were provided with all numbers of penny novelettes and most instalments of serials published in weekly miscellanies. But in order to sustain the interest of readers, and draw out particularly violent scenes, pictures of specific incidents were often scattered throughout the serial. From the examples of woodcuts from serial fiction included in this chapter, we can see how much care was taken to represent the murder as faithfully, if not as accurately, as possible, from the violent act itself – sucking blood from a victim's neck, stabbing or bludgeoning a victim, or sending a large sword through the centre of the bed of a sleeping victim – to the gory consequences, namely the tremendous blood flow. These early Victorian penny bloods almost literally dripped blood. The tremendous quantity of blood depicted, often spraying in various directions from fatal wounds, was harrowing and confrontational.

We have encountered similar illustrations of violence in this book already, on broadsides and even on playbills printed by popular theatres, and we will again in the final chapter, as woodcuts were used by Edward Lloyd in his first newspaper, the *Penny Sunday Times and People's Police Gazette*. But their particular prevalence and importance in new cheap fiction begs, at this stage, some discussion of the growth of the printed image in popular culture. Of course printed images had existed and circulated in pre-industrial plebeian culture, most notably appearing in chapbooks and on cheap broadsides. However, from *c.* 1820 onwards, as a result of the technological advances in printing mentioned above, images increased in number, became more widely available and demonstrated a much greater degree of diversity. Patricia Anderson has described at length the process of democratisation of high art as famous masterpieces were reproduced as wood engravings in periodicals produced for the middle and even lower classes. She has also shown how the image, in the form of topographical and scientific sketches, was used to impart 'useful knowledge' to the deprived masses in publications such as Charles Knight's *Penny Magazine*.[81]

But new images were not just imposed on the people from above. They also came from within as printers and publishers such as Jemmy Catnach, Edward Lloyd and G. W. M. Reynolds also exploited the new technologies and cheap materials available, their visual products reflecting the diverse but peculiar range of tastes, ideals and motivations encompassed by popular culture. At first, the great flood of woodcuts represented an expansion of pre-industrial visual culture, as broadside printers in London became more liberal in the inclusion of woodcuts especially on execution sheets, and the number of sheets printed and sold grew at an outstanding rate. The stock image of the gallows continued to occupy a central place, suggesting that its totemic power lingered until the abolition of public execution in 1868. However, as new printers and publishers began to make use of the image we can also see a gradual transformation of visual culture at work. Woodcuts became more elaborate, and much more closely tied to the narrative they were meant to represent. Eventually, they were replaced by ornate and detailed wood engravings, and as the people became more image-conscious, the stark symbols and codes which sustained the frequent application of a limited number of woodcuts to many different scenarios fell into disuse. The theme of violence, as it emerged as a prominent theme in early nineteenth-century popular culture, became intertwined in this process, its visual presentation, first in woodcuts and then in wood engravings, was intensified.

During the 1840s, at the very height of this process, publishers sought to capitalise on the voracious appetite of working men and women for elaborate pictures. Edward Lloyd and G. W. M. Reynolds regularly gave away specially printed woodcuts or wood engravings on oversized paper to subscribers of miscellanies. For instance, in 1848, subscribers to *Reynolds's Miscellany* were presented with, 'at an extra charge of only three half-pence, a splendid wood engraving, representing Wilkie's beautiful picture of "The Rent Day". – It will be larger than the sheet of the Miscellany when spread open!'[82] These and illustrations featured on the front pages of serials, were used by working people to decorate bare walls in their dwellings, in the same way broadsides had been used to decorate homes and public houses in the previous centuries, and for a good part of the nineteenth century. It was a practice caricatured in more polite publications, such as *Punch*, and even writers of popular fiction used the tendency to display more morbid pictures to highlight the villainy or violent tendencies of particular characters.[83] But these were exaggerated representations of what was reality, according to reports of social investigators. Henry Mayhew, visiting the home of a woman of the better class of sheep-trotter sellers found that a great portion of the walls of her room 'was covered with cheap engravings "given away with No. 6" of some periodical of "thrilling interest"'.[84] Mayhew found that the increasing prevalence of woodcuts and engravings in periodicals and newspapers had greatly diminished the sale of framed prints in the marketplace.[85]

Images, originally used to illustrate particular scenes in serials, therefore gained an extended life outside the story, perhaps as a reminder of favourite incidents in the tale, but foremost as a form of decoration. And we cannot help but imagine, in terms of their quantity in the serials, that some of those images selected must have been gory representations of very bloody murders, combats or suicides. The display of these images helps to tease out and make much more obvious something already equally present in the production of those images in the first place and the accompanying graphic descriptions of multiple murders that were devoured by large metropolitan audiences: the assertiveness of popular culture, and the way in which the range of entertainments it encompassed posed something of a challenge to respectability and the establishment.

The march of respectability?
The decline and rise of the bloody romance

When printer-compositor Thomas Catling arrived at Edward Lloyd's publishing office seeking employment in 1854, he found the business in the midst of an important transition. The flood of fiction projected from this centre through the streets of the metropolis had largely dried up. Authors 'no longer poured their manuscripts into Salisbury Square', as Lloyd had brought the miscellanies and novelettes to an end.[86] His focus had been diverted by his increasingly successful weekly newspaper, the subject of our next chapter.

Lloyd was not the only penny-blood publisher but he was the most prolific, and therefore his departure from this sector of the print industry was significant. The reasons, however, are less than clear and are in need of some rigorous exploration: why did the penny-blood trade, so popular over the preceding two decades, suddenly come to an end? As we know, Lloyd was a canny businessman with an overriding concern for profit. His publications were innovative in form, but drew upon the themes of the moment in popular culture. Lloyd's decision to close down such a thriving arm of his business would suggest that he was responding to a shift in popular taste, that readers had begun to lose interest in the gory serials and sales had fallen as purchasers had moved on to other literary products. This seems to be confirmed by the rise of several new penny periodicals from the late 1840s onwards, such as the *London Journal*, the *Family Herald* and *Cassell's Family Paper*, their growing circulation rates perhaps evidence of the gradual seduction of Lloyd's subscribers. While these publications continued to satisfy the desire for entertainment, especially through the provision of romantic serials, the tone of these had changed: although exciting, and even at times titillating, the fiction tended to be 'moralistic in tone and directly or indirectly supportive of the same sort of values that charac-terised [Charles Knight's] *Penny Magazine*'.[87] In the removal of the most protracted scenes of violence and gory illustrations, cheap fiction had become 'respectable'.

The decline of the early Victorian penny bloods and the simultaneous rise of a 'purified' penny press would then seem to confirm that which larger narrative histories have posited about nineteenth-century society: the civilisation of the crowd, or, in other words, the taming of popular culture. We could argue that penny bloods, melodramas in popular theatres and murder and execution broadsides represented the last location for the expression of unrespectable or unsuitable themes, such as gross violence. Their emergence in the 1820s and 1830s and rise to prominence in popular culture had assisted programmes pursued by the establishment to tame the streets of London as they formed an alternative outlet for the expression and celebration of disorder. After c. 1850, when the lower orders had supposedly been reformed and assimilated, these entertainments, as the final part of the jigsaw, required modification, namely pacification.

Though, unlike former attempts to tame popular culture, this was not to be achieved by the interference of the establishment, for example the imposition of new forms of entertainment or leisure from above. We have already noted the limited success of the rational recreationalists, including the efforts of Charles Knight, the SDUK and the RTS, to supply the labouring classes with alternative uplifting publications, and despite some public concern over the extremity of the penny bloods, at no stage did the government attempt to outlaw or regulate their production. And if the tastes of the penny-blood audience did change, they did not become more refined, or elevated, as some mid-century commentators hoped they would.[88] The cheap instalment fiction of the second half of the nineteenth century represented no vast improvement in terms of literary accomplishment. Rather, as David Vincent has argued, the genre was gradually emptied of 'the life it once contained', as the situations 'became ever more predictable and ever less recognisable'. Contemporaries similarly drew attention to its sameness and dullness. The systemisation of elementary education by the state had distanced readers from previous oral and literary forms of expression without guiding them on the selection and use of more challenging and fulfilling literary wares.[89]

Readers in the 1880s, for example, thus continued to purchase domestic romances with general storylines not unlike those tales produced by T. P. Prest and J. M. Rymer. However, the very gory or extreme elements had been eliminated. It may be that the gross violence penny-blood-style had become anachronistic. The stabilisation of society after 1850 demonstrated by the defeat of Chartism and subsidence of political unrest, the gradual rise in real wages, and the growing comfort with the urban environment and new structures of authority meant that the specific fears and anxieties that the penny bloods, as well as the melodramas in the previous chapter, gave vent to were no longer of relevance. We could, at this point, conclude that penny bloods, like a number of other entertainments explored in this book, were a part of a discrete phenomenon amongst a particular audience that emerged in response to a peculiar set of social tensions and faded away again in a relatively short period.

But that does not feel particularly satisfactory. In the decline or disappearance of specific phenomena or entertainments, it is too easy to cry change and ignore patterns of continuity. In other words, in looking at the cheap fiction produced for the masses from 1860 onwards for the continuation of a culture of violence, we might well be looking in the wrong place. For example, in this chapter and in previous chapters, we have tied the violent entertainments, especially their narratives, to the social experience of London in the period 1820 to 1870. The emergence of a new generation of Londoners combined with the nationalisation of a new mass culture from mid-century onwards may have called time on a series of phenomena that had served their purpose. This does not mean that violence, including gross or extreme representations of violence, did not appear in other locations. And even if violence ceased to be dominant in mass culture, that does not mean that it was not still prominent.

New printing technology in the mid-nineteenth century made mass audiences not only possible but essential for publishers. Large sums spent on purchasing machinery combined with the unprecedented production from the new equipment meant that it could be much more difficult and unprofitable to cater for smaller audiences. If we take a close look at the circulation rates of those journals of serial fiction present at mid-century and which survived through to the end of the century, we can see a significant leap in their circulation rates after *c.* 1850. For example, the *Family Herald* grew from 125,000 subscriptions in 1849 to 300,000 in 1855, the *London Journal* rose to 450,000 by 1855 and *Cassell's Family Paper* was selling around 285,000 in 1858.[90] These competitors to Lloyd's and Reynolds's weekly miscellanies certainly treated audiences to much less graphic, stomach-churning violence. But we cannot regard these publications as the successors to the penny bloods. They were not attracting a mass *metropolitan* audience.

Rather, improved communication and transportation networks, especially efficient railway, meant that their mass audience was a national one. This had two important implications. First, the violent tales of the penny bloods, so rooted in the metropolitan environment, could not satisfy the tastes of a mass national audience, week in, week out. If, as Vincent suggests, serial fiction became emptied of life and relevance, this was because publishers and authors need to present stories that would appeal across regional divides. Second, although these growing audiences seem to be, on paper, tremendously large, if we think in terms of the national context the numbers acquire a rather different significance. By courting mass, national audiences, publishers encouraged new divisions to open up in the market. Audiences were not just or even always split along class lines. Special journals were now produced for men, for women, for children, for adolescents and, by the last decades of the century, for those with specialist hobbies.

Within the weekly journal and serial fiction market, particularly gross violence re-emerged in the range of publications produced for children, especially adolescent boys. The taste for violence cut across class boundaries. Tales produced for public schoolboys featured youthful heroes ready to use their fists when challenged in order to prove their manliness; when confronted by untamed savages abroad, these heroes showed very little restraint. Lower down the social spectrum, new publishers such as Edwin J. Brett, and former penny-blood publishers, such as John Dicks and George Vickers, reprinted, remarketed and sometimes reinvented the gruesome stories of the penny bloods for a new, juvenile, male, working- and lower-middle-class audience (see figures 33 and 34). Crucial adjustments were made. Youthful heroes with whom readers could identify were inserted into the stories. Although attempts were made to curb the rise of these new penny dreadfuls (as they became known), these were largely unsuccessful, mostly because they were not pursued seriously.[91] The penny dreadfuls were as 'harmless' as their upmarket incarnations. And both were used to teach young males useful lessons about the proper channelling of aggression, including the right moments to resort to violence.[92]

Both sets of publications also provided a useful outlet for the bloodthirsty curiosity of adolescent males. As Peter Marsh has argued, aggressive fantasies are central to the maturation of males regardless of cultural context, and the late Victorians recognised the natural attraction of violence to young males.[93] As one parenting manual of 1880 stated, 'the love of romance and adventure is so strong in the boyish nature that it cannot be repressed and *will* have vent'.[94] The theme of violence was no longer connected to social turbulence, but rather inner turbulence, and as stories connected with the psyche as opposed to the community, they functioned as a different kind of outlet for tension and frustration.

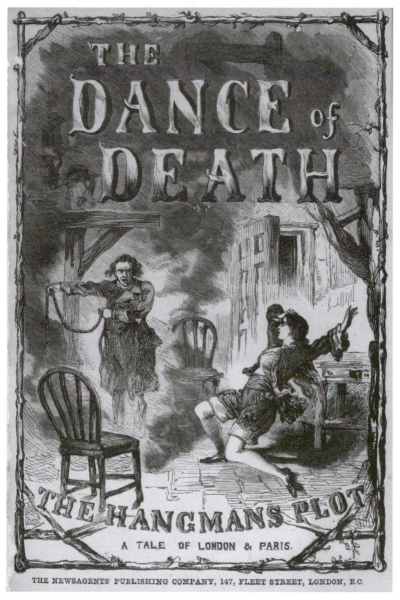

33. Front cover of the penny dreadful *The Dance of Death; or The Hangman's Plot* (1866)

34. The Red Man
of the Gibbet
prepares to 'shave'
a boy who dared
to mock him and
his frightening
Skeleton Crew. *The
Skeleton Crew; or
Wildfire Ned* (1867)

It was in a penny dreadful published by Charles Fox in 1878 and intended for an adolescent male audience that Sweeney Todd made his final nineteenth-century appearance in print. A comparison between this edition and Prest's original 1846 serial highlights the extent of the transformation from penny blood to penny dreadful, especially the dislocation of the story from its original settings. In this comic book, Sweeney Todd is turned into a character of horror, rather than terror, a type of bogeyman located in the world of nightmares instead of the everyday. The addition of a new word to the title of his story in print was no accident: Todd became the *Demon Barber of Fleet Street*. But most telling was the new attention given to the abnormalities and even supernatural occurrences surrounding his birth and childhood. We are told that even Todd did not know his own age, as the church he was christened at was burnt down the day after, his mother and father were dead, the nurse who cared for him was hanged and the doctor had cut his own throat.[95] Finally, at the very moment that Sweeney Todd was hanged, 'the ruins of his shop in Fleet Street fell with a thundering crash, and … the dust and ashes hovering in the air took the form of a huge gibbet, with the figure of a man suspended upon it'.[96]

Notes

1 G. D. Pitt, 'The String of Pearls; or, the Fiend of Fleet Street', February 1847, London, British Library (BL), Add. Mss 43000, pp. 753–815.

2 H. G. Hibbert, *A Playgoer's Memories* (London: G. Richards, 1920), p. 81, F. Hazleton, *Sweeney Todd, The Barber Fiend of Fleet Street; or, the String of Pearls* (London: S. French, 18??) [written for the Bower Saloon, 1862], Mrs H. Young, 'The String of Pearls; or, the Life and Death of Sweeney Todd' [for the Effingham Saloon], May to July 1862, BL, Add. Mss 53014, fo. bb, Anon., 'The String of Pearls', February to March 1861, BL, Add. Mss 53001, fo. f.

3 [T. P. Prest] 'The String of Pearls. A Romance', *People's Periodical and Family Library*, 1 (1846–47), 98–9.

4 Ibid., 361–3, 368 (quote).

5 The anonymity of penny-blood authors has encouraged debate among antiquarians anxious to attribute popular works to specific individuals, and many have argued that James Malcolm Rymer was in fact the author of 'The String of Pearls', among other works often attributed to Prest. Yet the fact of who actually put pen to paper really matters very little, the debate instead highlighting the degree of uniformity within the genre. See, for example, H. Smith, *New Light on Sweeney Todd, Thomas Peckett Prest, James Malcolm Rymer and Elizabeth Caroline Grey* (Bloomsbury: Jarndyce, 2002).

6 For example, J. Rose, *The Intellectual Life of the British Working Classes* (New Haven: Yale University Press, 2001), especially pp. 367–71. Historians who have attempted to explain the phenomenon: R. D. Altick, *The English Common Reader: A Social History of the Mass Reading Public, 1800–1900* (Chicago: University of Chicago Press, 1957), M. Dalziel, *Popular Fiction 100 Years Ago: An Unexplored Tract of Literary History* (London: Cohen & West, 1957), L. James, *Fiction for the Working Man, 1830–1850: A Study of the Literature Produced for the Working Classes in Early Victorian Urban England* (London: Oxford University Press, 1963), M. Vicinus, *The Industrial Muse: A Study of Nineteenth-Century British Working-Class Literature* (New York: Croom Helm, 1974), D. Vincent, *Literary and Popular Culture: England, 1750–1914* (Cambridge: Cambridge University Press, 1989). Antiquarians: M. Anglo, *Penny Dreadfuls and other Victorian Horrors* (London: Jupiter Books, 1977), P. Haining, *The Penny Dreadful: or, Strange, Horrid and Sensational Tales* (London: Gollancz, 1975), E. S. Turner, *Boys will be Boys: The Story of Sweeney Todd, Deadwood Dick, Sexton Blake, Billy Bunter, Dick Barton, et al* (London: Joseph, 3rd edn, 1975).

7 M. Spufford, *Small Books and Pleasant Histories: Popular Fiction and its Readership in Seventeenth-Century England* (Cambridge: Cambridge University Press, 1981), Vincent, *Literacy and Popular Culture*, pp. 197–9, Altick, *The English Common Reader*, pp. 38–41.

8 For example, see Altick, *The English Common Reader*, pp. 328–9.

9 R. S. Schofield, 'The measurement of literacy in pre-industrial England', in J. Goody (ed.), *Literacy in Traditional Societies* (Cambridge: Cambridge University Press, 1968), Schofield, 'The dimensions of illiteracy, 1750–1850', *Explorations in Economic History*, 10 (1973), 437–54.

10 For example, see G. Sutherland, 'Education', in F. M. L. Thompson (ed.), *Cambridge Social History of Britain, 1750–1950. Volume 3: Social Agencies and Institutions* (Cambridge: Cambridge University Press, 1996), pp. 126–31, 141–6, T. W. Laqueur, *Religion and Respectability: Sunday Schools and Working Class Culture 1780–1850* (New Haven: Yale University Press, 1976), P. Gardner, *The Lost Elementary Schools of Victorian England: The People's Education* (London: Croom Helm, 1984).

11 D. Mitch, *The Rise of Popular Literacy in Victorian England: The Influence of Private Choice and Public Policy* (Philadelphia: University of Pennsylvania Press, 1992), pp. 71–8.

12 R. K. Webb, *The British Working Class Reader, 1790–1848: Literacy and Social Tension* (London: Allen & Unwin, 1955), pp. 21–2, Webb, 'Working-class readers in early Victorian England', *English Historical Review*, 65 (1950), 333–51, and R. Crone, 'Reappraising Victorian literacy through prison records', *Journal of Victorian Culture*, 15 (2010), 3–37.

13 I. Dyck, *William Cobbett and Rural Popular Culture* (Cambridge: Cambridge University Press, 1992), P. Hollis, *The Pauper Press: A Study in Working-Class Radicalism of the 1830s* (London: Oxford University Press, 1970), E. P. Thompson, *The Making of the English Working Class* (London: Gollancz, 1963), pp. 781–886, M. Wood, *Radical Satire and Print Culture, 1790–1822* (Oxford: Clarendon Press, 1994).

14 T. Carter, *Memoirs of a Working Man* (London: Charles Knight & Co., 1845), p. 90.

15 C. Thomson, *Autobiography of an Artisan* (London: J. Chapman, 1847), pp. 79–80.

16 S. Pedersen, 'Hannah More meets Simple Simon: tracts, chapbooks and popular culture in late eighteenth-century England', *Journal of British Studies*, 25 (1986), 84–113.

17 D. Vincent, *Bread, Knowledge and Freedom: A Study of Nineteenth-*

Century Working-Class Autobiography (London: Europa, 1981), pp. 136–65.

18 P. Anderson, *The Printed Image and the Transformation of Popular Culture* (Oxford: Clarendon Press, 1991), p. 52.

19 Thomson, *Autobiography of an Artisan*, p. 319.

20 Anderson, *The Printed Image*, p. 81.

21 Select Committee on Newspaper Stamps (Parl. Papers, 1851, XVII.1), [hereafter SC (1851)], evidence of Collet Dobson Collet, p. 151, and evidence of William Edward Hickson, pp. 477–8, T. Frost, *Forty Years' Recollections* (London: Sampson Low, 1880), pp. 80–2, C. Knight, *Passages of a Working Life During Half a Century* (2 vols, London: Bradbury & Evans,1864–65), II, p. 328.

22 Carter, *Memoirs of a Working Man*, p. 90.

23 For more detailed analysis, see chapter 6.

24 I. McCalman, *Radical Underworld: Prophets, Revolutionaries and Pornographers in London, 1795–1840* (Oxford: Clarendon Press, 2nd edn, 2002), pp. 204–21.

25 Ibid., p. 205, V. A. C. Gatrell, *City of Laughter: Sex and Satire in Eighteenth-Century London* (London: Atlantic, 2006).

26 A. Humphreys, 'G. W. M. Reynolds: popular literature and popular politics', *Victorian Periodicals Review*, 16 (1983), 78–88, R. McWilliam, 'The mysteries of G. W. M. Reynolds: radicalism and melodrama in Victorian Britain', in M. Chase and I. Dyck (eds), *Living and Learning: Essays in Honour of J. F. C. Harrison* (Aldershot: Ashgate, 1996), I. Haywood, 'G. W. M. Reynolds and the radicalisation of Victorian serial fiction', *Media History*, 4 (1998), 121–39, Haywood, *The Revolution in Popular Literature: Print, Politics and the People, 1790–1860* (Cambridge: Cambridge University Press, 2004), and most recently the edited collection: A. Humphreys and L. James (eds), *G. W. M. Reynolds: Nineteenth-Century Fiction, Politics and the Press* (Aldershot: Ashgate, 2008).

27 R. McWilliam, 'Lloyd, Edward (1815–1890)', *Oxford Dictionary of National Biography* (Oxford University Press, 2004) [http://www.oxforddnb.com/view/article/16831, accessed 22 October 2008].

28 *People's Periodical and Family Library*, 1 (1846–47), 272.

29 *People's Periodical and Family Library*, 1 (1846–47), 352.

30 James, *Fiction for the Working Man*, p. 37.

31 Ibid., pp. 34–7, Haining, *Penny Dreadful*, p. 14.

32 Altick, *The English Common Reader*, p. 291.

33 *Lloyd's Penny Weekly Miscellany*, 1 (1843), preface.

34 Frost, *Forty Years' Recollections*, pp. 89–90.

35 H. Mayhew, *London Labour and the London Poor* (4 vols, London:

Griffin, Bohn & Co., 1861–62), I, pp. 25–6, 416, III, pp. 388–9, II, pp. 474, 495, T. Okey, *A Basket Full of Memories: An Autobiographical Sketch* (London: J. M. Dent, 1930), p. 20.

36 Mayhew, *London Labour and the London Poor*, I, pp. 25–6.

37 For example, *Turpin's Ride to York* (London: Glover, 1839), *George Barnwell, the City Apprentice* (London: Vickers, 1849), *The Life of Jack Sheppard the Housebreaker* (London: Glover, 1840), *Jack Rann, alias Sixteen String Jack* (London: Purkess, 1845), *Tyburn Tree, or the Mysteries of the Past* (London: Swift & Vickers, 1849). British Library, London (BL), Barry Ono Collection (BOC).

38 Anon., *The Bloody Innkeeper; or Sad and Barbarous News from Gloucester-shire: Being a True Relation how the Bodies of Seven Men and Women were Found Murthered in a Garden belonging to a House in Putley, near Gloucester* (London, 1675), Anon., *A Warning Piece against the Crime of Murder; or an Account of Many Extraordinary and Most Providential Discoveries of Secret Murders* (London, 1752), the tale of Jonathan Bradford in Anon., *The Cries of Blood, or the Juryman's Monitor* (London, 1767), pp. 41–7, M. G. Lewis, *The Monk* (London: Printed for J. Saunders, 1796), ch. 3.

39 *The History of Sawney Beane and his Family, Robbers and Murderers* (London, n.d., probably *c.* 1700), Scotland, National Library (NLS), Lauriston Castle Collection, LC.2737, no. 7, Captain A. Smith, *Memoirs of the Life and Times of the Famous Jonathan Wild, together with the History and Lives of Modern Rogues* (London, 1726), pp. 138–44, Captain C. Johnson, *A General History of the Lives and Adventures of most Famous Highwaymen, Murderers, Robbers and Thief-Takers* (London, 1758), pp. 155–61, Anon., *The History of Sawney Beane and his Family* (London, 1800?), Anon., *The Life of Richard Turpin, a Notorious Highwayman, to which is added, The Life of Sawney Beane, the Man-Eater* (London, 1800), pp. 43–8.

40 [T. P. Prest?], *Jonathan Bradford, or the Murder at the Roadside Inn. A Romance* (London: Lloyd, 1851), BL, BOC. Ronald Holmes refers to a penny-blood version of Sawney Beane written by Prest and published by Lloyd during the 1840s, entitled, *Sawney Beane; the Man-Eater of Mid-Lothian*. However, I can find no trace of this version. See Holmes, *The Legend of Sawney Beane* (London: F. Muller, 1975), p. 22.

41 R. Pratt, 'The Murderers', *Lloyd's Penny Atlas*, 1 (1843), 738–40, Anon., *The Bloody Innkeeper; or Sad and Barbarous News from Gloucester-shire*, p. 5. See also J. Kane, 'The Guilty Father; or, the Murderer of the Hovel', *Lloyd's Penny Atlas*, 1 (1843), 241–2, Anon., 'The Murderers of Penruddock', *Lloyd's Penny Miscellany*, 2 (1844), 1–3, J. Turner, 'The Murder at the Inn', *Lloyd's Penny Miscellany*, 2 (1844), 689–95.

42 [T. P. Prest or J. M. Rymer], *Retribution; or, the Murder at the Old Dyke* (London: Lloyd, 1846), pp. 1–20 (quote p. 17), BL, BOC.

43 Ibid., pp. 183–9.

44 W. P. Day, *In the Circles of Fear and Desire: A Study of Gothic Fantasy* (Chicago: University of Chicago Press, 1985), E. Markman, *The History of Gothic Fiction* (Edinburgh: Edinburgh University Press, 2000), J. E. Hogle (ed.), *The Cambridge Companion to Gothic Fiction* (Cambridge: Cambridge University Press, 2002), D. Punter, *The Literature of Terror: A History of Gothic Fictions from 1765 to the Present Day* (London: Longman, 1980), D. P. Varma, *The Gothic Flame: Being a History of the Gothic Novel in England: Its Origins, Efflorescence, Disintegration and Residuary Influences* (London: Scarecrow, 1987).

45 McWilliam, 'The mysteries of G. W. M. Reynolds'.

46 T. P. Prest, 'The Tribunal of Blood; or, the Skeleton Arm', *Calendar of Horrors*, 2 (1836), 153–5, 167–8, 223–4.

47 E. C. Grey, *Villeroy; or, the Horrors of Zindorf Castle* (London: Lloyd, 1844), BL, BOC.

48 W. E. Adams, *Memoires of a Social Atom* (London: Hutchinson & Co., 1903), pp. 101–6.

49 Vincent, *Literacy and Popular Culture*, p. 205.

50 Ibid., p. 206.

51 M. Vicinus, 'Helpless and unfriended: nineteenth-century domestic melodrama', *New Literary History*, 13 (1981), 128.

52 S. Powell, 'Black markets and cadaverous pies: the corpse, urban trade and industrial consumption in the penny blood', in A. Maunder and G. Moore (eds), *Victorian Crime, Madness and Sensation* (Aldershot: Ashgate, 2004), p. 46.

53 Ibid., pp. 46–8, R. Richardson, *Death, Dissection and the Destitute* (London: Routledge & Kegan Paul, 1988), pp. 51–60.

54 Powell, 'Black markets', pp. 49–50.

55 A. S. Wohl, *Endangered Lives: Public Health in Victorian Britain* (London: Dent, 1983), p. 48, J. Burnett, *Plenty and Want: A Social History of Food in England from 1815 to the Present Day* (London: Routledge, 3rd edn, 1989), pp. 86–98.

56 Powell, 'Black markets', pp. 51–3.

57 Evidence by Dr Guy Before the Sanitary Commission in Reference to Persons Employed in the Baking Trade (Parl. Papers, 1847–48, LI.367), pp. 1–3.

58 R. McWilliam, *The Tichborne Claimant: A Victorian Sensation* (London: Hambledon Continuum, 2007), p. 256.

59 'The String of Pearls', 380–3.

60 R. McWilliam, 'Melodrama and the historians', *Radical History Review*, 78 (2000), 59.

61 G. W. M. Reynolds, *The Mysteries of London* (2nd Series, 4 vols, London, 1844–48), II, pp. 187–8.

62 J. M. Rymer, 'Ada the Betrayed; or, the Murder at the Old Smithy', *Lloyd's Penny Weekly Miscellany*, 1 (1843), 87, 102–4.

63 'The String of Pearls', 98, [Prest] *The String of Pearls; or, the Barber of Fleet Street* (London: Lloyd, 1850), p. 2. BL, BOC.

64 'The String of Pearls', 98–9, 162–5, [Prest] *The String of Pearls; or, the Barber of Fleet Street*, pp. 4–7, 56–9.

65 'The String of Pearls', 115, 313–15, 367–8, [Prest] *The String of Pearls; or, the Barber of Fleet Street*, pp. 17–20.

66 L. D. Schwarz, *London in the Age of Industrialisation: Entrepreneurs, Labour Force and Living Conditions, 1750–1850* (Cambridge: Cambridge University Press, 1992), p. 128.

67 A. B. Hilton, *A Mad, Bad and Dangerous People? England, 1783–1846* (Oxford: Oxford University Press, 2006), pp. 574–6, S. Szreter and A. Hardy, 'Urban fertility and mortality patterns', in M. J. Daunton (ed.), *The Cambridge Urban History of Britain. Volume 3: 1840–1950* (Cambridge: Cambridge University Press, 2000), p. 671, S. Szeter and G. Mooney, 'Urbanisation, mortality and the standard of living debate: new estimates of the expectation of life at birth in nineteenth-century British cities', *Economic History Review*, 51 (1998), 84–112, F. M. L. Thompson, 'Town and city', in F. M. L. Thompson (ed.), *The Cambridge Social History of Britain, 1750–1900. Volume 1: Regions and Communities* (Cambridge: Cambridge University Press, 1990), p. 49.

68 Select Committee on the Improvement of the Health of Towns: Report on the Effect of Interment of Bodies in Towns (Parl. Papers, 1842, X.349) [hereafter SC (1842)], evidence of William Chamberlain, p. 130, Thomas Munns, p. 28, George Whittaker, p. 20.

69 For example, in *Lloyd's Weekly Newspaper*, 23 March 1845 p. 3, 24 August 1845 p. 5, 9 September 1849 p. 5, 16 September 1849 p. 5, 30 September 1849 p. 5, 21 October 1849 p. 5, 2 June 1850 p. 1, 18 December 1853 p. 7.

70 Richardson, *Death, Dissection and the Destitute*, p. 7.

71 Ibid., pp. 51–60.

72 M. A. Crowther, *The Workhouse System, 1834–1929: The History of an English Social Institution* (London: Batsford, 1981), p. 31.

73 SC (1842), evidence of Rev. John Channing Abdy, pp. 81–2.

74 Ibid., evidence of John Irwin, pp. 5–8, evidence of Moses Solomons, p. 12, evidence of George Whittaker, p. 20, James Michael Lane, p. 32, William Miller, p. 85.

75 SC (1840), evidence of George Alfred Walker, pp. 188, 211–13, 217, SC (1842), evidence of Samuel Pitts, pp. 8–11, evidence of William Burn, pp. 14–16, Rev. Henry John Knapp, p. 46, G. F. Collier, p. 114.

76 SC (1840), evidence of Alfred George Walker, p. 214, SC (1842), appendix, letter from G. A. Walker to W. A. McKinnon M.P., 3 May 1842, p. 211.

77 [Prest], *The String of Pearls; or, the Barber of Fleet Street*, Playbill from the Britannia Theatre, Monday 1 March 1847, BL.376.

78 *Ben Bolt; or, the Perils of a Sailor* (London: Lloyd, 1850), p. 22. BL, BOC.

79 J. M. Rymer 'Ada, the Betrayed; or, the Murder at the Old Smithy', *Lloyd's Penny Weekly Miscellany*, 1 (1843), especially pp. 1–5, 149–51, 229–32, 297–9, 824–8. The story was republished by Lloyd as a penny novelette in 1847. See also *Paul the Reckless; or the Fugitive's Doom* (London: Lloyd, 1846), T. P. Prest, *The Hampstead Murder; or, the Prediction* (London: Lloyd, 1845), especially p. 92. Both in BL, BOC.

80 Rymer, 'Ada', 750.

81 Anderson, *The Printed Image*. See also C. Fox, *Graphic Journalism in England during the 1830s and 1840s* (New York: Garland, 1988), B. Maidment, *Reading Popular Prints, 1790–1870* (Manchester: Manchester University Press, 1996).

82 *Reynolds's Miscellany*, 3 (1848), 224.

83 *Punch*, 17 (1849), 117, Reynolds, *The Mysteries of London*, series one, II, pp. 5–6.

84 Mayhew, *London Labour and the London Poor*, I, p. 171. See also I, pp. 47, 110, and III, pp. 1, 242, and Statistical Society of London, 'Report on St-George's-in-the-East', *Journal of the Statistical Society of London*, 11 (1848), 218, Anderson, *The Printed Image*, pp. 25–7.

85 Mayhew, *London Labour and the London Poor*, I, p. 304.

86 T. Catling, *My Life's Pilgrimage* (London: J. Murray, 1911), pp. 38–9.

87 Anderson, *The Printed Image*, pp. 119–20, 177–9.

88 H. Dixon, 'The literature of the lower orders', *Daily News*, 26 October 1847, 2 November 1847, 7 November 1847, SC (1851), evidence of William Edward Hickson, pp. 477–8, Collet Dobson Collet, p. 151, and John Cassell, p. 216, T. Burt, *An Autobiography* (London: Unwin, 1924), p. 115, Frost, *Forty Years' Recollections*, p. 94, C. Knight, *The Old Printer and the Modern Press* (London: J. Murray, 1854), p. 294.

89 Vincent, *Literacy and Popular Culture*, pp. 219–21, W. Collins, 'The unknown public', *Household Words*, 18 (1858), 217–22, J. Payn, 'Penny fiction', *Nineteenth Century*, 9 (1881), 145–54.

90 Altick, *The English Common Reader*, p. 394.

91 See report of an attempted prosecution against sellers of penny dreadfuls in *The Times*, 13 December 1877, p. 11. See also J. Greenwood, 'Penny

Awfuls', *St Paul's Magazine*, 12 (1873), 161–8, Greenwood, *The Wilds of London* (London: Chatto & Windus, 1874), pp. 159–69, J. M. Ludlow and L. Jones, *The Progress of the Working Class, 1832–1867* (London: A. Strahan, 1867), p. 181, 'The literature of the streets', *Edinburgh Review*, 165 (1887), 43, F. Hitchman, 'Penny fiction', *Quarterly Review*, 171 (1890), 152–5.

92 K. Boyd, *Manliness and the Boys' Story Paper in Britain: A Cultural History, 1855–1940* (Basingstoke: Palgrave, 2003), P. Dunae, 'New grub-street for boys', in J. Richards (ed.), *Imperialism and Juvenile Literature* (Manchester: Manchester University Press, 1989), Dunae, 'Penny-dreadfuls: late nineteenth-century boys' literature and crime', *Victorian Studies*, 22 (1978), 133–50, J. Springhall, *Youth, Popular Culture and Moral Panics: From Penny Gaffs to Gangsta-Rap* (Basingstoke: Macmillan, 1998), Springhall, 'A life story for the people? Edwin J. Brett and the London low-life penny dreadfuls of the 1860s', *Victorian Studies*, 33 (1990), 223–46, Springhall, 'Pernicious reading? The penny dreadful as a scapegoat for late Victorian juvenile crime', *Victorian Periodicals Review*, 27 (1994), 326–49, Springhall, '"Disseminating impure literature": the penny dreadful publishing business since 1860', *Economic History Review*, 27 (1994), 567–84, P. N. Stearns, 'Men, boys and anger in American society, 1860–1940', in J. A. Mangan and J. Walvin (eds), *Manliness and Morality: Middle-Class Masculinity in Britain and America, 1800–1940* (Manchester: Manchester University Press, 1987), p. 81

93 P. Marsh, *Aggro: The Illusion of Violence*, quoted in J. B. Twitchell, *Preposterous Violence: Fables of Aggression in Modern Culture* (Oxford: Oxford University Press, 1989), p. 36.

94 Quoted in Dunae, 'Penny-dreadfuls', 135.

95 [Charlton Lea?], *Sweeney Todd; the Demon Barber of Fleet Street* (London, 1878), pp. 211, 390. BL, BOC.

96 Ibid., p. 576.

6

The rise of modern crime reporting

D ESCRIBING THE RANGE OF ITEMS on sale at one of the largest Sunday markets in London, located on the border between the City and the East End, in 1850, Charles Manby Smith made reference to:

> the species of literature which finds encouragement among the frequenters of the Sunday Market. Books we saw none, but good store of single sheets of all sizes, and varying in price from one halfpenny up to sixpence. All the Sunday newspapers are regularly placarded and sold; and in addition to them, there was all abundance of the blood-and-murder, ghost and goblin journals.

Smith captured an important moment in the nineteenth century. The year 1850 marked the point when several different genres of literature, traditional and new, collided in the marketplace, their publishers and printers fiercely competing for the scarce pennies of the partially and newly literate lower orders. At this point, each form, namely the broadside, the penny blood and the weekly newspaper, seemed to command a more or less equal share of the market. And, crucially, each form was equally promiscuous, borrowing styles, methods and even text from the others. Violence, as Charles Manby Smith observed, was the common theme shared by all:

> It would seem that there is a charm in pistols, daggers, bludgeons and deadly weapons of all sorts, with the assaults and assassinations they suggest, that is irresistible to the population of London.[1]

This chapter focuses on this period of intense competition, roughly between 1840 and 1870, which ultimately witnessed the climax of several traditional and new genres of popular print and their take-over by the new Sunday press. A significant part of the established and thriving competition has already been described in the previous chapters: in chapter 3 we saw how the broadside trade, a hangover from the eighteenth-century popular literature of crime, was dramatically expanded and intensified during the early decades of the nineteenth century with developments in technology and changes in the penal code, while in chapter 5, we discussed the emergence of cheap instalment fiction, or penny bloods, from the 1830s onwards, through which several new publishers made small fortunes by appealing directly to the tastes of new readers. And we must add to these genres the radical unstamped press of the 1830s which, guided by popular literary trends, incorporated violence and sensation into their political rhetoric in order to increase and maintain their modest circulation rates.

Thus we have some sense of the climate into which the Sunday newspapers emerged. During the 1840s, a steady stream of new weekly newspapers became available: *Lloyd's Weekly London Newspaper* (1842), *News of the World* (1843), *Weekly Times* (1847) and *Reynolds's Weekly Newspaper* (1850). As demonstrated by their individual circulation rates, each attracting around 50,000 purchasers by the early 1850s, these newspapers quickly captured an unprecedented share of the market. Whilst drawing on evidence from all the weekly newspapers, this chapter will focus on one, *Lloyd's Weekly Newspaper*, the Sunday paper which always sold the most copies and, led by Edward Lloyd, an innovative, profit-minded entrepreneur, set the important trends in the industry. An in-depth analysis of *Lloyd's Weekly Newspaper* will be used in order to illuminate the complexities and contradictions inherent in the formation of the Sunday press, and especially in the development of modern crime reporting as a form of entertainment for lower-class Londoners which would overtake the other forms offered for sale at Charles Manby Smith's Sunday market.

There are, therefore, several parts to this chapter. As *Lloyd's Weekly Newspaper* emerged in the 1840s into an established popular print culture, one of the dominant themes of which was violence, we will first examine how Edward Lloyd deliberately incorporated styles and features from other genres, especially broadsides, into his newspaper in order to ensure its success. This transition from broadside to newspaper has been previously described by David Vincent, who argues that proprietors of weekly newspapers, by drawing on traditions in sensational fiction, the radical unstamped press and broadsides, translated news into a new category of popular leisure. Crudely put, the Sunday papers offered readers value for money and were better suited to an audience becoming more intimately acquainted with text and growing in their maturity as readers.[2] However, there were many more complications in this period of transition that need to be teased out and articulated. Even in 1850 it was not entirely certain that newspapers would triumph over broadsides as the preferred method of violent crime reporting. Thus we will look in more detail at how Lloyd, through skill and chance, was able to convert audiences of other forms of print to his newspaper, to make factual violent crime more entertaining and attractive to readers than rival semi-fictional and fictional accounts contained in broadsides and penny bloods, no matter how lifelike or culturally sensitive these might have been.

Next, we will turn to explore the styles of crime reporting used by the new weekly newspapers. While most historians have tended to avoid detailed analyses of the content of *Lloyd's Weekly Newspaper*, they have been quick to emphasise its violent and sensational character, perhaps taking too much at face value the critique provided by mid-nineteenth-century commentators.[3] They have, therefore, overlooked important parallels, networks of exchange and even dialogue that existed between the new weeklies and the established daily press, links and common-alities which enabled Edward Lloyd to feed violence and sensation back into mass and even respectable culture. Thus finally, we will see how, in this very way, *Lloyd's Weekly Newspaper* was able to survive and thrive while other popular genres fell into decline.

The popular Sunday press evolves

We have encountered the famous publisher Edward Lloyd before. In chapter 5, we discussed the way in which Lloyd, from very humble roots, launched his career in cheap instalment fiction, publishing a wide range of sensational periodicals, penny novelettes and penny miscel-lanies from the 1830s onwards. At a time when most books, even when sold second-hand, were beyond the working-class purse, Lloyd's cheap fiction was bound to be popular, his great success ensured by his ability to provide material suited to the tastes of his audience, to the great annoyance of the rational recreationalists who attempted to compete with him. Just as Lloyd's cheap fiction was approaching a climax in the 1840s, the canny entrepreneur sought to expand his business into the area of 'factual' reporting, his first dabble in the form of murder and execution broadsides.

As demonstrated in chapter 3, broadsides were an old genre, providing access for the lower orders to the popular literature of crime in the eighteenth century. During the opening decades of the nineteenth century, the trade dramatically expanded, and crime and its fatal punishment became a popular theme. Broadsides continued to be an important genre of crime reporting for the lower orders given the prohibitive price of and limited access to newspapers. Yet they were as much a form of entertainment as a method of passing on information. Reports often contained a judicious mixture of fact and fiction, providing accounts of extreme violence with which purchasers were comfortable, presented in an attractive way. As we saw in chapter 3, the tremendous appeal of these sheets was reflected in accounts of their sales, which biographers of printers and mid-century investigators claimed often reached the millions.

It is little wonder then that Edward Lloyd attempted to carve out a share of this booming trade for himself. He was a businessman focused on profits, and it was well known in 1840 that Jemmy Catnach, the leading broadside printer in Seven Dials, had just retired the year before with a small fortune of £10,000. Lloyd's only surviving set of broadsides was printed for the discovery of the mutilated body of Jane Jones and the trial of her murderer Daniel Good in April 1842 (see figures 35 and 36).[4] They certainly compare well to the competition. The woodcuts are suitably detailed and are instructive on the features of the case. They are also supported by captions, an increasingly popular addition to broadsides during the 1830s and 1840s. The text describing Good's examination at the police court and trial at the Central Criminal Court gives suitable attention to the violence of the murder, the evidence proving Good's guild and brief statements from other witnesses designed to fill gaps in the narrative. And finally, the verses, intended to be sung to the tune of 'The Gallant Poachers', conform to a general pattern for verses on crime at this time: calling people to gather and listen, giving an account of the violence of the murder, and emphasising the appropriateness of the punishment.

However, Edward Lloyd does not seem to have stayed in this business for very long. In May 1840, at the same time as his experiments in broadsides, Lloyd launched his first newspaper, the *Penny Sunday Times and People's Police Gazette*, a four-page weekly publication sold for one penny (see figures 37 and 38). Precise details about the *Penny Sunday Times* are hard to come by, mainly due to conflicting anecdotes about it in the sources. The much debated stamp tax, which prohibited the publication of news without the payment of a duty to the government, as well as the cost of paper duty, meant that Lloyd faced seemingly insurmountable problems in the publication of a penny

35, 36 *overleaf.* Edward Lloyd's broadsides, the first printed on the examination of Daniel Good at the police court, and the second on his trial, 1842

Trial of Good

For the MURDER of JANE JONES, at Putney.

Daniel Good, as he appeared in the Cell previous to his Trial.

Central Criminal Court.

Yesterday being fixed for the trial of Daniel Good, for the murder of Jane Jones, alias Good, the Court and all the avenues to it were besieged by numbers of the curious at an early hour. The doors of the Court were opened at eight o'clock, and before nine nearly every seat, both in the body of the Court and on the Bench was occupied, although no person was admitted without an order from one of the Sheriffs.

The counsel for the prosecution were the Attorney-General, Mr. Waddington, Mr. Adolphus, and Mr. Russell Gurney. The prisoner's counsel was Mr. Doane.

At a few minutes before ten o'clock the Duke of Sussex entered the Court and took his seat on the judges' bench.

At ten o'clock Lord Denman, Mr. Baron Alderson, and Mr. Justice Coltman, took their seats on the Bench. The prisoners Daniel Good and Mary Good were then brought in and placed in the dock to plead to the indictment. As soon as Good came to the front of the dock, he put his hand to his forehead, and respectfully bowed to the judges. The prisoner Mary Good, looked much better than when before her imprisonment.

Mr. Straat having read the indictment, called upon the prisoner, "What say you, Daniel Good, are you guilty or not guilty?"

The prisoner in a low tone of voice replied, "Not guilty."

The indictment against Mary Good, for feloniously harbouring and succouring the prisoner, was then read, and to the question "What say you, Mary Good, are you guilty or not guilty?" she replied in a strong Irish accent, "No, sir."

Mr. Doane said he appeared to defend the prisoner Daniel Good, and had an application to make to the Court to allow that there should be separate trials of the two prisoners.

The prisoner Daniel Good was then arraigned on the coroner's inquisition, to which he also pleaded "Not guilty."

The jury having been then sworn, the trial proceeded.

The Attorney-General rose, and said it was his duty to state the circumstances under which the prisoner at the bar was charged with the crime of murder. The learned gentlemen then described the stable, and their relative position, and detailed the circumstances attending the discovery of the body in one of the stalls of the stable, and the absconding of the prisoner.

Mr. Adolphus then called the first witness, Wm. Gardiner, the constable, who deposed to the circumstances attending the finding of the mutilated trunk of the murdered woman.

Thomas Houghton was the next witness examined by Mr. Russell Gurney—He was the gardener to Mr. Sicill, and went into the stable with the witnesses already examined. He stated that on the night of Wednesday he examined the fire-place, and found therein fuel three times as much in quantity as was necessary for an ordinary fire.

The next witness examined (by the Attorney-General) was Samuel Palmer, policeman V 6, who was at the stable a little before eleven the night Good escaped. This witness deposed to finding a fire, consisting of wood, coal, and straw, laid in the harness-room; and that under it he found the portions of calcined bones produced. He also produced the keys found in the same room.

Robert Tee, parish constable of Putney, examined by the Attorney-General, deposed to finding other keys (produced) on the top of the corn-bin in the stable opposite that in which the body was lying.

Josiah Tighe, constable, 199 V, deposed to finding in the cinders two pieces of bone on the Wednesday night, and on the Tuesday after, a small piece of flesh on the edge of the lid of the seat-box.

Inspector Busain (V) gave evidence of his having found some linen and books in a box in the harness-room, which he broke open, as well as a knife in the drawer of a table, which had blood marks on the handle and blade, the latter of which appeared to have been rusty and subsequently sharpened. In. On the 8th, assisted by Dr. Ridge, he sifted the cinders, and found more bones (now produced.)

John Houghton, son of Mr. Shiell's gardeners, examined by Mr. Gurney—This witness slept in a room over the stables, to which, however, he had no access, as the prisoner Good kept the key, and had it always locked. He deposed to observing on the Tuesday before the body was found a very unpleasant smell, like the singeing of horses. He remarked it to the prisoner, who told him he had been in liquor the overnight, and had been boasting some cheese to refresh himself. He had seen the youth named Daniel Good with the prisoner, and also a woman whom he had lately told witness was his sister; the last time he saw her was on Easter Monday.

The next witnesses called were the medical gentlemen, who deposed to the appearance of the body, and from which the deductions they made were, that it was that of a female, that the person did not appear to have died from apoplexy, that she had not been dead when found more than five days, that the marks on the arm were those of blood, that the fragments of bone found in the cinders were those of a human being; that the incisions by which the head been removed were made after death; that the heart and lungs were highly healthy; that death was not occasioned by disease, but from violence from the sudden loss (while in health and the muscular powers in action) of blood; and that deceased was pregnant.

The Lord Chief Justice having summed up the evidence, the jury immediately returned a verdict of "GUILTY," and sentence of death was then passed. The prisoner then made the following confession :—

My Lord,—Butcher was the cause of the death of the unfortunate Jane Jones. We went to Mrs. Hester's, from there we went to the stable. I wished Jones to remain in the stable all night, but she said she would go and commit suicide. I locked her in the stable, and when I returned at night I found her a corpse. A sharp pen-knife lay by her side, with which she had killed herself. The next morning a man called at the stables. I told him what had happened, when he advised me to conceal the body. I said I would give him a sovereign if he would do it for me, to which he agreed. He cut off the head, and then asked me to light a fire in the harness-room ; but on my refusing to do so, he made a fire himself, and then commenced burning part of the body. Ann Butcher has been the cause of all.

COPY OF VERSES.

Tune—"The Gallant Poachers."

Good people all, both young and old,
A dreadful tale I will unfold,
Will make your warm life blood run cold,
   Of Good I'll tell,
    That wretch so fell,
Who a cruel deed has done,
As e'er was witness'd 'neath the sun.
But his career of crime is done,
   His end is drawing near.

He helpless woman did betray,
His victim afterwards did slay ;
To hide his guilt from open day,
   The body hacked and hew'd,
    No mercy show'd,
   For none he know'd,
From pity he disdainful turne.
Compunction and remorse he spurns,
The quivering limbs with fire he burns,—
   Thou monster, Daniel Good.

Her tender limbs he sawed and tore,
The entrails, recking in their gore,
He gave the flames for to devour—
   Oh, what a deed of blood !
    Could no one speed,
   And stop the deed ?
Was there no one to save thee nigh,
When thou her succour loud did cry ?
No ; no one saw thy parting sigh,
   But cruel Daniel Good.

A scaffold soon thy end will be,
And hissing thousands flock to see,
For none will cheer or pity thee,
   Nor mourn the murderer's fate.
    Youth and age
    Will curse thy rage,
And ages yet unborn will tell,
And on thy crimes with anguish dwell,
And mourn thy cruel deed so fell,
   Deserving scorn and hate !   J. HUGHES.

Printed by E. LLOYD, 231, Shoreditch.

newspaper. It was a financial impossibility. Even proprietors of the radical unstamped press, many being successful flouters of these laws, found it difficult to attract a large enough audience to break even, let alone make a profit, by selling newspapers for a penny.[5] But Edward Lloyd avoided the payment of stamp tax by drawing upon traditions in the presentation of news in the broadside trade, liberally blending fact and fiction in reports.

Illustrations which adorned the front page were often (though not always) of factual events, either with or without accompanying explanations. Thus Lloyd relied on readers' awareness of the event, or their skills learnt from broadsides in interpreting stories from sequences of pictures. Human tragedy was the common theme (see figures 39 and 40). As one of Lloyd's illustrators, George Augustus Sala, remembered, 'murders were the topics which I generally treated in the Penny Sunday Times; and when there was a lack of assassinations, one had to fall back upon such topics as child-stealing, incendiarism, burglary under arms, and the infliction of the knout on Russian princesses'.[6] Woodcuts were very similar to those published simultaneously in the broadsides. They were graphic in their presentation of murder, capturing either the very moment of the infliction of gross violence or the shocking discovery of the victim's mangled body after the event. Blood was a crucial feature, rushing from wounds in terrific quantities or drenching the surrounding environment. Of course, such blood flow is fairly unrealistic, but its presentation suggests that the images were meant to be more representative than accurate, designed to impact heavily on viewers' senses and invoke their imaginations. Characters were cast in rigid theatrical poses, and the conventions of melodrama, in the form of exaggerated expressions and stock costumes, with which readers were familiar, were incorporated into the illustrations, designed to assist in the use of the imagination. That these features were so important to the success of the newspaper is evident in Edward Lloyd's instructions to Sala: 'The eyes must be larger, and there must be more blood – much more blood!'[7]

Sensational articles with eye-catching headings, probably fictional and typically set in a location outside Britain, coloured the pages of the newspaper. Although wholly unrelated to the lives of readers, they drew on the extremes of human tragedy, including accounts of shipwrecks, natural disasters and suicides, but gross violence was certainly a prominent characteristic. Particularly bloodthirsty and barbaric acts of savages frequently appeared. No details were considered unfit for publication. While Indonesian tribes devoured common criminals, Native Americans slaughtered farmers and their families

DANIEL GOOD, THE MONSTER MURDERER! !!

THE MURDER AND MUTILATION.

"Go, murderer. Hide thy deeds in the blackest night, yet will the Almighty God pierce them like a noon-tide sun."

BURNING OF THE MANGLED LIMBS.

"Can fire wash guilt from the Murderer's soul? No! Can it dry up the victim's blood? No! for rather will it make that blood arise to the altars of Heaven."

37, 38 *opposite*: Illustrations of Daniel Good's crime in Lloyd's *Penny Sunday Times*, 1842

"MOLLY" GOOD, AS SHE APPEARED WITH HER FRUIT-STALL IN BISHOPSGATE-STREET.

THE HARNESS-ROOM, WHERE THE BONES WERE BURNED.

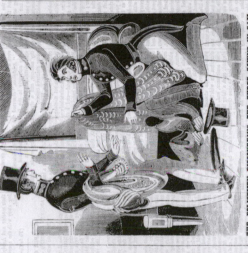

THE POLICEMEN DISCOVERING THE THREE GOWNS IN GAMBLE'S APARTMENTS, IDENTIFIED BY MRS. BROWN AS BELONGING TO JANE JONES.

THE INTERIOR, WHERE THE TRUNK WAS FOUND.

DANIEL GOOD, AS HE APPEARED BEFORE THE MAGISTRATES AT BOW-STREET.

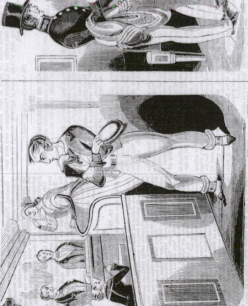

THE EXTERIOR OF MR. SHIELL'S STABLE, AT PUTNEY PARK LANE.

DREADFUL MURDER OF MRS. KEHOE, BY HER HUSBAND, AT LIVERPOOL.

39. Front page illustration for Lloyd's *Penny Sunday Times*, 1840

on the frontiers.[8] For example, this article, entitled 'Horrible Atrocity' appeared on the front page of the *Penny Sunday Times* on 3 May 1840:

> A female, now under the sentence of death, is expected to be executed next week, for a murder of more atrocious nature than any that has ever come to our knowledge. The husband of the woman in question had given his wife some mutton to curry for his supper, and the woman's paramour happening to come during the time of preparations, asked for, and obtained, the curry, which, being very hungry, he completely devoured: the woman, fearing her husband's anger, and having no means of replacing the mutton, actually killed her own child, curried it, and served it up to her husband, who, finding the bones smaller, and more tender than those of mutton, taxed her, with presenting him with a kid; but suddenly, as if suspecting the horrible catastrophe, he enquired for his child, when, dreadful to relate, the mother confessed the murder and the infernal fact of having made the flesh of her infant into curry for its father![9]

BARBAROUS MURDER OF MRS. WEBSTER, HER SISTER, AND THREE CHILDREN.

40. Front page illustration for Lloyd's *Penny Sunday Times*, 1841

The tale was probably entirely fictional. Moreover, Lloyd had in fact already published it in his periodical of fiction, *The Calendar of Horrors*, in 1835, thus demonstrating, in his very first newspaper, his intention to apply lessons learnt early on in his publishing career, a tendency which would continue in his compilation of a newspaper completely based on facts from late 1842.[10]

As clear from the title of the newspaper, police-court reports were also an important feature of the *Penny Sunday Times*. From the establishment of police courts in 1792, daily newspapers had included reports on proceedings as part of their general criminal intelligence coverage. However, by including police-court reports in the *Penny Sunday Times*, Lloyd was not imitating respectable press traditions, but rather drawing upon a key trend used by proprietors of the radical unstamped press during the 1830s to widen the appeal of their newspapers. As the popularity of various political movements fluctuated, these proprietors had begun to include sensational accounts of crimes and disasters, real or imaginary, to keep their journals afloat. The value of sensationalism had obviously been learnt from the contemporaneous broadside trade. As David Vincent notes, of all the titles in the unstamped press published between 1830 and 1836, no more than half could loosely be called political, 'and many of these employed satire, literary and dramatic criticism, or theological debate to attack the status quo'; another 'three in ten were miscellanies of literature and useful and entertaining knowledge, and the remainder included periodical versions of the ballads and sensational accounts' of crimes and disasters of the sort found in broadsides.[11]

Of these, the most successful was John Cleave's *Weekly Police Gazette*, achieving a circulation of about 40,000 in 1835.[12] It was undeniably a politically radical publication. Articles scattered throughout its four pages drew attention to the plight of the poor, their condition worsened by the severity of the New Poor Law, highlighted the injustice of the hated stamp tax and loudly criticised the policies of the government. Moreover, the weekly illustration adorning the front page loudly mocked the behaviour and beliefs of the Tories. Yet Cleave sought to attract additional readers by including more entertaining features, from theatrical reviews to police intelligence. Although Cleave's and many other radical journals that blatantly advertised their sensational content were short-lived, other more firmly entrenched publications followed a similar course of action. The *Northern Star*, an official Chartist newspaper often lauded by historians for its literary attributes, by the mid-1840s had begun to include regular columns of criminal intelligence alongside reports on various murders and executions. As Margot Finn has demonstrated, after the perceived defeat of Chartism in c. 1850, editors of radical publications continued to use sensation and narratives of violence in reports and editorials aimed at mobilising the working classes.[13]

When placed side by side, Cleave's *Gazette* and Lloyd's *Penny Sunday Times* look strikingly similar, especially in terms of layout and the display of police-court reports on the front page (see figures 41 and 42). But it is just about here that the comparison ends. Lloyd's paper contained almost no political comment. And his police intelligence seems to have been entirely fictional.[14] Reports were, for the most part, satirical portraits, designed to amuse rather than inform readers. Their purpose was to mock the misfortunes of others. Stereotypes were frequently used, from the drunken Irishman to cockney street-sellers. Witnesses and defendants spoke in comic dialects while the magistrate emerged as the sarcastic voice of reason. The reports provided comic relief, a balance to the stronger stories and illustrations featured in the newspaper, to ensure that the publication contained variety.

Predictably, the *Penny Sunday Times* attracted much concern and

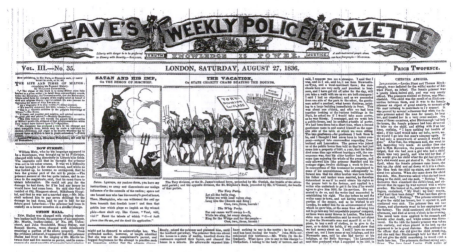

41. Front page of Cleave's *Weekly Police Gazette*, 1836

condemnation from the respectable classes. However, it did prove popular with its intended readership and its fictional content did not seem to trouble purchasers. Estimates of its circulation vary considerably. While Lloyd claimed it sold over 95,000 copies each week,[15] others have suggested that a more accurate figure might be about 20,000.[16] Moreover, evidence suggests that it also reached a provincial audience, for example in Ipswich and Preston.[17] But by late 1842, its position was usurped by Lloyd's new and factual weekly newspaper, *Lloyd's Illustrated London Newspaper*, priced at twopence halfpenny stamped. The *Penny Sunday Times* became mostly devoted to serial fiction, continuing in print for several more years. Yet its importance in this story should not be overlooked. The *Penny Sunday Times* was an important bridge, linking various traditions in a range of popular genres (a melting pot, if you like, of broadsides, radical newspapers and serial fiction), and then feeding these elements into Lloyd's new weekly and factual newspapers. Such continuity meant that Lloyd was able to draw audiences of each genre towards his new publication.

Violence, sensationalism and Lloyd's Weekly Newspaper

During 1843, Edward Lloyd removed the illustrations from his newspaper, expanded its contents to twelve pages, increased its price to threepence and renamed it *Lloyd's Weekly London Newspaper* (hereafter

THE PENNY
Sunday Times,
AND PEOPLE'S POLICE GAZETTE.

No. 25.   LONDON.—SUNDAY, SEPTEMBER 20, 1840.

Police.

DISCOVERY OF THE MURDER OF MR. & MRS. COOK, OF PEOVER, BY THE HOUSEMAID.

BOW-STREET.

HATTON GARDEN.

CEILING WRACKS—A BEL-FREY.

BELFAST.

A BELLY FULL OF GRAPES.

MARYLEBONE.

CHINESE PENAL CODE AND FORM OF PUNISHMENT.

TOO GOOD A WIFE.

MORE INDIAN TROUBLES.

---

42. Front page of Lloyd's *Penny Sunday Times*, 1840

referred to as *LWN*). From this time, the newspaper experienced a rapid rise in circulation, and sales always remained ahead of the competition, including the most popular London daily newspapers. Opening with an average of 21,000 weekly subscribers, by the end of the decade this number had risen to 49,000. It doubled again by 1855 and reached 350,000 by 1863.[18] These sales figures were boosted by changes in legislation between 1850 and 1870 which lowered the price of the newspaper. After the abolition of the stamp tax in 1855, Lloyd (and other proprietors of Sunday newspapers) dropped the price from threepence to twopence, and with the removal of the paper duty in 1861, Lloyd again reduced the price to one penny. Lloyd's ambition and entrepreneurial skills also supported this continuing increase in popularity among readers. In 1856, just after lowering prices, Lloyd purchased two of the newly invented Hoe Rotary presses, the first newspaper proprietor in Britain to do so, to enable the most up-to-date news to be printed cheaply and quickly for distribution on Sunday morning.

Although the circulation rates might at first appear a little small when compared with the sales of broadsides described in chapter 3, it must be remembered that *LWN* attracted only a share of the audience for the Sunday newspapers more generally, albeit a dominating one. Moreover, newspapers and broadsides encouraged different practices in purchasing and reading. While broadsides relied on impulse buyers, newspapers cultivated more committed subscribers. Both methods had benefits and drawbacks though the latter proved to be more durable in the long run. Lloyd, learning from his experience in publishing cheap fiction, knew exactly how to slide his newspaper into the rhythms of the working-class routine. Leisure time for reading was often only available on Sundays; hence the newspaper 'could be read on the only rest day of the week, and intermittently thereafter'.[19] As one reader, a street-buyer of waste paper, told Henry Mayhew, 'the only worldly labour I do on a Sunday is to take my family's dinner to the bakehouse, bring it home after chapel, and read *Lloyd's Weekly*'.[20] By 1886, one journalist wrote that 'few working-class homes fail to take in a newspaper on a Sunday', the most popular, he added, being *LWN*.[21] The clear text and physical toughness of *LWN* and other Sunday newspapers meant that they could withstand hard usage.[22] Copies would not only last until the end of the week, but might also be shared amongst family, friends and workmates. As historians have acknowledged, the 'buy your own' mentality did not prevail in the working classes until much later in the century.[23] Perhaps then a case could be made for doubling or even tripling these already large circulation rates.

Despite such impressive sales, the working-class reader, or for that matter any reader, of *LWN* is quite elusive. There is a real lack of solid evidence about which social groups purchased the paper and what they derived from reading it. On the one hand, revisionist historians have claimed that increasing circulations of the Sunday papers represent their success in appealing to the already literate lower-middle class of clerks, shopkeepers and master craftsmen, their primary audience, rather than attracting any new readers from the working classes.[24] Virginia Berridge, on the other hand, has stated that the revisionists have substantially overestimated the relative size of the lower-middle-class audience, arguing that at least some, such as *Reynolds's Newspaper*, were almost primarily supported by the working classes.[25]

Faced with few accounts of actual reading experience and the unreliable statements of respectable contemporaries with conflicting agendas, Berridge has suggested that patterns of readership might be revealed by a very close examination of the content of weekly newspapers, for example their correspondence columns, appeal funds lists, sections of advertising content and reports on labour problems such as strikes and negotiations. Through this, Berridge found that a good proportion of readers of *LWN* did belong to the ranks of the lower-middle class, including small shopkeepers, property owners in general and better-off tenants. However, also evident was a considerable working-class readership, but with no particular allegiance from any one section of workers, and encompassing skilled workers, mostly artisans of the old type, semi-skilled workers, females, from domestic servants to workers in the clothing trade, and perhaps the hint of an unskilled readership.[26]

Given Lloyd's earlier career in crude sensational fiction and the matching rises in circulation rates with internal changes in the newspaper, and taking into account the simultaneous decline of other genres in popular literature, the mixed lower-middle/ working-class audience for *LWN* is much more likely. Lower-middle-class readers supplemented a wide range of working-class readers rather than replacing them. This becomes even more certain when *LWN* is compared with its rival, *Reynolds's Newspaper*. G. W. M. Reynolds incorporated many important traditions of the radical unstamped press into his newspaper, including its strong political voice. Through this, Reynolds was able to attract large working-class support for his Sunday newspaper, but it also meant that circulation rates eventually stagnated. By avoiding such radical content, instead towing a much more liberal, mainstream political line, *LWN* represented a significant departure from the radical unstamped press, and Lloyd was therefore able to attract mass audiences to sustain his highly profitable commercial enterprise. To achieve this, Lloyd put into use an old lowest common denominator: sensationalism.

Lloyd's deliberate courting of the lower-middle-class audience for his newspaper might also account for the removal of illustrations from *LWN* in January 1843. As evident from the price of broadsides and Lloyd's earlier publications, illustrations were not a financial burden on the publication of the newspaper. It is likely that their exclusion was part of a general move towards a display of respectability which gathered momentum during the 1850s. As Berridge has noted, many in the lower-middle class who purchased *LWN* were not so very far removed from the higher ranks of the working class.[27] In chapter 1, we discussed the commonalities in culture and outlook that continued to exist between the lower-middle class and sections of skilled workers after the somewhat artificial division enforced by the Great Reform Act of 1832. The increasing importance of respectability might have begun to militate against their subscription to a penny blood or their purchase of a broadside, both of which contained such gross representations of violence. But the new Sunday newspapers were much more subtle in their incorporation of popular themes.

The very different physical character and presentation of *LWN* has also led Berridge to argue further that, in his own pursuit of respectability, Lloyd attempted to sever links with the early readers of his sensational fiction, a group she describes as a 'very low lot'.[28] But it is evident in the development of *LWN* through the 1840s and 1850s that Lloyd worked hard to maintain this audience too. Lloyd expertly intertwined elements from other forms of popular literature into his newspaper in order to appeal to these readers, only discarding some of these features much later and very gradually. And the exclusion of illustrations did not seem to repel these readers either. So far, this book has shown how the lower classes became much more image conscious during the first half of the nineteenth century, as illustrations became much more common, more elaborate and more accurate.[29] However, here we glimpse another important process at work: the growing comfort of the lower classes with text, a reflection of growing literacy rates and, perhaps more importantly, the growing number of readers from around 1840 onwards.[30]

In 1843 though, Lloyd still had to convince the working man to buy his newspaper instead of a broadside, especially in the event of a gruesome murder, followed by trial and execution, occurring in the metropolis. Despite such fast acceleration towards mass circulation, during the 1840s and even during the 1850s it was not entirely certain that the Sunday newspapers would replace the broadsides as the preferred method of violent crime reporting for the lower classes. Both genres offered different attractions to readers. Most obviously, the newspapers contained much more detail that was usually much more accurate. Where broadsides offered a few hundred words, newspapers might offer up to a thousand words or more. Poorer purchasers of the broadside *The Life, Trial, Confession and Execution of Harriet Parker for the Murder of Two Children in Golden Lane* (1848), for example, might have missed out on reading the sensational testimonies of key witnesses in the trial printed in *LWN*, including that of the father of the victims, who was forced to admit his sexual promiscuity and confess to how badly he had treated his common-law wife.[31] A rival broadside printed for the same execution did not include any details about the trial at all.[32]

With such limited space, broadside printers had to be selective. But apart from some general trends described in chapter 3 (from ways in which the violence of the murder was communicated to readers to comparisons made between different murders), there does not seem to have been a distinct pattern about precisely what details they decided to include. Printers certainly regularly and unashamedly copied text from the newspapers. Both broadsides printed for the execution of Harriet Parker copied Parker's final letter composed in the condemned cell for the father of her young victims from that printed in all the London newspapers, including *LWN* and *The Times*.[33] The account of the Criminal Court proceedings in *The Trial, Sentence and Execution of Samuel Wright at Horsemonger Lane* (1864) was directly lifted from the article in *LWN* of 20 December 1863.[34]

Yet also of interest are the times when broadside printers ignored factual details contained in the newspapers and chose instead to print fiction. The convict Thomas Hocker, sentenced to death for the brutal murder of James Delarue at Hampstead in 1845, wrote several letters from the condemned cell about his life and crime to the sheriff, the prison chaplain, Sarah and Olivia (presumably friends), all printed in the London papers.[35] But at least two broadside printers composed entirely fictional letters, the first to Hocker's parents, and the second to his 'dear friends', which bore no resemblance to the factual versions, instead following the traditional, sickly formula: Hocker confesses his crime, begs for forgiveness, acknowledges the justness of his punishment and asks the reader to take warning from his example.[36]

There are many other examples which all point to a preference among broadside printers for rigid formulas about crime and its punishment. These had not yet necessarily become antiquated, the proof being in the efforts of newspaper editors to incorporate these into their longer descriptions of murder and execution. The focus on the character of the felon remained important. The assessment of the murderer Emmanuel Barthelemy's character in *LWN* in January 1855, as well as in *The Times*, not only reflected the general Victorian concern with character and transparency of motivation, but also clearly echoed the narratives contained in the verses of the broadsides, which drew upon that early modern notion of the guilt of everyman: Barthelemy was portrayed as the son of poor, but honest, parents who chose the wrong path in life, resulting in a downward spiral of crimes that led to the double murder in Warren Street on 8 December 1854, and so to the scaffold.[37] Similarly, common euphemisms persisted across the board: for example, in all genres, a felon was typically 'launched into eternity' or simply 'ceased to exist' at the moment of execution.

And this might well have been the stalling point for the Sunday newspapers in their attempts to complete the seduction of the broadside purchasers up until 1868. There were certain narratives, principally those surrounding execution, with which the lower orders felt comfortable, no matter how fictional they were. Virtually the same account of the execution day was used for every convicted murderer, partly, of course, because the broadsides had to be printed before the actual execution in time for distribution. Thus, there are often discrepancies when compared with 'factual' reports in the newspapers. While one broadside printed for Hocker's execution in May 1845 described the respectful silence of the crowd, the reporter for *LWN* exclaimed that their continuous groans and yells were almost deafening. While the same broadside claimed that Hocker was deeply absorbed in prayer as Calcraft adjusted the rope, *LWN* drew attention to his convulsive sobs, the occasion overtaking him to the extent that he had to be carried onto the drop and supported whilst the rope was secured.[38]

Not only did the lower orders seem to find comfort or reassurance in stock accounts, but they also wanted them on that particular day. As executions were typically held on Monday or Tuesday, the reports in the Sunday newspapers were almost a week late. This insurmountable difficulty was parodied by *Punch* in 1849, when, after the hanging of Maria and Frederick George Manning, the editor printed a fictional petition from the proprietors of the Sunday press requesting that the execution day be changed, complaining that in 'the lapse of days between Tuesday and Saturday, the enthusiasm has had time to wear away; the glow has of necessity cooled; or the reader has slacked his thirst for knowledge at other and less authentic sources than those which we might supply'.[39] In part, broadsides lasted so long because they relied on the impulse buy at the scaffold; their main supporters were members of the large crowd seeking a souvenir of the day, and for whom daily newspapers were just too expensive. Thus, it was the abolition of public execution in 1868 which finally ensured the triumph of the weekly newspapers. As the significance of execution in the drama of crime and its punishment was reduced, the transition from broadside to weekly newspaper as the predominant crime-reporting genre for lower-class readers was completed.

If weekly newspapers inherited certain characteristics from the broadside trade, including eventually their audience, as evident from that *Punch* article, they were also subject to the same derision and censure from mid-century social commentators and respectable journalists. In 1848, a report on the condition of the poorer classes in St George's-in-the-east, an overcrowded parish with a population mainly composed of urban labourers, stated that of the 1,231 families who took in a newspaper, 514 read *LWN*, the investigator concluding that this was 'not a cheering picture; the great use made of the capacity to read being, so far as this statement indicates, in ministering to mere excitement'.[40] Similarly, a writer for *Chambers' Edinburgh Journal* attributed responsibility for a recent spate of particularly gruesome murders to the detailed reports published by the Sunday press. Such images, he argued, tended to excite the mentally weak: 'the vulgar drink in the details with a hideous delight and soon a new murder proclaims that these have come into contact with some predisposed mind'.[41] Historians have similarly drawn attention to the violent, lurid and sensational presentation of criminal intelligence in the popular press, especially *LWN*. But, in the reporting on criminal activity generally, and the reporting of infamous murders in particular, how far did *LWN* really differ from the press of the establishment, for example from that very respectable organ of news, *The Times*?

In the reporting of crime generally, important similarities existed between *LWN* and *The Times*. Both printed summaries of the business of the Central Criminal Court and the metropolitan police courts, weekly and daily respectively. Simon Devereaux has shown how newspapers such as *The Times* replaced publications such as *The Old Bailey Sessions Papers*, previously central to the eighteenth-century popular literature of crime, as newspapers began to publish in detail the proceedings of the metropolitan criminal courts.[42] With the founding of *LWN* at the very end of 1842, Lloyd had begun to publish factual police intelligence. The selection of cases for publication and their presentation in the reports were fairly similar to those in *The Times*. Both newspapers covered a wide spread of offences as well as cases in which applicants appeared before the magistrates to seek advice or apply for poor relief. As evident from table 1, offences involving interpersonal violence of

Table 1 Police-court reports in *Lloyd's Weekly Newspaper*, 1840–70

Date	Total cases reported	Offences against the person (violence)	Property offences	Other
Mar 1843	43	10	18	15
Sept 1843	67	22	22	23
Mar 1849	84	28	40	16
Sept 1849	72	20.5	25.5	21
Mar 1855	63	15	24	24
Sept 1855	92	31	41	19
Mar 1859	89	22	42	25
Sept 1859	75	18.5	38.5	18
Mar 1864	64	22	21	21
Sept 1864	62	18.5	17.5	26
Mar 1870	79	19.5	29.5	30
Sept 1870	89	36.5	34.5	18

some level, from threats to harm to manslaughter and murder, did not dominate the reports at all. Much more common were offences against property and often a range of cases included in that other category that the courts dealt with, including advice, various family disputes and anti-social behaviour (bad language and drunkenness). Considering the important role played by the police courts in the lives of working- and lower-middle-class people in the metropolis, it is easy to understand why some contemporaries viewed police reports as 'the most instructive and most desirable reading in the world ... Many individuals involve themselves in difficulties from an ignorance of the facts, which they might have learnt had they read the previous police reports.'[43] There is certainly evidence that some criminals made use of the intelligence provided. For example, a procuress of young prostitutes explained to W. T. Stead, editor of the *Pall Mall Gazette*, that she had been successful in her trade for many years because she had studied the application of the law as revealed by the proceedings of the metropolitan police courts: 'Always read the newspapers, they are useful. Every week I take in two, *Lloyd's* and *Weekly Dispatch*, and

I spend the great part of Sunday in reading all the cases in the courts which relate to this subject.'[44] But in any case, despite the choice of newspapers by this procuress, in assessing criminality and attributing blame for assaults both *LWN* and *The Times* applied the same rigid moral principles. For instance, violent men who beat their wives were described as brutes or ruffians, while wives who fought back were condemned as viragos and termagants.

Few records of trials at London's police courts survive, which makes any conclusions on the policy of selecting trials for newspaper publication limited. However, the survival of the *Central Criminal Court Proceedings* (*CCCP*) means that, by comparing the official transcripts of trials with the columns of Central Criminal Court intelligence, we might be able to gain a glimpse into what crime was considered to be newsworthy. Unsurprisingly, both *LWN* and *The Times* featured only a small number of trials; because it was a daily newspaper, *The Times* included more trials than *LWN*. On average, between 1845 and 1865, *LWN* covered around 10.6 per cent of the total number of trials in a session, and *The Times* approximately 19.9 per cent.[45] Table 2 shows the range of cases included in each newspaper from each sample session as well as the proportion of coverage for each offence category compared with the actual proportion of offences in each category in the *CCCP*. From these percentages, on the one hand we might conclude that readers of both *LWN* and *The Times* were not necessarily provided with an accurate, reflective summary of the trials at London's premier criminal court. Yet, on the other hand, it would be difficult to argue that certain categories of crime were consistently over-represented. For instance, the percentages suggest that neither *LWN* nor *The Times* were pandering to their readers' thirst for cases containing gratuitous descriptions of violence. The only direct hint provided by journalists of these reports is a recurring statement, especially in *The Times*, that cases excluded were judged not to present 'any feature of peculiar interest'.[46] A noteworthy statement when we consider that some of the trials reported were more or less non-starters in terms of content, as the defendant appeared before the bar, pleaded guilty and was sentenced. If these were considered to be in the 'public interest', we can identify a similar concern of subscribers to read about the business of the court in addition to stories of crime to that which we saw in the columns of police intelligence.

Even though space was limited in both newspapers, a surprising amount of detail on the cases selected for the reports was published. In fact, given the long descriptions of more sensitive cases which are not recorded in full detail in the *CCCP*, it might be fair to suggest that

Table 2 Categories of offences – proportion of the CCCP
and proportion of the coverage in *Lloyd's Weekly Newspaper* and *The Times*, 1840–70 (%)

Offence	Jan 1845			Sept 1850			Jun 1855			Apr 1860			Nov 1865		
	CCCP	LWN	Times	CCCP	LWN	Times	CCCP	LWN	Times	CCCP	LWN	Times	CCCP	LWN	Times
Person [a]	5.3	0	5.5	7.6	26.3	25.8	7.6	20	33.3	11.3	10	13.6	14.9	50	20
Property [b]	77.2	46.1	44.4	77.8	42.1	45.2	58.7	40	33.3	39.2	30	31.8	47.8	0	55
Deception [c]	11.4	46.2	38.9	12.2	26.3	22.6	31.5	40	33.3	46.4	50	50	26.9	25	20
Other [d]	6.1	7.7	11.1	1.5	5.3	6.5	2.1	0	0	2.1	10	4.5	10.4	25	5

Notes:

[a] Person: assault, manslaughter, murder, wounding, gbh, rape, indecent assault

[b] Property: theft, embezzlement

[c] Deception: forgery, coining, obtaining goods under false pretences, fraud

[d] Other: bigamy, being at large before expiration of sentence, concealing birth

for an accurate account of the sessions at the Old Bailey, even during the mid-nineteenth century, the *CCCP* should be read alongside the newspapers. For instance, in the *CCCP* for the September session of 1850, Ellen Hoar, charged with infanticide, is mentioned but no details of her trial are given. A note states that 'the particulars of this case were not of a nature for publication'.[47] However, both *LWN* and *The Times* published almost identical reports on this case describing the discovery of the dead infant in the room of the accused by her landlady.[48] More obvious is the case of Robert Hunter, a doctor charged with rape and tried in the November sessions of 1865. Only a brief reference to the existence of the case and the verdict of not guilty were recorded in the *CCCP*.[49] But both *Lloyd's* and *The Times* devoted substantial space to the trial in specially headed columns set apart from the general criminal intelligence. From the length of both reports it seems as if no detail was spared.[50] Given the almost prudish silence of the *CCCP* in these and other cases, it would be hard not to conclude that the publication of these trials in the newspapers was at least in part motivated by a desire to sell newspapers through the use of sensationalism.

The most striking similarities are evident in the simultaneous reporting of *LWN* and *The Times* on notorious murders in the metropolis, those which the public eagerly followed from the discovery, to the trial, to the execution of the convicted felon. Initial reports from both newspapers typically opened with the same, formulaic, sensational statement that the local community had been thrown into a state of excitement on the discovery of a terrible murder, often also claiming it to be the most horrendous crime ever discovered. When James Tapping murdered Emma Whiter on 28 January 1845, *The Times* published this report the next day:

> Yesterday an intense degree of excitement prevailed in the neighbourhood of Bethnal Green, in consequence of a rumour that a young woman named Emma Whiter, 21 years of age, had been shot dead with a pistol, by a young man named James Tapping, who had for some time past been paying her his addresses.[51]

That Sunday, the report in *LWN* opened with these words:

> On Tuesday an intense degree of excitement prevailed in the neighbourhood of Bethnal Green, in consequence of a rumour that a young woman named Emma Whiter, 21 years of age, had been shot dead with a pistol.[52]

First reports published on the murder of Mr Moore and Mr Collard by Emanuel Barthelemy in December 1854 were also more or less identical:

> *The Times*: 'A twofold murder of the most atrocious and determined character took place last night, about a quarter before 9 o'clock in Warren-street, Fitzroy-square.'[53]

> *LWN*: 'A twofold murder of the most atrocious and determined character took place on Friday night, about a quarter before nine o'clock, in Warren-street, Fitzroy-square.'[54]

Both newspapers printed graphic details about the level of violence involved in the crimes. Reporters for *The Times* and *LWN* attempted to reconstruct what probably happened in those fatal moments for the interest of readers. These narratives were usually supplemented by descriptive testimonies of police surgeons about the nature of the injuries received. Reports published in both newspapers were graphic; neither *LWN* nor *The Times* considered any details about violence and injuries unfit for publication. The surgeon's evidence at Emanuel Barthelemy's police-court examination was printed in the fullest manner possible by *The Times* and *LWN*:

> *LWN*: '[The surgeon] discovered a wound on the eye-brow, about half an inch from the root of the nose. On examining it he found that the wound reached into the brain, and that some of the brain was oozing out of the wound. On further examination he found two jagged wounds at the top of the head, penetrating to the scalp. There was likewise a wound on the back of the head. In the parlour to which the deceased was carried there was a broken chair, on which there were several spots or splashes of blood, at about the height a man's head would reach on sitting in the chair. There were similar marks on the covers and cushions of the sofa. He also saw a lump of lead, which he produced, weighing two or three pounds.'[55]

> *The Times*: 'About half-past eleven last night I was called to a house in Warren-street to see a person who had been shot, and found a man lying on his back in the passage quite dead, with a large quantity of blood flowing around him about the floor where his head was lying. I examined him and first discovered a wound just about half an inch from the root of the nose. On further examination and probing I found the wound extended to the left base of the skull, and some brain was protruding. I also discovered two torn and jagged wounds on the top of the head penetrating

to the bone. There was likewise a wound on the back of the head. That was all I noticed respecting the person of the deceased, but in the parlour where they carried him, was a broken chair, about the height of where a man would be sitting, and about the same height on the wall, about where his head would reach, were splashes of blood. I also saw the lump of lead (produced) in the room.'[56]

Similarly, reports on the murder of Mr Briggs in a train on the north London railway in July 1864 covered the same details, almost word for word, in order to build up a horrendous picture of events for readers. Both described the discovery of the outrage by a passenger who boarded the train at Hackney:

He had opened the door at Hackney with the intention of getting in, and had placed his hand on one of the cushions, which he found to be covered with blood. The guard ... found such to be the fact. Not only the cushions, but the floor, sides and windows were besmeared with blood; in some places there was quite a pool.'

Next both mentioned that the body of a gentleman was found by the tracks 'saturated with blood and apparently dead'. Briggs's injuries were then listed in great detail, both reporters drawing heavily on the statement of the attending surgeon. Finally, both printed long accounts of blood splatters emanating from the scene of the crime, including the complaint of several ladies to the guard

that some blood had been spurted through the window of their compartment when the train was passing near Victoria-park. The medical gentlemen account for this by suggesting that in the struggle, when Mr Briggs was forced out of the door of the carriage, one of the arteries in the wound on the side of the head burst from frightful exertion, and so would spurt the blood in the manner the ladies described.[57]

Reports in *The Times* and *LWN* on the trials of the accused at the police courts and the Central Criminal Court were thorough. Especially in the case of 'celebrity murderers', when reports are compared with the *CCCP* it is impressive to see just how much content editors managed to squeeze into their tightly packed newspaper columns. Both *LWN* and *The Times* attempted to regurgitate to readers as much of the witness statements as possible. In addition, in both newspapers slices of extra narrative were placed before, after and within witness statements for readers' enjoyment, so that they might feel as if they were participating in the event. The crowds gathering at the police courts and Central

Criminal Court were often referred to at the very opening of the article, their presence and behaviour at times attracting condemnation from both newspapers. Readers' attention was drawn to the presence of both the uncouth and the respectable. For instance, when Maria Manning appeared before the police magistrate charged with the murder of Patrick O'Connor on 1 September 1849, the newspapers opened with these words:

> *The Times*: 'At half-past nine o'clock the entrance was beset by an assemblage, which greatly increased in numbers as the day advanced. The court was at once filled when the doors opened at 10 o'clock. By the judicious arrangements and courtesy of Mr Edwin, the chief clerk, the scanty space at disposal for the public accommodation was turned as far as possible to account. Among those present were the Chief Secretary of the Austrian Embassy, the Hon. Mr Stanhope, the Rev. Mr Warton, rector of St George's, Southwark ...'[58]

> *LWN*: 'This morning having been fixed for the re-examination of Mrs Manning, long before ten o'clock, the hour at which the business of the court usually commences, the broad thoroughfare in front of the office was crowded, and a double row of police were on duty to keep the thoroughfare from being entirely blocked up ... Long before the business of the court commenced the interior was very much crowded with persons anxious to gain a glance at the accused, and amongst those were a great number of fashionably attired ladies. On the bench were numerous intimate friends of the magistrate.'[59]

In order to present information that appeared to be as accurate as possible, both *The Times* and *LWN* tended to print rather mundane accounts of witness statements, often in question-answer lists, the precise words being reconstructed from the short-hand of the court reporter. However, to spice up the reading experience as well as to assess the character and motivations of those involved in the crime, reporters added, often in parentheses, details about the reactions and behaviour of the accused and witnesses. When questioned by the coroner at the inquest for the children Robert and Amina Blake murdered by Harriet Parker in 1848, father Robert Blake, stating the time he last saw his children, 'was here much affected, and appeared to suffer from deep anguish of mind. Garner, the summoning officer, gave him some water.'[60] Similarly, as the surgeon presented his evidence at the examination of James Tapping for the murder of Emma Whiter

in February 1845, reporters for *The Times* and *LWN* wrote that the
following occurred:

> When he arrived at the description of the wound in the deceased's
> throat, the prisoner's younger sister, a girl of about eighteen years
> of age, who had stationed herself near the door of the clerk's
> office, and had been watching his evidence with intense anxiety,
> uttered a piercing scream, and fell to the ground in hysterics. She
> was instantly carried out by the officers but it was at least twenty
> minutes before she had returned to consciousness.[61]

Finally, accounts of executions were often surprisingly similar.
When Harriet Parker was executed on 22 February 1848, the report
that appeared in *LWN* the following weekend was an exact reprint of
that which had appeared in *The Times*.[62] This may have been because,
given the delay and the absence of additional sensational details,
plagiarism, or even perhaps the purchase of a report from a freelance
journalist, saved much time and money. *LWN* did dispatch its own
reporters to executions, but probably only in cases when boosted sales
and good profits were assured. Such a special occasion presented itself
in 1856, when the Rugeley poisoner, William Palmer, was executed at
Stafford on Saturday 14 June. Lloyd dispatched journalists to Stafford
for the composition of a special issue in the comfortable knowledge
that the Sunday papers would be the first to report on the event and
that Londoners would be anxious to read about the fate of an infamous
serial killer whose trial had been held in the capital.[63] Lloyd also used
the opportunity to publicise his purchase of a Hoe Rotary press, which
enabled the publication of the very latest details:

> THE EXECUTION OF PALMER. The Execution which took place
> at Stafford at eight o'clock on Saturday morning was printed and
> published in LLOYD'S WEEKLY LONDON NEWSPAPER AT NINE
> O'CLOCK (within one hour of the time), when, until late on
> Sunday night, the publishing office was besieged by newsagents
> anxiously waiting for the various Editions during that period.
> TWO HUNDRED THOUSAND COPIES were sold, and many more
> thousands would have been eagerly seized if they could have been
> printed; but from this difficulty the proprietor in future will be
> relieved by HOE's MONSTER ROTARY MACHINE.[64]

But William Palmer's execution was an exception to a general rule.
Even when reports published in *The Times* and *LWN* differed in length,
the general formula and message were the same: execution crowds
faced general condemnation, comment was made on the behaviour of

Table 3   Coverage of famous murders
by *Lloyd's Weekly Newspaper* and *The Times*, 1840–70

Murderer	LWN [a]		The Times [b]	
	Columns	Pages	Columns	Pages
Thomas Hocker, 1845	32.25	6.45	26.2	4.36
Harriet Parker, 1848	5.43	1.086	5.5	0.91
The Mannings, 1849	93.8	18.76	62.05	10.34
Emanuel Barthelemy, 1854–55	8.75	1.75	9.25	1.54
William Palmer, 1855–56	104.65	20.93	109.1	18.18
William Bousefield, 1856	4.6	0.92	3.0	0.5
William Godfrey Youngman, 1860	9.75	1.95	8.05	1.34
Franz Muller, 1864	72.5	14.5	74.8	12.46
John Wiggins, 1867	6.8	1.36	6.8	1.13

Notes:
[a] *Lloyd's Weekly Newspaper*: 5 columns of text per page
[b] *The Times*: 6 columns of text per page

the felon and euphemisms were employed to describe the moment of death.

Parallels in crime reporting in *The Times* and *LWN* are further evident when we consider just how much space each devoted to the narrative of crime and its punishment in the case of celebrity murderers. As table 3 demonstrates, it was more or less equal. For the Golden Lane murder in 1848 (Harriet Parker), *The Times* devoted approximately 5.5 columns, or 0.91 pages, to its coverage, while *LWN* published 5.43 columns, or 1.086 pages, on the crime. For Emanuel Barthelemy's murder of Mr Moore and Mr Collard in 1854–55, *The Times* filled 9.25 columns, or 1.54 pages, with reports, *LWN* about 8.75 columns, or 1.75 pages. They printed the same number of columns on John Wiggins's murder of his wife, Agnes Oates, in 1867, *LWN* reports covering just slightly more pages as fewer columns appeared on each page (*LWN*, 1.36 pages, *The Times*, 1.13 pages). Where *LWN* gained a lead over *The Times* in coverage, it was often because at the start of each week's report the editor would reprint part or even the whole of the report from the previous edition. Thus, based on this evidence – the space devoted to reporting infamous murders in addition to the common language and presentation of violence in the articles – we could conclude that reports of violent crime consumed by many working- and lower-middle-class readers were not so very different from those that the respectable classes were devouring in their fashionable West End clubs and semi-detached villas in suburbia.

However, there are some quirks in the style of crime reporting used by Lloyd that need to be flagged. These might seem rather minor to us, but they would have been full of significance for contemporaries. While both papers added extra narrative details to their accounts of police-court and Central Criminal Court proceedings to make them more digestible, LWN, at times, went much further than The Times. Often reports would contain slightly more description on the clothing and physical features of the accused. And particular features of a criminal case which The Times thought unfit for publication might appear in LWN. For instance, during the inquest on the death of James Delarue, and the examination and trial of Thomas Hocker for his murder, there were numerous hints that a homosexual relationship might have existed between the murderer and his victim. While The Times avoided any reference to this aspect of the case, LWN went into some depth on the topic, providing readers with regular snippets of evidence for their 'most revolting practices'.[65]

In addition, Lloyd not only incorporated traditions from the broadsides in his newspaper, but also popular styles he had developed in publishing penny instalment fiction. Whereas articles on infamous murders in The Times appeared only after specific events in the tale, thus leaving large gaps in the publishing sequence, in LWN, weekly instalments were issued, from the discovery of the murder until the execution, often in an unbroken sequence and even when there was no news or event from that week to report. As the occasion of a notorious murder would increase sales, Lloyd worked hard to keep those extra readers gained by the event, at least until the story of the crime came to a conclusion. The lengthy time between conviction and execution in the nineteenth century could be filled with smaller articles on the behaviour of the murderer in the condemned cell, on the visitors he or she might have received there, or even on the food they were being served.

In the case of particularly long delays, when all publishable news had been exhausted, Lloyd would instead print a prominent advertisement for the next week's edition, promising fresh and exciting intelligence. For example, in the time between the committal and trial of Thomas Hocker, this notice was published to reassure readers:

TRIAL OF THOS. HENRY HOCKER. In consequence of the increased circulation of 'LLOYD'S WEEKLY NEWSPAPER' (the sale of which is now upwards of 100,000) which the proprietor feels justified in attributing very largely, to the ample and correct reports that have appeared from time to time in its columns, and being anxious that it shall maintain that pre-eminence over every other Journal in the annals of Newspaper publication, of which it can now justly boast, has entered into extensive arrangements to have every particular connected with the TRIAL OF THOMAS HENRY HOCKER FOR THE MURDER OF MR DE LA RUE AT HAMPSTEAD, correctly reported, as also many facts hitherto unpublished, which will appear in the paper of NEXT WEEK.[66]

Similar advertisements appeared during the coverage of the murder of Patrick O'Connor by Maria and Frederick George Manning in 1849 and the conviction of the serial poisoner William Palmer in 1856.[67] Moreover, Lloyd was not adverse to publishing advertisements for crime ephemera related to the particular murder under investigation. During the pursuit, trial and execution of Franz Muller in 1864, for instance, small advertisements for Muller 'carte-de-visite' continued to appear.[68]

So far we have described very subtle contrasts between the coverage of murders in *The Times* and in *LWN*. By far the most obvious, and the one which probably led contemporaries and historians to emphasise the violence and sensationalism of *LWN*, was the actual proportion of space dedicated to crime reporting in relation to other news items. If we take another look at the space devoted by each newspaper to articles on famous murders from a different angle this becomes very clear. Table 4 shows the amount of space *The Times* and *LWN* used to cover a series of infamous murders out of the total number of pages published from the commission of the crime (the first reports to appear) until the execution (the last reports to appear). The difference in proportion is striking: 6.45 per cent of *LWN* was concerned with covering the crimes of William Palmer in 1856, compared with just 0.92 per cent of *The Times*. When William Godfrey Youngman brutally murdered his whole family in 1860, *LWN* used 2.7 per cent of available space, in contrast to *The Times* which filled no more than 0.26 per cent.

There are serious limits to this line of argument, mostly based on the fact that we are dealing with a daily and a weekly newspaper, and as such there will be significant differences in the presentation of news. But if we look at the content of *LWN* more generally, especially the topics of articles that surrounded the crime reports, it becomes very

Table 4 Proportion of total published pages devoted to famous murder coverage, *Lloyd's Weekly Newspaper* and *The Times*, 1840–70

Murderer	LWN[a]			The Times[b]		
	total pp	murder pp	% murder	total pp	murder pp	% murder
Thomas Hocker, 1845	132	6.45	4.8	672	4.36	0.64
Harriet Parker, 1848	108	1.086	1	540	0.91	0.16
The Mannings, 1849	168	18,76	11.1	960	10.34	1.07
Emanuel Barthelemy, 1854–55	96	1.75	1.8	468	1.54	0.32
William Palmer, 1855–56	324	20.93	6.45	1968	18.18	0.92
William Bousfield, 1856	108	0.92	0.85	600	0.5	0.08
William Godfrey Youngman, 1860	72	1.95	2.7	512	1.34	0.26
Franz Muller, 1864	192	14.5	7.5	1408	12.46	0.88
John Wiggins, 1867	156	1.36	0.8	1120	1.13	0.1

Notes:

[a] LWN: published 12 pages per week

[b] *The Times*: published 12 pages per day, from 1860 published 16 pages per day

Table 5   Proportion of *Lloyd's Weekly Newspaper*
devoted to sensational news, 1840–70 (%)

Date	Sensational content
March 1843	27.56
September 1843	25.05
March 1849	25.37
September 1849	34.81[a]
March 1855	12.33
September 1855	18.8
March 1859	20.81
September 1859	26.81
March 1864	27.39
September 1864	34.30[b]
March 1870	20.42
September 1870	20.50

Notes:
[a] Coverage of the Bermondsey murder this month (the Mannings) took up approximately 12.5% of coverage; without this murder for month: 22.31%; therefore, coverage added on top of month
[b] Coverage of the train murder this month (Franz Muller) took up approximately 7.37% of coverage; without this murder for month: 26.93%; therefore, coverage added on top of month

clear why proportion matters. Editors of weekly newspapers had to make important judgements about what news of that week to include. At Lloyd's publishing house in Salisbury Square, stories of human tragedy from around the country, and even from around the globe, seemed to take precedence. Table 5 shows just how much of *LWN* was devoted to sensational news from 1843 to 1870, the average being around 24 per cent. Virginia Berridge estimates that the proportion increased further after 1870, reaching around 50 per cent in 1886.[69] Yet the category of sensationalism covers a wide variety of news, from criminal intelligence, to reports of accidents and natural disasters, to accounts of scandals such as divorce and adultery in high life. Thus, if we break down the sensational content into a series of subsections

Table 6   Categories of sensationalism
in *Lloyd's Weekly Newspaper*, 1840–70 (%)

Date	Violence and crime		Accidents/ natural disasters	Scandal	Misc.
	Total	(violence)[a]			
Mar 1843	81.38	(33.87)	16.98	0.22	0.0
Sept 1843	82.90	(31.48)	14.16	1.33	1.33
Mar 1849	81.19	(41.52)	11.08	7.3	0.0
Sept 1849	89.69	(50.91)	8.59	0.15	0.83
Mar 1855	82.60	(32.96)	10.60	3.37	0.0
Sept 1855	82.03	(37.44)	17.81	0.16	0.0
Mar 1859	83.51	(36.17)	10.34	4.0	0.28
Sept 1859	59.02	(34.67)	38.74	1.80	0.30
Mar 1864	68.30	(33.48)	27.65	3.57	0.0
Sept 1864	81.29	(56.39)	17.12	0.85	1.20
Mar 1870	69.73	(32.88)	12.69	18.72	0.26
Sept 1870	76.39	(42.38)	19.0	3.40	0.0

Note:
[a] % of total sensational content

(table 6), although crime and violence dominate, the actual proportion of violence is much less than we might otherwise assume, averaging at around one-third of the total sensational content. And finally, if we look at the violent content in *LWN* as a whole, it rarely comprises more than 10 per cent of the newspaper, and often a good deal less than that (see table 7).[70]

This hard evidence is certainly useful, especially in debunking or at least challenging some of the long-held assumptions about the publishing practices in the mid-century popular press. But hard evidence also has limits and does not tell us a great deal about the actual experience of reading *LWN* each week. The category of violence is limited to articles on interpersonal violence, including suicides and also a very tiny number of cases of cruelty towards animals. However, a different, though equally valid, type of violence was contained in tales about various accidents and natural disasters too. Through often graphic descriptions, these articles captured the tragedy encountered by

Table 7   Proportion of whole of *Lloyd's Weekly Newspaper*
devoted to violent content (%)

Date	Violence
March 1843	9.31
September 1843	7.80
March 1849	10.53
September 1849	17.7
March 1855	4.06
September 1855	7.04
March 1859	7.53
September 1859	9.30
March 1864	9.17
September 1864	19.34
March 1870	6.71
September 1870	8.68

victims, for example lives lost in shipwrecks, bodies mutilated in boiler explosions. The images invoked by these narratives are important as they contributed to the general sentiment expounded by the newspaper, and the atmosphere created for the reader.

A good proportion of violent content, and even more general sensational news, was presented to readers of *LWN* in regular columns. Intelligence from the police courts was typically published in two headed sections on pages 3 and 12, with cases from other law courts, such as the Central Criminal Court, the Middlesex Sessions and the Provincial Assizes, placed alongside these and also always with distinctive headings. Regular readers would also know to find short sensational articles in the column reserved for provincial news. The subheadings presented in this section of news on 11 August 1867 were typical: 'Bedfordshire: murder and robbery; Cheshire: poaching and affray near Macclesfield; Cumberland: murder and suicide; Lancashire: wife murders in Liverpool; Staffordshire: two men scolded to death in a boiler; Surrey: death of a gentleman shot by his brother; Yorkshire: the alleged murder at Beverly'.[71] The arrangement of these narratives in regular columns is important, but equally so are the number of articles, small and large, on murder, infanticide, assault and suicide, not to mention various disasters and accidents, scattered throughout the pages of *LWN* each week, inserted randomly, wherever there was a space that needed to be filled.

Finally, some effort was made to tentatively link particularly violent crimes in separate reports. Multiple columns of text covering more prominent murders in the metropolis were sometimes surrounded by smaller articles drawing attention to similar crimes around the country. As the tale of the Rugeley poisoner William Palmer unfolded in the pages of *LWN* in 1856, other cases of poisonings, harmful and fatal, accidental and deliberate, were published alongside the dominant story. Similarly, reports on various outrages and unfortunate incidents in railway carriages increased substantially as the newspaper covered the murder of Mr Briggs by Franz Muller on the north London railway in 1864. Furthermore, Lloyd expanded that minor trait found in some broadsides of making reference to previous, infamous murders. The opening report for the murder of Patrick O'Connor by the Mannings in August 1849 began with these words: 'One of the most appalling and cold-blooded murders that has probably been heard of since that perpetrated by the notorious Daniel Good, was discovered yesterday afternoon.'[72] Thomas Hocker's murder of James Delarue was compared with that of William Weare by John Thurtell in 1823.[73] Through this technique, reporters invoked the memories readers had of these murders so that they might be able to imagine and visualise the extent of the violence involved in the recent event.

Readers were already well acquainted with this practice. Invoking the names of murderers past was part of a common language of violence used throughout the Victorian period at least. Evidence of the use of this language can be glimpsed in trials for various assaults as perpetrators were sometimes said to have used the name of an infamous murderer to describe their intentions to their victims. After the especially gruesome murder and mutilation of Hannah Brown by James Greenacre in 1837, several criminal trials followed in which witnesses claimed that the accused had invoked the name of Greenacre much to their concern and fright. During a robbery in June 1837, victim Catherine Crawford of the Hutchinson Arms in Ratcliffe claimed that the thief stated: '"If you do not give [the money] to me, it will be the worst day's work you ever did, for I will serve you as Greenacre served Mrs Brown" – I am quite sure he used that expression – he repeated several times about Greenacre, and I was very much alarmed.'[74] Similarly, in September 1849 drunken bricklayer John Ryan made this threat to Mr Tucker, a pianoforte maker, that he would 'serve him as Manning had O'Connor'.[75]

Volume combined with disorderly presentation and loose, suggestive connections between acts of gross violence led this reader, interviewed by Henry Mayhew, to announce, 'I read *Lloyd's Weekly Newspaper* on a Sunday, and what murders and robberies there is now!' We know from the statistical evidence available that interpersonal violence generally was in decline throughout the nineteenth century.[76] We cannot assume that just because a high proportion of violence was reported in the newspapers that the incidence of murder and assault was particularly high at this time. But reader perception is important and might point towards some deeper meanings. John Archer and Joanne Jones have suggested that the representation of violent crime in newspapers, especially when graphic, identified certain behaviours as deviant and unacceptable, thus defining criminality for readers by invoking their moral outrage.[77] Other historians have also demonstrated how newspapers, in their presentation of specific types of violent crime in large quantities, could initiate a moral panic in society, such as the garrotting panic during the early 1860s.[78]

But the narratives of violent crime contained in *LWN* were, on the whole, just too random to create specific panics or to fan fears of specialised crimes amongst readers. Moreover, messages contained in the various reports were often too contradictory to suggest set patterns of criminal behaviour or to present a critique on the response of authority and systems of punishment. There was just too much range and variety in the content. While several reports from the police courts might condemn assaults on police officers, others might be concerned with crimes committed by police constables, or even the haphazard nature of their evidence against the accused in a murder trial. Statements about the justness of public execution for murderers sat alongside articles expressing disapprobation at the behaviour of the crowds who watched the felons die. Journalists would bemoan the public excitement and curiosity about murders at the opening of their reports about police-court examinations and criminal trials, while also openly encouraging and excusing such interest when promoting the coverage of these cases provided by the newspaper. In one sense, then, crime reporting in *LWN* was rather similar to that of the late eighteenth- and early nineteenth-century London press recently described by Peter King: 'the newspapers' lack of in-depth accounts, their collage-like style and their multi-vocal nature ... forced readers to forge their own sense of the degree to which printed discourses might offer them any real insights into, or strategies for understanding, both the prevalence of crime and the effectiveness of authorities' reactions to it'.[79]

In the mid-nineteenth century, for the readers of *LWN*, it was the quantity and the variety that were of primary importance, as each week readers would devour several different stories about violent crime, alongside tales of other types of human tragedy, which highlighted the dangerous possibilities of modern life. Snippets of evidence suggest that these reports were read aloud in family or social groups and discussed. In the trial of James Greenacre for the murder of his former paramour, Hannah Brown, Henry Wignall, landlord of his supposed partner in the crime, Sarah Gale, told the court that in the days following the crime, he read reports from the newspaper describing the discovery of the body parts of Brown to his wife, sister and friend.[80] It was with great glee that the crime reporter for *LWN* told readers that Abraham Austin and Charlotte Ffrench had shared a copy of that newspaper containing detailed reports on the murder of James De la Rue with James Hocker, brother of the murderer Thomas Hocker.[81]

This practice in addition to the links clearly established with other printed genres, namely the broadsides and penny bloods, indicate that reading about violent crime was enjoyable, a form of entertainment. But the process of sharing and, in particular, the act of vocalising the very graphic descriptions of violence contained in the newspaper reports are at odds with notions of respectable reading, whereby readers might choose to skip over such reports, or at least peruse them silently and discreetly. Thus the consumption of stories about crime and human tragedy by the growing mass readership for *Lloyd's Weekly Newspaper* and its competitors smoothed over divisions within and between classes, providing a means of cultural expression which gave vent to fears about the modern city but also, through its clear assertiveness, set some firm boundaries on the potential reach and implications of respectable ideals.

Violence, respectability and the New Journalism

As we have seen in previous chapters, by 1860 a number of genres that formed part of the 'culture of violence' had begun to decline. In this chapter, we have shown how *LWN* emerged into this environment, drew much inspiration from its range of expressions, and used different genres to shape its style of crime reporting and much of its presentation of violence and sensation. How was *LWN* (and other popular Sunday newspapers) going to survive without this supportive and reaffirming network?

Traditionally, some historians have argued that Edward Lloyd, aware of the winds of change, pragmatically decided to ditch his penny-blood business and concentrate on making his thriving newspaper more respectable. First, we have been told, Lloyd tried to erase his 'unrespectable' publishing history by destroying all evidence of his previous business. Some have said that during the late 1850s Lloyd and his agents visited street stalls, newsagents' stands and chandlers' shops in an attempt to purchase and eliminate any penny numbers still displayed for sale.[82] Lloyd's success in this endeavour is perhaps evident in the omission of his penny fiction publishing in many accounts of his life, from obituaries on his death, to his original entry in the *Dictionary of National Biography*, to the favourable portraits written by early newspaper historians.[83] Second, Lloyd employed a new, well-known and respectable editor on a handsome salary to run his newspaper in 1856: the famous Douglas Jerrold.[84] Reflecting on this appointment, London publisher Henry Vizetelly stated that *LWN* was previously 'of a poor standing … Jerrold found it, as it were, in the gutter, and annexed it to literature'.[85]

The story of Lloyd's pursuit of respectability and move to distance himself and his publications from their roots does fit with other general trends. For example, we can see how, during the mid-1860s, the theme of violence and its committed audience were picked up by a new marginal press which, with simultaneous increases in literacy, incomes and distribution capabilities could attract a large enough specialised audience to survive. In particular, I am referring to the founding of the *Illustrated Police News* in 1864 and its smaller competitors, such as the *Police Budget* (see figure 43). These publications represented a throwback and an intensification of the broadside traditions. The use of wood engraving for the illustrations which covered the front page meant that images of violence were much more detailed and realistic. Some casual readers of these publications remember being haunted by the pictures of murder and violence they consumed.[86] The most famous of these pictorial papers, the *Illustrated Police News*, never achieved a national circulation higher than about 100,000, its marginal status as a publication further confirmed by the risqué advertisements it tended to run, from cheap biographies of murderers, to pornography, and cures for sexually transmitted diseases.[87]

So far so good. However, when we look back in detail at the actual content of *LWN* for the rest of the nineteenth century, not to mention at some of the readers it continued to attract, does this particular story about respectability really stand up? The very limited evidence on reading experience for the last decades of the nineteenth century that we have tends to show that the audience did not really change at all. New readers seemed to come from the same social groups, the greater numbers being attracted as Lloyd, and his succession of canny editors,

THE ILLUSTRATED
POLICE NEWS
LAW COURTS AND WEEKLY RECORD.

[No. 327. SATURDAY, MAY 21, 1870. [PRICE ONE PENNY.

PRISONER RE-CAPTURED | HORRIBLE DOUBLE MURDER IN CHELSEA | POLICE EFFECTING AN ENTRANCE IN MR HUELIN'S HOUSE

HOUSE IN PAULTONS SQUARE—MILLER GIVEN INTO CUSTODY | BREAKING OPEN THE BOX—DISCOVERY OF MURDERED WOMAN | FINDING THE BODY OF THE REVD MR HUELIN | HOUSE IN WELLINGTON SQUARE WHERE THE BODY OF MR HUELIN WAS FOUND

HEADS OF THE GREEK BRIGANDS | MEN IN WOMEN'S CLOTHES—THE DRESSING ROOM

43. The graphic front page of the *Illustrated Police News* (1870)

continued to include a wide mix of elements and themes to ensure mass appeal. With its soft liberal politics, the newspaper was seen by many in the higher classes as harmless but not really very respectable. Molly Hughes (b. 1866), for example, daughter of a stockbroker, remembered 'how horrified my father was on discovering that the servants had been reading little bits to me out of *Lloyd's Weekly*'.[88] In the main, this reaction was encouraged by the fact that much of the content remained unchanged. Tables 6 and 7 show that the employment of a respectable editor really did very little to reduce the proportion of violence and sensation in *LWN* before 1870. Virginia Berridge argues that sensation had increased even more by the mid-1880s, the concluding years of her study.[89]

Instead, the survival and unprecedented success of *LWN* in the latter decades of the nineteenth century is largely a story of appropriation, and a much more interesting one at that. This process has already been glimpsed above, in the comparison of the coverage of infamous murders by *The Times* and *LWN*. Violence, especially in the form of crime reporting, did not always have to be unrespectable. Knowing this, Edward Lloyd just moved to consolidate his position during the 1850s. He was aware that popular culture was changing and so severed the potentially unprofitable arm of his business, the penny bloods. But it was clear that factual violence would not fall out of fashion so quickly. Thus Lloyd ensured that his newspaper would attract a mass audience, and in the process of increasing its circulation, to the unheard of figure of 1 million in 1896, he managed to channel some of that violence and sensation into the mainstream press of the late nineteenth century. These characteristics certainly emerged in the New Journalism of 1880–1914. Historians point to the general shift away from parliamentary and political news to sport, gossip, crime and sex, emphasising the significant part played by crime reporting, while also acknowledging the important legacy of the mid-century Sunday press.[90] As Aled Jones argues, the period of the New Journalism in England was partly defined by a decreasing concern with respectability matched with a new pursuit of profit.[91]

Respectability, as least in its purest form, mattered very little to profit-hungry news proprietors when collecting and publishing reports on gruesome murders in the last two decades of the nineteenth century. For example, the Ripper murders of autumn 1888 guaranteed the success of the new halfpenny evening paper *The Star*, launched in January of that year.[92] And as L. Perry Curtis has shown, there was really very little difference between the styles of reporting on the event in the highbrow, middlebrow and lowbrow press: 'while they had smaller and less sensational headlines and fewer subheads, *The Times* and *The Morning Post* served up almost as much morbid detail as any mass circulation newspaper with the obvious exception of *Lloyd's Weekly Newspaper* ... If the London press differed in the volume of gore produced, almost every paper published material capable of shocking or thrilling readers.' Curtis concludes that much of the detail, especially that derived from the autopsy reports, would not be considered fit to print in today's tabloids.[93] The same could be said for many of the murder reports published by *The Times* and *LWN* during the 1840s, 1850s and 1860s.

Thus, through tracing the development, fine-tuning and appropriation of popular crime-reporting genres, this chapter, and indeed this book, has shown how violence can be considered a kind of cultural amoeba, always present in British society, but changing its shape and meaning depending on various external pressures, and the audience it attracts at a given moment. For the late nineteenth-century mass newspaper audience, its presence symbolised something very different from what it had meant to the mid-century artisan or dock labourer, newly literate, in search of entertainment, and coming to grips with the changing urban and social environment of the metropolis. In other words, the deeper motivations which drove readers of all classes to buy newspapers with the latest intelligence on the Ripper murders, and to repeat those narratives in different forms, might have changed, but the extent to which these readers could claim to be 'civilised' needs to be questioned.

Notes

1 C. M. Smith, *Curiosities of London Life* (London: A. W. Bennett, 1853), pp. 256–7.

2 D. Vincent, *Literacy and Popular Culture: England, 1750–1914* (Cambridge: Cambridge University Press, 1989), p. 252.

3 The most detailed analysis of the content of *Lloyd's Weekly Newspaper* remains V. S. Berridge's often-cited 1972 dissertation: 'Popular journalism and working-class attitudes, 1854–1886: a study of *Reynolds's Newspaper, Lloyd's Weekly Newspaper* and the *Weekly Times*' (PhD diss., University of London, 1972). See also Berridge, 'Popular Sunday papers and mid-Victorian society', in G. Boyce, J. Curran and P. Wingate (eds), *Newspaper History from the Seventeenth Century to the Present Day* (London: Constable, 1978). More attention has centred on *Reynolds's Newspaper* with its strong political radicalism and clear links with G. W. M. Reynolds's fiction:

e.g. A. Humphreys, 'G. W. M. Reynolds: popular literature and popular politics', in J. H. Wiener (ed.), *Innovators and Preachers: The Role of the Editor in Victorian England* (Westport: Greenwood, 1985), pp. 3–21, Humphreys, 'Popular narrative and political discourse in *Reynolds's Weekly Newspaper*', in L. Brake, A. Jones and L. Madden (eds), *Investigating Victorian Journalism* (Basingstoke: Macmillan, 1990), and R. Williams, 'Radical and/or respectable', in R. Boston (ed.), *The Press we Deserve* (London: Routledge & Kegan Paul, 1970). For other works on the rise of the Sunday newspaper, see R. Williams, 'The press and popular culture: an historical perspective', in Boyce *et al.*, *Newspaper History*, R. D. Altick, *The English Common Reader: A Social History of the Mass Reading Public, 1800–1900* (Chicago: University of Chicago Press, 1957), D. Mitch, *The Rise of Popular Literacy in Victorian England: The Influence of Private Choice and Public Policy* (Philadelphia: University of Pennsylvania Press, 1992), A. J. Lee, *The Origins of the Popular Press in England* (London: Croom Helm, 1976), A. Jones, *Powers of the Press: Newspapers, Power and the Public in Nineteenth-Century England* (Aldershot: Ashgate, 1996), L. Brown, *Victorian News and Newspapers* (Oxford: Oxford University Press, 1985).

4 *Apprehension of Good for the Barbarous Murder of Jane Jones* (London, 1842), London, British Library (BL), 1881.d.8, *Examination of Good for the Barbarous Murder of Jane Jones* (London, 1842), Oxford, Bodleian Library (Bod.), John Johnson Collection (JJ), Murder and Execution Broadsides, 10 (40), *Trial of Good for the Murder of Jane Jones at Putney* (London, 1842), Bod., JJ, Murder and Execution Broadsides, 5 (41). These are the only broadsides published by Lloyd that I have been able to recover. There may be more in other collections of broadsides.

5 P. Hollis, *The Pauper Press: A Study in Working-Class Radicalism of the 1830s* (London: Oxford University Press, 1970), Berridge, 'Popular journalism and working-class attitudes', p. 21.

6 G. A. Sala, *The Life and Adventures of George Augustus Sala* (2 vols, London: Cassell & Co., 3rd edn, 1895), I, p. 209.

7 Ibid.

8 For example, see *Penny Sunday Times and People's Police Gazette*, 7 February 1841, p. 1, 20 September 1840, p. 1, 3 May 1840, p. 1, 4 July 1841, p. 1.

9 *Penny Sunday Times*, 3 May 1840, p. 1.

10 *Calendar of Horrors*, 1 (1835), 155.

11 Vincent, *Literacy and Popular Culture*, pp. 246–7, J. H. Wiener, *A Descriptive Finding List of Unstamped British Periodicals, 1830–1836* (London: Bibliographical Society, 1970).

12 Altick, *The English Common Reader*, p. 393.

13 M. Finn, *After Chartism: Class and Nation in English Radical Politics, 1848–1874* (Cambridge: Cambridge University Press, 1993), pp. 110–12.

14 Clear from the style of reporting, and reports do not appear in other newspapers. Also claimed by Thomas Catling, an editor for *Lloyd's Weekly Newspaper* during the 1850s: Catling, *My Life's Pilgrimage* (London: J. Murray, 1911), pp. 44–5.

15 L. James, *Fiction for the Working Man, 1830–1850: A Study of the Literature Produced for the Working Classes in Early Victorian Urban England* (London: Oxford University Press, 1963), p. 41.

16 Berridge, 'Popular journalism and working-class attitudes', p. 40.

17 Select Committee on Criminal and Destitute Juveniles (Parl. Papers, 1852, VII.1), evidence of Rev. John Clay, p. 196, 'General report founded on the reports of the Visiting Justices, the reports of the Chaplain and the Certificates of the Keeper of the Gaol and House of Correction at Ipswich in the County of Suffolk', Reports and Schedules pursuant to Gaol Acts (Parl. Papers, 1843, XLIII.1), p. 154.

18 Altick, *The English Common Reader*, pp. 394–5, J. Hatton, *Journalistic London* (London: S. Low, 1882), pp. 191–4.

19 Lee, *The Origins of the Popular Press in England*, p. 35.

20 H. Mayhew, *London Labour and the London Poor* (4 vols, London: Griffin, Bohn & Co., 1861–62), II, p. 113. See also 'Investigation into the state of the poorer classes in St George's-in-the-east', *Journal of the Statistical Society of London*, 11 (1848), 216.

21 E. G. Salmon, 'What the working classes read', *Nineteenth Century*, 20 (1886), 110–111.

22 Brown, *Victorian News and Newspapers*, p. 27.

23 Ibid., p. 29.

24 Williams, 'The press and popular culture', Brown, *Victorian News and Newspapers*.

25 Berridge, 'Popular Sunday papers and mid-Victorian society'.

26 Berridge, 'Popular journalism and working-class attitudes', pp. 74–86.

27 Ibid., p. 77.

28 Ibid., p. 71.

29 P. Anderson, *The Printed Image and the Transformation of Popular Culture* (Oxford: Clarendon Press, 1991).

30 R. K. Webb, *The British Working-Class Reader, 1790–1848: Literacy and Social Tension* (London: Allen & Unwin, 1955), R. S. Schofield, 'The dimensions of illiteracy, 1750–1850', *Explorations in Economic History*, 10 (1973), 437–54, Vincent, *Literacy and Popular Culture*, Mitch, *The Rise of Popular Literacy in Victorian England*.

31 *The Life, Trial, Confession and Execution of Harriet Parker for the*

Murder of Two Children in Golden Lane (London, 1848), BL 1881.d.8; *LWN*, 6 February 1848, p. 12.

32 *Life, Trial Confession and Execution of Harriet Parker for the Murder of Amina and Robert Blake, in Cupid's Court, Golden Lane* (London, 1848), Bod., JJ, Murder and Execution Broadsides, 11 (11).

33 Ibid., *The Life, Trial Confession and Execution of Harriet Parker*, BL 1881.d.8, *LWN*, 13 February 1848, p. 7, *The Times*, 15 February 1848, p. 8.

34 *Trial, Sentence and Execution of Samuel Wright at Horsemonger Lane* (London, 1864), Bod., JJ, Murder and Execution Broadsides, 11 (24), *LWN*, 20 December 1863, p. 7.

35 For example, *LWN*, 4 May 1845, p. 10, *The Times*, 29 April 1845, p. 7.

36 *Full Particulars of the Trial, Sentence and Execution of Thomas Hocker who was Executed at the Old Bailey this Morning for the Wilful Murder of James De la Rue* (London, 1845), BL 1881.d.8, *Life, Trial, Confession and Execution of Thomas Hocker for the Murder of Mr De La Rue. With the Copy of his Letter and the Condemned Sermon* (London, 1845), BL 1881.d.8.

37 *LWN*, 14 January 1855, p. 2, *The Times*, 11 January 1855, p. 9, *The Life, Trial, Sentence and Execution of Emanuel Barthelemy* (London, 1855), BL 1881.d.8, *Trial, Sentence and Execution of Emanuel Barthelemy who was Executed at the Old Bailey this morning for the Murder of Mr Collard and Mr Moore of Warren Street, Tottenham-Court Road, on the evening of the 8th of December last* (London, 1855), BL 1881.d.8.

38 *Life, Trial and Execution of T. H. Hocker for the Murder of Mr J. De La Rue* (London, 1845), BL 1881.d.8, *LWN*, 4 May 1845, p. 10.

39 'The proper time for public executions', *Punch*, 17 (1849), 214.

40 'Investigation into the state of the poorer classes in St George's-in-the-east', 216.

41 'Murder mania', *Chambers' Edinburgh Journal*, N.S. 12 (6 October 1849), 209–11.

42 S. Devereaux, 'The City and the Sessions Paper: public justice in London, 1770–1800', *Journal of British Studies*, 35 (1996), 466–503.

43 Select Committee on Newspaper Stamps (Parl. Papers, 1851, XVII.1), evidence of Michael James Whitty, editor of the *Liverpool Journal*, pp. 106–9. See also T. Wright, *Some Habits and Customs of the Working Classes* (London: Tinsley Brothers, 1867), p. 193. For the important role played by police courts in the community, see J. Davis, 'A poor man's system of justice: the London police courts in the second half of the nineteenth century', *Historical Journal*, 27 (1984), 309–35.

44 W. T. Stead, 'The maiden tribute of modern Babylon – II', *Pall Mall Gazette*, 7 July 1885, pp. 2–3.

45 The exception to this is June 1855, when the coverage dipped well below that of *LWN*. The reason for this may be extended coverage of the Crimean War. But then it is interesting that the War does not have the same impact on the coverage of court proceedings in *LWN*.

46 *The Times*, 5 April 1860, p. 11

47 *Old Bailey Proceedings Online* (www.oldbaileyonline.org) [*OBP*], September 1850, trial of Ellen Hoar (t18500916–1590).

48 *LWN*, 22 September 1850, p. 3, *The Times*, 19 September 1850, pp. 6–7.

49 *OBP*, November 1865, trial of Robert Hunter (t18651120–50).

50 *LWN*, 26 November 1865, p. 5, *The Times*, 25 November 1865, p. 12.

51 *The Times*, 29 January 1845, p. 7.

52 *LWN*, 2 February 1845, p. 10.

53 *The Times*, 9 December 1854, p. 10

54 *LWN*, 10 December 1854, p. 12.

55 *LWN*, 10 December 1854, p. 12. Identical to the report published in *Reynolds's Newspaper*, 10 December 1854, p. 16.

56 *The Times*, 11 December 1854, p. 10. Identical to the report published in the *Morning Chronicle*, 11 December 1854, p. 6.

57 *The Times*, 11 July 1864, p. 9, *LWN*, 17 July 1864, p. 5.

58 *The Times*, 1 September 1849, p. 5.

59 *LWN*, 2 September 1849, p. 10.

60 *The Times*, 1 January 1848, p. 6, *LWN*, 2 January 1848, p. 12.

61 *The Times*, 5 February 1845, p. 8, *LWN*, 9 February 1845, p. 10.

62 *LWN*, 27 February 1848, p. 5, *The Times*, 22 February 1848, p. 7.

63 *LWN*, 15 June 1848, p. 12, Catling, *My Life's Pilgrimage*, p. 59.

64 *LWN*, 22 June 1848, p. 6. Lloyd claimed that with the two machines he had purchased he would be able to print 30,000 copies of the newspaper per hour.

65 *LWN*, 2 March 1845, p. 3, and 13 April 1845, pp. 9–10.

66 *LWN*, 6 April 1845, p. 7.

67 *LWN*, 21 October 1849, p. 6, 11 November 1849, 22 June 1856, p. 6.

68 *LWN*, 16 October 1864, p. 9, 8 June 1856, p. 5, 21 October 1849, p. 6.

69 Berridge, 'Popular journalism and working-class attitudes', pp. 184–9. However, in her statistics, Berridge only looks at the proportion of editorial material, excluding advertising. As advertising increased after 1870, the proportion of sensational content to the whole newspaper might not have increased all that much.

70 For the two occasions in the table where it does rise above 10 per cent we must take into account that in these months the newspaper was covering two very famous, long-running murders: the Mannings (September 1849) and Franz Muller (September 1864).

71 *LWN*, 11 August 1867, p. 8.

72 *LWN*, 19 August 1849, p. 12.

73 *LWN*, 23 February 1845, p. 12.

74 *OBP*, June 1837, trial of William Gaskin and Mary Dowling (t18370612-1579). See also *OBP*, February 1839, trial of Jane Reeves (t18390204-684), and *OBP*, November 1843, trial of Edward Dwyer (t18431127-267). Judith Walkowitz identified the operation of this language of violence during the Jack the Ripper murders in London in 1888 also. See J. R. Walkowitz, 'Jack the Ripper and the myth of male violence', *Feminist Studies*, 8 (1982), 543–74.

75 *LWN*, 9 September 1849, p. 3.

76 The exception being of course domestic violence, which probably did not decline and might have even increased. See V. A. C. Gatrell, 'The decline of theft and violence in Victorian and Edwardian England and Wales', in V. A. C. Gatrell, B. Lenman and G. Parker (eds), *Crime and the Law: The Social History of Crime in Western Europe since 1500* (London: Europa, 1980), and M. J. Wiener, *Men of Blood: Violence, Manliness and Criminal Justice in Victorian England* (Cambridge: Cambridge University Press, 2004), pp. 2–8.

77 J. Archer and J. Jones, 'Headlines from history: violence in the press, 1850–1914', in E. Stanko (ed.), *The Meanings of Violence* (London: Routledge, 2003), pp. 17–31.

78 J. Davis, 'The London garrotting panic of 1862: a moral panic and the creation of a criminal class in mid-Victorian England', in Gatrell *et al.*, *Crime and the Law*, R. Sindall, *Street Violence in the Nineteenth Century: Media Panic or Real Danger?* (Leicester: Leicester University Press, 1990), Sindall, 'The London garrotting panics of 1856 and 1862', *Social History*, 12 (1987), 351–9.

79 P. King, 'Newspaper reporting and attitudes to crime and justice in late eighteenth and early nineteenth-century London', *Continuity and Change*, 22 (2007), 73–112, quote p. 77. See also P. Williams and J. Dickinson, 'Fear of crime: read all about it? The relationship between newspaper crime reporting and fear of crime', *British Journal of Criminology*, 33 (1993), 33–56.

80 *OBP*, April 1837, trial of James Greenacre and Sarah Gale (t18370403-917).

81 *LWN*, 9 March 1845, p. 9.

82 Berridge, 'Popular journalism and working-class attitudes', pp. 71–4.

83 *The Times*, 9 April 1890, p. 9, *Daily Chronicle*, 9 April 1890, p. 5, *LWN*, 13 April 1890, p. 7, V. E. Neuburg, *Popular Literature: A History and Guide* (Harmondsworth: Penguin, 1977), p. 171, Hatton, *Journalistic London*, pp. 188–93.

84 Berridge, 'Popular journalism and working-class attitudes', p. 73.

85 H. Vizetelly, *Glances Back through Seventy Years* (2 vols, London: Kegan Paul, 1893), I, pp. 270–80.

86 For example, E. Muir, *The Story and the Fable: An Autobiography* (London: G. G. Harrap, 1940), pp. 84–5, J. Stamper, *So Long Ago* (London: Hutchinson, 1960), pp. 161–2.

87 Altick, *The English Common Reader*, pp. 394–5.

88 M. V. Hughes, *A London Family, 1870–1900* (London: Oxford University Press, 1946), p. 73.

89 Berridge, 'Popular journalism and working-class attitudes', p. 186.

90 J. H. Wiener, 'How new was the New Journalism', in J. H. Wiener (ed.), *Papers for the Millions: The New Journalism in Britain, 1850s to 1914* (New York: Greenwood, 1986), pp. 49–65, Brown, *Victorian News and Newspapers*, p. 31, J. R. Walkowitz, *City of Dreadful Delight: Narratives of Sexual Danger in Late Victorian London* (Chicago: University of Chicago Press, 1992), p. 84, Jones, *Powers of the Press*, pp. 137–9, Lee, *The Origins of the Popular Press in England*, pp. 101, 128.

91 Jones, *Powers of the Press*, p. 137.

92 J. Goodbody, '*The Star*: its role in the rise of the New Journalism', in Wiener, *Papers for the millions*, pp. 143–63.

93 L. P. Curtis, *Jack the Ripper and the London Press* (New Haven: Yale University Press, 2001), p. 272.

Epilogue:

1870 – the civilising moment?

IDENTIFYING A TURNING POINT in history, a moment at which society became noticeably different, can be a relatively simple task. Explaining why that date holds significance, and accounting for the change that happened, is much more difficult. That is why this epilogue was long in the writing and went through many versions. Then in the first half of November 2010, a series of events occurred which encouraged me to think much more critically about the violent entertainments that feature in this book, in particular their function and legacy in British society.

At first, these events seemed rather trivial, as I encountered them not just in my 'everyday life', but at its most mundane moments. At the start of the month, I went to the cinema in Cambridge. The queue for tickets was long, and I soon realised the main attraction was a new film released that weekend for Halloween: *Saw 3D*. The film was the last instalment in a series of *Saw* films, each concerned with the machinations of a serial 'killer' called Jigsaw, who does not directly kill his victims but places them in 'traps' which they can only escape by undergoing severe psychological and physical violence. Since the release of the first *Saw* in 2004, each film has become progressively more horrific and gory. *Saw 3D*, as clear from the trailer playing in the ticket hall, took things to a new level: eyewear and special projection hardware meant that audiences were transported into the film, experiencing the violence of Jigsaw's traps first hand. Although the professional critics expressed some dissatisfaction with the film, notably its poor plot, they understood its attraction for the masses, that audiences 'enjoy the sight of limbs being hacked off and heads exploding'.[1] The film's popularity is undisputable. Not only did *Saw 3D* top the British charts for the month of November, but the *Saw* franchise has become the most successful horror movie ever, including seven films, two computer games and even a scary ride at Thorpe Park, just outside London.

A week later, while eating breakfast, I watched a news item about the release of a new computer game just in time for Christmas: *Call of Duty: Black Ops*. On 9 November, thousands of committed 'gamers' queued at shops around the country to get hold of a copy. These combined with post-release sales suggested that *Black Ops* would break international sales records. *Black Ops* is the latest in an established genre of first-person shooter games, the first being the controversial but popular *Wolfenstein 3D* released in May 1992. In these games, the human player is directly invited to participate. Instead of directing soldiers (or other protagonists) from above, the action is presented from the point of view of the player: s/he looks into the game, over the butt of a rifle or other weapon, moving around spaces and shooting enemies as they appear. Since 1992, these games have become ever more realistic, the latest, *Black Ops*, almost deceptively so. Nor are 'war games' the only first-person shooters on the market. For example, in *Left 4 Dead* you are placed in the midst of an apocalyptic pandemic of 'green flu', and as you kill the infected humans with various guns, bombs, or even a chainsaw, the blood and human debris is thrown at the screen – it feels as if you are literally covered in it. And there is a long history of street-fighting and boxing games which have also become more interactive over the past five years. Only the day after *Black Ops* arrived in the shops, Microsoft released *Kinect*, a new controller-free 3D gaming system. Among the family-friendly games available to play, customers could choose *Fighters Uncaged*. Instead of directing the protagonist to punch and kick his opponents with a controller, the player performs the actions which are detected by motion sensors and translated into fight-moves on the screen. In other words, now you can literally beat up a virtual person.

Horror movies and other extremely violent films and violent computer games have been popular for several decades now. November 2010 seemed to mark a crucial moment in the levels of audience interaction and participation in these entertainments which, with further techno-logical development in the next few years, will only become more seamless and feel 'more real'. What surprised me, however, was that this new technology failed to spark any notable discussion in our so-called 'civilised' society about the great quantities of graphic and gratuitous violence on movie, television and computer screens, not to mention as part of the spin-off products from merchandise (including T-shirts, mugs and key rings) to theme-park rides. Most of the products described above do carry a rating restricting their sale or admission to those over the age of eighteen. The limited debate encouraged by the release of *Black Ops* focused not on the violence of the game, but on concerns about younger players: from those who might be given the game for Christmas, to those who might encounter the game at a friend's house when their conscientious parents had decided not to purchase it in the first place.[2] Ratings are imposed on these products because responsible adults worry about the impact gratuitous violence might have on the young and impressionable. Proponents of the civilising process argue that this demonstrates the operation of civilised impulses as we actively protect those social groups that are as yet 'uncivilised'.[3] But there is a paradox in this argument: if we, as adults, have become civilised, and so are immune to any ill-effects of exposure, surely the fact that we are 'civilised' would mean that we would not want to experience exposure in the first place?

Moreover, I could not help but see in these entertainments a clear line of continuity with those I have described in this book. The central narratives of violence have changed. For example, whereas in this book we have been confronted with stories of violence in the nineteenth-century city and often in everyday life, the science fiction plots, mutant plagues and modern warfare missions do appear to be very late twentieth/ early twenty-first century. But then, as I have argued in this book, narratives of violence are time-bound. The display of violence is not, and if anything the audience for violent entertainments is larger and less defined by class and gender than it may have been at any point in the nineteenth century.

The year 1870 is frequently held up as a significant turning point in studies of nineteenth-century Britain and London. This book would seem to support that position. Over the course of the 1860s, many of the entertainments described in its chapters went through some sort of change so that after 1870 most did not exist in their original form. For instance, the working classes deserted the popular theatres in favour of the new, bright music halls, the repertoire of which contained much less graphic violence than the bloody melodramas. The penny bloods disappeared; the cheap fiction purchased by most labourers in the late nineteenth century was characterised by watered-down rags to riches stories with little gore or other titillation. As execution was removed from public view there was a notable decline in the broadside trade.

To explain this evident decline, leisure historians would point to the emergence of a mass, commercial leisure industry during the second half of the nineteenth century. As impresarios and new entrepreneurs in the entertainment business needed to appeal to larger audiences to maintain profits, violence was removed as it no longer proved to be a point of attraction for increasingly diverse audiences. A less boisterous world of leisure existed from about the 1870s onwards, characterised by the weekend football match, the glittering music hall and the seaside holiday. The masses also enjoyed the more improving recreations supplied in approved institutions such as the library and the mechanics' institutes. And domestic forms of leisure began to flourish, for example specialist magazines which supported an array of new hobbies from cycling to pigeon-fancying.[4] Some historians have sought to qualify our understanding of the content of this mass culture, but few have questioned its tameness. For instance, Garth Stedman Jones, in examining music hall culture, has argued that it was not necessarily respectable, as apparent in the importance of the drink trade to the halls and even the content of some of the songs, but this did not make it subversive; the culture supported by the working classes was conservative and inward looking, a 'culture of consolation'.[5]

Many social historians of the nineteenth century argue that changes in popular culture reflected changes in the lifestyle and living conditions of the working classes. After the defeat of Chartism in the late 1840s and with the emergence of a new generation of workers there was a general acceptance of industrial capitalism accompanied by a settling down of society. Rises in real wages after 1850 helped to smooth tensions, and allowed for the appearance of a labour aristocracy who, especially after the development of commuter rail services, were able to move to the suburbs and begin to ape the lifestyles of those above them. In their new environments, they certainly rubbed shoulders with the growing numbers of low-paid white-collar workers, for example clerks and shopkeepers. Along with improving living conditions, workers enjoyed shorter working hours which provided time for the enjoyment of new leisure pursuits.[6]

Better living standards, improved working conditions and a noticeably tamer culture have prompted a large number of historians to assert that by the end of the 1860s, at least the upper echelons of the working classes, if not the semi-skilled labourers as well, had embraced respectable culture. They were rewarded with the extension of the franchise in 1867, a move which, by drawing attention to divisions within the working classes, also promoted the image of the respectable working-class man as something for those immediately below to aspire to. Those who did were welcomed into the political community in 1884. Respectability has continued to be the lens through which we view and assess Victorian, especially late Victorian, society. Although first viewed as a challenge, Peter Bailey's work, which suggested that, for the working classes, respectability should be regarded as a role they played when circumstances demanded or suited, has helped to reinforce the cultural and social power of respectability.[7] It became increasingly necessary for working people to play along.

Those who did not were confined to the dregs of society. Crime historians often point to the emergence of a new construction of criminality in the 1860s. The working classes as a whole were no longer seen as a dangerous class, where crime, violence and sedition fermented indiscriminately. Instead, a new dividing line was inserted between the respectable working class and the unrespectable or undeserving poor, a large criminal underclass responsible for the majority of crime in late nineteenth-century London. The police used this stereotype as the basis for fighting crime, and so it became a self-fulfilling prophecy.[8] Nineteenth-century criminal statistics lend further support to this thesis. From about 1850 onwards, in England generally and in London in particular, serious theft and violence demonstrated a clear decline.[9] As violence, especially actual violence, was confined to a small section of society which sat outside the boundaries of the social sphere, on the margins, historians have argued that 1870 represents the moment when the civilising offensive was triumphant over the customary mentality. As John Carter Wood writes, the 'expressive language of violence was … denied a legitimate social space' and the customary mentality was 'marginalised in the social discourse of all classes'.[10]

However, I wonder whether this story is too neat. In particular, I cannot help but feel that the triumph of the civilising process sits a little uneasily with a late Victorian culture which abounds with images of 'Darkest London' and the 'City of Dreadful Delight'.[11] Can we reconcile a civilising process with the dark and violent fantasy of Jack the Ripper which was shared by all metropolitan inhabitants in the 1880s largely regardless of class?

Many historians would argue that we can. At the same time that society was divided into the respectable and the unrespectable, the topography of London, in both a physical and imaginative sense, was recast. The East End was presented as the habitat of the underclass, a place of gut-wrenching poverty, sinister alleys, crime and violence. It symbolised urban decay, the very worst results of a century of urbanisation. The Jack the Ripper murders of 1888 not only occurred at the very gateway to the East End, his prostitute victims representative of the degenerate folk of the neighbourhood, but 'Jack' became the embodiment of that very environment.[12] In many ways, Jack the Ripper, and the media frenzy that surrounded the murders, represented the loudest and most famous representation of the violence of the late nineteenth-century East End.

Although London had always attracted the attention of writers, and a new type of male urban explorer, the flâneur, provided reams of copy on the exploits of the inhabitants of the growing metropolis from *c*. 1820 to *c*. 1850, from the late 1860s onwards the representation of London acquired a new character as an increasing number of people (women as well as men) from a wide range of backgrounds put pen to paper to describe the scandals and misery of everyday life in the East End.[13] Their literary and visual products have been used to support the notion of the civilising process. In particular, the repeated characterisation of the Eastenders as savages, not unlike the natives of deepest, darkest Africa, provided a convenient other, a vital prop for civilising narratives. Moreover, missions were established in the East End in the hope of spreading enlightenment among the people, in other words, of civilising them.

But that argument is only skin deep. If we peel away the rhetoric and look not only at the narratives, but also at the reception of these tales, then we might question the civilised behaviour of those who devoured them often in the comfort of their drawing rooms. Media scandals about the dark and violent East End, from James Greenwood's 'Night in a workhouse' (1866) and W. T. Stead's 'Maiden tribute of modern Babylon' (1885) to the daily reports on the pursuit of Jack the Ripper, were consumed by record numbers of people in London. There is no doubt that they enjoyed the stories in large part because these publications offered a means of vicarious participation. In other words, they were a powerful and appealing form of entertainment for both high and low.

Nor did they just read about the East End in newspapers, journals and books. During the last third of the nineteenth century, large numbers of affluent people decided to visit the neighbourhood themselves, a practice which acquired the appropriate appellation, 'slumming'. Some of those who went slumming did so for charitable reasons, because they genuinely thought that they could help make a difference, and the institutions they founded were held up as beacons of light amidst the darkness.[14] But these institutions were also included in guidebooks for London, to help the visitor find their way around the East End. And many considered a trip down to the docks or a walk up Commercial Road an afternoon or evening's entertainment.[15] The Rev. James Adderley, a clergyman who lived and worked in the heart of the East End, made reference to the lady who 'dined out' on tales of her slum exploration, as well as the numbers of 'rich people' who were disappointed on touring the East London parishes because they were not 'slummy' enough.[16] Slumming, both as a charitable but especially as a tourist activity, took the notion of participation to yet another level.

Furthermore, delight in gazing upon dark and violent spectacles was not just limited to the everyday lives of the Eastenders, but was also apparent in patterns of crime reporting in the press. In this respect, the late Victorian press was far from respectable or civilised. Hardly any detail of the mutilation Jack the Ripper inflicted on his victims was kept from readers of lowbrow and highbrow newspapers alike.[17] Similarly, hanging may have been relocated away from public sight inside the walls of the prison, but the use of reporters to reassure the public that the punishment did take place combined with the increasing distance of the people from the spectacle may have led to an increase in the detail of execution reports along with a decrease in the use of euphemisms.[18] Certainly these tales exercised power over imaginations, as evident from the unprecedented number of unsolicited applications from so-called respectable, willing executioners received by the Lord Mayor, the metropolitan sheriffs and the Home Secretary on the death of the hangman William Marwood in September 1883.[19] Most of all, as we saw in chapter 6, the sensationalism and particular methods of reporting violent crime used by the new popular press in the mid-nineteenth century were not toned down after 1860 but instead fed into the rise of New Journalism, a style that dominated the production of news during the last third of the century.

Appropriation, rather than decline, is a much more fitting term to describe the fate of the entertainments presented in this book. For the most part, the violent entertainments that characterised popular culture in London between 1820 and 1870 did not disappear into a vacuum, but instead, in many cases, were remoulded to serve new purposes in the late Victorian period, repopulating mainstream culture alongside a number of new violent pastimes, some of which I have just outlined.[20] That these entertainments could tempt new or expanded audiences at the end of the century should not surprise us, especially given the glimpses in previous chapters of polite, if distant spectators.

Although *Punch and Judy* was given a new veneer of respectability, through the advertisement of respectable showmen for indoor parties and through spin-off products that attempted to explain the violence to young audiences and present an alternative image of a loving and stable family, the puppet show continued to be violent. The show survived because the more affluent enjoyed watching it. Execution broadsides declined with the privatisation of the spectacle of hanging. But scaffold culture persisted, not just in the descriptions of punishment in the press, but also in venues such as Madame Tussaud's in London. The Chamber of Horrors continued to attract large numbers of visitors from London and from the provinces, its popularity reflected in its expansion in 1860 and again in 1884 when the Tussaud's moved their waxwork gallery to their current premises next to Baker Street Station.[21] Famous murder melodramas, such as *Maria Marten and the Murder in the Red Barn* and *Sweeney Todd,* continued to delight the new polite audiences at the theatre, even if the working classes had long deserted the venue; and just as penny dreadfuls, or mass-produced boys' story papers, gratified the grubby boys in the East End, they also captured the imagination of adolescent males in the working and lower-middle classes across London and even the whole of Britain, while equally violent tales of adventure were served up to the offspring of the affluent in an attempt to instil the virtues of pluck and manliness.[22]

In addition to these representations of violence, forms of actual violence were also preserved in tiny corners, where social discourses such as respectability and civilisation did not attempt to eradicate but, instead, to regulate them. Domestic violence, for example, persisted, despite new legislation in the last quarter of the nineteenth century, as patriarchal society upheld the utility of certain forms of violence to keep women under control.[23] While prizefighting and bare-knuckle boxing were outlawed, boxing as a sport was protected through the introduction of the Queensbury Rules in 1867 and thrived in the late Victorian period with cross-class support. Cockfighting and dogfighting may have been outlawed, but the foxhunt remained.[24]

The continued presence of violence in Victorian culture during the last third of the nineteenth century, or even more than this, the appropriation or reintegration of violence into so-called respectable culture, strongly suggests that we might have misunderstood the nature of change at 1870. Respectability has come to dominate our perceptions of the Victorians. I do not doubt its presence, or its power, as a social discourse; but I do wonder whether its great presence within the sources, or in that record largely created by the more affluent, has led us to overemphasise its hold over Victorian society and the actions and tastes of the people.

Some years ago, historians were convinced that the doctrine of Separate Spheres, by which women were confined to the private or domestic sphere (the home) while men made their way in the public sphere (the world of work), shaped women's lives in a cultural and physical sense from about 1780 through to the First World War. During the 1990s, a group of revisionist historians challenged conceptions of Separate Spheres, first insisting on patterns of continuity in women's lives stretching back through the pre-industrial period, and second questioning whether the great insistence on Separate Spheres in the sources might actually be evidence of its unreality, as contemporary authors attempted to encourage a stricter adherence to its central tenets.[25] Since then, our understanding of the lives of women in the nineteenth century has become far more nuanced; the concept of Separate Spheres is still used by many gender historians, but with greater sensitivity to the nature of its influence over women and men, and few would argue that the concept provides a literal description of people's behaviour in the period.[26]

I do wonder whether we might be on the cusp of a similar revolution with respect to our understanding of respectability in Victorian England. This is not the only book to have emerged recently which suggests that the power of respectability over the cultural imagination and social action in the nineteenth century may have been more limited than so far appreciated.[27] Moreover, new digital technologies have been harnessed by public libraries and commercial publishers in the past two or three years to expose the range of sources charting 'unrespectable' behaviour and pastimes in Britain during the nineteenth century; interestingly, the focus on digitising these sources springs largely from continued modern tastes for gore and sensationalism.[28] It may be that we have taken respectability at face value and interpreted it too literally. In other words, we might have too readily adopted a set of social binaries, such as respectable/ unrespectable, and moral/ immoral, constructed by contemporaries and used to bolster the social hierarchy. As many recent studies have shown, behaviour on the ground was much more difficult to categorise absolutely.

If respectability was part and parcel of the civilising process, where does this new interpretation of Victorian society leave us? Contrary to many other studies of violence in this era, I would argue that the progress of violent entertainments over the course of the nineteenth century allowed for the triumph of the customary mentality at 1870. I have represented this process diagrammatically in diagram 1. But it might also be worth explaining exactly how this came about.

The term 'customary mentality', coined by John Carter Wood, has been referred to at several points in this book. As explained in the preceding chapters, Wood, and some subsequent historians, have used the customary mentality to refer to a shared culture in pre-industrial England in which violence was seen as a legitimate form of expression: violence was used to regulate society, resolve disputes and as a means of releasing social tensions.[29] For the most part, this violence was in the form of actual violence, including retributive physical punishments, forms of combat – from reactionary brawls to staged bare-knuckle

Diagram 1   The remaking of the customary mentality in the
nineteenth century

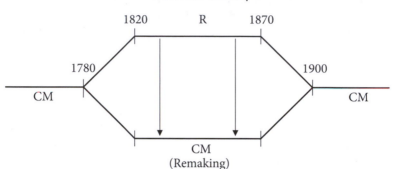

Note: Where 'R' stands for 'respectability' and 'CM' the 'customary mentality'.

fights and duels – and brutal animal sports. The representation of
violence featured in some forms of entertainment, for example as part
of the popular literature of crime (described in chapter 3), or in some
entertainments of the fairground (such as beheading puppets in chapter
2), but these were sub-forms, supporting other larger themes, rather
than dominant.

From about 1780, the middle and upper classes withdrew their
support for the customary mentality, and by 1820 had established a
separate dominant culture: respectability. As a result, they sought
to regulate society in new ways, and also to tame the behaviour of
those below, the lower orders. This led to an assault, in the form of
legislation and new law-enforcement agencies, on actual violence –
some forms were outlawed while others were supervised or managed in
new ways. Arguably, this process was most intense in the large towns
and cities of England, and especially in London, because the desire to
control violence was not just a product of shifts in mentality but also
had a functional explanation. In the increasingly densely populated
and spatially restricted urban environments, social relations needed
to be transformed.[30] In the process of taming, actual violence, in
sports and social relations, persisted where it continued to perform
an important function and did not interfere with daily operations
especially commerce.

Moreover, taming, when or if it occurred, failed to displace the
customary mentality. As this book has shown, from 1820 the customary

mentality found a new expression in the form of the graphic representation of high-level violence. These representations dominated popular
culture, a culture by this stage synonymous with working-class culture,
and were largely received as a form of entertainment. This popular
culture ran parallel to respectable culture. The presence of such gross
displays of violence, and the writings of some contemporaries who
expressed concern about the extent to which such entertainments
could debilitate the morality of the lower orders, suggests that these
two cultures sat in opposition, that they were diametrically opposed.
But that was not entirely the case. There were very few attempts by
the respectable establishment to suppress or even regulate violent
entertainments. Instead, at times the so-called civilised classes formed
part of their audience (hence the drill points, indicators of connections,
in diagram 1). Furthermore, the narratives of violence did not indicate
that actual violence, especially murder, was necessarily appropriate or
should go unpunished.

Rather, these entertainments constituted a celebration of the
representation of gross violence, providing an alternative and more
suitable way to experience and even participate in violence. Social
and economic change at the turn of the nineteenth century not
only encouraged the substitution of violent entertainments for actual
violence; the narratives which accompanied these representations also
reflected the people's experience of that change, from the pressures of
urbanisation, to the challenges of new social relations and everyday
interactions. Violence, but as violent representations rather than
physical conflict, continued to be a useful social safety valve, ultimately
preserving the social hierarchy rather than threatening it.

Thus the process we see at work in the nineteenth century is not
the erosion of the customary mentality, but its evolution, or remaking,
as part of the process of making modernity. The fifty years between
1820 and 1870 form a key period in which the use of violence as a form
of expression shifts from actual violence to the gross representation
of high-level violence accompanied by a series of reaffirming, tightly
regulated spaces for physical confrontation. The site for this remaking
was primarily London, because here the experience of rapid and
dramatic social and economic change collided with a high population
density and accompanying innovations in the entertainment industry.
However, around 1850, with developments in technology and improved
communications, the products of the metropolitan industry were
transported to the provinces where, combined with local initiatives,
they helped to speed up the remaking of the customary mentality.
Moreover, during this period of remaking, the use of violence as a tool

of expression in popular culture became dominant. Violence had an overwhelming presence, and the various forms in which it appeared overlapped, and became mutually supporting.

During the last third of the century, or in the period roughly between 1870 and 1900, the customary mentality became triumphant, because in its new form it was able to expand its base of support, from the metropolitan working classes, to the national masses, and increasingly the more affluent. Violence as entertainment became a form of expression across the social spectrum and the customary mentality (if it is still appropriate to call it by that name) was able to sit comfortably alongside other social discourses, including respectability and civilisation. It was not a shadow of the latter, but equally important; participation did not pose an open challenge to the rhetoric of respectability or the civilising process. The two cultures had been successfully enmeshed so that contradictions in social discourse had been stabilised and no longer posed a threat to the social hierarchy. Furthermore, during this period, as part of a general settling down in society, representations of violence became prominent, rather than dominant, in English culture.

Finally, in the twentieth century, violent entertainment was successfully assimilated into a more global culture, or at least into the culture of the Western English-speaking world. This brings us full circle, back to the point at which we started in this epilogue – the continued prominence of graphic violence in pastimes that we enjoy in the early twenty-first century. The violent films and computer games we encountered at the opening of the epilogue await their historian to uncover the links between them and chart the meaning of their time-bound narratives to post-modern British society. But surely the eagerness which we display in securing tickets to 3D horror movies, and the dedication we show to increasing our record body counts in first-person shooter games, challenge our claims to be 'civilised' in the purest sense of the word.

Notes

1 M. Hale, 'Ending a lethal game and all its gory details', *New York Times*, 29 October 2010.

2 Similarly, the release of the previous *Call of Duty* game, *Modern Warfare 2*, provoked debate not about the level of violence in the game, but about whether it was appropriate to provide plots based on current terrorist events.

3 C. Emsley, *Hard Men: Violence in England since 1750* (London: Hambledon & London, 2005), pp. 179–80.

4 F. M. L. Thompson, *The Rise of Respectable Society: A Social History of Victorian Britain, 1830–1900* (London: Fontana, 1988), pp. 246–306, H. Cunningham, *Leisure in the Industrial Revolution, 1780–1880* (London: Croom Helm, 1980), J. Walvin, *Leisure and Society, 1830–1950* (London: Longman, 1978), J. K. Walton, *The English Seaside Resort: A Social History, 1750–1914* (Leicester: Leicester University Press, 1983), J. K. Walton, 'Respectability takes a holiday: disreputable behaviour at the Victorian seaside', in M. Hewitt (ed.), *Unrespectable Recreations* (Leeds: Centre for Victorian Studies, 2001), R. McKibbin, *Ideologies of Class: Social Relations in Britain, 1880–1950* (Oxford: Oxford University Press, 1991).

5 G. S. Jones, *Languages of Class: Studies in English Working-Class History, 1832–1982* (Cambridge: Cambridge University Press, 1983), pp. 179–238, especially p. 237.

6 Thompson, *Rise of Respectable Society*, pp. 203–5, E. J. Hobsbawm, 'The labour aristocracy in nineteenth-century Britain', in Hobsbawm, *Labouring Men: Studies in the History of Labour* (London: Weidenfeld & Nicolson, 1964), pp. 272–315, K. T. Hoppen, *The Mid Victorian Generation, 1846–1886* (Oxford: Oxford University Press, 1998), pp. 56–90, G. Best, *Mid-Victorian Britain, 1851–1875* (London: Weidenfeld & Nicolson, 1971), p. 267.

7 P. Bailey, '"Will the real Bill Banks please stand up?" Towards a role analysis of mid-Victorian respectability', *Journal of Social History*, 12 (1979), 336–53. See also M. Huggins, 'More sinful pleasures? Leisure, respectability and the male middle classes in Victorian England', *Journal of Social History*, 33 (2000), 585–600.

8 J. Davis, 'The London garrotting panic of 1862: a moral panic and the creation of a criminal class in mid-Victorian England', in V. A. C. Gatrell, B. Lenman and G. Parker (eds), *Crime and the Law: The Social History of Crime in Western Europe since 1500* (London: Europa, 1980), J. Davis, 'Jennings Buildings and the Royal Borough: the construction of the underclass in mid-Victorian England', in D. Feldman and G. S. Jones (eds), *Metropolis London: Histories and Representations since 1800* (London: Routledge, 1989), V. Bailey, 'The fabrication of deviance: "dangerous classes" and "criminal classes" in Victorian England', in J. Rule and R. Malcomson (eds), *Protest and Survival: The Historical Experience: Essays for E. P. Thompson* (London: Merlin, 1993), M. J. Wiener, *Reconstructing the Criminal: Culture, Law and Policy in England, 1830–1914* (Cambridge: Cambridge University Press, 1990), pp. 149–56.

9 V. A. C. Gatrell, 'The decline of theft and violence in Victorian and Edwardian England', in Gatrell *et al.*, *Crime and the Law*.

10 J. C. Wood, *Violence and Crime in Nineteenth-Century England: The Shadow of our Refinement* (London: Routledge, 2004), pp. 139, 144. See also G. T. Smith, 'Violent crime and the public weal in England, 1500–1900', in R. McMahon (ed.), *Crime, Law and Popular Culture in Europe, 1500–1900* (Cullompton: Willan Publishing, 2008).

11 These are quotes from the times, but have also formed the titles of various studies on late Victorian society, which is suggestive.

12 D. Gray, *London's Shadows: The Dark Side of the Victorian City* (London: Continuum, 2010), p. 17.

13 J. R. Walkowitz, *City of Dreadful Delight: Narratives of Sexual Danger in Late Victorian London* (Chicago: University of Chicago Press, 1992), pp. 15–39, A. Potts, 'Picturing the modern metropolis: images of London in the nineteenth century', *History Workshop Journal*, 26 (1988), 28–56, Wiener, *Reconstructing the Criminal*, pp. 215–56.

14 S. Koven, *Slumming: Sexual and Social Politics in Victorian London* (Princeton: Princeton University Press, 2004), G. Ginn, '"Slumming it": the intellectuals and the masses in late Victorian London', *Proceedings of the University of Queensland History Research Group*, 6 (1995), 29–43, E. Ross (ed.), *Slum Travellers: Ladies and London Poverty, 1860–1920* (Berkeley: University of California Press, 2007).

15 Koven, *Slumming*, pp. 1–4.

16 J. Adderley, 'Is slumming played out?', *English Illustrated Magazine*, 119 (August 1893), 834. See also A. Mayne, *The Imagined Slum: Newspaper Representation in Three Cities* (Leicester: Leicester University Press, 1993).

17 L. P. Curtis, *Jack the Ripper and the London Press* (New Haven: Yale University Press, 2001).

18 A study of execution reporting after the privatisation of hanging awaits its historian, though hints are provided by J. Tullock, 'The privatising of pain: Lincoln newspapers, "mediated publicness" and the end of public execution', *Journalism Studies*, 7 (2006), 437–51. I am grateful to Alice Smalley for this valuable reference.

19 G. T. Smith, '"I could hang anything you can bring before me": England's willing executioners in 1883', in S. Devereaux and P. Griffiths (eds), *Penal Practice and Culture, 1500–1900: Punishing the English* (Basingstoke: Palgrave Macmillan, 2004), pp. 285–308.

20 In contrast to the work of Wiener, who has argued that during the last quarter of the century the detective takes over imaginative centre stage from the criminal in terms of literary productions, and violence takes place 'off stage'. But we are in need of a broader approach to measure the representation of *violence* in culture. Wiener, *Reconstructing the Criminal*, pp. 219–20. Richard Price similarly argues that popular

culture was appropriated by the more affluent at around 1870, though, in the process, it was emptied of its meaning. Price, *British Society, 1680–1880* (Cambridge: Cambridge University Press, 1999), pp. 316–18.

21 P. Pilbeam, *Madame Tussaud and the History of Waxworks* (London: Hambledon & London, 2003), pp. 159, 169.

22 K. Boyd, *Manliness and the Boys' Story Paper in Britain: A Cultural History, 1855–1940* (Basingstoke: Palgrave, 2003).

23 A. J. Hammerton, *Cruelty and Companionship: Conflict in Nineteenth-Century Married Life* (London: Routledge, 1995), M. J. Wiener, *Men of Blood: Violence, Manliness and Criminal Justice in Victorian England* (Cambridge: Cambridge University Press, 2004), Wood, *Violence and Crime in Nineteenth-Century England*, p. 40.

24 D. C. Itzkowitz, *Peculiar Privilege: A Social History of English Foxhunting, 1753–1885* (Hassocks: Harvester Press, 1977), E. Griffin, *Blood Sport: A History of Hunting in Britain* (New Haven: Yale University Press, 2007).

25 Led by Amanda Vickery with her seminal, 'From Golden Age to Separate Spheres? A review of the chronologies and categories of English women's history', *Historical Journal*, 36 (1993), 383–414.

26 For an example of a very sensitive approach which is able to demonstrate in a sophisticated way the continuing usefulness of Separate Spheres, see A. Summers, *Female Lives, Modern States: Women, Religion and Public Life in Britain* (Newbury: Threshold Press, 2000), pp. 5–26.

27 For example, R. McWilliam, *The Tichborne Claimant: A Victorian Sensation* (London: Hambledon Continuum, 2007), but see also Hewitt, *Unrespectable Recreations*.

28 For example, *The John Johnson Collection: An Archive of Printed Ephemera* (Bodleian Library and ProQuest, released 2009), *London Low Life* (Adam Matthew Digital, released 2010), *The Word on the Street: Broadsides at the National Library of Scotland* (NLS, released 2004), *Dying Speeches and Bloody Murders: Crime Broadsides Collected by the Harvard Law School Library* (Harvard, released 2007), *Victorian Popular Culture* (Adam Matthew Digital, released 2008), *Old Bailey Online: The Proceedings of the Old Bailey, 1675–1913* (University of Sheffield, 2003). Even the recent British Library Nineteenth Century Newspapers could not resist including in their digitisation the *Illustrated Police News* (British Library and Gale Cengage, 2007).

29 Wood, *Violence and Crime in Nineteenth-Century England*, pp. 3–4.

30 R. B. Shoemaker, *The London Mob: Violence and Disorder in Eighteenth-Century England* (London: Hambledon & London, 2004), pp. 295–9.

Bibliography

Primary sources

Archival collections

Bodleian Library, Oxford
Francis Douce Collection of Ballads and Broadsides, vols I and II (microfilm edition).
John Johnson Collection:
  Actors, Actresses and Entertainers, Catnach, Circulating Libraries Catalogues, Crime, Murder and Execution Broadsides, Miniature Theatre, Printsellers' Catalogues, Provincial Playbills, Waxworks.

Brighton Museum, Brighton
Willet Collection of Popular Pottery.

British Library, London
Add. Mss 42865–43038: Plays submitted to the Lord Chamberlain's Office for Licensing, February 1824 to December 1851.
Add. Mss 52929–53701: Plays submitted to the Lord Chamberlain's Office for Licensing, 1852–1899.
Barry Ono Collection of Penny Dreadfuls.
Collection of Playbills for the City of London Theatre and Grecian Saloon, 1837–58: London III – Miscellaneous Institutions, Societies, and other Bodies, Playbills.370.
Collection of Playbills for the Royal Albert Saloon, Bower Saloon and Britannia Saloon, 1841–54: London III – Miscellaneous Institutions, Societies and other Bodies, Playbills.376.
Collection of Playbills for the Effingham Saloon, 1841–63: London III – Miscellaneous Institutions, Societies and other Bodies, Playbills.397.
Nineteenth-century Broadsides: 1881.d.8.

Eighteenth-century microfilm collection
Robert Sheppard, 'By His Majesty's Permission. Here is come to this place, and is to be seen a play call'd, Dives and Lazarus', An Advertisement for a Puppet Show, London *c.* 1720 (reel number 10389).

Harvard University, Cambridge, Massachusetts
Harvard Theatre Collection, 'Theatre Playbills from the Harvard Theatre Collection' (Microfilm Edition, Research Publications, Woodbridge, 1982).

National Library of Scotland, Edinburgh
Lauriston Castle Collection.

Public Record Office, The National Archives, Kew, Richmond, Surrey
Lord Chamberlain's Papers, LC1: Department Correspondence.
Lord Chamberlain's Papers, LC7: Records of Licensing of Entertainments and Theatres.

Contemporary books (including plays and novelettes not included in the above archival collections)

Adams, W. E. *Memoires of a Social Atom* (London: Hutchinson & Co., 1903).
Anon., *The Bloody Innkeeper; or Sad and Barbarous News from Gloucester-Shire: Being a True Relation how the Bodies of Seven Men and Women were Found Murthered in a Garden Belonging to a House In Putley, near Gloucester* (London, 1675).
Anon., *A Warning Piece against the Crime of Murder; or an Account of Many Extraordinary and Most Providential Discoveries of Secret Murders* (London, 1752).
Anon., *The Cries of Blood, or the Juryman's Monitor* (London, 1767).
Anon., *The History of Sawney Beane and his Family* (London, 1800?).
Anon., *The Life of Richard Turpin, a Notorious Highwayman, to which is added, The Life of Sawney Beane, the Man-Eater* (London, 1800).
Anon., *Pug's Visit; or, the Disasters of Mr Punch* (London: J. Harris, 1806).
Anon., *A Peep at Bartholomew Fair* (London: R. Macdonald, 1837).
Anon., *Punch's Pleasantries: The Tragical Comedy of Punch and Judy* (London, 1838?).
Anon., *Madame Tussaud & Sons Catalogue, Bazaar, Baker Street. Portman Square* (London, 1869).
Baker, H. B. *The London Stage* (London: W. H. Allen & Co., 1889).
Ballantine, W. *Some Experiences of a Barrister's Life* (2 vols, London: R. Bentley, 5th edn, 1882).
Barrymore, W. *Trial by Battle; or, Heaven Defend the Right* (London, J. Duncombe, n.d.).

Boswell, J. *Boswell's London Journal, 1762–1763*, ed. F. A. Pottle (London: W. Heinemann, 1952).

Boulton, W. B. *The Amusements of Old London* (2 vols, London: J. C. Nimmo, 1901).

Brayley, E. W. *Historical and Descriptive Accounts of the Theatres of London* (London: Printed for J. Taylor, 1826).

Bunn, A. *The Stage* (3 vols, London: R. Bentley, 1840).

Burn, J. D. *The Language of the Walls: And a Voice from the Shop Windows* (London: Abel Heywood, 1855).

Burt, T. *An Autobiography* (London: Unwin, 1924).

Carter, T. *Memoirs of a Working Man* (London: Charles Knight & Co., 1845).

Catling, T. *My Life's Pilgrimage* (London: J. Murray, 1911).

Chambers, R. *Book of Days* (2 vols, London: W. R. Chambers, 1863).

Collier, J. P. *Punch and Judy, with twenty-four illustrations designed and engraved by George Cruikshank* (London: Printed for S. Prowett, 1828).

Colman, G. *The Review; or, the Wags of Windsor* (London: J. Cawthorn, 1808).

Daniel, G. *Merrie England in the Olden Time* (2 vols, London: R. Bentley, 1842).

Dickens, C. *The Old Curiosity Shop* (London: Chapman & Hall, 1841).

Eliot, G. *Scenes from Clerical Life* (London: Blackwood, 1858).

—— *The Mill on the Floss* (London: Blackwood, 1860).

Erle, T. *Letters from a Theatrical Scene Painter* (London: Printed for private circulation, 1880).

Fielding, H. *The Author's Farce* (London: Printed for J. Roberts, 1730).

Fitzball, E. *Thirty-five Years of a Dramatic Author's Life* (London: T. C. Newby, 1859).

Fonblanque, A. *England under Seven Administrations* (3 vols, London: R. Bentley, 1837).

Frost, T. *The Old Showmen and the Old London Fairs* (London: Tinsley Brothers, 1874).

—— *Forty Years' Recollections* (London: Sampson Low, 1880).

Godwin, G. *Town Swamps and Social Bridges* (London: Routledge, 1859).

Grant, J. *The Great Metropolis*, 2nd Ser. (2 vols, London: Saunders & Otley, 1837).

—— *The Great Metropolis*, 1st Ser. (2 vols, London: Saunders & Otley, 3rd edn, 1838).

—— *Sketches in London* (London: W. S. Orr & Co., 1838).

Greenwood, J. *The Seven Curses of London* (London: Rivers, 1869).

—— *The Wilds of London* (London: Chatto & Windus, 1874).

Hamilton, A. H. *The Summer Guide to the Amusements of London and Provincial Excursionist for 1848* (London: Kent & Richards, 1848).

Hatton, J. *Journalistic London* (London: S. Low, 1882).

Hazleton, F. *Sweeney Todd, The Barber Fiend of Fleet Street; or, the String of Pearls* (London: S. French, 18??).

Hibbert, H. G. *A Playgoer's Memories* (London: G. Richards, 1920).

Hindley, C. *The Life and Times of James Catnach (Late of the Seven Dials), Ballad Monger* (London: Reeves & Turner, 1878).

—— *The History of the Catnach Press* (London: C. Hindley, 1886).

Hollingshead, J. *My Lifetime* (2 vols, London, 2nd edn, 1895).

Hone, W. *The Every-Day Book* (2 vols, London: Hunt & Clarke, 1825–26).

Howard, J. H. *Winding Lanes* (Caernarvon: Calvinistic Methodist Printing Works, 1938).

Hughes, M. V. *A London Family, 1870–1900* (London: Oxford University Press, 1946).

Jerrold, D. and G. Doré, *London: A Pilgrimage* (London: Grant & Co., 1872).

Johnson, Captain C. *A General History of the Lives and Adventures of Most Famous Highwaymen, Murderers, Robbers and Thief-Takers* (London, 1758).

Kilgarriff, M. (ed.), *The Golden Age of Melodrama: Twelve Nineteenth-Century Melodramas* (London: Wolfe, 1974).

Knight, C. *The Old Printer and the Modern Press* (London: J. Murray, 1854).

—— *Passages of a Working Life During Half a Century* (2 vols, London: Bradbury & Evans, 1864–65).

Lewis, A. *Grace Clairville; or, the Crime at the Symon's Yat* (London: J. Dicks, 1883).

Lewis, M. G. *The Monk* (London: Printed for J. Saunders, 1796).

Ludlow, J. M. and L. Jones, *The Progress of the Working Class, 1832–1867* (London: A. Strahan, 1867).

McNally, L. *The Apotheosis of Punch; a Satirical Masque: with a monody on the death of the late Master Punch* (London, 1779).

Mayhew, E. *Stage Effect: or, the Principles which Command Dramatic Success* (London: C. Mitchell, 1840).

Mayhew, H. *London Labour and the London Poor* (4 vols, London: Griffin, Bohn & Co., 1861–62).

—— *London's Underworld*, ed. P. Quennell (London: Bracken, 1950).

Miller, T. *Picturesque Sketches of London, Past and Present* (London: Office of the National Illustrated Library, 1852).

Moncrieff, W. T. *The Red Farm; or, the Well of St Marie. A Domestic Drama in Two Acts* (London: J. Dicks, 1842).

Morley, H. *Memoirs of Bartholomew Fair* (London: Chapman & Hall, 1859).

—— *Journal of a London Playgoer* (London: Routledge, 1866).

Muir, E. *The Story and the Fable: An Autobiography* (London: G. G. Harrap, 1940).

Okey, T. *A Basket Full of Memories: An Autobiographical Sketch* (London: J. M. Dent, 1930).

Pepys, S. *The Diary of Samuel Pepys*, ed. R. Latham and W. Matthews (11 vols, London: Bell, 1970–83).

Pirsson, J. P. *The Discarded Daughter; A Comedy in Five Acts* (New York: W. Stodart, 1832).

Place, F. *The Autobiography of Francis Place, 1771–1854*, ed. M. Thale (Cambridge: Cambridge University Press, 1972).

Pope-Hennessy, J. *Monckton Milnes. Volume 1: The Years of Promise* (London: Constable, 1949).

Puckler-Muskau, Prince H. von, *A Regency Visitor: The English Tour of Prince Puckler-Muskau*, ed. E. M. Butler and trans. S. Austin (London: Collins, 1957).

Reynolds, G. W. M. *The Mysteries of London* (2 series, 4 vols, London: G. Vickers, 1844–48).

—— *The Mysteries of the Court of London* (4 series, 8 vols, London, J. Dicks, 1848).

Ritchie, J. E. *The Night Side of London* (London: W. Tweedie, 1857).

Sala, G. A. *Twice Round the Clock; or the Hours of Day and Night in London* (London: John & Robert Maxwell, 1858).

—— *The Life and Adventures of George Augustus Sala* (2 vols, London: Cassell & Co., 3rd edn, 1895).

Scott, C. *The Drama of Yesterday and Today* (London: Macmillan, 1899).

Simmons, G. *The Working Classes: Their Moral, Social and Intellectual Condition; with Practical Suggestions for their Improvement* (London: Partridge & Oakey, 1849).

Smith, Captain A. *Memoirs of the Life and Times of the Famous Jonathan Wild, together with the History and Lives of Modern Rogues* (London, 1726).

Smith, C. M. *Curiosities of London Life* (London: A. W. Bennett, 1853).

Smith, J. T. *Nollekens and his Times* (London, 1828).

Stamper, J. *So Long Ago* (London: Hutchinson, 1960).

Strutt, J. *The Sports and Pastimes of the People of England* (London: Printed for Thomas Tegg, 1801).

Thomson, C. *Autobiography of an Artisan* (London: J. Chapman, 1847).

Thornbury, W. and E. Walford, *Old and New London* (2 vols, London: Cassell, 1878).

Thorndike, R. and R. Arkell, *The Tragedy of Mr Punch: A Fantastic Play and Prologue in One Act, with an introductory essay by Max Beerbohm* (London: Duckworth, 1923).

Tomlins, F. G. *A Brief View of the English Drama from the Earliest Period to the Present Time* (London: C. Mitchell, 1840).

Vizetelly, H. *Glances Back through Seventy Years* (2 vols, London: Kegan Paul, 1893).

Westmacott, C. M. *The English Spy* (2 vols, London: Sherwood, Jones & Co., 1826).

Williams, M. *Round London: Down East and Up West* (London: Macmillan, 1892).

Wontner, T. *Old Bailey Experience* (London: J. Fraser, 1833).

Wright, T. *Some Habits and Customs of the Working Classes* (London: Tinsley Brothers, 1867).

Contemporary newspapers and journals

Ainsworth's Magazine
All the Year Round
Blackwood's Edinburgh Magazine
Calendar of Horrors
Chambers's Edinburgh Journal
Chambers' Journal of Popular Literature
Cleave's Weekly Police Gazette
Daily News
The Drama; or, Theatrical Magazine
The Drama; or, Theatrical Pocket Magazine
Edinburgh Review
English Illustrated Magazine
The Era
Fraser's Magazine for Town and Country
Harper's Weekly
Household Words
Illustrated Police News
Journal of the Statistical Society of London
Literary Speculum
Lloyd's Penny Atlas
Lloyd's Penny Weekly Miscellany
Lloyd's Weekly Newspaper
The Morning Chronicle
New Monthly Magazine
Nineteenth Century
Pall Mall Gazette
Penny Sunday Times and People's Police Gazette
People's Periodical and Family Library
Pocket Magazine
Punch
Quarterly Review
Reynolds's Miscellany
Reynolds's Newspaper
St Paul's Magazine
The Spectator
The Stage; or, Theatrical Inquisitor
Strand Magazine
The Theatre: A Monthly Review
The Times

Official sources

Evidence by Dr Guy Before the Sanitary Commission in Reference to Persons Employed in the Baking Trade (Parl. Papers, 1847–48, LI.367).

Old Bailey Proceedings (www.oldbaileyonline.org).

Reports and Schedules pursuant to Gaol Acts (Parl. Papers, 1843, XLIII.1).

Royal Commission on Capital Punishment (Parl. Papers, 1866, XXI.1).

Select Committee on Criminal and Destitute Juveniles (Parl. Papers, 1852, VII.1).

Select Committee on Dramatic Literature (Parl. Papers, 1831–32, VII.1).

Select Committee on the Health of Towns (Parl. Papers, 1840, XI.277).

Select Committee of the House of Lords to Consider the Present Mode of Capital Punishments (Parl. Papers, 1856, VII.9).

Select Committee on the Improvement of the Health of Towns: Report on the Effect of the Interment of Bodies in Towns (Parl. Papers, 1842, X.349).

Select Committee on Newspaper Stamps (Parl. Papers, 1851, XVII.1).

Select Committee on Public Libraries (Parl. Papers, 1849, XVII.1).

Select Committee on Theatrical Licences and Regulations (Parl. Papers, 1866, XVI.1).

Websites

Old Bailey Proceedings Online (www.oldbaileyonline.org).

UK Reading Experience Database, 1450–1945 (www.open.ac.uk/Arts/reading/UK).

Secondary sources

Books

Adams, A. and R. Leach, *The World of Punch and Judy* (London: Harrap, 1978).

Altick, R. D. *The English Common Reader: A Social History of the Mass Reading Public, 1800–1900* (Chicago: University of Chicago Press, 1957).

—— *Victorian Studies in Scarlet: Murders and Manners in the Age of Victoria* (London: Dent, 1972).

—— *The Shows of London* (London: Belknap Press, 1978).

Anderson, P. *The Printed Image and the Transformation of Popular Culture* (Oxford: Clarendon Press, 1991).

Anglo, M. *Penny Dreadfuls and other Victorian Horrors* (London: Jupiter Books, 1977).

Bailey, P. *Leisure and Class in Victorian England: Rational Recreation and the Contest for Control, 1830–1885* (London: Routledge & Kegan Paul, 1978).

—— *Popular Culture and Performance in the Victorian City* (Cambridge: Cambridge University Press, 1998).

Best, G. *Mid-Victorian Britain, 1851–1875* (London: Weidenfeld & Nicolson, 1971).

Bettelheim, B. *The Uses of Enchantment: The Meaning and Importance of Fairy Tales* (Harmondsworth: Penguin, 1978).

Booth, M. R. *English Melodrama* (London: H. Jenkins, 1965).

—— *Theatre in the Victorian Age* (Cambridge: Cambridge University Press, 1991).

Boyd, K. *Manliness and the Boys' Story Paper in Britain: A Cultural History, 1855–1940* (Basingstoke: Palgrave, 2003).

Brailsford, D. *Bareknuckles: A Social History of Prizefighting* (Cambridge: Lutterworth, 1998).

Bratlinger, P. *The Reading Lesson: The Threat of Mass Literacy in Nineteenth-Century British Fiction* (Bloomington: Indiana University Press, 1998).

Brewer, J. *Sentimental Murder: Love and Madness in the Eighteenth Century* (London: HarperCollins, 2004).

Briggs, A. *Victorian Things* (London: Batsford, 1988).

Brooks, P. *The Melodramatic Imagination: Balzac, Henry James, Melodrama and the Mode of Excess* (New Haven: Yale University Press, 1976).

Brown, L. *Victorian News and Newspapers* (Oxford: Oxford University Press, 1985).

Burnett, J. *Plenty and Want: A Social History of Food in England from 1815 to the Present Day* (London: Routledge, 3rd edn, 1989).

Clark, A. *The Struggle for the Breeches: Gender and the Making of the British Working Class* (Berkeley: University of California Press, 1995).

Crowther, M. A. *The Workhouse System, 1834–1929: The History of an English Social Institution* (London: Batsford, 1981).

Cunningham, H. *Leisure in the Industrial Revolution, 1780–1880* (London: Croom Helm, 1980).

Curtis, L. P. *Jack the Ripper and the London Press* (New Haven: Yale University Press, 2001).

Davis, J. and V. Emeljanow, *Reflecting the Audience: London Theatregoing, 1840–1880* (Hatfield: University of Hertfordshire Press, 2001).

Davis, N. Z. *Society and Culture in Early Modern France* (Stanford: Duckworth, 1975).

Day, W. P. *In the Circles of Fear and Desire: A Study of Gothic Fantasy* (Chicago: University of Chicago Press, 1985).

Dalziel, M. *Popular Fiction 100 Years Ago: An Unexplored Tract of Literary History* (London: Cohen & West, 1957).

Daunton, M. J. *Progress and Poverty: An Economic and Social History of Britain, 1700–1850* (Oxford: Oxford University Press, 1995).

D'Cruze, S. *Crimes of Outrage: Sex, Violence and Victorian Working Women* (De Kalb: Northern Illinois University Press, 1998).

Dolan, F. *The Taming of the Shrew: Texts and Contexts* (Basingstoke: Macmillan, 1996).

Donajgrodski, A. P. (ed.), *Social Control in Nineteenth Century Britain* (London: Croom Helm, 1977).

Dyck, I. *William Cobbett and Rural Popular Culture* (Cambridge: Cambridge University Press, 1992).

Elias, N. *The Civilising Process*, trans. E. Jephcott (Oxford: Oxford University Press, rev. edn, 2000).

Emsley, C., *Crime and Society in England, 1750–1900* (London: Longman, 2nd edn, 1996).

—— *The English Police: A Political and Social History* (London: Longman, 2nd edn, 1996).

—— *Hard Men: Violence in England since 1750* (London: Hambledon & London, 2005).

Faller, L. B. *Turned to Account: The Forms and Functions of Criminal Biography in Late Seventeenth and Early Eighteenth Century England* (Cambridge: Cambridge University Press, 1987).

Finn, M. *After Chartism: Class and Nation in English Radical Politics, 1848–1874* (Cambridge: Cambridge University Press, 1993).

Fox, C. *Graphic Journalism in England during the 1830s and 1840s* (New York: Garland, 1988).

Foyster, E. *Marital Violence: An English Family History, 1660–1857* (Cambridge: Cambridge University Press, 2005).

Gardner, P. *The Lost Elementary Schools of Victorian England: The People's Education* (London: Croom Helm, 1984).

Gatrell, V. A. C. *The Hanging Tree: Execution and the English People, 1770–1868* (Oxford: Oxford University Press, 1994).

—— *City of Laughter: Sex and Satire in Eighteenth-Century London* (London: Atlantic, 2006).

Geertz, C. *The Interpretation of Cultures: Selected Essays* (London: Hutchinson, 1975).

Golby, J. M. and A. W. Purdue, *The Civilisation of the Crowd: Popular Culture in England, 1750–1900* (London: Batsford, 1984).

Goodway, D. *London Chartism, 1838–1848* (Cambridge: Cambridge University Press, 1982).

Gray, D. *London's Shadows: The Dark Side of the Victorian City* (London: Continuum, 2010).

Gretton, T. *Murders and Moralities: English Catchpenny Prints, 1800–1860* (London: British Museum, 1980).

Griffin, E. *England's Revelry: A History of Popular Sports and Pastimes, 1660–1830* (Oxford: Oxford University Press, 2005).

—— *Blood Sport: A History of Hunting in Britain* (New Haven: Yale University Press, 2007).

Hadley, E. *Melodramatic Tactics: Theatricalised Dissent in the English Marketplace, 1800–1885* (Stanford: Stanford University Press, 1995).

Haining, P. *The Penny Dreadful: or, Strange, Horrid and Sensational Tales* (London: Gollancz, 1975).

Halttunen, K. *Murder Most Foul: The Killer and the American Gothic Imagination* (Cambridge, Mass.: Harvard University Press, 1998).

Hammerton, A. J. *Cruelty and Companionship: Conflict in Nineteenth-Century Married Life* (London: Routledge, 1995).

Haywood, I. *The Revolution in Popular Literature: Print, Politics and the People, 1790–1860* (Cambridge: Cambridge University Press, 2004).

Heilman, R. B. *Tragedy and Melodrama: Versions of Experience* (Seattle: University of Washington Press, 1968).

Hewitt, M. (ed.), *Unrespectable Recreations* (Leeds: Centre for Victorian Studies, 2001).

Hilton, A. B. *A Mad, Bad and Dangerous People? England, 1783–1846* (Oxford: Oxford University Press, 2006).

Hogle, J. E. (ed.), *The Cambridge Companion to Gothic Fiction* (Cambridge: Cambridge University Press, 2002).

Hollingsworth, K. *The Newgate Novel, 1830–1847: Bulwer, Ainsworth, Dickens and Thackeray* (Detroit: Wayne State University Press, 1963).

Hollis, P. *The Pauper Press: A Study in Working-Class Radicalism of the 1830s* (London: Oxford University Press, 1970).

Holmes, R. *The Legend of Sawney Beane* (London: F. Muller, 1975).

Hoppen, K. T. *The Mid Victorian Generation, 1846–1886* (Oxford: Oxford University Press, 1998).

Horn, P. *Pleasures and Pastimes in Victorian Britain* (Stroud: Sutton, 1999).

Humphreys, A. and L. James (eds), *G. W. M. Reynolds: Nineteenth-Century Fiction, Politics and the Press* (Aldershot: Ashgate, 2008).

Itzkowitz, D. C. *Peculiar Privilege: A Social History of English Foxhunting, 1753–1885* (Hassocks: Harvester Press, 1977).

James, L. *Fiction for the Working Man, 1830–1850: A Study of the Literature Produced for the Working Classes in Early Victorian Urban England* (London: Oxford University Press, 1963).

Jones, A. *Powers of the Press: Newspapers, Power and the Public in Nineteenth-Century England* (Aldershot: Ashgate, 1996).

Jones, G. S. *Outcast London: A Study in the Relationship between Classes in Victorian Society* (Harmondsworth: Penguin, 1976).

—— *Languages of Class: Studies in English Working-Class History, 1832–1982* (Cambridge: Cambridge University Press, 1983).

Kalikoff, B. *Murder and Moral Decay in Victorian Popular Literature* (Michigan: UMI Research Press, 1986).

Kitson Clark, G. S. R. *The Making of Victorian England* (London: Methuen, 1965).

Koven, S. *Slumming: Sexual and Social Politics in Victorian London* (Princeton: Princeton University Press, 2004).

Laqueur, T. W. *Religion and Respectability: Sunday Schools and Working Class Culture 1780–1850* (New Haven: Yale University Press, 1976).

Leach, R. *The Punch and Judy Show: History, Tradition and Meaning* (London: Batsford, 1985), p. 33.

Lee, A. J. *The Origins of the Popular Press in England* (London: Croom Helm, 1976).

McCalman, I. *Radical Underworld: Prophets, Revolutionaries and Pornographers in London, 1795–1840* (Oxford: Clarendon Press, 2nd edn, 2002).

Macfarlane, A. *The Justice and the Mare's Ale: Law and Disorder in Seventeenth-Century England* (Oxford: Blackwell, 1981).

McKenzie, A. *Tyburn's Martyrs: Execution in England, 1675–1775* (London: Hambledon Continuum, 2007).

McKibbin, R. *Ideologies of Class: Social Relations in Britain, 1880–1950* (Oxford: Oxford University Press, 1991).

McMahon, V. *Murder in Shakespeare's England* (London: Hambledon & London, 2004).

McWilliam, R. *The Tichborne Claimant: A Victorian Sensation* (London: Hambledon Continuum, 2007).

Maidment, B. *Reading Popular Prints, 1790–1870* (Manchester: Manchester University Press, 1996).

Malcolmson, R. *Popular Recreations in English Society, 1700–1850* (Cambridge: Cambridge University Press, 1973).

Markman, E. *The History of Gothic Fiction* (Edinburgh: Edinburgh University Press, 2000).

Mayne, A. *The Imagined Slum: Newspaper Representation in Three Cities* (Leicester: Leicester University Press, 1993).

Melman, B. *The Culture of History: English Uses of the Past, 1800–1953* (Oxford: Oxford University Press, 2006).

Mitch, D. *The Rise of Popular Literacy in Victorian England: The Influence of Private Choice and Public Policy* (Philadelphia: University of Pennsylvania Press, 1992).

Moody, J. *Illegitimate Theatre in London, 1770–1840* (Cambridge: Cambridge University Press, 2000).

Nead, L. *Victorian Babylon: People, Streets and Images in Nineteenth-Century London* (New Haven: Yale University Press, 2000).

Neuburg, V. E. *Popular Literature: A History and Guide* (Harmondsworth: Penguin, 1977).

Newton, H. *Chance Crime and the Drama: or Dark Deeds Dramatized* (London, 1927).

Pickard, P. M. *I Could A Tale Unfold: Violence, Horror and Sensationalism in Stories for Children* (London: Tavistock Publications, 1961).

Pilbeam, P. *Madame Tussaud and the History of Waxworks* (London: Hambledon & London, 2003).

Porter, R. *London: A Social History* (London: Hamish Hamilton, 1994).

Price, R. *British Society, 1688–1880* (Cambridge: Cambridge University Press, 1999).

Pugh, P. D. G. *Staffordshire Portrait Figures and Allied Subjects of the Victorian Era* (London: Barrie & Jenkins, 1970).

Punter, D. *The Literature of Terror: A History of Gothic Fictions from 1765 to the Present Day* (London: Longman, 1980).

Rawlings, P. *Drunks, Whores and Idle Apprentices: Criminal Biographies of the Eighteenth Century* (London: Routledge, 1992).

Richardson, R. *Death, Dissection and the Destitute* (London: Routledge & Kegan Paul, 1988).

Rose, J. *The Intellectual Life of the British Working Classes* (New Haven: Yale University Press, 2001).

Ross, E. (ed.), *Slum Travellers: Ladies and London Poverty, 1860–1920* (Berkeley: University of California Press, 2007).

Schwarz, L. D. *London in the Age of Industrialisation: Entrepreneurs, Labour Force and Living Conditions, 1750–1850* (Cambridge: Cambridge University Press, 1992).

Scott, J. C. *Weapons of the Weak: Everyday Forms of Peasant Resistance* (New Haven: Yale University Press, 1985).

—— *Domination and the Arts of Resistance: Hidden Transcripts* (New Haven: Yale University Press, 1990).

Shepard, L. *The History of Street Literature* (Newton Abbott: David & Charles, 1973).

Shershow, S. C. *Puppets and 'Popular' Culture* (Ithaca: Cornell University Press, 1995).

Shoemaker, R. B. *The London Mob: Violence and Disorder in Eighteenth-Century England* (London: Hambledon & London, 2004).

Sindall, R. *Street Violence in the Nineteenth Century: Media Panic or Real Danger?* (Leicester: Leicester University Press, 1990).

Smith, H. *New Light on Sweeney Todd, Thomas Peckett Prest, James Malcolm Rymer and Elizabeth Caroline Grey* (Bloomsbury: Jarndyce, 2002).

Speaight, G. *Punch and Judy: A History* (London: Studio Vista, 1979).

Spierenburg, P. *The Spectacle of Suffering: Executions and the Evolution of Repression: From a Pre-Industrial Metropolis to the European Experience* (Cambridge: Cambridge University Press, 1984).

—— *A History of Murder: Personal Violence in Europe from the Middle Ages to the Present* (Cambridge: Polity, 2008).

Spraggs, G. *Outlaws and Highwaymen: The Cult of the Robber in England from the Middle Ages to the Nineteenth Century* (London: Pimlico, 2001).

Springhall, J. *Youth, Popular Culture and Moral Panics: From Penny Gaffs to Gangsta-Rap* (Basingstoke: Macmillan, 1998).

Spufford, M. *Small Books and Pleasant Histories: Popular Fiction and its Readership in Seventeenth-Century England* (Cambridge: Cambridge University Press, 1981).

Stephens, J. R. *The Censorship of English Drama, 1824–1901* (Cambridge: Cambridge University Press, 1980).

Stewart, S. *On Longing: Narratives of the Miniature, the Gigantic, the Souvenir, the Collection* (Baltimore: Johns Hopkins University Press, 1984).

Stocker, M. *Judith, Sexual Warrior: Women and Power in Western Culture* (New Haven: Yale University Press, 1998).

Storch, R. D. (ed.), *Popular Culture and Custom in Nineteenth-Century England* (London: Croom Helm, 1982).

Summers, A. *Female Lives, Modern States: Women, Religion and Public Life in Britain* (Newbury: Threshold Press, 2000).

Taylor, D. *The New Police: Crime, Conflict and Control in Nineteenth-Century England* (Manchester: Manchester University Press, 1997).

Thompson, E. P. *The Making of the English Working Class* (London: Gollancz, 1963).

—— *Customs in Common: Studies in Traditional Popular Culture* (New York: New Press, 1993).

Thompson, F. M. L. *The Rise of Respectable Society: A Social History of Victorian Britain, 1830–1900* (London: Fontana, 1988).

Turner, E. S. *Boys will be Boys: The Story of Sweeney Todd, Deadwood Dick, Sexton Blake, Billy Bunter, Dick Barton, et al* (London: Joseph, 3rd edn, 1975).

Twitchell, J. B. *Preposterous Violence: Fables of Aggression in Modern Culture* (Oxford: Oxford University Press, 1989).

Varma, D. P. *The Gothic Flame: Being a History of the Gothic Novel in England: Its Origins, Efflorescence, Disintegration and Residuary Influences* (London: Scarecrow, 1987).

Vicinus, M. *The Industrial Muse: A Study of Nineteenth-Century British Working-Class Literature* (New York: Croom Helm, 1974).

Vincent, D. *Bread, Knowledge and Freedom: A Study of Nineteenth-Century Working-Class Autobiography* (London: Europa, 1981).

—— *Literacy and Popular Culture: England, 1750–1914* (Cambridge: Cambridge University Press, 1989).

Walkowitz, J. R. *City of Dreadful Delight: Narratives of Sexual Danger in Late Victorian London* (Chicago: University of Chicago Press, 1992).

Walton, J. K. *The English Seaside Resort: A Social History, 1750–1914* (Leicester: Leicester University Press, 1983).

Walton, J. K. and J. Walvin (eds), *Leisure in Britain, 1780–1939* (Manchester: Manchester University Press, 1983).

Walvin, J. *Leisure and Society, 1830–1950* (London: Longman, 1978).

Webb, R. K. *The British Working Class Reader, 1790–1848: Literacy and Social Tension* (London: Allen & Unwin, 1955).

Weightman, G. *Bright Lights, Big City: London Entertained, 1830–1850* (London: Collins & Brown, 1992).

White, J. *London in the Nineteenth Century: A Human Awful Wonder of God* (London: Jonathan Cape, 2007).

Wiener, J. H. *A Descriptive Finding List of Unstamped British Periodicals, 1830–1836* (London: Bibliographical Society, 1970).

Wiener, M. J. *Reconstructing the Criminal: Culture, Law and Policy in England, 1830–1914* (Cambridge: Cambridge University Press, 1990).

—— *Men of Blood: Violence, Manliness and Criminal Justice in Victorian England* (Cambridge: Cambridge University Press, 2004).

Wilson, A. E. *East End Entertainment* (London: A. Barker, 1954).

Wiltenburg, J. *Disorderly Women and Female Power in the Street Literature of Early modern England and Germany* (Charlottesville: University Press of Virginia, 1992).

Winter, J. *London's Teeming Streets, 1830–1914* (London: Routledge, 1993).

Wohl, A. S. *Endangered Lives: Public Health in Victorian Britain* (London: Dent, 1983).

Wood, J. C. *Violence and Crime in Nineteenth-Century England: The Shadow of our Refinement* (London: Routledge, 2004).

Wood, M. *Radical Satire and Print Culture, 1790–1822* (Oxford: Clarendon Press, 1994).

Worrall, D. *Theatric Revolution: Drama, Censorship and Romantic Period Subcultures, 1773–1832* (Oxford: Oxford University Press, 2006).

Articles and chapters

Archer J. and J. Jones, 'Headlines from history: violence in the press, 1850–1914', in E. Stanko (ed.), *The Meanings of Violence* (London: Routledge, 2003).

Assael, B. 'Music in the air: noise, performance and the contest over the streets of the mid-nineteenth-century metropolis', in T. Hitchcock and H. Shore (eds), *The Streets of London: From the Great Fire to the Great Stink* (London: Rivers Oram, 2003).

Bailey, P. '"Will the real Bill Banks please stand up?" Towards a role analysis of mid Victorian respectability', *Journal of Social History*, 12 (1979), 336–53.

Bailey, V. 'The fabrication of deviance: "dangerous classes" and "criminal classes" in Victorian England', in J. Rule and R. Malcomson (eds), *Protest and Survival: The Historical Experience: Essays for E. P. Thompson* (London: Merlin, 1993).

Barker, C. 'A theatre for the people', in K. Richards and P. Thompson (eds), *Essays on Nineteenth-Century British Theatre* (London: Methuen, 1971).

—— 'The audiences of the Britannia Theatre, Hoxton', *Theatre Quarterly*, 9 (1979), 27–41.

Berridge, V. S. 'Popular Sunday papers and mid-Victorian society', in

G. Boyce, J. Curran and P. Wingate (eds), *Newspaper History from the Seventeenth Century to the Present Day* (London: Constable, 1978).

Berry, H. 'Rethinking politeness in eighteenth-century England: Moll King's coffee house and the significance of flash talk', *Transactions of the Royal Historical Society*, 6th Ser., 11 (2001), 65–81.

Booth, M. 'East End and West End: class and audience in Victorian London', *Theatre Research International*, 2 (1977), 98–103.

Chassaigne, P. 'Popular representations of crime: the crime broadside – a subculture of violence in Victorian Britain?', *Crime, Histoire et Sociétés*, 3 (1999), 23–55.

Clark, A. 'Rape or seduction? A controversy over sexual violence in the nineteenth century', in London Feminist History Group (ed.), *Men's Power, Women's Resistance: The Sexual Dynamics of History* (London: Pluto, 1983).

—— 'The politics of seduction in English popular culture, 1748–1848', in J. Radford (ed.), *The Progress of Romance: The Politics of Popular Fiction* (London: Routledge & Kegan Paul, 1986).

—— 'Domesticity and the problem of wife-beating in nineteenth-century Britain: working-class culture, law and politics', in S. D'Cruze (ed.), *Everyday Violence in Britain, 1850 -1950: Gender and Class* (Harlow: Longman, 2000).

Cockburn, J. S., 'Punishment and brutalisation in the English Enlightenment', *Law and History Review*, 12 (1994), 155–79.

Crafts, N. F. R. 'Some dimensions of the "quality of life" during the British industrial revolution', *Economic History Review*, 50 (1997), 617–39.

Crone, R. 'Reappraising Victorian literacy through prison records', *Journal of Victorian Culture*, 15 (2010), 3–37.

Cunningham, H. 'Metropolitan fairs', in A. P. Donajgrodski (ed.), *Social Control in Nineteenth-Century Britain* (London: Croom Helm, 1977).

—— 'Leisure and culture', in F. M. L. Thompson (ed.), *The Cambridge Social History of Britain, 1750–1950. Volume 2: People and their Environment* (Cambridge: Cambridge University Press, 1992).

Daunton, M. J. 'Industry in London: revisions and reflections', *London Journal*, 21 (1996), 1–8.

Davis, J. 'The London garrotting panic of 1862: a moral panic and the creation of a criminal class in mid-Victorian England', in V. A. C. Gatrell, B. Lenman and G. Parker (eds), *Crime and the Law: The Social History of Crime in Western Europe since 1500* (London: Europa, 1980).

—— 'A poor man's system of justice: the London police courts in the second half of the nineteenth century', *Historical Journal*, 27 (1984), 309–35.

—— 'Jennings Buildings and the Royal Borough: the construction of an underclass in mid-Victorian England', in D. Feldman and G. S. Jones (eds), *Metropolis London: Histories and Representations since 1800* (London: Routledge, 1989).

Davis, J. and T. C. Davis, 'The people of the "People's Theatre": the social demo-graphy of the Britannia Theatre (Hoxton)', *Theatre Survey*, 32 (1991), 137–65.

Davis, J. and V. Emeljanow, 'New views of cheap theatres: reconstructing the nineteenth-century theatre audiences', *Theatre Survey*, 39 (1998), 53–72.

Devereaux, S. 'The City and the Sessions Paper: public justice in London, 1770–1800', *Journal of British Studies*, 35 (1996), 466–503.

—— 'Recasting the theatre of execution in London: the end of Tyburn', *Past & Present*, 202 (2009), 127–74.

Dunae, P. 'Penny-dreadfuls: late nineteenth-century boys' literature and crime', *Victorian Studies*, 22 (1978), 133–50.

—— 'New grub-street for boys', in J. Richards (ed.), *Imperialism and Juvenile Literature* (Manchester: Manchester University Press, 1989).

Dyos, H. J. and D. A. Reeder, 'Slums and suburbs', in H. J. Dyos and M. Wolff (eds), *The Victorian City: Images and Realities. Volume 2* (London: Routledge, 1973).

Eastwood, D. 'The age of uncertainty: Britain in the early nineteenth century', *Transactions of the Royal Historical Society*, 8 (1998), 91–115.

Eisner, M. 'Modernisation, self-control and lethal violence: the long-term dynamics of European homicide rates in theoretical perspective', *British Journal of Criminology*, 41 (2001), 618–38.

—— 'Long-term historical trends in violent crime', *Crime and Justice: An Annual Review of Research*, 30 (2003), 83–142.

Elkins, C. 'The voice of the poor: the broadside as a medium of popular culture and dissent in Victorian England', *Journal of Popular Culture*, 14 (1980), 262–74.

Faller, L. B. 'Criminal opportunities in the eighteenth century: the "ready-made" contexts of the popular literature of crime', *Comparative Literature Studies*, 24 (1987), 120–45.

Feinstein, C. H. 'Pessimism perpetuated: real wages and the standard of living in Britain during the industrial revolution', *Journal of Economic History*, 58 (1998), 625–58.

Foyster, E. 'Boys will be boys? Manhood and aggression, 1660–1800', in T. Hitchcock and M. Cohen (eds), *English Masculinities, 1660–1800* (London: Longman, 1999).

—— 'Creating a veil of silence? Politeness and marital violence in the English household', *Transactions of the Royal Historical Society*, 6th Ser., 12 (2002), 395–415.

Garside, P. 'London and the home counties', in F. M. L. Thompson (ed.), *The Cambridge Social History of Britain, 1750–1900. Volume 1: Regions and Communities* (Cambridge: Cambridge University Press, 1992).

Gatrell, V. A. C. 'The decline of theft and violence in Victorian and Edwardian England', in V. A. C. Gatrell, B. Lenman and G. Parker (eds), *Crime and the Law: The Social History of Crime in Western Europe since 1500* (London: Europa, 1980).

—— 'Crime, authority and the policeman-state', in F. M. L. Thompson (ed.), *The Cambridge Social History of Britain, 1750–1950. Volume 3: Social Agencies and Institutions* (Cambridge: Cambridge University Press, 1992).

Ginn, G. '"Slumming it": the intellectuals and the masses in late Victorian London', *Proceedings of the University of Queensland History Research Group*, 6 (1995), 29–43.

Goodbody, J. '*The Star*: its role in the rise of the New Journalism', in J. H. Wiener (ed.), *Papers for the Millions: The New Journalism in Britain, 1850s to 1914* (New York: Greenwood, 1986).

Griffin, E. 'Popular culture in industrialising England', *Historical Journal*, 45 (2002), 619–35.

Gurr, T. R. 'Historical trends in violent crime: a critical review of the evidence', *Crime and Justice: An Annual Review of Research*, 3 (1981), 295–393.

Halttunen, K. 'Humanitarianism and the pornography of pain in Anglo-American culture', *American Historical Review*, 100 (1995), 303–34.

Haywood, I. 'G. W. M. Reynolds and the radicalisation of Victorian serial fiction', *Media History*, 4 (1998), 121–39.

Hobsbawm, E. J. 'The labour aristocracy in nineteenth-century Britain', in Hobsbawm, *Labouring Men: Studies in the History of Labour* (London: Weidenfeld & Nicolson, 1964).

Huggins, M. 'More sinful pleasures? Leisure, respectability and the male middle classes in Victorian England', *Journal of Social History*, 33 (2000), 585–600.

Humphreys, A. 'G. W. M. Reynolds: popular literature and popular politics', *Victorian Periodicals Review*, 16 (1983), 78–88.

—— 'G. W. M. Reynolds: popular literature and popular politics', in J. H. Wiener (ed.), *Innovators and Preachers: The Role of the Editor in Victorian England* (Westport: Greenwood, 1985).

—— 'Popular narrative and political discourse in *Reynolds's Weekly Newspaper*', in L. Brake, A. Jones and L. Madden (eds), *Investigating Victorian Journalism* (Basingstoke: Macmillan, 1990).

Hunt, M. 'Wife-beating, domesticity and women's independence in eighteenth-century London', *Gender and History*, 4 (1992), 10–33.

Inwood, S. 'Policing London's morals: the metropolitan police and popular culture, 1829–1850', *London Journal*, 15 (1990), 129–46.

James, L. 'Taking melodrama seriously: theatre and nineteenth-century studies', *History Workshop Journal*, 3 (1977), 151–8.

Judd, M. 'The oddest combination of town and country: popular culture and the London fairs, 1800–1860', in J. K. Walton and J. Walvin (eds), *Leisure in Britain, 1780–1939* (Manchester: Manchester University Press, 1983).

King, P. 'Newspaper reporting and attitudes to crime and justice in late eighteenth and early nineteenth-century London', *Continuity and Change*, 22 (2007), 73–112.

Langton, J. 'Urban growth and economic change: from the late-seventeenth century to 1841', in P. Clark (ed.), *The Cambridge Urban History of Britain. Volume 2: 1540–1840* (Cambridge: Cambridge University Press, 2000).

Lindert, P. H. and J. G. Williamson, 'English workers' living standards during the industrial revolution: a new look', *Economic History Review*, 36 (1983), 1–25.

McGowen, R., 'The image of justice and reform of the criminal law in early nineteenth-century England', *Buffalo Law Review*, 32 (1983), 89–125.

—— 'A powerful sympathy: terror, the prison and humanitarian reform in early nineteenth-century Britain', *Journal of British Studies*, 25 (1986), 312–34.

—— 'Civilising punishment: the end of public execution in England', *Journal of British Studies*, 33 (1994), 257–82.

—— 'Revisiting the Hanging Tree: Gatrell on emotion and history', *British Journal of Criminology*, 40 (2000), 1–13.

McKenzie, A. 'Making crime pay: motives, marketing strategies and the printed literature of crime in England, 1670–1770', in S. Devereaux, A. May and G. T. Smith (eds), *Criminal Justice in the Old World and the New: Essays in Honour of J. M. Beattie* (Toronto: Centre of Criminology, University of Toronto, 1998).

McPharlin, P. 'The Collier-Cruikshank Punch and Judy', *Colophon*, 1 (1936), 371–87.

McWilliam, R. 'The mysteries of G. W. M. Reynolds: radicalism and melodrama in Victorian Britain', in M. Chase and I. Dyck (eds), *Living and Learning: Essays in Honour of J. F. C. Harrison* (Aldershot: Ashgate, 1996).

—— 'Melodrama and the historians', *Radical History Review*, 78 (2000), 57–84.

—— 'The theatricality of the Staffordshire figurine', *Journal of Victorian Culture*, 10 (2005), 107–14.

Neuburg, V. E. 'The literature of the streets', in H. J. Dyos and M. Wolff (eds), *The Victorian City: Images and Realities. Volume 1* (London: Routledge, 1973).

Pedersen, S. 'Hannah More meets Simple Simon: tracts, chapbooks and popular culture in late eighteenth-century England', *Journal of British Studies*, 25 (1986), 84–113.

Pedley, C. 'Maria Marten, or the Murder in the Red Barn: the theatricality of provincial life', *Nineteenth-Century Theatre and Film*, 31 (2004), 26–40.

Potts, A. 'Picturing the modern metropolis: images of London in the nineteenth century', *History Workshop Journal*, 26 (1988), 28–56.

Powell, S. 'Black markets and cadaverous pies: the corpse, urban trade and industrial consumption in the penny blood', in A. Maunder and G. Moore (eds), *Victorian Crime, Madness and Sensation* (Aldershot: Ashgate, 2004).

Reed, M. 'The transformation of urban space, 1700–1840', in P. Clark (ed.), *The Cambridge Urban History of Britain. Volume 2: 1540–1840* (Cambridge: Cambridge University Press, 2000).

Reid, D. A. 'Interpreting the festival calendar: wakes and fairs as carnivals', in R. D. Storch (ed.), *Popular Culture and Custom in Nineteenth-Century England* (London: Croom Helm, 1982).

Ross, E. '"Fierce questions and taunts": married life in working-class London, 1870–1914', *Feminist Studies*, 8 (1982), 575–602.

Roth, R. 'Homicide in early modern England, 1549–1800: the need for a quantitative synthesis', *Crime, Histoire et Sociétés*, 5 (2001), 33–67.

Samuel, R. 'Reading the signs', *History Workshop Journal*, 32 (1991), 88–109.

—— 'Reading the signs II', *History Workshop Journal*, 33 (1992), 220–51.

Schofield, R. S. 'The measurement of literacy in pre-industrial England', in J. Goody (ed.), *Literacy in Traditional Societies* (Cambridge: Cambridge University Press, 1968).

—— 'The dimensions of illiteracy, 1750–1850', *Explorations in Economic History*, 10 (1973), 437–54.

Schwarz, L. D. 'The standard of living in the long run: London, 1700–1860', *Economic History Review*, 38 (1985), 24–49.

—— 'English servants and their employers during the eighteenth and nineteenth centuries', *Economic History Review*, 52 (1999), 236–56.

—— 'London, 1700–1840', in P. Clark (ed.), *The Cambridge Urban History of Britain. Volume 2: 1540–1840* (Cambridge: Cambridge University Press, 2000).

Sharpe, P. 'Population and society, 1700–1840', in P. Clark (ed.), *The Cambridge Urban History of Britain. Volume 2: 1540–1840* (Cambridge: Cambridge University Press, 2000).

Shershow, S. C. 'Punch and Judy and cultural appropriation', *Cultural Studies*, 8 (1994), 541–6.

Shoemaker, R. B. 'The decline of public insult in London, 1660–1800', *Past & Present*, 169 (2000), 97–131.

—— 'Male honour and the decline of public violence in eighteenth-century London', *Social History*, 26 (2001), 190–208.

Sindall, R. 'The London garrotting panics of 1856 and 1862', *Social History*, 12 (1987), 351–9.

Smith, G. T., 'Civilised people don't want to see that kind of thing: the decline of public physical punishment in London, 1760–1840', in C. Strange (ed.), *Qualities of Mercy: Justice, Punishment and Discretion* (Vancouer: University of British Columbia Press, 1996).

—— '"I could hang anything you can bring before me": England's willing executioners in 1883', in S. Devereaux and P. Griffiths (eds), *Penal Practice and Culture, 1500–1900: Punishing the English* (Basingstoke: Palgrave Macmillan, 2004).

—— 'Violent crime and the public weal in England, 1500–1900', in

R. McMahon (ed.), *Crime, Law and Popular Culture in Europe, 1500–1900* (Cullumpton: Willan Publishing, 2008).

Springhall, J. 'A life story for the people? Edwin J. Brett and the London low-life penny dreadfuls of the 1860s', *Victorian Studies*, 33 (1990), 223–46.

—— 'Pernicious reading? The penny dreadful as a scapegoat for late Victorian juvenile crime', *Victorian Periodicals Review*, 27 (1994), 326–49.

—— '"Disseminating impure literature": the penny dreadful publishing business since 1860', *Economic History Review*, 27 (1994), 567–84.

Stearns, P. N. 'Men, boys and anger in American society, 1860–1940', in J. A. Mangan and J. Walvin (eds), *Manliness and Morality: Middle-Class Masculinity in Britain and America, 1800–1940* (Manchester: Manchester University Press, 1987).

—— 'Girls, boys and emotions: redefinitions and historical change', *Journal of American History*, 80 (1993), 36–74.

Stephens, J. R. 'Jack Sheppard and the licensers: the case against the Newgate plays', *Nineteenth-Century Theatre Research*, 1 (1973), 1–13.

Stevenson, J. 'Social aspects of the industrial revolution', in P. O'Brien and R. Quinalt (eds), *The Industrial Revolution and British Society* (Cambridge: Cambridge University Press, 1993).

Stone, L. 'Interpersonal violence in English society, 1300–1980', *Past & Present*, 101 (1983), 22–33.

Storch, R. D. 'The policeman as domestic missionary: urban discipline and popular culture in northern England, 1850–80', *Journal of Social History*, 9 (1976), 481–509.

—— 'Police control of street prostitution in Victorian London: a study in the contexts of police action', in D. H. Bayley (ed.), *Police and Society* (London: Sage Publications, 1977).

—— 'Introduction', in Storch (ed.), *Popular Culture and Custom in Nineteenth-Century England* (London: Croom Helm, 1982).

Sutherland, G. 'Education', in F. M. L. Thompson (ed.), *Cambridge Social History of Britain, 1750–1950. Volume 3: Social Agencies and Institutions* (Cambridge: Cambridge University Press, 1996).

Szreter, S. and G. Mooney, 'Urbanisation, mortality and the standard of living debate: new estimates of the expectation of life at birth in nineteenth-century British cities', *Economic History Review*, 51 (1998), 84–112.

Szreter, S. and A. Hardy, 'Urban fertility and mortality patterns', in M. J. Daunton (ed.), *The Cambridge Urban History of Britain. Volume 3: 1840–1950* (Cambridge: Cambridge University Press, 2000).

Thompson, F. M. L. 'Town and city', in F. M. L. Thompson (ed.), *The Cambridge Social History of Britain, 1750–1900. Volume 1: Regions and Communities* (Cambridge: Cambridge University Press, 1990).

Tomes, N. 'A "torrent of abuse": crimes of violence between working-class men and women in London, 1840–1875', *Journal of Social History*, 11 (1977), 328–45.

Tullock, J. 'The privatising of pain: Lincoln newspapers, "mediated publicness" and the end of public execution', *Journalism Studies*, 7 (2006), 437–51.

Vicinus, M. 'Helpless and unfriended: nineteenth-century domestic melodrama', *New Literary History*, 13 (1981), 127–43.

Vickery, A. 'From Golden Age to Separate Spheres? A review of the chronologies and categories of English women's history', *Historical Journal*, 36 (1993), 383–414.

Walkowitz, R. 'Jack the Ripper and the myth of male violence', *Feminist Studies*, 8 (1982), 543–74.

Walters, R. G. 'Signs of the times: Clifford Geertz and historians', *Social Research*, 47 (1980), 537–56.

Walton, J. 'Respectability takes a holiday: disreputable behaviour at the Victorian seaside', in M. Hewitt (ed.), *Unrespectable Recreations* (Leeds: Centre for Victorian Studies, 2001).

Webb, R. K. 'Working-class readers in early Victorian England', *English Historical Review*, 65 (1950), 333–51.

Wiener, J. H. 'How new was the New Journalism', in J. H. Wiener (ed.), *Papers for the Millions: The New Journalism in Britain, 1850s to 1914* (New York: Greenwood, 1986).

Wiener, M. J. 'Alice Arden to Bill Sikes: changing nightmares of intimate violence in England, 1558 to 1869', *Journal of British Studies*, 40 (2001), 184–212.

Williams, P. and J. Dickinson, 'Fear of crime: read all about it? The relationship between newspaper crime reporting and fear of crime', *British Journal of Criminology*, 33 (1993), 33–56.

Williams, R. 'Radical and/or respectable', in R. Boston (ed.), *The Press we Deserve* (London: Routledge & Kegan Paul, 1970).

—— 'The press and popular culture: an historical perspective', in G. Boyce, J. Curran and P. Wingate (eds), *Newspaper History from the Seventeenth Century to the Present Day* (London: Constable, 1978).

Wiltenburg, J. 'True crime: the origins of modern sensationalism', *American Historical Review*, 109 (2004), 1377–404.

Unpublished

Bell, K. 'The magical imagination and modern urbanisation' (PhD thesis, University of East Anglia, 2007).

Berridge, V. S. 'Popular journalism and working-class attitudes, 1854–1886: a study of *Reynolds's Newspaper*, *Lloyd's Weekly Newspaper* and the *Weekly Times*' (PhD diss., University of London, 1972).

Index

Page numbers in *italic* refer to illustrations.
Literary works can be found under authors' names where known.
Publications (newspapers, periodicals, serials etc) are listed by title.